PENGUIN CLASSI

THE ROMAN HISTORY
THE REIGN OF AUGUSTUS

ADVISORY EDITOR: BETTY RADICE

The Greek historian Cassius Dio was born in Bithynia in about
A.D. 163. Coming to Rome as a young man, he entered the senate
under Commodus; he held the praetorship in 194 and a provincial
governorship and then the consulship some years later during the
reign of Septimius Severus. A long interval, occupied in preparing
and writing much of his *History*, preceded his return to public life
after the death of Septimius's odious son and successor Caracalla.
He went on to hold the pro-consulship of Africa and the governorships of Dalmatia and Pannonia, and crowned his official career
with a second consulship in 229, when the emperor Alexander
Severus was his colleague.

Dio's *Roman History* was his major literary achievement and
covered the period from the arrival of Aeneas in Italy to his own
second consulship. He wrote it in eighty books, of which those
dealing with the period from the Second Mithridatic War (69
B.C.) to the reign of Claudius (A.D. 46) have survived substantially
intact. His other important works were a biography of Arrian and
an account of the portents that foretold the reign of Septimius
Severus. Dio spent the last few years of his life in Bithynia and
died in about A.D. 235.

IAN SCOTT-KILVERT was Director of English Literature at the
British Council. He was Editor of *Writers and their Work* and also
translated Plutarch's *The Rise and Fall of Athens: Nine Greek Lives*,
The Age of Alexander, *Makers of Rome* and Polybius's *The Rise of
the Roman Empire* for the Penguin Classics. He died in 1989.

JOHN CARTER is Senior Lecturer in Classics at Royal Holloway
and Bedford New College in London University. Other published work includes a history of Augustus's rise to power, *The
Battle of Actium* (1970), and an edition of Suetonius's life of Augustus, *Divus Augustus* (1982).

CASSIUS DIO

THE ROMAN HISTORY

THE REIGN OF AUGUSTUS

TRANSLATED BY
IAN SCOTT-KILVERT

WITH AN INTRODUCTION BY
JOHN CARTER

PENGUIN BOOKS

PENGUIN BOOKS

Published by the Penguin Group
Penguin Books Ltd, 27 Wrights Lane, London w8 5tz, England
Viking Penguin, a division of Penguin Books USA Inc.
375 Hudson Street, New York, New York 10014, USA
Penguin Books Australia Ltd, Ringwood, Victoria, Australia
Penguin Books Canada Ltd, 2801 John Street, Markham, Ontario, Canada l3r 1b4
Penguin Books (NZ) Ltd, 182–190 Wairau Road, Auckland 10, New Zealand

Penguin Books Ltd, Registered Offices: Harmondsworth, Middlesex, England

This translation first published 1987
5 7 9 10 8 6 4

Introduction copyright © John Carter, 1987
Translation and Notes © Ian Scott-Kilvert, 1987
All rights reserved

Printed in England by Clays Ltd, St Ives plc
Filmset in Monophoto Bembo

IN MEMORY OF
BETTY RADICE

CONTENTS

INTRODUCTION

Cassius Dio, often referred to as Dio Cassius, was a Greek of an important family of Bithynia, who entered the senate towards the end of the third century A.D. and rose to hold the consulship twice, the second time in A.D. 229 as colleague to the emperor. His *Roman History* runs from the foundation of the city by Romulus up to his own times. Of it we have substantial portions covering the years 68 B.C. to A.D. 46, while some idea of most of the rest can be gained from summaries made in the Byzantine era. The Augustan books survive almost complete, and are important because they constitute the only narrative of the reign which pretends to any degree of fullness.

The present volume contains Books 50–56, running from 32 B.C. to A.D. 14. They span the point of division in Dio's work, at the end of Book 50, between the republic and the empire, and inevitably require to be set in their historical as well as their literary and historiographical context. This introduction therefore falls into two chief sections. The first aims to provide a sketch of the events leading up to the crisis with which Book 50 opens, and then to discuss some features of Augustus's reign which call for comment in the light of Dio's narrative. The second deals with Dio himself and with the composition and nature of his *History*, which was profoundly influenced by his own experiences and by the literary culture of the epoch.

AUGUSTUS AND HIS HISTORICAL CONTEXT

I. The end of the republic

In the beginning kings ruled the city of Rome; Lucius Brutus brought freedom and instituted consuls. On occasion there were dictatorships; the Decemvirate lasted no more than two years, and the military tribunes with consular power not long. Neither Cinna nor Sulla exercised mastery for more than a brief space; the power of Pompey and Crassus swiftly passed to Caesar, the armed strength of Lepidus and Antony to Augustus; and he, now that the whole state was exhausted by civil war, assumed the name of *princeps*, and took it under his command.

Thus Tacitus, greatest of the Roman historians, setting the scene at the start of his sombre tale of the years between the death of Augustus and that of Nero. It is clear enough to us, and was clear enough to Tacitus, that the periods of temporary mastery over the state enjoyed by such as Sulla and Caesar were a logical prelude to the establishment of the permanent and institutionalized domination which we call the principate; but this must have been far from clear to the participants in the events of the dramatic sixty years between 91 and 31 B.C.

The republic had existed for over four hundred years, ever since the expulsion of the last king at the end of the sixth century. During that time there had been major changes in the constitution, and major changes in the way in which power was exercised in society. There had been many internal and external crises in which ambitious and fortunate men had challenged for, or actually enjoyed for a while, a share of power greater than would ordinarily have been tolerated. Yet the republic had survived them all, for in spite of the Roman reverence for *mos maiorum*, the way their ancestors behaved, a conspicuous characteristic of their state was its capacity to absorb and resolve conflict within the framework of a set of institutions which retained the names, and often apparently the powers, which they had always had, but which in practice were perceptibly modified. Adaptation there might be, but the basic elements endured: a pair of annual consuls elected by a popular assembly and governing with the advice of a senate composed of those who had been, were, or aspired to be magistrates themselves, while legislation came before the popular assembly and all citizens except the poorest had an obligation to serve as required in the army for a certain number of campaigning seasons. So there was no necessity to suppose that with a modification here, an adjustment there, the state could not last indefinitely, still recognizably the republic, still the same but different. Even the civil war which broke out in 49 B.C. between Pompey and Caesar had its predecessor in the far bitterer conflict of Sulla and the supporters of Marius in the eighties. So the bout of armed struggle which lasted, with changes of protagonists and intervals of uneasy calm, from Caesar's crossing of the Rubicon down to Augustus's capture of Alexandria in 30 B.C., was surely not seen by contemporaries as the 'death of the republic'.

It was the great achievement of Augustus to perform a kind of conjuring trick, by which all the traditional organs of the state continued to function, while he himself, taking no power that was without precedent, retained a position within the constitutional framework that effectively allowed him to control the state – that is, the *res publica*. Augustus, by contriving that Tiberius should succeed to all his powers, established at his death a quasi-hereditary monarchy; and it was not until then that the conceptual difference, familiar to us, between 'republic' and 'empire' could be formulated. The idea that *principatus*, 'the principate' (in effect, a soft term for 'monarchy', which Roman political susceptibilities did not allow), can stand in opposition to, and not simply describe a form of, *res publica*, does not appear until a hundred years later, in the writings of Tacitus. So if Augustus or his supporters ever claimed – and they probably did not – to have 'restored the republic', they were not trying to gull an unsuspecting public.

What Augustus had done, by his victory over Antony and subsequent diplomatic arrangements, was to bring a period of freedom from threat by internal or external enemies. Peace, and a measure of *de facto* political stability, allowed the normal organs of government, the consuls, Senate and people, to resume their accustomed roles. Augustus came to occupy a somewhat special place, but other great men of the recent past had likewise enjoyed positions which strayed outside the bounds set by strict application of constitutional norms. *Princeps* indeed he was, but not the first in Rome's history. All societies possess their 'leading men', which is all the word means. However, he remained sole *princeps* for the whole of the rest of his life, and Dio is right when he remarks that 'from his time a monarchy, strictly speaking, was established' (53.17.1). The means by which Augustus achieved this are discussed below (section III), but first something needs to be said about how the character of the Roman army and Roman politics changed in the last century of the republic.

The fundamental changes are associated with the names of Gracchus and Marius. In the second century B.C. the peasant economy of Italy was severely jolted by the huge influx of slaves and money produced by the successful overseas wars of 200–146 B.C. The city of Rome grew enormously by immigration from the countryside. In 133 B.C. the young aristocrat Tiberius Gracchus decided to make use of the normally dormant independent legislative powers of the office of tribune of the plebs to redistribute to the landless poor Roman public land occupied by the rich, in an attempt to reverse the economic developments which favoured large-scale specialist farming and were displacing the traditional peasantry on whom the state relied for its soldiers. Bitter passions were aroused and Tiberius was killed. Ten years later his brother Gaius again demonstrated how a tribune with a popular programme could override conservative control of the Roman assemblies by appealing to the rootless and often poverty-stricken urban population. Then in 108 B.C. Gaius Marius was elected against strong opposition and on an avowedly popular platform to the consulship of the next year and a command in Numidia, in order to end a war which the normal senatorial system of appointments had failed to bring under control.

Succeeding dramatically in Numidia, Marius was then swept by the same popular tide to a technically illegal sequence of five further consulships when Italy was menaced from the north by mass wanderings of Germanic tribesmen who had overwhelmed several Roman armies. His importance for this analysis lies in two things. The first is that he decisively breached the theoretical principle on which the Roman army was based, that it was a citizen militia recruited for limited periods from those who had a stake in the state, defined as the possession of a certain minimum amount of property. All qualified citizens had an obligation to serve for sixteen years on foot or ten years in the cavalry. These arrangements were patently an anachronism after the wars with Carthage, when overseas campaigns, often for more than a year at a time, became frequent. The scale of Rome's militarism in the second century had already made it necessary to reduce the minimum property qualification for service in the legions to a very low figure, so as to obtain an adequate pool of recruits and to avoid keeping men overseas for very long periods. Marius went further, and recruited those who did not even possess this very small amount. These volunteers, lacking any base in civilian life to return to, depended entirely on him to provide for them, whether by winning booty or arranging some form of land settlement when their service was over. This required political muscle, and leads to the second significant point. Marius's string of consulships was largely the fruit of the alliance he formed with an ambitious and energetic tribune, Lucius Saturninus, who was able to use the votes of Marius's veterans and soldiers, and of the urban proletariat, to support Marius in office and put through a series of laws in the interest of the various parties to this anti-senatorial coalition. The alliance was revolutionary, and powerful, and seems only to have collapsed because of Saturninus's excessive use of violence to attain his political ends.

That was in 100 B.C. Another ten years later war broke out in Italy over the demand of Rome's allies to be admitted to her citizenship. A complicated series of events then led to a situation in which Lucius Sulla twice used his army against the authority of the state: first, when he led it on Rome in 88 in order to prevent himself losing to Marius the prestigious and potentially lucrative command against King Mithridates of Pontus, and then again in 84–82 when he returned at its head to take bloody revenge on his enemies, the heirs of Cinna and Marius, who had violently overthrown the men he had left behind in charge of Rome. Becoming dictator, he carried through a number of constitutional changes designed to emasculate the demagogic features of the tribunate and restore power to the Senate, and he paid his veterans the price for their readiness to follow him on his path of illegal violence: land was sequestered from all those who had dared to oppose him, communities as well as individuals, in order to give smallholdings to a hundred thousand men. They, as the beneficiaries of this legalized rape, would serve as a useful guarantee both of it and of the rest of his arrangements. At the end of 80 he resigned his powers, to die only a little over a year later.

As Tacitus observed, Sulla's mastery of the state was brief. But the chain of events which led to it reveals all the elements which tore the republic apart. Perhaps the most significant single episode was the march on Rome in 88. By recruiting the landless, Marius had taken the vital step in the creation of a professional army which depended for its longer-term rewards (pay being merely at subsistence levels and booty unpredictable) on the success, prestige and political power of its commander. What the soldiers looked for, ultimately, was the ancient equivalent of a good pension, that is a small farm, on discharge. The state, not acknowledging that its army was no longer drawn only from the propertied, made no provision for such a thing. Now it was an important peculiarity of the Roman constitution that the authority (*imperium*) with which it invested its highest magistrates, the consuls and praetors, was simultaneously civil and military, so that a Roman general was inescapably also a 'career politician'. Since organized parties were unknown, success in politics depended on the ability to build up personal support and to form effective links with others who could command it for you. The alliance between Marius and Saturninus had shown how powerful the votes of the soldiers who identified their interests with those of Marius could be. They made this identification because they depended on Marius's ability, as a politician, to pass the legislation necessary to give them their hoped-for rewards. Marius had not in fact wished to use his army in any improper manner, but the political link between commander and soldiers had been created. Sulla, by his march, brought out its full implications. The army of the state no longer behaved like the state under arms. It had become an alienated part of that state. In the civil wars that followed the murder of Caesar, soldiers were repeatedly induced to change sides by promises of better rewards.

Looked at in another way, this behaviour means that the army was willing to use its strength to seize back some of the agricultural wealth of Italy which the economic changes of the second century had diverted into richer hands. This truth was never expressed in such terms by the Romans, but it was the fundamental fact which underlay the escalating struggle for power that characterized the fifty years between Sulla's death and Augustus's ending of the civil wars. There were of course many other factors: the greed, ambition and quarrelsome pride of the Roman aristocracy; the vast scale of the rewards to be wrung from the provinces; the huge gap between rich and poor; the continued existence of political institutions which were unsuitable for governing Italy, let alone an empire; the growth of the city of Rome into a metropolis; the inbuilt militarism of the state; and the social acceptance of violence as a means of self-help – to name only some of the more important. But in the breakdown of politics into armed struggle, the allegiance of armies to their commanders rather than to Rome (for what had 'Rome' done for them?) was crucial. Augustus, as it happened, was not naturally a military man; on the other hand there can be no real doubt that he attained power, and held on to it, because he was able to command the loyalty of soldiers. He was a revolutionary, not indeed in a modern sense, because what the warlords of the late republic were fighting for was status not social justice, but a revolutionary none the less, who used force to overturn the government of the day and ultimately brought in a new order. That new order, in spite of its republican detail, rested firmly on its architect's personal army.

II. From 44 to 32 B.C.

The murder of Julius Caesar by Brutus, Cassius and other disaffected senators on the Ides of March 44 B.C. brought his eighteen-year-old heir and great-nephew Octavian back to Rome to demand vengeance on the murderers, to claim his inheritance, and to challenge the consul Antony for the leadership of the Caesarian party. Claiming adoption by Caesar's will and assuming the potent name of Caesar, he won the favour of the city plebs and was able to raise a private army from amongst his 'father's' veterans to such good effect that before the end of 43 he and Antony, with Marcus Lepidus, had established a tyranny sanctioned by law, holding quasi-dictatorial power as 'Triumvirs for the Organization of the State' and carrying out a savage purge of their opponents. After the defeat of Brutus and Cassius at Philippi in 42 B.C., Antony, as the senior partner, took the choice assignment of dealing with the provinces and semi-independent kingdoms of the eastern Mediterranean, while Lepidus took the western provinces, and to Octavian fell the thankless task of taking land in Italy from ordinary Italians in order to fulfil the promises by which the triumvirs had induced their troops to fight against their fellow-citizens.

This stirred up a hornets' nest. Antony's wife Fulvia and brother Lucius expressed the outrage of Italy by raising armed revolt against the triumviral authority of Octavian. They were almost successful, but in the end were besieged in Perusia (Perugia) and starved out in the spring of 40 B.C. Antony, meanwhile, in all ignorance of these events, was spending the winter as the honoured guest of Cleopatra, Queen of Egypt, sometime mistress of Julius Caesar, and mother of a boy known familiarly as Caesarion ('little Caesar'). Antony's serious concern was with the Parthians, but the news of Perusia brought him rapidly back to Italy. A violent struggle was only prevented by the refusal of the soldiers on either side to fight those who had recently been their comrades in arms. Eventually a reconciliation was arranged, the guarantee of it being a marriage between Octavian's beautiful and recently widowed sister Octavia and Antony, likewise bereaved by the opportune death of Fulvia. The next year saw the triumvirs reach an accommodation with the remaining son of Pompey the Great, Sextus, who had built up a strong navy and had managed to establish himself in Sicily as the last focus of opposition to the triumvirs. Civil discord apparently laid to rest, Antony took his bride to Greece and busied himself with preparations for his long-deferred campaign against the Parthians.

Harmony did not last. Sextus and Octavian fell out, and without reference to Antony, Octavian embarked on war. Meeting no success in 38, he had to pacify an irate Antony, from whom he also wanted to borrow naval reinforcements. Through the good offices of Octavia the two men reached yet another agreement at Tarentum in 37. Under its terms Octavian got the ships and promised in return to lend Antony legions, while the triumvirate, which had technically expired the previous November, was retrospectively renewed for another five years so that it ended on the last day of 33. But when Antony left Italy in the autumn of 37, having lost yet another campaigning season on account of his difficult and over-ambitious young brother-in-law, he also left his wife behind – on excellent grounds, as she was pregnant with their second child – and went to meet Cleopatra. The queen was not only the mother of his twins, whom he had never seen, but could provide him with essential money and supplies for the great expedition he was to lead against Parthia in the following year.

That expedition was a disaster, and Antony's retreat through Armenia in the snows of early winter can be compared with Napoleon's retreat from Moscow. At the same time Octavian, thanks largely to the brilliance of Agrippa, was defeating Sextus. He also managed to eliminate Lepidus from the triumvirate when the latter made an ill-judged attempt to suborn Octavian's legions. Thus by the end of 36 B.C. the balance of prestige, if not yet of power, decisively altered. Furthermore, Antony had not been seen in Rome for more than three years, and Rome was still the centre of power. Octavian's marriage to Livia early in 38 marked the beginning of the drift of the republican aristocracy towards accepting him. Meanwhile, Antony's entanglement with the Egyptian queen stood in patent contrast with the loyalty of his abandoned but faithful wife, who had borne him two daughters and was bringing up his younger son by Fulvia – not to speak of her own three children by her first marriage.

When the news of the Parthian débâcle filtered back to Rome, Octavian saw his chance to wrest the primacy from Antony in order to become, like his adoptive father, master of the Roman world. Antony's chief military weakness was that he was cut off from recruiting in Italy, and Italians were the best soldiers to be had. Octavian never sent him the legions he had promised him at Tarentum, and made it clear by his other actions that support would not be forthcoming unless he returned to Octavia and abandoned Cleopatra both as lover and as monarch of the only remaining Mediterranean power that had the resources to stand up to Rome. Antony read the signals, and made his choice: to remain independent of the odious Octavian and his virtuous sister, base himself on Alexandria, and concern himself with promoting the joint advantage of Rome and Egypt in the area between Greece and Mesopotamia. He would leave it to his supporters, who were neither few nor undistinguished, to fight his corner in Rome and see that his interests were not damaged by whatever Octavian chose to do in the other half of the empire. Unfortunately Octavian's ambition did not allow him to reciprocate. He had no intention of playing second fiddle to a new sort of quasi-monarch lording it in Alexandria under the fiction of Roman constitutional propriety.

And so Octavian set out to put pressure on Antony by denying him cooperation and presenting his actions in an unfavourable light. He built up his own strength, both political and military; he won over supporters from Antony, and created a battle-hardened army by a series of campaigns in Illyria in 35–33 B.C. Antony meanwhile took some redress for his defeat of 36 by invading and capturing Armenia and its king Artavasdes. At the end of the campaign, late in 34, a splendid ceremony, whose first part resembled a Roman triumph, was staged in Alexandria. Antony sent his royal prisoners and other captives ahead of him, as they would have walked in a triumph at Rome; he followed them, driving in a chariot, and presented Artavasdes and his family, with other spoils, to Cleopatra, who sat on a gilded chair on a silvered dais in front of a vast crowd. A day or two later the populace, assembled in the stadium, were treated to the sight of Antony and Cleopatra and their children, with Cleopatra's son Caesarion, enthroned above the throng, and heard Antony affirm that Caesarion (or Ptolemy Caesar, to give him his proper name) was Julius Caesar's legitimate son and was to be joint ruler of Egypt with his mother. They were to be called King of Kings and Queen of Kings and be overlords of a number of territories which were given to the younger children: the six-year-old Alexander Helios ('the Sun'), wearing a Median costume, received Armenia and (in hopeful anticipation) Media and Parthia; to his twin sister Cleopatra Selene ('the Moon') were granted Cyrenaica and Libya; and to Ptolemy Philadelphus, just two years old, wearing the Macedonian costume appropriate to the Ptolemaic house, came the Egyptian possessions in Syria and Cilicia along with a general suzerainty over the dynasts of Asia Minor. These grants have become known as the 'Donations of Alexandria' and without doubt they mark the beginning of the final clash. Why?

The reason is simple. Antony's grants to his children by Cleopatra were of no particular significance, since the territories concerned were almost exclusively those hitherto ruled by foreign princes, and that was exactly what their newly designated rulers were. Antony did not divorce Octavia until 32. In Roman law and in Roman eyes, the three were simply scions of the line of Ptolemy. But it was otherwise with Caesarion. Octavian's extraordinary rise to power had been founded on his designation as Julius Caesar's son and on the name of Caesar (which was what he always called himself). Adoption (at any age) was not uncommon in Roman society, so there was no hypocrisy in Octavian's describing Caesar as his father; but if there existed a real and legitimate son, and moreover one whose mother was a queen, the whole basis of Octavian's position was undermined. Antony had thrown down a direct challenge.

Hence a frigid silence from Rome at the news of the Armenian success, no customary thanksgiving to the gods, no ratification of Antony's acts. The message was clear: cooperation was dead. One of the two would have to take second place to the other. And so there followed in 33 and 32 B.C. an intense propaganda war, by which each man attempted to place the other in the wrong and induce his supporters to change sides. At the same time, there was a gradual build-up for real war. The powers of the triumvirate expired at the end of 33 B.C., leaving (by long-standing agreement) two consuls, who happened to be partisans of Antony, in charge of the Roman state. This is the point at which Dio's fiftieth book begins.

III. The position of Augustus after 27 B.C.

The development of Augustus's constitutional position was a topic beloved of historians of the later nineteenth and earlier twentieth centuries, who believed that it held the key to his power. We, who have learnt that power comes out of the barrel of a gun, see things differently. But it is still true that if Augustus had failed to devise a formula which made his *de facto* power acceptable, he might have met the same fate as Julius Caesar. The Romans were particularly conservative and unenthusiastic about change, and very proud of the stability and excellence of their constitution. Augustus showed himself astonishingly skilful in devising a position for himself which made use of no elements that were not familiar and accepted.

The significance of the arrangements made in January 27 B.C. cannot be fully appreciated without some knowledge of the system as it operated at the end of the republic. The men who had charge of the state were the two consuls, assisted by eight praetors. All were elected annually, spent their year of office (except in emergency) in Rome, and were invested with *imperium*, that is the legal authority to give commands to citizens in their military or civil capacity. The provinces, not all of which would contain legions, or require the presence of them, were governed by ex-consuls and ex-praetors, on whom was conferred for the purpose an *imperium* that could only be exercised within their province but was classified as consular (*pro consule*). The governor was primarily and originally the commander of the Roman forces operating in the province, and civil functions followed as a consequence of his authority. Governors were appointed by the Senate, normally for a year, though there might be special reasons which delayed the appointment of a successor. In the late republic special long-term commands were created by popular legislation for particular purposes, like Pompey's offensives against the pirates and Mithridates in the sixties, or Caesar's conquest of Gaul in the fifties.

In practice a provincial governor was a temporary monarch. Slowness of communications, and lack of information available to Senate and consuls, meant that little effective control could be exercised. What restrained a governor was fear of prosecution when he returned to Rome and became a private citizen unprotected by office. Men coveted provincial commands because this gave an opportunity to conduct wars and win glory – quite apart from the pickings that were to be had. The civil war of 49 B.C. broke out over the refusal of both Caesar and Pompey to abandon their long-term governorships of Gaul and Spain respectively. Through these they enjoyed many advantages, including the command of large armies loyal to themselves (see p. 6 above); immunity from prosecutions that might be brought by their enemies on political grounds for alleged misbehaviour in the past; ability to dispense patronage both to senators, by way of staff appointments, and to businessmen, by way of contracts and favours; opportunity to enrich themselves and their troops; and the exclusion of rivals from potential sources of military glory.

These facts explain why the allocation of the provinces in 27 B.C. was so important. By it Augustus acquired for ten years (and hitherto the longest period had been five) control of those provinces which contained the bulk of the legions and offered the principal chances for winning that all-important political commodity, military glory. Not that Augustus stood in much need of it (though rather too many of his successes had been won against his fellow-citizens), but he needed to prevent any would-be competitors from acquiring it. Because the Senate had made the allocation, Augustus depended on no special law for his position. In theory, he was a proconsul on a par with all other proconsuls designated by the Senate, except that he had charge of more than a single province and for longer than a single year. The problem raised by the fact that he could not be in more than one place at once was solved by the perfectly republican device of the *legatus* – a personal representative to whom Augustus's authority could be delegated. Thus Augustus did not need to visit any of his provinces, and could appoint whom he chose to govern them for him; but the responsibility, and the credit, remained his alone.

The Roman plebs continued to elect Augustus to the consulship every year. His popularity with them was overwhelming, and the office of course gave him all the constitutional power he needed in Rome, but it had certain disadvantages as a means of running the state. Repeated holding of the consulship was against the law and practice of the last 150 years, and the recent examples (Marius, Cinna and Julius Caesar) not altogether comfortable. The consuls had to perform a number of routine duties, nor was it in accord with tradition to be absent from Rome for long periods or to enter on a consulship elsewhere than at Rome – as Augustus in fact did in 26 and 25 B.C. A consul's acts could also be vetoed, by his colleague or a tribune. Although such a possibility was highly unlikely at this time, Fortune might one day bring in her changes. And by monopolizing one of the two highest offices of state, Augustus halved the number of men who could reach it. That was no way to win support amongst the senatorial aristocracy, who, deprived of power, longed all the more for status.

He therefore decided to resign from the consulship in 23 B.C. The Roman people did not like this. They tried to elect him on more than one occasion in the following years, but he would have none of it except in 5 and 2 B.C., when his grandsons entered public life. To compensate for the powers he surrendered, he received enhanced proconsular authority (*imperium maius*) and a grant of tribunician power (*tribunicia potestas*). The former enabled him to give orders to all other provincial governors, disposing of the fiction that he was equal to them, and freeing him from the necessity of proceeding through the Senate and consuls. The latter gave him back most of the powers he had lost in Rome (where proconsular power was not valid) through surrendering the consulship: power of veto, of summoning and putting business to the Senate, of taking legislation to the people, of holding public meetings, of enforcing obedience to his orders. In addition, the symbolic value of the tribunate was enormous, for the office had originated in the class struggles of the fifth century B.C., when the ordinary people of Rome were resisting an oppressive aristocracy. The tribunes were above all the protectors of the people. What better association could Augustus, heir of Caesar, patron of the plebs, look for? The office itself he had no wish to hold. That would have entailed elections, colleagues and formal obligations; and besides, he was a patrician. So, taking its power, he used it to mark the years of his reign, and turned it into a title of imperial authority.

The brilliance of this arrangement lies in its dissociation of the powers of an office from the office itself. The history of the late republic shows clearly that the two most important political power-bases were the tribunate in Rome and the proconsulate (with an army) outside. In conjunction they were capable of dominating the state, but individuals held them only for relatively short periods – a mere year in the case of the tribunate. Augustus not only united the two in his own person, but also freed himself from any real limitation of time, because his tribunician power was conferred for life and his proconsular *imperium* for blocks of ten (rarely five) years at a time. He had also freed himself from the actual offices, and therefore from any kind of 'democratic' challenge from colleagues and from any necessity to carry out formal duties. While still embracing the forms and words of power evolved over centuries, he had in fact placed himself in a totally new relation to the old constitutional framework. The final step was to add consular *imperium*, that is *imperium* valid in Rome itself, which he lacked after 23 B.C. This was done in 19 B.C., so that after that date he exercised the power of a consul without being consul, the power of a tribune without being tribune, and the power of a proconsul (who was by law superior to all others) without being in the ordinary sense a proconsul, for it was his *legati* who occupied that position.

None of the foregoing should obscure the fact that the constitutional arrangements were merely a vessel to accommodate Augustus's mastery of the state, won by violence and justified by success. In making them work the Senate was of considerable importance. Great prestige attached to it, because it was the body whose collective wisdom had traditionally guided Rome and its members were the men of most consequence in the state. But since it was essentially an advisory body, it had no real constitutional power. Augustus took great care to cultivate friendly relations with it, both collectively and individually, so that although it was the place where dissent might be expected (and was, in the early years, found), in fact it came to serve as a pool from which the magistrates, officers and administrators of the Empire were drawn. The emperor and the Senate were natural allies once the new order was established. After the old nobility of the republic, or what was left of them after the wars, had accepted that Augustus had moved beyond their reach, they settled down to cooperate with him and to secure position and advantage for themselves.

Augustus's real power was unchallengeable, based solidly on three chief elements: his popularity with the people of Rome, his support among the non-political upper classes of the Italian towns and the loyalty of the army to the name of Caesar. These were reinforced in many ways. The soldiers swore a personal oath of loyalty to their commander, who was in nearly all cases Augustus himself. After 12 B.C. the spirit (*Genius*) and household gods of Augustus were not only worshipped empire-wide by all, but shared shrines in the legionary camps with those talismanic objects of military reverence, the eagles. Until A.D. 6 the emperor funded discharge pensions out of his own resources. All appointments to officer service in the legions were in his gift, and with it membership of the equestrian order, which in turn gave access to a senatorial career or to responsible and privileged posts in the service of the emperor. The army was thus an avenue to the status sought by men whose families were locally prominent but aspired to higher things. The regions of Italy had suffered badly in the civil wars, but had nothing to gain from them – except finally a more rational system of government. Julius Caesar had made a point of cultivating them, and now they had every reason to offer their support and gratitude to the regime. And as for the people of Rome, Augustus looked after them handsomely: he provided food, water supplies, shows, splendid new buildings and proper administration of the city. Not for nothing did he receive the title 'Father of his Country' (*Pater Patriae*). His power and patronage were all-pervasive, his images in public places and on the coinage ubiquitous, his very father a god. His control of the state went deep, and rested on far firmer foundations than constitutional legality; but constitutional legality was still necessary.

IV. The frontier policy of Augustus

In the east, Augustus's main problem was with the Parthians. They had seen Antony off in 36, capturing some of his standards, and had previously done the same to two earlier Roman commanders, Crassus in 53 and Decidius Saxa in 40. They had also overrun Armenia in 32–31, reversing Antony's conquest and installing a pro-Parthian king, Artaxes, son of the captured Artavasdes. The safety of Syria, which bordered Parthia, and the honour of Rome, which did not accept defeat, seemed to demand action. But neither Armenia nor Parthia was fundamentally aggressive, and at no time did Augustus attempt a conquest of either. His policy was to secure a pro-Roman occupant of the throne of Armenia and maintain calm on the borders of Syria and Parthia. A friendly Armenia safeguarded the north of Syria and confirmed in their allegiance to Rome the less important client-kingdoms of that area. In contrast, the expeditions of the twenties mounted by the prefects of Egypt into Arabia and Ethiopia seem to be clear cases of aggression. No serious defensive justification can be found for them, and in the light of what is now known about the spice trade and the contacts of the Greek world with India there can be little doubt that Augustus's Arabian venture was intended to bring control of this lucrative part of the world. Presumably, similar motives lay behind the forays into Ethiopia. However, success was not to be had, and Augustus seems to have decided that this was not a fruitful corner of the world for imperial expansion.

Neither Spain nor Gaul had been completely conquered by 27 B.C. In Spain, Augustus personally conducted a full-scale war in 26 and 25 against the Cantabrians of the north, but although he represented the result as decisive much remained to be done before Agrippa in 18 carried out a characteristically ruthless and efficient subjugation of those tribes of the north and west which still held out. Gaul, thanks to the work of Julius Caesar and the subsequent campaigns of others, presented less of a problem and was effectively reduced by the mid-twenties. Its main importance in military terms was that its eastern border, the Rhine and the mountains of Switzerland, abutted against territory occupied by a variety of independent German tribes. The story in Dio (53.22.5) that Augustus planned to make an attack on Britain from Gaul is unlikely to reflect a serious project, even though it is echoed in the poetry of Horace: Strabo, who was a contemporary, explicitly comments on the pointlessness of annexing Britain, since the revenues from duty on trade exceeded the likely return from conquest and occupation (C 116).

In 17 B.C. Augustus felt ready to turn to the conquest of 'Germany' – an elastic term embracing an undefined and ill-understood area, whose size the Romans seriously underestimated, lying north and east of the Rhine and the Alps. The ground was prepared by the campaigns of Tiberius and his brother Drusus in Rhaetia (the Swiss and western Austrian Alps) in 15 B.C., and those of M. Vinicius and Agrippa in 14 and 13 in Pannonia (northern Yugoslavia, to the Danube valley). In 12 B.C., after Agrippa's death, Tiberius took over the reduction of Pannonia while Drusus struck eastward from the Rhine in what was probably intended as a kind of pincer movement. In 9 B.C. Drusus died and Tiberius, having completed the conquest of Pannonia, replaced him in command of the armies on the Rhine. After his sudden departure into self-imposed exile on Rhodes, a succession of senior and experienced generals continued to operate in Germany, gradually grinding down the independence of the tribesmen until Tiberius, after his reappearance in A.D. 4, was able to establish Roman control up to the Elbe, with the exception of an area roughly corresponding to Bavaria and Bohemia. In these years Roman power also advanced to the lower Danube, where the province of Moesia was created.

Thus by A.D. 6 Augustus had almost succeeded in bringing within the empire everything to the west and south of the Elbe and Danube. Then came disaster. Pannonia revolted in the autumn of that year, and it took Tiberius three years to restore control. Fortunately he had completed the task when in A.D. 9 the German leader Arminius, pretending cooperation, lured Varus, the governor of Germany, into a trap and totally destroyed him and his three legions. It is obvious from the sources that Varus was behaving as though Germany was actually an administrative province, albeit a newly conquered and inchoate one. The news brought near-panic at Rome. Emergency troops had to be conscripted, which casts an interesting light on the lack of spare capacity in the Augustan army. Augustus even feared for the security of the capital. In the event, the line of the Rhine was easily held, but Germany as a province was gone for ever, and Augustus, old and bitterly disappointed, attempted no more conquests. He is also said to have passed on to Tiberius the deathbed advice not to expand the empire.

There was of course military activity elsewhere in the empire at various times, but it always seems to have been in response to specific rebellion, attack, or threat, and not to have involved sustained effort over years. Conquest did not result, nor were Augustus or his sons or stepsons seen in the field – with the single exception of Gaius's expedition to the east in A.D. 1–3, which was more in the nature of a display of Roman force for diplomatic purposes. The cases discussed above are clearly different: massive effort was put into them and a corresponding quantity of glory came (or was supposed to come) from them.

It is very hard to maintain that Augustus was actuated by primarily defensive considerations and that the vast additions he made, or tried to make, to the empire were nothing more than the product of a process of tidying-up and making safe the frontiers. Such a view is in any case partly the product of modern maps. It is true that certain operations were forced on him, and he was notably cautious to avoid being drawn into a conflict with Parthia; but the pushing forward of Roman frontiers to the Danube along the whole length of the river, and the attempted incorporation of Germany into the empire, were a matter of choice, and preoccupied him for twenty-five years. There can be very little doubt that Augustus's ambitions were exactly the same as those of the great men of preceding generations: to win first place in the state and to increase the power and greatness of Rome. Translated into the terms of his epoch, that meant to be master of the state and to advance the boundaries of the empire by conquest. Nor should one forget the insistence of the Augustan poets on the Roman destiny to rule the world. But in this, as in many other ways, the reign of Augustus was truly transitional. He succeeded in being the last and greatest of the republican war-lords, and at the same time the man who discovered that there were limits to Roman expansion.

DIO AND HIS HISTORY

V.   Dio's life

For an ancient historian, Dio is unusually informative about himself. He was born at Nicaea, a leading town of Bithynia, in A.D. 163 or 164, the son of Cassius Apronianus, who was consul in an unknown year and served as governor of Lycia-Pamphylia, Cilicia and Dalmatia. He came to Rome about A.D. 180, saw the start of Commodus's reign, and accompanied his father on his governorship of Cilicia, probably in A.D. 182/3. He presumably held the quaestorship in 188 or 189, thereupon entering the Senate. Pertinax in 193 designated him praetor for 194 or perhaps 195, and the appointment was confirmed by Severus, who had by then become emperor. When Severus returned to Rome, either in 197 after defeating Clodius Albinus in Gaul, or more probably in 202 after the Mesopotamian expedition, Dio gave the emperor his history of the wars that had recently ended. He then began to prepare for the writing of his *Roman History*. He subsequently held a provincial governorship and a suffect consulship, probably in A.D. 205 or 206. (The arguments for a later date, *c.* 222, are not convincing, since they require the belief that the province of Numidia had not at that time been created, and Dio's own words at 76.14.4 strongly imply a consulship under Septimius Severus. Whichever view one takes there is a very large interval to be accounted for in his career. Presumably his lack of enthusiasm for Severus's regime and obvious revulsion from Caracalla (211–17) and Elagabalus (218–22) provide the explanation.) He was, however, distinguished enough to become a member of Severus's imperial council from at least 204, though he did not accompany Severus to Britain in 208. Perhaps, as a Greek with a consular father (an untypical combination), he had both status and a special viewpoint. We find him at Nicomedia in his native Bithynia in the winter of 214–15, in the thankless role of 'companion' (*comes*) to the unspeakable Caracalla. As one of the local rich, he also had to make his contribution to the feeding and entertainment of the emperor and his troops. He then returned to Italy until 218, when he was appointed by the new emperor Macrinus to be overseer (*curator*) of Pergamum and Smyrna (80.7.4). A period of illness, spent at Nicaea, intervened between this post and the governorship of Africa (that is Tunisia), which can hardly be before 221. He then proceeded almost immediately to the governorship of Dalmatia, followed directly by that of Upper Pannonia, with two legions under his command (80.1.2–3). Coming back to Rome, in 229 he achieved the distinction of holding a second consulship as colleague to the emperor Severus Alexander, but returned home almost at once with an ailment in his legs to die at Nicaea at an unknown date.

VI. Composition and circumstances of the History

Dio tells us himself how he came to write his *Roman History*:

> After this there occurred very violent wars and civil strife, and I wrote an account of these for the following reason. I had written and published a memoir about the dreams and portents which led Severus to hope for the imperial power, and after he had read the copy I sent him he wrote me a handsome acknowledgement. Receiving the letter in the evening, I soon went to sleep, and as I slept the divine power commanded me to write history. Thus I came to compose the present account. And since it found great favour, not only with others, but with Severus himself, I felt the desire to put together the whole history of the Romans; therefore I decided not to leave my composition as a separate work but to incorporate it into this present history ... I spent ten years collecting everything that the Romans did from the beginning until the death of Severus, and another twelve years in working it up; later events will be recorded as fortune allows. (73.23.1–3, 5)

From this it appears that Dio cannot have started writing before the death of Severus in 211. On the other hand, if he did not begin until after Caracalla died (217), he would surely have named that event, and not the death of Severus, as the point up to which he took notes. Thus the twelve years of composition must have begun between 211 and 217 and ended between 223 and 229. If one assumes that his string of governorships from c. 222 reduced his leisure for writing, and that he started taking notes fairly soon after he had completed and presented to Severus his work on the wars (perhaps 202 or 203), the most probable hypothesis is that he took notes c. 203–13 and wrote them up c. 214–26. Other evidence is hard to use: for example, references like those in Book 49 (36.4, 37.3), which show that this narrative was written during or after Dio's governorship of Dalmatia and Pannonia; but since we have no idea how he actually worked, nor how fast he wrote, nor to what extent he might have rewritten sections in the light of later knowledge, it is unsafe to argue that he was only a little over half-way through by c. 225.

He must, then, have started to write in the reign of Caracalla, who ranks as one of the most odiously cruel, greedy and autocratic of the emperors of Rome. By comparison with such a man Augustus was bound to seem a paragon. A fairer, but equally telling, comparison existed with Caracalla's father and predecessor, Septimius Severus. Severus, like Augustus, had come to power as a result of struggles in Rome over the mastery of the state and after a period of civil war in which his actions were as unscrupulous and as effective as those of Augustus had been. Like Augustus, he inherited a situation in which domestic peace should have been attended by reconciliation, stability and goodwill. Like Augustus, he saw himself as a great conqueror, making major expeditions to Mesopotamia and to Scotland. Like Augustus, his power was solidly based on the loyalty of his soldiers and his attention to the welfare of the ordinary people of Rome. But he and his son after him never attempted to conceal that theirs was a military despotism. They brought out quite openly the absolutism latent in the principate, and treated the Senate for what it was, a kind of court to perform certain ceremonial and validatory functions. Dio's reactions were probably typical of the upper classes (he has just described Severus's entry into Rome in 193 to assume the imperial power):

Entering the city in this way, he made some fine promises to us like the emperors of old, that he would put no senator to death; and he took an oath to this effect, and furthermore ordered it to be confirmed in a joint decree that the emperor and anyone who aided him in such a deed, both themselves and their children, were to be declared public enemies. Yet he himself was the first to transgress and not keep this law, executing many senators ... He did many things that we disliked, and he was blamed for disturbing the city with the numbers of his soldiers and for burdening the state with excessive expenditure, and most of all because he placed his hopes of safety not in the goodwill of his companions but in the strength of his army. (75.2.1–3)

Dio's interpretation of the way emperors ought to behave was also shaped by the events which occurred before the reign of Severus. Marcus Aurelius had unwisely chosen his son Commodus to succeed him. Aged nineteen when his father died in 180, Commodus quickly freed himself from the influence of the counsellors given him by the philosophic and virtuous Marcus and took to a life of tyrannical luxury and self-indulgence. He put to death his wife and his sister, and also many prominent men. When he was at last done away with, strangled in his bath on the last day of 192 at the behest of his chamberlain and his praetorian prefect, the treasury was practically empty. It was a testimony to the strength of the system set up by Augustus that it could survive a twelve-year reign of this nature. The next emperor was Pertinax, a senior senator of probity, experience and military reputation won under Marcus Aurelius. But he moved too fast in bringing back decency and self-restraint to public service. He antagonized the praetorians and was killed confronting a mob of them in the palace after a reign of only eighty-seven days. 'He failed to comprehend,' says Dio, 'though a man of wide practical experience, that one cannot with safety reform everything in a moment, and that the restoration of a state in particular requires both time and wisdom' (74.10.3). Dio surely had the example of Augustus very much in mind when he made this comment. As for the notorious auction of the imperial throne which the praetorians then conducted, when the city prefect, Flavius Sulpicianus, father-in-law of Pertinax, bid against the rusticated spendthrift from Milan, Didius Julianus, to offer the larger donative, it makes its own point. In the light of this disgrace, even Severus, Didius's successor, must have seemed like an avenging angel, and Augustus to have richly deserved his deification.

VII. Dio as a historian

There were rules for writing history – indeed Lucian's essay on the subject, written about the time of Dio's birth, survives – and Dio could not escape them. He obeys the precept not to write either too elaborately or too simply, and took care to study the artificial literary language of his day, which looked back to classical Attic Greek, by reading approved exponents of it. The style of the speeches also gives variety, being fuller and more antithetical than that of the narrative.

Another requirement was to have assimilated one's material and, so to speak, homogenized it, so that a smooth, continuously flowing narrative emerged without citation of sources or argument over the true version of events. Thus it is that we know virtually nothing about the sources Dio used for the reign of Augustus. A certain amount of detective work has been done by comparing Dio with other ancient writers on Augustus; for instance it is clear that Dio knew Suetonius, Seneca and Tacitus, as well as the emperor's own autobiography and the hostile writings of Cremutius Cordus; but it has recently been shown by Manuwald that Livy is not, as used to be assumed, the fount of the narrative of the triumviral period.

Any attempt to estimate Dio's quality and reliability as a historian by identifying his sources is fruitless. What is certain is that a substantial proportion of the material in the Augustan books is original to Dio (notably the speeches, and the digressions on the imperial system in Book 53 and on the legions in Book 55) and we should be prepared to admit that an ancient historian was no less capable than his modern counterpart of reshaping what he had read – though the placing of the improving tale of Cinna Magnus's conspiracy in A.D. 5 instead of where Seneca puts it, in *c.* 15 B.C., is probably only a mistake. Dio's Augustan books are very much his own creation, setting out the mature views of a senior statesman on an age that was at once very similar to and very different from his own.

History was also supposed to be interesting and entertaining as well as truthful and improving. In practice, the latter function often came a poor second to the former, except in the case of the rare writers like Polybius who had an exalted view of the usefulness and seriousness of history. This meant that history was enlivened by anecdotes (if possible, with a moral), by colourful descriptions (especially of unusual customs, places, or things), by accounts of dreams and prodigies (of which Dio is fond, not unnaturally in view of his literary debut), and by avoidance of tedious detail (such things as exact dates, times and places, to the frustration of moderns). Personalities and notable deeds bulk large, the common man and the price of bread very small.

We are ignorant of the aim Dio set himself. There are signs that he was considerably influenced by Thucydides: the annalistic structure, the probing of motive, the use of speeches, the fondness for antithesis. If we had his preface, unfortunately lost along with all the earlier part of his *History*, we might know whether he consciously rejected the Livian view of history as an extended moral lesson in favour of the Greek tradition of Thucydides and Polybius which saw the value of history in the insights it offered into the ways men actually behave. If we measure him by the criteria of Lucian, who details at length the shortcomings of contemporaries, he shows up quite well. He possessed 'the two supreme qualities, political understanding and power of expression'; he is no panegyricist and is willing to set down the truth; he had patience in investigating and collecting facts before he set out to clothe them in acceptable style; for the most part his ordering of the facts is lucid, even though the precise chronological relationships of different chains of events is not always clear; his narrative moves swiftly (it had little choice); he does not linger long on descriptions; and his speeches (see below) are at least not out of general character with the individuals who deliver them.

What then are the main features of the narrative? First, it is supposedly annalistic. But in fact there are cases where a topic, broached under the appropriate year, is followed to its conclusion in a later year (generally not specifically identified) before Dio comes to the next pair of consuls' names. In other words, there is a certain amount of disguised chronological displacement. A spectacular example of this is the way the description of the division of the provinces, and of how they were governed, at 53.12–13 leads into a 'timeless' sketch of provincial organization under the empire and of the position and powers of the emperor. Sometimes a topic arises by association of ideas rather than time, as when the mention of Agrippa's dedication of the Saepta in 26 B.C. leads on to his modesty and self-effacement, which in turn brings up the boasting and downfall of Cornelius Gallus (53.23). Yet that belongs to 27 B.C. at the latest, a thing the unwary reader would never suspect. There is, therefore, a certain tension between topical and annalistic presentation; but on the whole the picture remains clear apart from some chronological vagueness.

Next, Dio's preoccupations are, as one can only expect, those of a man of his class and time. The subject-matter consists of things that concerned a senator: conspiracies against the emperor; unrest in Rome; laws affecting social order, status and senatorial careers; doings of members of the imperial family; succession to the imperial power; prodigies and portents (which the state religion, at least, took seriously); and, of course, military campaigns, whether conducted by Augustus himself or by others. What we are not told are the details of things Dio either took for granted, like the network of personal connection and patronage which contributed so much to the strength of the emperor's position, or found too trivial to mention, like the way in which power was actually exercised through the formal working of the constitution (cf. 55.8.2). Nor is Dio (or any other ancient historian) concerned to bring out the slow processes of social and economic development which we have learnt to recognize as prime movers of political change. If one thinks of such topics as the prosperity of Italy as compared with the provinces, the effects of citizen settlement overseas, the changes set in train by the creation of a large standing army at the borders of an enlarged empire, the mechanisms by which wealth became concentrated in the hands of the emperor, and the impact of taxation – all these are of no concern to Dio, although sundry facts which bear on these questions emerge incidentally. They have no power of explanation until a historian takes a longer view of the historical process than Dio did.

This brings us to a third feature of the *History*. Dio was treating nearly a thousand years of Roman history, but he is not a good enough writer to iron out variations of attitude and interpretation in his sources and to impose a unified vision on his vast mass of material. He remains close to the performers as the great procession of Roman history winds its way past him, and for him, as for the annalists of the Augustan age, Livy and Dionysius of Halicarnassus, the backdrop hardly changes. Rome was the mistress of the world, her métier empire, and her rule eternal. Such a viewpoint does not encourage a man who has absorbed it as an essential feature of the culture of his age to indulge in a Toynbee-esque hunt for growth, maturity and decay, or attempt to unravel the causes of these things. It also leads him into anachronism, particularly when he talks about succession to the principate (cf. 53.31). On the other hand, he often brings out, like Thucydides, the contrast between appearance and reality, truth and allegation; and in his consistent interpretation of the great figures of the late republic as driven on by the desire for power one feels that personal judgement and personal experience are at work. Lastly, there is the effect of the high place accorded to rhetorical accomplishment in the educational process and the polite society of Dio's day. Apart from style, there are two obvious ways in which this shows in his work. One is the working-up of a set-piece, typically a battle, like Varus's disaster (56.20 ff.), or Actium (50.34–35). In the latter case we have other information and it is apparent that Dio (or possibly his source) has let his imagination run riot in order to turn a somewhat disappointing battle into something worthy to serve as the 'birth-legend in the mythology of the principate' (Syme).

The other rhetorical feature is the presence of imaginary speeches. In ancient history-writing there appears to be a shortage of reflection and analysis. This apparent lack is due to a convention which goes back to the earliest surviving Greek historian, Herodotus, and was used with powerful effect by his immediate successor Thucydides. Public speaking was important in the ancient world. Generals harangued their troops before battles, and politicians argued cases before large audiences. Speeches could therefore properly be inserted in the historical narrative to depict character and to give variety, drama and emphasis. Thucydides goes further than his predecessor and uses speeches to give the reader an analysis of the situation or an insight into the motives and reasoning of his characters in a vivid and dramatic way, while still retaining the appearance of objective reporting; and although he claims to be giving the substance of what was said, internal evidence is against the claim. Thus the convention of fictitious speeches was established. They also gave the writer an opportunity to display his rhetorical skill and entertain his readers. The fiction itself could be trivial or total, ranging from attributing to a known speaker on a known occasion something different from what he (perhaps) said, to complete invention of both speech and occasion. Dio makes full use of this convention, most interestingly perhaps in the speech of Maecenas in Book 52, where he is obviously giving his own opinions. Likewise the advice given to Augustus by Livia on the occasion of Cinna Magnus's conspiracy (55.14–21) seems to embody his own reflections on how a ruler should temper justice with mercy. By contrast, the speech he puts into Augustus's mouth at the crucial meeting of the Senate early in 27 B.C. (53.3–10) contrives to say very little at some considerable length.

VIII. Dio's view of Augustus

Dio laments, in a celebrated passage, how difficult it became after the establishment of the principate to discover the truth of events. Before that time, he says, government was open and actions and decisions a matter of public knowledge. 'But in later times most events began to be kept secret and were denied common knowledge, and even though it may happen that some matters are made public, the reports are discredited because they cannot be investigated, and the suspicion grows that everything is said and done according to the wishes of the men in power at the time and of their associates' (53.19; cf. 54.15). Such a complaint also makes very clear what Dio thought the focus of history should be: politics and war, famous men and notable events. Within these limits, the picture that Dio paints of Augustus is generally favourable (that is, once the civil wars were over). He does not avoid the occasional discreditable item, nor does he suspend his critical faculties – for example his own experience must have told him that the private funds of the emperor were not really private at all, and so he refuses to distinguish between Augustus's private expenditure and that of the state treasury (53.22.4).

As to the principate itself, from the point of view of an admirer of old-fashioned republican freedom like Tacitus, its very institution was a calamity. In two famous chapters of his *Annals* (1.9–10), Tacitus makes Augustus's detractors, after his death, accuse him of being driven by a desire for mastery, while his apologists justify his seizure of sole power by saying that it was the only way in which the state could be saved. Dio frankly accepts that Augustus brought monarchy back to Rome after a lapse of nearly five hundred years, and he sees through the republican façade of the Augustan constitution, but does not condemn it. He marks the moment of transition more than once (51.1.1, 52.1.1, 53.17.1), seeming to contradict himself but in fact granting emphatic recognition to the birth of a new order, and then goes on to relate, so far as he can, how Augustus used his power, and what the fortunes of the Roman people and their empire were under his direction. Power is amoral, a fact of political life. The important thing, to Dio, is that it take an acceptable form and enable all classes in society to enjoy freedom under the law and perform their various functions as citizens, from privileged senator down to humble fisherman, without unjust and capricious interference. In these terms, he regarded Augustus as a benefactor of mankind, though one should perhaps beware of interpreting the eulogy delivered by Tiberius at Augustus's funeral as a statement of Dio's own views: it is wiser to regard this as a virtuoso exercise in panegyric, showing how even the unsavoury start of Augustus's political career could be justified, than as an 'editorial' judgement by the author – and in fact such a judgement follows the end of the speech and is noticeably more restrained in tone (56.43–45). Dio was perfectly well aware of the distinction between history and panegyric, and his general view of Augustus was based on the record as it was known to him. Unpleasant but true facts about Augustus required neither suppression nor justification. On the other hand, his sense of the quite literally epoch-making nature of the reign is evident in the way in which he structures Books 52 and 53 and in the emphasis he gives to certain aspects of Augustus's policies through the speeches in Books 55 and 56.

His own political views are expressed very clearly in the speech of Maecenas in Book 52, answering one by Agrippa. The debate serves to emphasize Augustus's single most important political decision, and to present it in the agonistic form natural to Graeco-Roman literary culture. It is in essence an elaboration of reflections he has already given us *in propria persona* on Caesar's murder (44.2), and other remarks elsewhere (53.19.1, 54.6.1) leave the reader in no doubt that Dio thoroughly approved of monarchy in principle. The speakers purport to be offering advice to Augustus as to what he should do now that he has restored peace and normality to the Roman world – lay down his power, or retain it? If there ever was such a debate in Augustus's circle, it would certainly not have taken the form Dio gives it. Nor are either of the protagonists known to have held the views attributed to them here. Agrippa, however, had an impressive record of concern for the welfare of the people of Rome, and so democrat Dio made him.

Dio chose these men as mouthpieces because they were the two most influential and important of Augustus's supporters. Marcus Vipsanius Agrippa, a man of obscure, probably central Italian origin, who liked to suppress his revealingly un-Roman family name, had been a fellow-officer of Augustus's in 44 B.C. and accompanied him to Italy on his quest for Caesar's inheritance. He became prominent in the war of Perusia, and thereafter was Augustus's chief marshal, as competent by sea as by land. He was responsible for the defeat of Sextus Pompey, played a vital part in the campaign before Actium, and was admiral on the day of the battle. He took charge of a great programme of public works to improve the amenities of Rome in 33 B.C. (and later), and held consecutive consulships, with Augustus, in 28 and 27 – the years which marked the return of constitutional government. His most outstanding qualities were his ruthlessness, efficiency and utter loyalty. Gaius Maecenas was altogether different. Born into the old Etruscan aristocracy of Arretium (Arezzo), he affected descent from kings and never felt the need to hold Roman public office or even become a senator. Subtle, immensely cultured, effeminate and given to luxury, his languor concealed formidable powers of organization and control. Like Agrippa, he had been with Augustus from the beginning – thanks doubtless to previous links with Caesar. He is on record as a diplomat and as unofficial governor of Rome at certain vital moments. His greatest value to Augustus will have been behind the scenes, as political adviser and judge of men. It is entirely appropriate that he should speak for monarchy.

Agrippa's speech is very much shorter than Maecenas's and deals almost entirely in clichés which pay no heed to the particular circumstances of the moment nor to the peculiar nature of Roman democracy. 'Democracy' is used by Greek writers to mean a republican as opposed to a monarchical form of government; but none the less the concept as handled here by Agrippa appears rather theoretical. If Dio knew Polybius's analysis of the Roman constitution, he preferred to ignore it here. Oligarchy is not mentioned. The monarch is referred to as a 'tyrant' (perhaps a less emotive translation would be 'autocrat', the point of the Greek word being that his power is absolute). The necessity to tax his subjects is said to make him unpopular – yet at this date Roman citizens were barely taxed at all. The problems raised concerning the administration of justice are unreal, in the light of the system which actually operated in the early empire. In short, what we have here is a rhetorical presentation of arguments which might once have applied to a Greek city-state, long before the days of Augustus, but had very little relevance to Rome in 29 B.C. The ghosts of thousands of school declamations on the topic haunt this unconvincing exercise. One feels that Dio's heart is not in it – unless of course he is really saying that democracy is an irrelevant concept, but leaving it to his readers to work this out for themselves.

Maecenas's answer falls into two main parts. The first is almost as theoretical as the case put on the other side by Agrippa, but it stays a good deal closer to Roman reality and acknowledges specific historical facts like the size of the state and the occurrence of the civil wars (though it must be said that the historical examples he produces to bolster his argument are used no more accurately than Agrippa's: Caesar, for example, is said to have lost his life because he was thinking of giving up his power!). Maecenas does not seriously attempt a justification of Augustus's present position beyond saying that it was forced on him as a result of the actions of others, starting with the assassins of Caesar. Still less does he pretend that the rise to power was blameless. He prefers simply to take the fact for granted and advise Augustus how best to use it.

This advice constitutes the second and by far the longer part of the speech (chapters 19–40). In it Dio sketches a kind of ideal principate, in which various features from different periods, or from none, coexist in a composite picture. Some of the recommendations made by Maecenas were actually features of the Augustan constitution, for example the prescribed minimum ages for office-holding, which lowered those al-lowed under the republic by five years. Some were never carried out, like the proposal for a 'sub-censor' (ch.21), which seems to be an idea of Dio's own. And some, like the proposal to appoint senior ex-magistrates to oversee individual cities and districts within provinces (and indeed within Italy) look forward to practices which were instituted long after Augustus's day, but were part of the administrative scheme of the late second-century empire.

It is quite clear that Dio—Maecenas believes essentially in an ideal form of the status quo. The system sketched by Maecenas is recognizably the system we know, improved in detail, maybe, and restoring to the Senate some of its lost responsibility, but it is nevertheless not fundamentally different. It is remarkable that Dio's own experience of the abuse of autocratic power did not lead him to propose more radical changes. For him, Augustus had laid down the main outlines of his world. The ruler is simply assumed to be actuated by the highest motives, namely his wish to benefit the whole empire and be thought worthy by all of his exalted position. Dio says nothing about how he should be educated or selected or, once selected, stopped from abusing his power. Dio accepts the division of the upper class of the empire into two (the senatorial and equestrian orders), a division whose original basis had become quite irrelevant by his day. He does not question the social order and its existing stratification. He is, in short, a staunch upholder of the view propounded two generations earlier by another upper-class Greek, Aelius Aristides, and found elsewhere in the literature of the time, that the empire, paradoxically, represented a kind of perfect democracy (or republic): 'there is an abundant and beautiful equity of the humble with the great', thanks to the existence of the emperor as supreme judge, and 'a common democracy of the earth has been set up under one man, the best, as ruler and orderer; and all come together, as in a common market-place, each to receive what is worthy of him' (*To Rome*, 39, 60). If this is so, no fundamental change is needed, and the difference between a statement of the ideal and a plan for practical action largely vanishes. Perhaps the speech of Maecenas is a political manifesto directed at Severus Alexander, perhaps not: the theory that it could have been intended for Caracalla requires one to suppose that it was written separately and later embodied in the main text, which is far too hostile to both Caracalla and Elagabalus to have seen the light of day in their reigns. However that may be, the speech is most certainly a document for its own age, and it shows Dio doing, albeit without great finesse, what any historian worth the name must do: show how the past is relevant to the present.

BIBLIOGRAPHICAL NOTE

An excellent sketch of the reign of Augustus can be found in Colin Wells, *The Roman Empire*, chapters 3–4 (Fontana, 1984); more substantial is D. C. Earl, *The Age of Augustus* (1968, reissued London, 1980), while the full-scale treatment of R. Syme, *The Roman Revolution* (Oxford, 1939), has become a classic. Both Earl and Wells provide extensive annotated bibliographies. Further discussion of some of the features of the late republic picked out in this Introduction may be found in A. W. Lintott, *Violence in Republican Rome* (Oxford, 1968), W. V. Harris, *War and Imperialism in Republican Rome* (Oxford, 1979), D. C. Earl, *The Moral and Political Tradition of Rome* (London, 1967), E. Gabba, *Republican Rome, the Army, and the Allies* (English trans., London, 1976), and many other studies of the period, to which Michael Crawford, *The Roman Republic* (Fontana, 1978), is a very good introduction. The practical working of political institutions is fully analysed by C. Nicolet, *The World of the Citizen in Republican Rome* (English trans., London, 1980), while T. P. Wiseman (ed.), *Roman Political Life 90 B.C.–A.D. 69* (Exeter, 1985) is an extremely useful survey of the aims, motivation and behaviour of the Roman governing class and also contains excellent bibliographical notes.

On Dio, the monograph of Fergus Millar, *A Study of Cassius Dio* (Oxford, 1964), is fundamental, superseding the article of E. Schwartz in *Paulys Realenzyklopädie* (Bd. III, 1684 ff.); and B. Manuwald, *Cassius Dio und Augustus* (Wiesbaden, 1979) exhaustively examines how Dio presents Augustus–Octavian in Books 45–56. The review of Manuwald's book by C. B. R. Pelling in *Gnomon* 55 (1983) 221–6 is illuminating, and on the composition of the history see G. W. Bowersock's review of Millar in *Gnomon* 37 (1965) 469–74, and T. D. Barnes 'The composition of Cassius Dio's *Roman History*', *Phoenix* 38 (1984) 240–55. For the text, the critical edition of U. P. Boissevain (5 vols., Berlin, 1895–1931) is standard and is the basis of E. Cary's text, with parallel English translation, in the Loeb Classical Library (9 vols., London and New York, 1914–27). It is the latter which has been used here, the variations from Boissevain being insignificant. There also exist commentaries on Books 53 (H. T. F. Duckworth, Toronto, 1916) and 54 (F. B. Bender, Univ. of Pennsylvania, 1961). Forthcoming are commentaries by M. Reinhold and M. Swan on Books 45–56 (the first volume, on Books 49–52, is due in 1986) and by J. W. Rich on selected portions of Books 51–56.

ACKNOWLEDGEMENTS

I should like to express my gratitude for various kinds of help and encouragement to Fergus Millar, Stephen Usher, Susan Sherwin-White, Ian Scott-Kilvert, and especially John Rich, none of whom should bear any responsibility for the shortcomings of the introductory pages.

J. M. CARTER

In preparing the translation my thanks are due to John Carter for his invaluable and constructive criticism of the text and notes and for adding many important notes. Also to Professor Michael Grant for his advice on the events of the period and the Augustan background.

IAN SCOTT-KILVERT

NOTE ON THE TEXT

AUGUSTUS'S NAMES

Augustus did not acquire this name, which was a title of honour, until 27 B.C. (see Book 53, ch. 16). His original name was Gaius Octavius, but after the Ides of March he became Gaius Julius Caesar as a result of his posthumous adoption by the dictator's will. Dio, in common with all other ancient writers, therefore correctly calls him 'Caesar' between 44 and 27 B.C. To avoid confusion with his adoptive father, who had exactly the same names, the modern convention is to call him 'Octavian' in this period, although he never used this name himself. This is the practice that has been followed here.

TEXTUAL LACUNAE

There are gaps in the original text of Books 55 and 56, where leaves have dropped out from the single manuscript on which we depend at this point. These gaps can be partly filled from the excerpts and summaries made in the eleventh and twelfth centuries by two Byzantine scholars, Xiphilinus and Zonaras, and from other less important collections of excerpts. They occur between 55.9.4 and 55.10.2 (2 leaves); 55.10.15 and 55.10A.1 (2 leaves); 55.11.2 and 55.13.2 (2 leaves); 55.33.2 and 55.34.1 (4 leaves); at 56.22.2 (1 leaf); between 56.24.5 and 56.25.1; (1 leaf); 56.28.6 and 56.29.3 (1 leaf); and 56.31.3 and 56.34.2 (1 leaf, almost completely replaced). Each leaf contains about the same amount of text as each leaf of the present translation. We have enclosed the inserted material, chiefly from Xiphilinus and Zonaras, between square brackets; but note that where only a handful of words are enclosed in this way (as at the opening of 55.10A), these are purely an editorial convenience to give a mutilated sentence some intelligibility and make no claim to represent what Dio may once have written.

THE ROMAN HISTORY
THE REIGN OF AUGUSTUS

BOOK 50

The following is contained in the Fiftieth Book of Dio's *Rome*:

How Octavian and Antony began to fight one another (chs. 1-14)
How Octavian conquered Antony at Actium (chs. 15-35)

1.   Although the Roman people's republican form of government had been taken away from them, they had still not reached the situation, strictly speaking, of being ruled by a monarchy.[1] Antony and Octavian, who controlled the affairs of state, did so with equal authority, since they had divided by lot most of the functions of government. For the rest, although in theory they regarded themselves as exercising these in common, in practice each strove to arrogate powers to himself, according to the success of either in gaining an advantage over the other. But later, when Sextus Pompeius[2] had been put to death, when the king of Armenia[3] had been captured by Antony, when hostilities against Octavian's forces had ceased, and no trouble threatened in Parthia, then the two men openly turned against one another, and the Roman people was undeniably enslaved.

The causes of the war and the pretexts which each leader put forward were as follows. Antony accused Octavian of having removed Lepidus[4] from his office of triumvir, and of having appropriated both the territory and the troops which had been under the last-named and Sextus's control, and which ought to have been shared with Antony: he demanded that Octavian should transfer to him half of these forces, and in addition half the soldiers who had been conscripted in those parts of Italy which belonged to them both. Octavian countered[5] with the charge that Antony was still keeping possession of Egypt and other territories without having drawn them by lot; that he had executed Sextus Pompeius, whom Octavian had willingly spared, so he claimed; and that by having tricked, arrested and put in chains the king of Armenia, he had brought the Roman people into great disrepute. He likewise demanded a half share of Antony's conquests, and above all denounced Antony for his union with Cleopatra, for begetting their children whom he had acknowledged as his own, and for the gifts he had made to them.[6] In particular he attacked Antony because he was using the name Caesarion for Cleopatra's son by Julius Caesar, and thus making him a member of the Caesarian family.

2.   These were the accusations which they brought against one another, and so in a sense employed to defend their actions. They were exchanged partly through private letters and partly through public speeches delivered by Octavian and written pronouncements despatched by Antony. On the same pretext they repeatedly sent envoys back and forth, partly because they wished to create the impression that their respective charges were well founded, but also to try to discover one another's strength. All this time they were gathering funds, avowedly for some different purpose, and making all the other preparations for war, as though it were against some different opponent, until the moment when Gnaeus Domitius[7] and Gaius Sosius,[8] both supporters of Antony, became consuls. From that time they dropped all further concealment and set their course uncompromisingly for war. These events came about as follows.

Domitius, as a man who had experienced many reverses in public life, did not openly introduce any measures of radical change. Sosius, on the other hand, was a stranger to shifts of fortune, and so on the first day of the next month[9] he delivered a speech which praised Antony and attacked Octavian at length. Indeed he would have immediately proposed a motion hostile to Octavian, had not Nonius Balbus, one of the tribunes, interposed his veto. Octavian, it seems, had suspected Sosius's intention, and judged that he should neither ignore it nor, by opposing it, create the impression that he was taking the first step in the war. He therefore refrained from entering the Senate during this period, and even ceased to reside in the capital at all. He invented some excuse and proceeded to stay outside the city, not only for the reasons already given, but also so as to study at leisure the reports he received, and then decide after due consideration what action he should take.

But not long afterwards he returned and summoned a meeting of the Senate which he attended, surrounded with a guard of soldiers and a number of personal supporters who carried daggers concealed about them. Then, sitting upon his chair of state with the consuls, he made a long speech defending his actions in moderate terms, and launching many accusations against Sosius and Antony. Neither of the consuls nor any of the senators dared to utter a word in reply, whereupon Octavian named a date for a further meeting of the Senate, and announced that he would establish the injustice of Antony's actions by means of certain documents. Then the consuls, since they did not dare to speak in opposition but did not tolerate being silenced, left the city secretly before the date fixed for the next meeting. Later they travelled to join Antony, and not a few of the other senators joined them. When Octavian discovered this, he gave it out that he had sent them away of his own accord: he was anxious that nobody should think they had abandoned him for any wrongful action on his part, and he added that any other senators who wished to join Antony were free to leave in safety.

3.   The departure of these men from the Senate was offset by the arrival of other senators, who in turn had fled from Antony and now joined Octavian. These included Titius[10] and Plancus,[11] in spite of the fact that they were among the men whom Antony had honoured most highly and who knew all his secrets. The sequence of events had been as follows. After the consuls had left, as I have described, and Octavian had summoned the Senate in their absence, spoken at length and read out the documents he wished to make public, these matters were reported to Antony. He in turn summoned a kind of senatorial council drawn from his supporters: the choice between war and peace was debated at length on both sides, and finally Antony decided in favour of war and of renouncing his marriage to Octavia. It was then that Titius and Plancus, either on account of some personal quarrel with Antony, or because they had grounds for resentment against Cleopatra, abandoned Antony's cause.

Octavian welcomed them most warmly and learned from them all about Antony's affairs – his present actions, his future plans, the provisions of his will and the name of the man who held the document – for Titius and Plancus had been among the witnesses to it. These discoveries angered Octavian even more violently than before, and he did not scruple to search out the will, seize it, bring it into the Senate and later the assembly, and read it out in public. Although Octavian had no right whatever to do this, yet the provisions of the will were such that none of the citizens blamed him for his action.[12] Antony had testified to Caesarion that he was without doubt Julius Caesar's son, had made enormous settlements upon his children by the Egyptian queen, whom he was bringing up, and had ordered that his body should be buried in Alexandria by Cleopatra's side.

4.   The Romans were so outraged by these disclosures that they were willing to believe that other rumours current at the time were equally true, namely that if Antony were victorious, he would hand over the city of Rome to Cleopatra and transfer the seat of government to Egypt. Public hostility became so intense that not only Antony's enemies, and those who had not hitherto taken sides, but even his closest friends, utterly condemned his action. They were dismayed at what had been read out, and in their anxiety to dispel any suspicion of themselves on Octavian's part, spoke in the same terms as the rest. They stripped Antony of the consulship for which he had been designated in advance,[13] and of all other authority vested in him. They did not formally declare him a public enemy, since they feared that his supporters would also have to be classed as enemies if they did not abandon Antony, but their actions showed their feelings more clearly than any form of words. They passed a resolution that Antony's adherents would be pardoned and commended, if they would desert him. They then declared war outright upon Cleopatra, put on their military cloaks, as if Antony were close at hand, and went to the temple of Bellona.[14] There, with Octavian officiating as *fetialis*,[15] they carried out the rites which are customary before a declaration of war. These proceedings were directed formally against Cleopatra, but in reality against Antony.

5.   She had, it was believed, enslaved him so completely that she had persuaded him to act as gymnasiarch[16] for the Alexandrians; she was saluted by him as 'queen' and as 'mistress', and she had Roman soldiers in her bodyguard, all of whom had her name inscribed upon their shields. She visited the market-place with Antony, presided with him over festivals and at the hearing of lawsuits, rode with him on horseback even in the cities, or else was carried in a litter, while Antony followed on foot together with her eunuchs. He also referred to his headquarters as 'the palace',[17] sometimes carried an Oriental dagger in his belt, wore clothes which were completely alien to Roman custom, and appeared in public seated upon a gilded couch or chair. Painters and sculptors depicted him with Cleopatra, he being represented as Osiris or Dionysus,[18] and she as

Selene or Isis, and it was this practice more than anything else which gave the impression that she had laid him under some spell and deprived him of his wits. Indeed she so enchanted and enthralled not only Antony but all the others who counted for anything with him that she came to entertain the hope that she would rule the Romans as well, and whenever she took an oath, the most potent phrase she used were the words, 'So surely as I shall one day give judgement on the Capitol.'

6.   This was the reason why the Romans voted to declare war against Cleopatra, but they passed no such declaration against Antony. They knew very well that he would be at war with them in any event, since there was no prospect that he would give up the queen and come over to Octavian's side, and they wished to have this additional charge to lay against him – that he had of his own accord declared war for the sake of the Egyptian woman[19] against his own country, even though nobody there had caused him any personal harm whatever.

Both sides, then, set themselves urgently to mobilize the men of fighting age, money was raised from every quarter, and warlike stores and material were assembled with all possible speed. The preparations far exceeded anything that had been seen before, for all the nations I shall mention took part in the war on one side or the other.

Octavian, in the first place, controlled Italy. He had brought over to his side all those who had been given land by Antony, partly by frightening them since they were few in number, and partly by benefiting them in various ways: for example, among other acts, he personally granted a new charter to the colonists who had settled in Bononia,[20] so as to give the impression that the colony had originally been established by him. Besides Italy, he controlled Gaul; Spain; Illyricum; the provinces of Africa,[21] including not only those people who had previously been under Roman rule (except for the inhabitants of Cyrenaica), but also those who had been subjects of Bogud[22] and later of Bocchus; Sardinia; Sicily; and the other islands adjacent to those parts of the mainland I have mentioned.

Antony's territories included the provinces ruled by the Romans on the continent of Asia; the regions of Thrace, Greece and Macedonia; the Egyptians; the Cyrenaicans and the surrounding country; the islanders living in their vicinity; and virtually all the kings and princes whose territories bordered that part of the Roman empire which was under his control. Some of these rulers took the field themselves: others were represented by subordinates. Both sides entered the war with such intense conviction that the alliances they made with the two leaders were confirmed by oaths of allegiance.

7.   Such, then, was the strength of the two sides. For his part Antony vowed to his troops that he would carry on the war with no thought of truce, and he further promised that within two months after his victory he would lay down his command and restore to the Senate and the people the whole of their authority. Indeed he was only persuaded with difficulty by some of his supporters to extend the time limit for this action to six months, so as to avoid undue haste in settling the affairs of state. And even if he had little intention of carrying out this undertaking, he apparently offered it with the utmost confidence that a complete victory was certain. He saw that his forces were greatly superior in numbers, and besides this he hoped to weaken those of his opponents by means of bribes. Accordingly he now began to send gold in every direction,[23] especially to Italy, and above all Rome: his object was to undermine the loyalty of individuals and win them to his side. This caused Octavian to keep a stricter watch on affairs and to distribute grants of money to his own troops.

8.   Such were the strong feelings which animated both sides, and such were their preparations. Meanwhile human imagination was busy circulating rumours of the most diverse kinds, and the hand of the gods was seen in many unmistakable portents. For example, an ape entered the temple of Ceres and caused complete confusion during a ceremony; an owl flew first into the temple of Concord, and then into almost all the other most holy shrines. Finally, when it had been driven away from the others, it perched on the temple of the Genius Populi Romani, and there not only evaded capture, but did not fly off until late in the day. The chariot of Jupiter, which stands in the Circus Maximus[24] in Rome, was destroyed, and for many days a flaming torch was seen to rise over the sea in the direction of Greece, and to soar aloft in the sky. A storm also wrought havoc in the capital: thus, a trophy which stood on the Aventine hill was overturned; a statue of Victory was dislodged from the back wall of the theatre, and the wooden bridge over the Tiber was completely wrecked. At the same time many objects were destroyed by fire, and a

great stream of lava erupted from Mount Aetna and laid waste many cities and fields.

When the Romans witnessed these occurrences or heard of them, they recalled the phenomenon of the serpent, and recognized this too as a sign which was related to the present events. Not long before a two-headed serpent no less than eighty-five feet long had suddenly appeared in Etruria, and after causing much damage had been killed by lightning. All these signs were regarded as concerning the whole Roman people, since it was the Romans who would bear the brunt of the conflict on both sides alike; moreover it was inevitable that great numbers would die in each army at this time, and that all who survived would come under the rule of the victor.

Another presentiment of Antony's defeat came from the children of Rome. Although nobody had proposed this, they had divided themselves into two parties, one calling itself the Antonians, the other the Caesarians. They fought each other for two days, at the end of which the Antonians were defeated. Antony's death was also foreshadowed by the spectacle of a statue of him which stood on the Alban Mount beside that of Jupiter, and which was seen, although made of marble, to send forth streams of blood.

9.   On both sides, then, feelings were aroused to a high pitch of excitement by these events, but in that year nothing further took place. Octavian was busy putting affairs in order in Italy, especially when he found out that the sums of money sent by Antony had been received there, and so he could not take the field before the winter. In Antony's case, he had set out intending to launch an attack upon Italy before the enemy could detect his movements. But when he reached Corcyra and learned that the fleet sent out in advance from Italy to reconnoitre his position was lying off the Acroceraunian mountains,[25] he concluded that Octavian had arrived with his whole naval force, and so ventured no further. Instead, as the autumn was already far advanced, he sailed back to the Peloponnese and wintered in Patras. He despatched bodies of troops in all directions to secure the main approaches and to ensure that his supplies would be plentiful.

Meanwhile men were freely transferring their allegiance from one side to the other, both senators and persons of lower rank. Octavian caught a spy, one Lucius Messius, but released him after showing him his whole force, in spite of the fact that he was one of those who had earlier been captured at Perusia.[26] Then Octavian sent Antony a letter. He asked his opponent to withdraw inland to the distance of a day's journey on horseback and allow him to disembark his troops safely, on condition that the armies should engage within five days; alternatively he proposed that Antony should sail across to Italy on the same understanding. He did not expect that this manoeuvre would have any result, and indeed Antony ridiculed it and asked, 'Who is to judge between us if the agreement is broken in any way?' But he hoped that the fact of making this offer would put heart into his own troops and strike dismay into his opponent's.

10.   Now Octavian and Antony were due to become consuls for the following year. At the time when these appointments had been made, all the offices of state had been chosen for eight years in advance and this was the last year of the period.[27] However, as Antony had been deposed from the consulship, as I have mentioned above, Valerius Messalla, whom the Triumvirs had once proscribed, became consul with Octavian. At about this time a madman ran into the public theatre at one of the festivals, seized the crown which adorned the chair of Julius Caesar,[28] and put it on, whereupon he was torn to pieces by the bystanders. Then a wolf was caught and killed as it ran into the temple of Fortuna, and a dog killed and devoured another dog while a horse-race was actually in progress in the Circus Maximus. A large part of the Circus was damaged by fire, and the temple of Ceres, a shrine dedicated to the goddess Hope,[29] and a number of other buildings were burned down.

These acts of arson were believed to have been committed by the freedmen, since all of them who resided in Italy and possessed property worth 200,000 sesterces or more had been compelled to pay an eighth of its value.[30] This measure was the cause of many murders, riots and the firing of buildings on their part, and order was not restored until the freedmen had been subdued by armed force. The result was that other citizens who owned any land in Italy took fright and kept quiet, for they had also been ordered to pay a quarter of their annual income. They had been on the point of rising in revolt against this levy; but as matters turned out, they did not dare to cause any disturbance, and paid their contributions grudgingly, but without resistance. For this reason it was believed that the conflagrations were the outcome of a plot organized by the freedmen, but because of the great number of buildings that were destroyed, the fires were recorded as if they were portents, not the work of human hands.

11. Although these occurrences were known to the two leaders, they were neither alarmed nor did they abate their preparations for war, but spent the winter spying upon and harassing one another. Octavian had set sail from Brundisium and had reached Corcyra with the intention of making a surprise attack upon the enemy fleet as it lay off Actium, but he met a storm, suffered damage to his ships, and was forced to withdraw.

When spring arrived,[31] Antony made no move in any direction. The crews of his triremes were drawn from many different nationalities, they had spent the winter at a distance from him, had had no opportunities for training, and their strength had been reduced both by sickness and by desertions. Besides this, Octavian's admiral Agrippa had stormed the port of Methone in the Peloponnese and killed Bogud, the former king of Mauretania. This success enabled him to lie in wait for the merchant vessels which put in there, and from time to time to make raids upon the coast of Greece. All these events were as unsettling to Antony as they were encouraging to Octavian. The latter wished to take advantage as soon as possible of the fighting spirit of his troops, who were splendidly trained, and to carry the war into Greece near the enemy's positions rather than to fight in Italy in the neighbourhood of Rome.[32]

Accordingly he assembled at Brundisium all his troops who were of military value[33] and all the men who carried weight in public life, both senators and knights. His object was to win the cooperation of the soldiers and to prevent the others from making trouble for him, as they might do if they were left to themselves. But his main purpose was to demonstrate publicly that he had the largest and strongest body of support among the Roman people on his side. He sent instructions from Brundisium to all these men that they should bring with them a specified number of servants, and that, with the exception of the soldiers, they should all be furnished with their own supplies. Then he crossed the Ionian sea with his whole expedition.

12. His objective was not the Peloponnese or Antony's base at Patras, but rather Actium, where the main body of his opponent's force was stationed. He hoped to secure possession of the enemy's fleet, whether voluntarily or not, before Antony could arrive. With this object he

disembarked his army at the foot of the Acroceraunian mountains. Then, finding that Antony's troops, which were supposedly garrisoning Corcyra, had left, he took possession of the island with his fleet and anchored in the Fresh Harbour, which is so named because it is purified by the river flowing into it. There he established a naval station, which he made his base for movements against Actium. However, although he challenged the enemy either to come to terms or to fight, no vessel came out of the bay there to parley or to oppose him. Antony's forces declined the former course out of confidence, and the latter out of fear.

Octavian then occupied the peninsula where Nicopolis now stands, and encamped on the high ground there. This location on one side overlooks the whole stretch of the outer sea which surrounds the islands of Paxos and Anti-Paxos, and on the other the Ambracian Gulf and the waters in between, where the harbour of Nicopolis is situated. He fortified the position and built walls which ran down to Comarus, the outer harbour of Nicopolis. These dispositions enabled him to command Actium both by land and by sea: he could keep watch over the bay with his army from above, and blockade it with his fleet. I have even heard it reported that he managed to transport triremes from the outer sea to the Ambracian Gulf across the fortifications by means of newly flayed hides covered with olive oil, which he used instead of runways. But I can find no record of anything achieved by these ships inside the gulf, and so cannot credit this account. It would certainly have required no small effort to haul triremes on hides across a stretch of ground which was so cramped and so uneven. Still, the feat is said to have been accomplished in this way.

Now Actium is a place sacred to Apollo,[34] and stands in front of the mouth of the strait which leads into the Ambracian Gulf: it is situated opposite the harbours of Nicopolis. This narrow waterway stretches for a long distance and is of the same breadth throughout; both the channel itself and the waters in front of it afford excellent shelter in which ships can anchor and lie in wait. Antony's troops had occupied these positions in advance. They had built towers on either side of the mouth of the strait, and had placed ships in the channel at intervals so that they could sail in or out with safety. The troops were stationed on the southern shore of the strait near the sanctuary on a broad and level stretch of plain, but this was better suited for a battlefield than for an encampment: it was above all on account of its low-lying position that they suffered great hardship from disease,[35] not only in the winter but much more in the summer.

13.   As soon as Antony received news of Octavian's arrival, he lost no more time but hurried to Actium with his supporters. He arrived there soon after his opponent, but did not immediately venture a trial of strength. Octavian, on the other hand, repeatedly drew up his infantry in battle order in front of Antony's camp, threatened the enemy with his fleet, and carried off their transports. The object of these tactics was to bring on a battle against the limited numbers which were then facing him, before Antony could concentrate his whole strength. For the same reason Antony was unwilling to stake everything on an engagement; instead, for a number of days, he attempted nothing more than skirmishes and probing operations to test the enemy's strength, until he had assembled his legions.

When these arrived, and especially since Octavian had ceased to harass him as before, he crossed the strait with his main body and encamped not far from the enemy; next he despatched a force of cavalry across the Ambracian Gulf, so that his opponent was hemmed in from both sides. It was then Octavian's turn to stay quiet, and he no longer accepted any risk that he could avoid; instead, he detached some troops to invade mainland Greece and Macedonia, in the hope of diverting Antony to move in that direction. While these manoeuvres were going on, Agrippa launched a surprise attack with his fleet and seized Leucas and the shipping which was lying there. He then defeated Quintus Nasidius in a sea battle which enabled him to capture Patras, and he went on to take possession of Corinth.

After these events Marcus Titius and Statilius Taurus took the offensive with a sudden attack upon Antony's cavalry: they defeated them and won over Philadelphus, the king of Paphlagonia. At the same time Gnaeus Domitius Ahenobarbus, who had been angered in some way by Cleopatra, went over to Octavian. As it happened, he proved to be of no service to his new master, for he fell sick and died soon afterwards. Still, the belief gained ground that it was because Domitius had come to disapprove of the situation on Antony's side that he had deserted him, for many of Antony's other supporters followed his example. This undermined Antony's confidence, and he became suspicious of everybody. For this reason he had Iamblichus, the king of one of the Arabian tribes, tortured and put to death, and Quintus Postumius, a senator, was condemned to be torn asunder. Finally Antony became alarmed at the prospect that Quintus Dellius[36] and Amyntas the Galatian, two officers whom, as it happened, he had sent into Macedonia and Thrace to recruit mercenaries, would also go over to Octavian. He therefore set off to overtake them, on the pretext of giving them help in case they were attacked by an enemy force.

14.   Meanwhile a naval engagement took place. Antony's commander Sosius found a small force of ships under Lucius Tarius Rufus anchored opposite him, and thought he could strike an important blow by attacking them before the arrival of Agrippa, who had been placed in command of the whole fleet. Sosius therefore waited for a thick mist, so that it would be impossible for Tarius to discover his superior numbers and escape. Then he suddenly sailed out just before dawn, routed his opponent in the first onslaught, and followed but could not capture him. But during the pursuit, by a stroke of bad luck, he met Agrippa's fleet, so that he not only gained nothing from his victory, but perished together with Tarcondimotus and many others.[37]

Partly because of this defeat and also because he himself on his return from Macedonia had been worsted by Octavian's advance guard in a cavalry battle, Antony decided not to have his forces divided between two separate camps. So he withdrew his men by night from their entrenchments, which were close to the enemy's, and retreated to the other side of the straits, where his main body was encamped. There his provisions began to run short, because he was cut off from the means of bringing in grain. Accordingly he held a council of war to decide whether they should remain where they were and risk a battle, or move to another position and prolong the campaign.

15.   Various officers gave different advice, but it was Cleopatra's opinion which prevailed.

Her view was that they should leave garrisons to hold the best defensive positions, and that the rest of the army should return with Antony and herself to Egypt. In reaching this conclusion, she had been influenced by various omens which had disturbed her. Some swallows had built their nests about her tent and under the poop of the flagship in which she was sailing, and milk and blood together had oozed out of beeswax. At this time too the statues of her and of Antony attired as gods, which the Athenians had placed on the Acropolis, had been struck by thunderbolts and flung down into the theatre. These portents, which depressed the spirits of the army, and the sickness which weakened their strength, caused Cleopatra to lose heart, and this in turn affected Antony. They did not wish to sail away secretly, nor yet openly, as if they were turning tail, for fear of the effect upon their allies; it seemed best to disguise their departure under the semblance of preparing for a sea battle, for such a plan would allow them to force their way through should they meet with resistance. Accordingly they selected the best of their ships and set fire to the rest.[38] This action was plausible because the numbers of the crews had been reduced through losses and desertions, and, next, they secretly loaded all their most valuable possessions aboard by night. Finally, when the ships were ready, Antony summoned his troops and addressed them as follows.

16.   'Soldiers, all the preparations for the war which it was my duty to undertake have been completed in good time. You belong to an army whose strength is as overwhelming as its quality is unsurpassed, and with you are the picked troops of our subject peoples and our allies. Your training has given you such a mastery of every form of combat that is known in our times that each of you, man for man, can strike fear into our adversaries. You can see for yourselves the size and excellence of our fleet and the superiority of our infantry, cavalry, slingers, targeteers and archers, both mounted and on foot. Most of these special troops the enemy do not possess at all, and those that they have are fewer and less well equipped than ours. The money in their treasury is running low, and that though it has been raised by force, nor can it last for long.[39] It follows that those who have had to pay are more friendly towards us than to the men who have robbed them: the population of Italy not only feels no goodwill towards them, it is on the point of open revolt. Our preparations are based on a state of prosperity, no man has been injured by our demands, and our resources will aid us all alike.

17.   'All these material factors are important, but when I come to speak of myself besides, I do not wish to add anything which might seem boastful. But this too is one of the elements which determine victory in war, and is universally recognized to be of supreme importance. I mean that men who are to succeed in war need a general of the highest quality to lead them. So I have no choice but to speak about myself, and you will then understand this truth even better than you do now – that you yourselves are the kind of soldiers who can conquer even without a good

leader, and I am the kind of leader who can win even with inferior soldiers. I have reached the age at which men are at the height of their powers, both in body and in mind.[40] At this time of life they are handicapped neither by the impetuosity of youth nor the sluggishness of old age: they perform at their best because they have attained the mean between these extremes.

'Besides this I possess a combination of natural gifts and of training, so that I have no difficulty in making the right decision in all circumstances, nor in putting that decision into words. It is experience, as you know, which enables even the uneducated and the ignorant to appear to be of value, and I have added to my experience throughout the whole of my political and military career. From my boyhood to the present day I have continuously trained myself in public life. I have spent long years both in being ruled and in ruling; in this way I have learned the whole range and nature of the orders which the leader must give, and likewise the duties which the subordinate must obediently perform. I know what it is to be afraid and what it is to have confidence: from such situations I have accustomed myself not to take fright at anything too easily, nor to take undue risks through recklessness. I have known success and failure, and in consequence I can avoid despair and arrogance alike.

18.   'I tell you now what I know to be true, and I make you who listen to my words the witnesses of their truth. I say these things not to utter idle boasts about myself – your knowledge of what I have done is fame enough for me – but to help you to understand clearly how much better prepared we are than our opponents. They are the weaker not only in numbers, but in the whole range of their equipment, but above all they are at a disadvantage in the youth and the inexperience of their commander. I do not need to dwell on his shortcomings in every detail; but to sum them up, I will remind you of what you know – that he is a puny creature in body and has never by his own efforts won a victory in any important battle by land or sea. Indeed at Philippi, in the very same battle in which he and I fought as allies,[41] it was I who conquered, and he who was defeated.

'These are the differences between us, and they are great. However, as a general rule, victory goes to the side which is the better equipped. Now, if our enemies are strong in any department, it is in their heavy infantry and their strength on land, for you will find that their ships are not even able to come out and challenge us. You can see for yourselves the size and the stoutness of our vessels, which are such that even if the enemy could equal them in numbers, yet because of our superiority in construction, they could cause us no damage, either by meeting us head-on or by ramming our sides. In the first case the thickness of our timbers, and in the second the height of our topsides, would stop them, even if there were no defenders on board. Where can anybody find a point of assault against ships which carry such a complement of archers and slingers and also have the advantage of shooting down from their turrets upon any attackers?

'Finally, if the enemy succeeded in getting to close quarters, how could they fail to be sunk by the mass of our oars or founder under the hail of missiles from the soldiers stationed on our decks and in our turrets?

19.   'You need not think that they have any special skill in seamanship because Agrippa won a naval battle off Sicily, for they were not fighting against Sextus Pompeius but against his slaves, whose equipment was nothing like ours, but far inferior. And if anyone is greatly impressed by his success on that occasion, it is only right for him to set off against this the defeat which Octavian himself suffered from Sextus.[42] If he remembers that, he will see that our chances are not just evenly balanced; on the contrary, the advantages we can count on our side are far more numerous and more important than they possess.

'To put it shortly, how large a part does Sicily form of the whole empire, and what proportion of our expedition did Sextus's force represent? The point is that Octavian's force is exactly the same size as before. Anyone who understands this will have no cause to fear any increase in its strength – his good luck has not made his army any larger or any better – but should rather take courage from its defeat. Because I had this in mind, I was unwilling to risk a battle on land – where they appear to possess a certain strength – as our first encounter, so that none of you should become disheartened by a reverse in that arm. Instead, I preferred to engage them where we are strongest and have complete superiority, so that when we have beaten them at sea, we can look down on them on land too.

'You know very well that in this war the turn of the scale for both sides depends entirely upon this factor, our fleet: if we prevail at sea, we have nothing to fear from their other forces either. We shall cut them off on some islet, as it were, since all the surrounding territory is in our hands, and we shall overcome them without difficulty – if by no other way, then by starvation.

20.   'I have said enough, I believe, to show you that we shall not be fighting for any petty or trifling stakes. If we are resolute, we shall win the greatest prizes of all; if we are careless, we shall suffer the worst of misfortunes. What would they not do to us, since they have already put to death almost all the followers of Sextus who were of any importance, and killed many of the supporters of Lepidus, even though these men helped Octavian's cause? I need not dwell on this, since they have already deposed Lepidus himself, although he had committed no offence, and had even fought on their side. They keep him under guard, as though he were a prisoner of war, and they have extorted money from all the freedmen in Italy and from all the rest of the population who own any land; they have obliged some of these even to resort to arms, and on that account put many of them to death. So how can we expect that those who have not spared their own allies will spare us? Will the men who have levied tribute on the property of their own supporters leave our possessions alone? Will the men who have committed atrocities of every kind even before they gained power now show humanity if they conquer us?

'I shall not digress into reporting the experiences of others, but I shall tell you of their overbearing actions towards ourselves. You all know that I was chosen to be a colleague and a partner of Octavian: I was entrusted with the direction of public affairs on equal terms with him and was granted similar honours, which I continued to hold for many years. I have now been stripped of all these, so far as lay in Octavian's power. From commander I have been demoted to private citizen, and from consul to a disfranchised person. This was not done on the authority of the people nor of the Senate – how could it be, when both the consuls and a number of senators fled at once from the Senate to avoid casting any such vote? – but at the bidding of this one man and his supporters, who do not grasp that they are training up a monarch to make them his first subjects.

'This is the man who has the effrontery to hunt out my will, seize it from those who had been given it, open it and read it in public, and all this while I am still alive, commanding a powerful army, and conquering the Armenians. Is this the sort of man who will spare you or anyone else? After he has behaved in this way to me, who have been his friend and shared his table and am related to him by marriage, what kind of humanity will he show to those with whom he has no ties at all?

21.   'Suppose we were to try to interpret his decrees. He makes open threats – at any rate he has declared most of you enemies outright – but he has made no such pronouncement against me, although he is at war with me, and all his actions are those of a man who has not only conquered but murdered me besides. When he has treated me in this way, whom even now he professes not to regard as an enemy, he is hardly likely to exonerate you, with whom he declares in the plainest terms that he is at war. What is his purpose, then, when he threatens us all alike with arms, but in his decree proclaims that he is at war with some, but not with others? You can be sure, at least, that it is not to make any distinction between us, nor, should he win the war, to treat one class in one way and one in another. No, it is to divide us, to create clashes between us, and in that way weaken us. He knows very well that so long as we are united and act as one in all our undertakings, he can never in any way master us, but that if we fall out, with some choosing one policy and some another, he may perhaps overcome us. That is why he adopts this attitude towards us.

22.   'Now I and my Roman supporters, though we have been exempted after a fashion from Octavian's decrees, still foresee the danger, are aware of his scheme, and shall on no account abandon you, nor look to our private interests. And so you too, whom even Octavian does not deny that he regards as his enemies, yes, even his bitterest enemies, must keep all these facts before you. You should see both our dangers and our hopes as prospects which we all share, join your efforts to ours in every way in the common cause, and put your hearts into the struggle as we do. Weigh up the alternatives in your minds – what will be our fate, as I have explained, if we are defeated, and what we shall gain if we are victorious.

'Certainly it is a great thing to be delivered from being the victims of our enemies' insolence and greed, as we would be if we chanced to be defeated; but the greatest prize of all is to conquer and to accomplish everything that we could pray for. The most shameful choice of all, for us who have so many men of such mettle on our side, who possess weapons and money and ships and horses, would be to accept the worse fate in place of the better, to prefer a slavery we would share with our enemies, when we could win liberty both for them and for ourselves. Octavian's aims are completely opposite to mine. He desires to reign as a king over you all: I wish to free his supporters as well as you, and this I have sworn to do. It falls to us, then, to fight for both sides alike and to win rewards which all will share. And so, my soldiers, let us nerve ourselves to conquer this day, and secure our happiness for all time.'

23.   When he had delivered this speech, Antony ordered all his most prominent supporters to embark, to forestall any possibility that they might change their allegiance if left on their own, as Dellius and some other deserters had done. He also took aboard large contingents of archers, slingers and heavy infantry. He had noted that the size of Octavian's ships and the numbers of his marines had played a great part in the defeat of Sextus Pompeius, and so he had given his ships much higher sides than those of his opponents. He had built only a few triremes, but some of his ships were 'fours' and some 'tens',[43] and the rest were of intermediate size. He had constructed high turrets on their decks and embarked large numbers of soldiers, who could fight as it were from battlements. Octavian for his part was taking note of his opponents' armament and making his own preparations. When he learned of their intentions from Dellius and from others, he called his troops together and addressed them as follows.

24.   'Soldiers, there is one conclusion that I have reached, both from the experience of others and at first hand: it is a truth I have taken to heart above all else, and I urge you too to keep it before you. This is that in all the greatest enterprises of war, or indeed in human affairs of any kind, victory comes to those whose thoughts and deeds follow the path of justice and of reverence for the gods. No matter how great the size and strength of our force might be – great enough perhaps to make the man who had chosen the less just course of action expect to win with its help – still I base my confidence far more upon the principles which are at stake in this war than upon the advantage of numbers. We Romans are the rulers of the greatest and best parts of the world, and yet we find ourselves spurned and trampled upon by a woman of Egypt.

'This disgraces our fathers, who defeated Pyrrhus,[44] Philip of Macedon,[45] Perseus[46] and Antiochus[47]; who uprooted the Numantines[48] and the Carthaginians[49] from their homes; whose swords slew the Cimbri[50] and the Ambrones. It disgraces our own generation, who have conquered the Gauls,[51] subdued the Pannonians,[52] marched as far as the Danube and beyond the Rhine, and crossed the sea to Britain. The men who achieved these feats of arms I have named would be cut to the heart if ever they knew that we have been overcome by this pestilence of a woman. Would we not utterly dishonour ourselves if, after surpassing all other nations in valour, we then meekly endured the insults of this rabble, the natives of Alexandria and of Egypt, for what more ignoble or more exact name could one give them? They worship reptiles and beasts as gods, they embalm their bodies to make them appear immortal, they are most forward in effrontery, but most backward in courage. Worst of all, they are not ruled by a man, but are the slaves of a woman, and yet they have dared to claim our possessions, and to employ our fellow-countrymen to lay hands on them, as if we would ever consent to surrender the prosperity which belongs to us.

25. 'Who would not tear his hair at the sight of Roman soldiers serving as bodyguards of this queen? Who would not groan at hearing that Roman knights and senators grovel before her like eunuchs? Who would not weep when he sees and hears what Antony has become? This man has twice been consul and many times Imperator.[53] He was appointed with me to take charge of the affairs of state and entrusted with the government of many cities and the command of many legions. Now he has abandoned his whole ancestral way of life, has embraced alien and barbaric customs, has ceased to honour us, his fellow-countrymen, or our laws, or his fathers' gods. Instead, he makes obeisance to that creature as if she were an Isis or a Selene, names her children Sun and Moon,[54] and finally adopts for himself the title of Osiris or Dionysus. And to crown it all, he bestows gifts of whole islands and parts of continents as though he were master of the entire earth and sea.[55] These things must seem to you amazing and hardly to be believed, but that should only make you the more angry. For if an event which defies belief turns out to be true, if Antony's self-indulgence leads him into actions of which even the bare mention is painful to hear, it is only reasonable that your anger should exceed all bounds.

26. 'And yet, I myself was at first so attached to him that I granted him a share in our command, gave to him my sister in marriage,[56] and transferred legions to his army. After that, I was so kindly and warmly

disposed to him that I shrank from waging war merely because he insulted my sister, neglected the children she had borne him,[57] preferred the Egyptian to her, and presented that woman's children with almost all your possessions – or indeed because of any other of his provocations. I acted so, first, because I did not think it right to treat Antony in the same way as Cleopatra. I considered her, on account both of her foreign birth and of her actions, to be an enemy of Rome, but Antony to be a citizen of Rome, who could still, I believed, be brought to reason.

'Later still I hoped that he might, if not voluntarily, at least under pressure, decide to change his course in consequence of the decrees that were passed against her. It was for these reasons that I did not declare war upon him at all. But he has treated all my efforts with contempt and disdain, and refuses to be pardoned, although we offer him our pardon, or pitied, although we offer him our pity. He is either blind to reason or mad, for I have heard and can believe that he is bewitched by that accursed woman, and therefore disregards all our efforts to show him goodwill and humanity. And so, being enslaved by her, he plunges into war with all its attendant dangers which he has accepted for her sake, against ourselves and against his country. What choice, then, remains to us, save our duty to oppose him together with Cleopatra and fight him off?

27. 'Henceforth, then, let nobody consider him to be a Roman citizen, but rather an Egyptian: let us not call him Antony, but rather Serapis, nor think of him as ever having been consul or Imperator, but only gymnasiarch. He has made these choices of his own accord: he has discarded all the august titles of his native land and become a cymbal player from Canopus.[58]

'And let no one fear him as a soldier, whose efforts could decide the issue of the war. Even in the past he was of no real consequence, as those of you who defeated him at Mutina[59] know well enough. And even if at one time he showed some valour when he served with our army, you can rest assured that he has now lost it beyond recall through the change in his manner of life. It is impossible for anyone who indulges in a life of royal luxury and pampers himself as a woman to conceive a manly thought or do a manly deed, since it cannot but follow that a man's whole being is moulded by the habits of his daily life. A proof of this is that in the one war he has waged in all this time and the one expedition he has undertaken, he threw away the lives of huge numbers of citizens in his battles, returned in complete disgrace from Phraaspa, and incurred further terrible losses in his retreat.[60]

'To sum up, if it were a matter of being called upon to cavort in some ridiculous dance or cut some erotic caper, Antony would have no rival – for these are the specialities in which he has trained himself. But when it comes to weapons and fighting, what has anyone to fear from him? The fitness of his body? But he has become effeminate and his homosexuality has worn him out.[61] His piety towards our gods? But he has declared war upon them and upon his native land. His loyalty towards his allies? Everyone knows how he tricked and then imprisoned the king of Armenia. His kindness to his friends? We have all seen the men who have died a cruel death at his hands. His popularity among his troops? But who, even among them, has not condemned him? The evidence for this is the number of his soldiers who join us every day. I believe that all our citizens will do this, just as happened once before, when he was on his way from Brundisium to Gaul.[62] So long as they hoped to get rich without danger, some were happy to take his side. But they will not choose to fight against us, their own countrymen, for what does not belong to them, least of all when by joining us they can protect their lives and their property without risk.

28. 'Someone will say that Antony has many allies and great wealth on his side. Tell me then, what has been our record in the past in conquering the inhabitants of Asia? The famous Scipio Asiaticus[63] can answer for this, or Sulla the Fortunate, or Lucullus, or Pompey the Great, or my father, Julius Caesar. Or for that matter you yourselves, when you defeated the armies of Brutus and Cassius. It follows, then, that if you believe that the wealth of Antony and his allies is so much greater than that of the earlier kingdoms of Asia, you should be all the more eager to take it for yourselves. It is the greatest contests which offer the greatest rewards, and make it worth while to engage in them. But, in the end, I cannot describe to you any greater prize than that of upholding the renown which your forefathers won, of preserving the proud tradition of your native land, of punishing those who have rebelled against us, of conquering and ruling over all mankind, and of allowing no woman to make herself equal to a man.

'You who are serving with me here fought valiantly against the Taurisci,[64] the Iapydes,[65] the Dalmatians and the Pannonians, and often it was only to take a few walls and a patch of barren soil. You subdued all those tribes, although they are among the most warlike opponents in the world; you fought against Sextus Pompeius to win nothing more than Sicily, and against this very Antony only to capture Mutina, and you fought so bravely that you overcame both of them. I cannot believe that you will show any less courage against this woman who covets all your possessions, against her husband who has settled all your property upon her children, and against their fine comrades and table companions, whom they themselves nickname "councillors of the privy". How could this be? Because of the size of their army? No army can overcome valour by sheer numbers. Because of their race? Theirs has been trained to carry loads rather than to bear arms. Because of their experience? They know more about rowing than about fighting at sea. For my part I can even feel ashamed to go into action against such opponents, since we can win no fame by conquering them; only disgrace should we be defeated.

29. 'You must not imagine that the size of their ships or the stoutness of their timbers is any match for our courage. What ship has ever killed or wounded any by its own efforts? I believe that their height and their solid construction will make them more difficult for their rowers to keep under way, and less responsive for their helmsmen to steer. What use can ships like these be to the fighting-men aboard when they can attack neither head-on nor abeam, the two manoeuvres which you know are essential in naval warfare? I do not suppose that they intend to use infantry tactics against us at sea, nor are they thinking of shutting themselves up behind wooden walls and inviting a siege, so to speak, since it could only be to our advantage if we were faced with an immobile wooden barrier. If their ships remain motionless, as if they were moored there, we can rip them open with our rams, or else bombard them from a distance with our siege engines, or burn them to the water's edge with our incendiary missiles. On the other hand, if they do venture to move, they will be too slow either to overtake or to escape our vessels: their weight makes them too cumbersome to cause damage to us, and their size makes them most liable to suffer it themselves.

30. 'I need not waste any more words on their fleet, since we have already had many encounters with it, both off Leucas and lately in these waters. So far from finding ourselves inferior to them, we have every

time gained the upper hand. You can take heart now not so much from my words as from your own actions, and resolve to put an end to the whole war without further delay. And you can rest assured that, if we conquer today, we shall have no more to do. It is a general rule of human nature that when a man fails at his first trial of strength, he becomes discouraged for any others. In our case, we are so indisputably superior to our enemies on land that we could beat them even if they were coming fresh to the contest.

'They themselves know this so well – and here let me give you the intelligence I have received – that they have lost their nerve at what has already happened, and despair of saving their lives if they remain in their positions. So they are trying now to flee to some destination or other, and are making this sortie not to offer battle but to find a way of escape. They have loaded into their ships the best and most valuable of their possessions in the hope of breaking out with them if they can. And so, since they have clearly admitted that they are weaker than us, and since they carry the prizes of victory in their ships, let us not allow them to slip away anywhere else, but defeat them here on the spot and make all these treasures our own.'

31.   Such was the speech that Octavian delivered.[66] After this he drew up a plan to allow Antony's ships to sail through, and then to attack from the rear as they fled. For his part, he hoped that his vessels could muster enough speed to capture Antony and Cleopatra quickly, and he calculated that once it became clear that they were trying to escape, he could, through their action, persuade the rest to surrender without fighting. But this scheme was opposed by Agrippa, who feared that their ships, which were using oars, would be too slow to catch the fugitives, who intended to hoist sails. Also a violent rainstorm accompanied by a tremendous wind had in the meanwhile struck Antony's fleet, leaving it in total confusion, though it had not touched his own, and this gave him some confidence that he would win easily enough. So he abandoned his plan, and, like Antony, posted large numbers of infantry on his ships. He also embarked his subordinates in auxiliary craft: they were to move rapidly between the ships, giving the necessary instructions to the men in action, and reporting back all that he needed to know. Then he waited for the enemy to sail out.

At the sound of the trumpet Antony's fleet began to move, and, keeping close together, formed their line a little way outside the strait, but then advanced no further. Octavian put out, as if to engage should the enemy stand their ground, or else to make them retire. But when they neither came out against him, nor turned away, but stayed in position and even increased the density of their closely packed formation, Octavian halted his advance, being in doubt as to what to do. He ordered his rowers to let their oars rest in the water, and waited for a while; after this he suddenly made a signal and, advancing both his wings, rounded his line in the form of an enveloping crescent. His object was to encircle the enemy if possible, or, if not, at least to break up their formation. Antony was alarmed by this outflanking and encircling manoeuvre, moved forward to meet it as best he could, and so unwillingly joined battle with Octavian.

32. So the fleets came to grips and the battle began. Each side uttered loud shouts to the men aboard, urging the troops to summon up their prowess and their fighting spirit, and the men could also hear a babel of orders being shouted at them from those on shore.

The two sides used different tactics. Octavian's fleet, having smaller and faster ships, could advance at speed and ram the enemy, since their armour gave them protection on all sides. If they sank a vessel, they had achieved their object; if not, they would back water before they could be engaged at close quarters, and either ram the same ship suddenly a second time, or let it go and turn against others. When they had damaged these as much as they could in a short time, they would seek out fresh opponents over and over again, constantly switching their attack, so that their onslaught always came where it was least expected. They feared their adversaries' long-range missiles no less than their superior strength in fighting at close quarters, and so they wasted no time either in the approach or the clash. They would sail up suddenly so as to close with their target before the enemy's archers could hit them, inflict damage or cause enough confusion to escape being grappled, and then quickly back away out of range.

Antony's tactics, on the other hand, were to pour heavy volleys of stones and arrows upon the enemy ships as they approached, and then try to entrap them with iron grapnels. When they could reach their targets, Antony's ships got the upper hand, but if they missed, their own hulls would be pierced by the rams and they would sink, or else, in the attempt to avoid collision, they would lose time and expose themselves to attack by other ships. Two or three of Octavian's vessels would fall upon one of Antony's, with some inflicting all the damage they could, while the others bore the brunt of the counter-attack.

On the one side the helmsmen and rowers suffered the heaviest casualties, on the other the marines. Octavian's ships resembled cavalry, now launching a charge, and now retreating, since they could attack or draw off as they chose, while Antony's were like heavy infantry, warding off the enemy's efforts to ram them, but also striving to hold them with their grappling-hooks. Each fleet in turn gained the advantage over the other: the one would dart in against the rows of oars which projected from the ships' sides and break the blades, while the other fighting from its higher decks would sink its adversaries with stones and ballistic missiles. At the same time each side had its weaknesses. Antony's ships could do no damage to the enemy as they approached: Octavian's, if they failed to sink a vessel when they had rammed it, would find the odds turned against them once they were grappled.

33. For a long while the struggle was evenly poised and neither side could gain the upper hand anywhere, but the end came in the following way. Cleopatra, whose ship was riding at anchor behind the battle lines, could not endure the long hours of uncertainty while the issue hung in the balance: both as a woman and as an Egyptian she found herself stretched to breaking-point by the agony of the suspense, and the constant and unnerving effort of picturing victory or defeat. Suddenly she made her choice – to flee – and made the signal for the others, her own subjects. So when her ships immediately hoisted their sails and stood out to sea, a favourable wind having luckily got up, Antony supposed that they were turning tail, not on Cleopatra's orders, but out of fear because they felt themselves to have been defeated, and so he followed them.

At this, dismay and confusion spread to the rest of Antony's men, and they resolved likewise to take whatever means of escape lay open. Some raised their sails, while others threw the turrets and heavy equipment overboard to lighten the vessels and help them to get away. While they were thus engaged, their opponents again attacked: they had not pursued Cleopatra's fleeing squadron, because they themselves had not taken sails aboard and had put out prepared only for a naval battle. This meant that there were many ships to attack each one of Antony's, both at long range and alongside. The result was that the struggle took many forms on both sides and was carried on with the greatest ferocity. Octavian's soldiers battered the lower parts of the ships from stem to stern, smashed the oars, broke off the rudders, and, climbing on to the decks, grappled with their enemies. They dragged down some, thrust others overboard, and fought hand to hand with others, since they now equalled them in numbers. Antony's men forced their attackers back with boat-hooks, cut them down with axes, hurled down stones and other missiles which had been prepared for this purpose, forced down those who tried to scale the ships' sides, and engaged all who came within reach. A witness of the battle might have compared it, if one can reduce the scale, to the spectacle of a number of walled towns or islands set close together being besieged from the sea. Thus one side strove to clamber up the sides of the ships, as it might be up a cliff or fortress, and brought to bear all the equipment which is needed for such an assault, while the others struggled to repel them, using all the weapons and tactics which are known to defenders.

34.   As the fighting remained evenly balanced, Octavian, who found himself in doubt what to do next, sent for fire from his camp. Until then he had been unwilling to use it, since he was anxious to capture Antony's treasure intact. He now resorted to it because he saw that it was impossible to win in any other way and believed that this was the only weapon which would help him. The battle then changed its character. The attackers would approach their targets from many different points at once, bombarding them with blazing missiles and hurling by hand javelins with torches attached to them; from a longer range they would also catapult jars filled with charcoal or pitch. The defenders tried to ward off these missiles one by one, but when some got through, they ignited the timbers and immediately started a blaze, as is bound to happen on a ship. The crews first put out the flames with the drinking water which they carried on board, and when that ran out, they used sea water. If they managed to throw this on the fire in great quantities at once, they could sometimes quench it by the sheer volume of the water. But this was not always possible, since their buckets were few and of no great size. In their confusion they sometimes only half filled them, and in that case instead of reducing the blaze they only increased it, since small quantities of salt water poured on a fire make it burn all the more strongly. So when they found that they were failing to check the flames, they threw on their heavy cloaks and even dead bodies, and for a time these stifled the

conflagration, which seemed to die down. But later, and especially when the wind blew strongly, the flames leaped up more violently than ever, fed by their own efforts.

So long as only a section of the ship was on fire, the men would stand close by and jump into it, cutting away some of the planks and scattering others; in some instances the men threw the timbers into the sea, and in others against their adversaries, in the hope that they might cause them some hurt. Others would take up position in the part of the ship that was undamaged, and would ply their long spears and grappling-hooks more desperately than ever, in the hope of making some enemy ship fast to theirs and boarding her, or, if not, setting her alight as well. But when none of the enemy came near enough, since they were guarding against this very possibility, and when the fire spread to the encircling sides of the ship and descended into the hold, they found themselves in the most terrible plight of all. Some, especially the sailors, were overcome by the smoke before the flames ever came near them, while others were roasted in the midst of the holocaust as if they were in ovens. Others were incinerated in their armour as it grew red-hot. Others, again, to avoid such a fate, or when they were half burned, threw off their armour and were wounded by the missiles shot at them from long range, or jumped into the sea and were drowned, or were clubbed by their enemies and sank, or were devoured by sea-monsters. The only men to find a death which was endurable in the midst of such sufferings were those who either killed one another in return for the service, or took their own lives before such a fate could befall them. These were spared the torments I have described, and their corpses were burned on board the ships, as though they were on a funeral pyre.

When Octavian's men saw that the battle had taken this turn, they at first held off from the enemy, since some of the latter could still defend themselves. But when the fire had taken hold of the ships, and the men aboard them, so far from being able to injure an opponent, could no longer even defend themselves, they eagerly sailed up to Antony's vessels in the hope of seizing their treasure, and tried to put out the fires which they themselves had started. The result was that many of them perished, both from the flames and from their own greed.

BOOK 51

᠎᠎᠎᠎᠎᠎᠎᠎

The following is contained in the Fifty-First Book of Dio's *Rome*:

Duration of time: the remainder of the consulship of Octavian (his third) and of M. Valerius Corvinus Messalla. Also two additional years in which the magistrates here enumerated became consuls:

30 B.C. Octavian (his fourth): M. Licinius Crassus
29 B.C. Octavian (his fifth): Sextus Appuleius

1. Such was the sea battle which took place between them on the second day of September. I do not mention this date without cause, for it is not my custom to do so. The reason is that at this point for the first time Octavian alone held all the power of the state in his hands, and accordingly the calculation of the years of his reign should, strictly speaking, be made from that day. In honour of the date he dedicated to Apollo of Actium from the captured vessels a trireme, a quadrireme and one each of the other sizes of warship up to a 'ten',[1] and he built another and larger temple on the spot. He also founded a musical and gymnastic contest, which included horse-racing, to be held every four years; the festival was to be 'sacred', as such celebrations are termed in which there is a distribution of food, and he named it Actia. Besides this he established a city on the

ground where he had pitched his camp; this was effected by bringing together some of the neighbouring peoples and evicting others, and the place was named Nicopolis. On the spot where his tent had stood, he built a plinth of square stones, which was ornamented with the rams of the captured ships,[2] and erected on it a shrine for Apollo, which was open to the sky.

All this was done later.[3] Immediately after the battle he despatched part of his fleet to pursue Antony and Cleopatra. These ships made chase after the fugitives, but when they could see that they were not going to overtake them, they sailed back. With the help of the rest of the fleet Octavian captured the enemy's entrenchments, meeting no resistance because of the small number of troops which occupied them. He then overtook the rest of the army, which was withdrawing into Macedonia, and managed to bring the troops over to his side without fighting. Others of Antony's principal supporters had already made their escape; of these the Romans joined their leader, while the allies dispersed to their homes. However, the latter no longer carried on the war against Octavian. Both they and all the peoples which had previously been under Roman rule remained at peace and came to terms with him, some immediately, others after an interval.

2.   Octavian proceeded to punish the city-states, levying money from them and depriving them of the limited authority over their citizens which had hitherto rested with their assemblies. As for the princes and kings, all with the exception of Amyntas[4] and Archelaus[5] were stripped of the lands they had been granted by Antony: Philopator, the son of Tarcondimotus,[6] Lycomedes, the king of part of Cappadocian Pontus, and Alexander the brother of Iamblichus[7] were deposed. The last-named, because he had received his kingdom as a reward for denouncing Iamblichus, was led in the triumphal procession in Rome and later executed. Octavian bestowed Lycomedes's kingdom upon a man named Medeius, because he had detached the Mysians of the province of Asia from Antony's cause before the battle of Actium, and had fought with them against Antony's supporters. He also granted the peoples of Cydonia and Lampe[8] their freedom from Roman rule because they had given him help, and in the case of the Lampaeans he assisted them to rebuild their city, which had been destroyed.

In the case of the senators, knights and other prominent men who had collaborated with Antony to any significant extent, many were fined and many others executed, but some were actually spared. Among these a notable example was Sosius;[9] this man had often fought against Octavian, was then hiding in exile, and was not tracked down until later, but was nevertheless let go. In the same way Marcus Scaurus, a half-brother of Sextus Pompeius on his mother's side, had been condemned to death, but was later set free for the sake of his mother Mucia.[10] Of those who were executed it was the two Aquilii Flori and Curio who attracted most attention. The latter was a son of that Curio who had once rendered great services to Julius Caesar.[11] In the case of the Florii, when Octavian gave orders that the one who drew the lot should be put to death, both of them died. They were father and son, and when the son, without waiting to draw lots, volunteered to undergo execution, the father was overcome with grief, and killed himself over his son's dead body.

3. Such was the end of these men. The majority of Antony's troops were enrolled into Octavian's legions. Later, however, Octavian posted back to Italy all those Roman citizens serving both in his forces and in Antony's who were over military age, without making them grants either of money or of land; the rest of the army was then dispersed. The reason for this action was that Octavian's own troops had given him cause to fear them after his victory in Sicily over Sextus Pompeius. He was afraid that they might again become restive, and so, before there was the least indication of any disorder, he acted with speed, discharging some of the soldiers from any future service and dispersing most of the rest. At this time he was also suspicious of the freedmen, and so he exempted them from the fourth instalment which they still owed of the tax levied the year before. The result was that the freedmen ceased to bear him any grudge on account of the money already paid out, but rejoiced as if they had actually been given what they had merely been exempted from paying. As for the rank and file who were still serving in the legions, they too remained quiet, partly because they were kept under control by their commanders, but chiefly because of their hopes that the riches of Egypt would fall into their hands.

However, the men who had been discharged after having helped Octavian to win his victory felt aggrieved that their efforts had gone unrewarded, and soon afterwards began to mutiny. Octavian was expecting trouble from this quarter. At this time Maecenas had been placed in charge not only of Rome, but also of the rest of Italy. Octavian feared that the soldiers would despise him as a mere knight, and so he despatched Agrippa to Italy, ostensibly on another mission. He also delegated such great authority in all matters of government both to Agrippa and to Maecenas that they were even allowed to read in advance the letters he wrote to the Senate and to other officials, and then alter whatever they thought fit in these documents.

For this purpose they were also given a ring, so that they could seal his letters up again. He had had a duplicate made of the seal he used most frequently at that time. The design of this was a sphinx, an identical form of which was impressed upon each copy; it was not until later that he had his own likeness engraved on the seal and sealed every document with that. It was this ring that succeeding emperors used, except for Galba, who employed an ancestral device, which showed a dog looking out of a ship's prow. It was Octavian's habit in these letters to his two ministers and to others of his closest friends, if he ever needed to give them secret information, to substitute in each case for the appropriate letter in a word the letter immediately following it in the alphabet.

4. After this, Octavian concluded that the discharged veterans would cause him no further trouble, so he proceeded to settle affairs in Greece, and took part in the Mysteries of the two goddesses, Demeter and Persephone. He then crossed to Asia and dealt with affairs of state there, while at the same time vigilantly awaiting any news of Antony's activities. He had received no positive information as to where his enemy had taken refuge, and so was making preparations to attack him in the event of receiving precise details. But meanwhile the discharged veterans, now that he had put so great a distance between himself and them, were openly creating disturbances, and Octavian began to fear that, if they could find a leader, they might weaken his position. He therefore delegated the task of tracking down Antony to his local commanders and himself hastened to Italy. He arrived in the middle of the winter of the year[12] in which he was holding the consulship for the fourth time, together with Marcus Crassus:[13] this man was Octavian's fellow-consul, even though he had not previously held the praetorship, and had actually been a supporter both of Sextus Pompeius and of Antony.

Octavian then arrived at Brundisium, but travelled no further. When the Senate learned that his ship was approaching Italy, all its members flocked to the port to meet him, with the exception of the tribunes and two praetors, who remained in the capital by decree. The equestrian order likewise left the city, together with the greater part of the population, and various other groups also gathered at Brundisium in large numbers, some coming as envoys, others quite spontaneously. Thus in view of Octavian's impending arrival and of the evident enthusiasm of the majority for his cause, there were no further signs of opposition from any part of the population.

The veterans also marched to Brundisium, some impelled by fear, others by hopes of reward, and others again in response to a summons. This time Octavian distributed money to some, while those who had served with him throughout his campaigns were rewarded with a grant of land. By evicting those communities in Italy which had taken Antony's side, he was able to settle his soldiers both in their cities and on the lands of his opponents. Octavian compensated most of those who had been penalized in this way by allowing them to settle in Dyrrachium, Philippi, and elsewhere; the remainder were either compensated in cash for their land, or promised that they would be helped in this way. The fact was that although Octavian had come into possession of great sums of money from his victories, he was still spending far more than he received. For this reason he put up for auction both his own possessions and those of his principal supporters, so that anyone who wished to purchase any of them, or take any in exchange for something else, might do so. Of course nothing was either purchased or exchanged, for who would dare to risk a transaction of this kind? But through this manoeuvre he gained a plausible cause for the delay in fulfilling his promise to the soldiers, and later he paid them out of the plunder which was taken in Egypt.[14]

5.   This was how he dealt with the foregoing and other urgent matters of business. These included granting to those who had received an amnesty permission to live in Italy, a concession which had not previously been made, and also pardoning that part of the populace which had remained behind in Rome for not having come out to greet him. Then on the thirtieth day after his arrival, he again left Italy for Greece. Because it was winter, he had his ships hauled across the isthmus of Corinth,[15] and crossed to Asia so quickly that Antony and Cleopatra only learned of his departure and his return simultaneously.

It seems that after their flight from the sea battle at Actium they had sailed together as far as the Peloponnese. There they dismissed a number of their supporters whom they suspected of disloyalty, but many others deserted them against their wishes. From the Peloponnese Cleopatra then sailed on with all haste to Egypt, for she feared that her people might rise in revolt if they learned of her defeat before she arrived. So in order to make her approach at any rate safe, she had the ships' prows hung with garlands, as though she had actually won a victory, and had songs of triumph chanted to the accompaniment of flute-players.

Once she was safely ashore, she had many of the leading Egyptians executed, on the grounds that they had always been ill-disposed to her and were now exulting in her defeat. Their estates yielded her great wealth, and she also drew upon other sources, both sacred and secular; in the effort to equip her forces and seek fresh allies, she did not exempt even the most holy shrines. She had Artavasdes,[16] the king of Armenia, put to death and his head sent to the king of Media, who she hoped would be influenced by this act to help her cause and Antony's.

Meanwhile Antony had sailed to Cyrenaica to Pinarius Scarpus and the army which had been assembled there under his command to defend Egypt. However, Scarpus not only refused to receive him, but killed the delegation which Antony had sent ahead to approach him, and even executed some of the soldiers under his own command who had protested against this action. In consequence Antony too returned to Alexandria without having achieved anything.

6.   Besides the other preparations which they made for an immediate resumption of the war, Cleopatra enrolled her son Caesarion among the youths who were of age for military service, and Antony did the same for Antyllus, who was his son by his first wife, Fulvia, and was then with him. The object of this action was to put heart into the Egyptians, who could then feel that they had a man to rule over them, and to encourage the rest of their allies to persevere in their resistance, since they would have these boys as their leaders, should any disaster overtake their parents. As far as the boys were concerned, this enrolment was to bring about their destruction. In the event Octavian spared neither, but treated them as grown men, who had been vested with some semblance of authority.

As for Antony and Cleopatra, they continued to make arrangements to carry on the war in Egypt both at sea and on land, and for this purpose they summoned all the neighbouring tribes and rulers who were on friendly terms to come to their help. But they also made alternative plans, should the need arise, either to sail to Spain and stir up rebellion there, using their huge resources of money or other means, or even to shift the theatre of operations to the Persian Gulf. Meanwhile they despatched emissaries to Octavian carrying peace proposals for him and bribes of money for his supporters; their purpose here was to conceal the schemes they were preparing for as long as they could, and either outwit Octavian in some way, or actually kill him by treachery. At the same time Cleopatra sent to Octavian a golden sceptre, a golden crown, and the royal throne of Egypt, signifying that through these gifts she was offering him the kingdom as well, and she did this without Antony's knowledge. She hoped that even if Octavian regarded Antony as a mortal enemy, he would take pity on her at least. Octavian accepted her gifts as an auspicious event, but sent no answer to Antony's proposals. As far as Cleopatra was concerned, his official response was a threatening one, including the pronouncement that if she would disband her forces and renounce her throne, he would then consider what should be done with her. But he also sent her a secret message that, if she would kill Antony, he would grant her pardon and leave her kingdom untouched.

7.   While these manoeuvres were in progress, the Arabians[17] were persuaded by Quintus Didius, the governor of Syria, to burn the fleet which Cleopatra had assembled in the Red Sea[18] for the voyage to the Persian Gulf, and all the neighbouring peoples and rulers to whom she and Antony had appealed, refused support. Indeed I am bound to wonder at the fact that while many other associates of theirs, in spite of having received a great number of gifts, now deserted them, yet the men who were being trained for gladiatorial combats, an occupation generally held in the lowest regard, showed the greatest loyalty to them, and fought with the greatest courage. These men were training in Cyzicus[19] for the triumphal games which Antony and Cleopatra were hoping to hold in celebration of Octavian's defeat, and as soon as they heard what had happened, they started for Egypt to help their rulers. They fought many actions against Amyntas in Galatia, against the sons of Tarcondimotus in Cilicia – these rulers had previously been well disposed towards them, but because of the change in circumstances had gone over to Octavian – and later against Quintus Didius, who barred their passage through Syria, but in the end they were unable to break through to Egypt. Yet even

when they were encircled on all sides, they would not accept surrender on any terms, although Didius made them a number of offers. Rather than this, they sent for Antony, since they believed that they would fight better even in Syria if he were with them. Only when he neither came himself nor sent any message did they conclude at last that he had been killed, and reluctantly came to terms, on the condition that they should never again have to fight as gladiators. Didius allowed them to live in Daphne, the suburb of Antioch, until their case should be brought to Octavian's notice. These men were later deceived by Messalla and posted to various places on the pretext that they were to be enlisted in the legions; then they were put to death in some convenient manner.

8.   When Antony and Cleopatra learned from Octavian's envoys what terms he demanded from them, they sent him further proposals. Cleopatra promised to give him large sums of money, while Antony reminded him of their friendship and of their kinship by marriage. He also sought to defend his association with the Egyptian queen, and reminded Octavian of the various amorous encounters and youthful escapades they had shared in the past. Finally, he handed over to Octavian Publius Turullius,[20] a senator who had been one of the assassins of Julius Caesar and who was then living with Antony as a friend, and he offered to take his own life if Cleopatra might be saved by this action. Octavian had Turullius put to death: it so happened that the man had cut down trees from the grove of Aesculapius[21] in Cos to build ships for Antony, and since his execution took place in Cos, it was believed that he was paying the penalty to the god as well as to Julius Caesar. But once again Octavian made no reply to Antony.

Antony then made a third approach, sending his son Antyllus with a large sum of gold. Octavian accepted the money, but sent the boy back empty-handed with no message for Antony. But to Cleopatra, just as on the first occasion, so in these second and third exchanges he sent back a combination of threats and promises. He was still afraid of several possible eventualities. Either the two might despair of ever obtaining a pardon from him and so continue to resist. In that case they might either defeat him through their own efforts, or sail to Spain or Gaul. Alternatively they might destroy their wealth, which he was repeatedly informed was enormous. Cleopatra had collected all her treasure in the tomb which she was building in the grounds of the palace, and she threatened to burn it all and herself with it, if she failed to obtain the least of her demands. So Octavian sent one of his freedmen named Thyrsus to charm her with a flow of fine words, and in particular to intimate that he was in love with her. He hoped that by this approach at least, since she believed that she had the power to inspire passion in all mankind, she might dispose of Antony and keep herself and her treasure unharmed. So it turned out in the event.

9.   However, before this happened, Antony received news that Cornelius Gallus[22] had taken command of Scarpus's army in Cyrenaica, and had suddenly advanced with these troops to Paraetonium[23] and occupied it. So although he had wished to march to Syria to answer the appeal of the gladiators, he did not do this, but moved against Gallus. He believed that he had a chance of winning over these troops without a struggle, since they had served under him in various campaigns, and still had some regard for him. Otherwise he intended to subdue them by force, since his expedition comprised a strong force of infantry and a powerful fleet. But he found that he could not communicate with them, even though he came close to their ramparts and raised a great shout, for Gallus ordered his trumpeters to sound all their instruments at once, and made it impossible for anyone to hear a word. After this Antony attempted a surprise attack which failed, and later his fleet also suffered a reverse. Gallus arranged for chains to be stretched at night across the mouth of the harbour, but beneath the surface: he appeared to be taking no steps to guard the entrance, but contemptuously allowed the enemy to sail in unmolested. Then, once they were inside, he raised the chains by means of winches, surrounded Antony's ships from all sides – from the land, the houses and the sea – burned some, and sank others.

In the meanwhile Octavian captured Pelusium,[24] to appearances by assault, but in reality because it was betrayed by Cleopatra. She had understood that none of their allies now supported them, and that resistance to Octavian was impossible. Above all she had been convinced by what Thyrsus had told her, and believed that Octavian really loved her, first of all because she wished this to happen, and secondly because she had in the same way captivated Julius Caesar and Mark Antony. Thus she had come to expect that she would not only be pardoned and retain the kingdom of Egypt, but gain the empire of the Romans as well. So she at once surrendered Pelusium to Octavian, and later, when he advanced upon the capital, she prevented the Alexandrians from making secret sorties; at the same time, so far as could be judged from the outcry she made, she spiritedly urged them to resist.

10.   When Antony learned of the loss of Pelusium, he returned from Paraetonium and marched to face Octavian before Alexandria. His cavalry fell upon the enemy when they were exhausted from their advance and scored a success. Elated by this and by the fact that he had shot arrows into Octavian's camp which carried leaflets promising the soldiers six thousand sesterces each, he attacked with his infantry and was defeated. Octavian of his own accord read out the leaflets to his soldiers and did his utmost to counter their effect, on the one hand to incite feelings of shame at the treachery they were being invited to commit, and on the other to arouse enthusiasm for his own cause. In the end, the very episode itself stirred his men's emotions: they were angry at the attempt to undermine their loyalty and were anxious to prove that they did not deserve to be regarded as traitors.

After this unexpected defeat on land, Antony fell back on his fleet, and made ready to give battle at sea, or at least to set sail for Spain. But when Cleopatra saw this, she prevailed upon the crews to desert, and herself fled in haste to the mausoleum. She gave out that she feared Octavian, and wished by one means or another to forestall his plans by taking her own life, but in reality she was inviting Antony to enter the place with her. For his part, he half suspected that he was being betrayed, and yet because of his love for her could not believe this, but pitied her even more, it might be said, than himself. Cleopatra, no doubt, understood this very well, and hoped that once he heard that she was dead, he would not survive her, but straightaway follow her example. So she hastened to take refuge in the tomb with a eunuch and two of her women attendants, and from there sent a message to make him believe that she was dead.

He, when he heard it, did not hesitate, but longed to follow and join her in death. First he begged one of his attendants to kill him, but the man drew his sword and turned it on himself. Antony, wishing to match his courage, then stabbed himself and fell face downwards, so that the bystanders believed that he was dead. A great cry of lamentation went up, and when Cleopatra heard this, she peered out over the top of the tomb. Its doors had a locking device, so that, once closed, they could not be opened again, but the upper part of the building near the roof was not yet quite completed. When some of Antony's companions saw her looking out from there, they uttered a shout which even Antony could hear, and learning that Cleopatra was still alive, he struggled to his feet as though he still had strength enough to live. But as he had lost much blood, he knew that his end was near, and implored his companions to carry him to the monument and lift him up by the ropes which had been left hanging to raise the stone blocks. This was done, and Antony died there in Cleopatra's bosom.

11. She now believed that she could place some degree of trust in Octavian and at once sent word to him of what had happened, and yet she could not feel completely confident that no harm would befall her. She therefore remained in seclusion within the building, so that even if there were no other reason for keeping her alive, she could at least trade upon Octavian's fear concerning her treasure to obtain a pardon and keep her throne. Even when she had sunk to such depths of misfortune, she remembered that she was queen and preferred to die bearing the title and majesty of a sovereign rather than live in a private station. At any rate she kept ready fire to destroy her treasure, and asps and other reptiles to end her life; she had experimented before on human beings to discover how these creatures caused death in each case.

Now Octavian was much concerned not only to make himself master of her wealth, but also to capture her alive and lead her in his triumph at Rome. However, as he had given her a pledge of a kind, he did not wish to be seen as having tricked her; rather he wanted to make her appear as his captive, who had been to some extent subdued against her will. He therefore sent Gaius Proculeius,[25] a knight, and Epaphroditus, a freedman, to visit her, and instructed them carefully as to what they should say and do. The two accordingly obtained an audience with Cleopatra, began by discussing a number of reasonable proposals, and then, before anything had been agreed, suddenly laid hands on her. After this they removed from her any means of ending her life, and allowed her to spend some days in the monument where she was engaged in embalming Antony's body. They moved her to the palace, but did not dismiss any of her accustomed retinue or attendants: their object was that she should continue to cherish the hope of obtaining her wishes, and so do nothing to harm herself. At any rate, when she sought an audience with Octavian, her request was granted, and to further the deception he promised that he would visit her himself.

12. So she prepared a superbly decorated apartment and a richly orna-mented couch, dressed herself with studied negligence – indeed her appearance in mourning wonderfully enhanced her beauty – and seated herself on the couch. Beside her she arranged many different portraits and busts of Julius Caesar, and in her bosom she carried all the letters Caesar had sent her. Then as Octavian entered, she sprang to her feet, blushed, and cried, 'Greetings, my lord, for now the gods have given supremacy to you and taken it from me.[26] But now you can see with your own eyes how Caesar looked when he visited me so many times, and you have heard tell of how he honoured me and made me queen of Egypt. You should learn something of me from his own words; these are the letters which he wrote with his own hand: take them and read them.'

So saying, she went on to read many of Caesar's passionate expressions of his feelings for her. At one moment she would weep and kiss the letters, and then she would kneel and bow her head before Caesar's portraits. She kept turning her eyes towards Octavian and lamenting her fate in a plaintive musical tone. Her voice melted as she murmured, 'How can thy letters, Caesar, help me now?' and 'And yet in this man thou livest for me again,' then, 'Would that I had died before thee,' and still again, 'But if I have him, I have thee.'

Such were the subtle tones of speech and changes of expression with which she addressed Octavian, casting sweet looks towards him and murmuring tender words. Octavian understood the passion with which she was speaking and the seductive power of her gestures; however, he acted as if he were unaware of these, looked towards the ground and merely replied, 'Do not distress yourself, lady, take heart, no harm shall come to you.' But her spirits were utterly cast down, because he neither looked at her, nor made any mention of her kingdom, nor uttered so much as a word of love. She threw herself on her knees, burst out weeping, and said, 'I have no desire to live, nor can I live. But this favour I beg of you, in memory of your father, that since the gods gave me to Antony after him, I too may die with Antony. I wish that I had perished at the very instant after Caesar's death. But seeing that it was my fate to suffer that parting from him, send me to Antony. Do not grudge that I should be buried with him: as I die because of him, so may I live with him, even in Hades.'

13.   So she spoke, in the hope of arousing his pity, but Octavian made no reply. As he was afraid that she might still end her own life, he urged her yet again to take heart. After this he did not dismiss any of her attendants, but treated her with especial care in his desire that she should make a brilliant spectacle at his triumph. She guessed that this was his plan, and since she felt such a fate to be worse than any number of deaths, she now truly longed to die. She begged Octavian time and again that her life should be ended by one means or another, and of her own accord she thought of many ways to bring this about. Finally, when she could put none of these into effect, she professed to have undergone a change of heart and to place great hopes for the future both in Octavian and in Livia. She said that she would sail to Rome of her own free will, and prepared a number of specially treasured chosen ornaments to take as gifts. In this way she hoped to convince them that she did not intend to die, and hence that she would be less closely guarded and thus enabled to kill herself.

So it came about. As soon as the others, and in particular Epaphroditus, who had been charged with her safe keeping, had become convinced that her state of mind was as she described it and so relaxed their strict surveillance, she prepared to die as painlessly as possible. First she gave a sealed paper to Epaphroditus himself to deliver, in which she begged Octavian to give orders for her to be buried beside Antony. She pretended that the letter concerned some other matter, and using this pretext to get the freedman out of the way, she set about her task. She put on her finest robes, seated herself with majestic grace, took in her hands all the emblems of royalty, and so died.

14.   No one knows for certain by what means she perished, for the only marks that were found on her body were tiny pricks on the arm. Some say that she applied to herself an asp,[27] which had been brought to her in a water jar, or perhaps covered beneath some flowers. According to others she had smeared a pin with some poison whose composition rendered it harmless if the contact were external, but which, if even the smallest quantity entered the bloodstream, would quickly prove fatal, although also painless; according to this theory, she had previously worn the pin in

her hair as usual, but now made a small scratch in her arm and caused the poison to enter the blood. In this or some similar way she had died, and her two waiting women with her. As for the eunuch, he had of his own accord delivered himself up to the serpents at the time when Cleopatra had been seized by Proculeius, and after being bitten by them, had leaped into a coffin prepared for him.

When Octavian heard of Cleopatra's death, he was astounded,[28] and not only came to see her body, but called in the aid of drugs and of the Psylli in an attempt to revive her. The Psylli are male – there is no such thing as a Psylla – and they are able, if sent for immediately, to suck out the venom of any reptile before the victim dies; moreover they suffer no harm themselves if they are bitten by any such creature. They are propagated from one another, and they test their children either by having them thrown among serpents as soon as they are born, or having their swaddling clothes thrown on the serpents. The reptiles do not harm the children in the first case, and find themselves drugged by the clothing in the second.

So much for this matter of the Psylli. As for Octavian, when he found that it was impossible to revive Cleopatra, he felt both admiration and pity for her, but he was bitterly chagrined on his own account, as if all the glory of his victory had been taken away from him.

15. Antony and Cleopatra were the cause of many misfortunes to the Egyptians and many to the Romans. These were the circumstances in which they fought the war and met their deaths. They were both embalmed in the same manner and buried in the same tomb. The qualities of character which they possessed, and the fortunes which they experienced, may be described as follows. Antony had no superior in recognizing where his duty lay, and yet he committed many senseless acts. There were times when he excelled in courage, and yet he often failed through cowardice: he was capable equally of true greatness of spirit and of extreme baseness. He would plunder the property of others and squander his own. He showed compassion to many without cause, and punished even more without justice. Thus although he rose from most weak beginnings to a position of great power, and from the depths of poverty to the possession of great riches, yet he gained no profit from either situation. Instead, after hoping that he alone would rule the empire of the Romans, he took his own life.

Cleopatra was a woman of insatiable sexuality and insatiable avarice. She often displayed an estimable ambition, but equally often an overweening arrogance. It was by means of the power of love that she acquired the sovereignty of the Egyptians, and when she aspired to obtain dominion over the Romans in the same fashion, she failed in the attempt and lost her kingdom besides. Through her own unaided genius she captivated the two greatest Romans of her time, and because of the third, she destroyed herself.[29]

Such was the nature of these two, and so they ended their lives. Of their children, Antyllus[30] was immediately put to death, although he was betrothed to Octavian's daughter Julia and had taken refuge in his father's shrine, which Cleopatra had built; while Caesarion,[31] who was attempting to escape to Ethiopia, was overtaken on the road and murdered. Cleopatra was married to Juba,[32] the son of Juba. This young man had been brought up in Italy and Octavian rewarded him for his service in various campaigns by giving him his own ancestral kingdom and the hand of the princess. As a further favour to them Octavian spared the lives of Alexander and of Ptolemy, Antony's sons by Cleopatra. For his own nieces, the two daughters whom Octavia had borne to Antony and brought up, he set aside money from Antony's estate. He also commanded Antony's freedmen to hand over immediately to Iullus,[33] Antony's other son by Fulvia, all the possessions they would have been obliged by law to bequeath him after their own death.

16.   Of the rest of those who had served Antony's cause up to this time he punished some and pardoned others, in certain instances according to his own inclinations, in others for the sake of his friends. He found that there were many children of various princes and kings who were being kept at Antony's court, some as hostages, but others in a spirit of arrogance. A number of these he restored to their homes, for others he arranged marriages with one another, others, again, he detained. Of all these I shall mention only two. The Median king Artavasdes[34] had taken refuge with Octavian after his defeat, and to him Octavian returned Artavasdes's young daughter, Iotape, of his own accord. But when the Armenian king Artaxes requested that his brothers should be sent back to him, Octavian refused, because this ruler had put to death the Romans who had been left in Armenia.

These captives who had been held in Egypt were dealt with in the way that I have described. At the same time all the Egyptians and the Alexandrians were spared, and there were no executions. The truth was that since the population of Egypt was so large and might in many ways be of great use to the Romans, he decided against doing anything irremediably harmful; to explain his leniency he gave it out that he had been influenced by their god, Serapis, by their founder, Alexander the Great, and thirdly by their compatriot, Areius, whose learning and companionship he had enjoyed. The speech which announced these measures of clemency was addressed to the people in Greek for their better understanding. Later Octavian viewed the body of Alexander, and actually touched it, with the result that a piece of the nose was broken off, so the story goes. But he was unwilling to look at the remains of the Ptolemies, although the Alexandrians were very anxious to show them; Octavian commented, 'I wished to see a king, not corpses.' For this same reason he declined to enter the presence of Apis, remarking that he was accustomed to worship gods, not cattle.[35]

17.   After this he imposed a tribute upon Egypt and entrusted it to Cornelius Gallus to govern. Because of the great size of the population both in the cities and in the country, and of the impressionable and fickle nature of the inhabitants, the quantity of the grain supply, and the wealth of the whole country, so far from venturing to entrust the territory to any senator,[36] he would not even allow one to live there, unless he personally gave permission to the individual by name. Nor, on the other hand, did he allow Egyptians to become members of the Roman Senate.[37] He made various arrangements for the government of the other Egyptian cities, but in the case of the Alexandrians he ordered them to conduct their affairs without a city council,[38] so strongly, we must suppose, did he consider them to be addicted to radical change. Most of the features of the administration which Octavian imposed upon them at that date have been strictly preserved even to the present day. However, the Egyptians now have councillors in Alexandria, where they were first introduced under the emperor Severus, and they have also become senators in Rome, where they were first enrolled under Severus's son, Caracalla.

This was how the enslavement of Egypt took place. All those who carried on resistance for a time were subdued, as indeed various divine portents made clear that they would be. For not only did rain fall in places where no drop had ever been seen before, but blood besides, and the flash of weapons appeared from the clouds, as the showers of blood mingled with water poured down. In other places the clash of drums and cymbals and the notes of flutes and trumpets were heard, and a serpent of enormous size suddenly appeared and uttered a hiss of incredible volume. Meanwhile comets were observed in the heavens, the apparitions of dead men were seen, statues frowned, and the bull-god Apis bellowed a groan of lamentation and shed tears.

So much for these events. Great quantities of treasure were found in the palace, for Cleopatra had removed almost all the offerings from even the holiest of the shrines, and in this way the Romans were enabled to amass their spoils without committing any act of sacrilege. Heavy fines were also collected from all who were charged with any misdemeanour. Apart from these, all the rest, even though no specific accusation could be brought against them, were required to surrender two-thirds of their property. These resources were used to provide all the soldiers with the pay that was due to them, and those who were serving with Octavian at that time received a further thousand sesterces[39] on condition that they did not plunder the city. All those who had advanced loans to Octavian's cause were repaid in full, and both the senators and the knights who had taken part in the war received large sums of money. In all the Roman empire gained greatly in wealth and its temples in ornaments.

18.   After making the arrangements I have described, Octavian founded a city on the spot where the battle had taken place, and gave it the same name and the same games as the city he had founded previously.[40] He also cleared some of the canals, dug out others afresh,[41] and dealt with other problems which required attention.

Then he travelled through Syria to the province of Asia and spent the winter there, settling the affairs of the subject nations, as well as attending to those of the Parthians. It seems that strife had broken out amongst the latter, and a certain Tiridates had risen against the ruling king, Phraates. Until then, so long as the war with Antony continued even after Actium, Octavian had refrained from siding with either party, although both had sought his support; indeed he had not even sent a reply, except to say that he would give the matter his consideration. His excuse was that he was fully occupied with Egypt, but in fact he hoped that they would wear one another out in fighting. However, now that Antony was dead, and Tiridates had been defeated and had fled to Syria, and Phraates, the victor, had sent a delegation to him, Octavian entered into friendly negotiations with the envoys; at the same time he allowed Tiridates to live in Syria, but gave no promise to help him. He received one of Phraates's sons as an apparent gesture of goodwill, but he took him to Rome and kept him there as a hostage.

19.   Meanwhile, and even before this date, the Romans at home had passed many resolutions in honour of Octavian's naval victory. They voted him a triumph for his defeat of Cleopatra, and decreed that an arch adorned with trophies should be erected at Brundisium, and another in the Forum at Rome. They also decreed that the base of the shrine of Julius Caesar should be adorned with the rams of the captured warships; that a festival should be held at five-yearly intervals in honour of Octavian; that there should be a ceremony of thanksgiving on his birthday and the day of the announcement of his victory; and that when he entered the city of Rome, the Vestal Virgins, the Senate and the people, together with their wives and children, should go out to meet him. I need not record the details of the prayers, the effigies of Octavian, the privilege of the front seat, and all the other distinctions of this kind. At first the Romans not only voted these honours, but also removed or obliterated all the monuments which commemorated Antony, pronounced the day of his birth as accursed, and forbade any of his kinsmen to use the name Marcus. Later, when they learned of Antony's death, it so happened that the news arrived while the younger Cicero, the son of Marcus Tullius, was consul for a part of the year, and some people professed to see the hand of the gods in this coincidence, since it was Antony who had been largely responsible for the elder Cicero's death. They then voted Octavian many more crowns and ceremonies of thanksgiving and granted him another triumph, this time over the Egyptians.

But in neither the earlier nor the later announcements of these commemorations did they mention the name of Antony, nor of the other Romans who had been conquered with him, and so imply that it was proper to celebrate their defeat. They pronounced the day of the capture of Alexandria to be an auspicious day, and ordered that for the future the Alexandrians should take that date as the starting point for their chronology. They also decreed that Octavian should be vested with tribunician power for life, and that he should give his protection to those who appealed to him both within the city limits and beyond, to the distance of one mile, a prerogative which none of the other tribunes possessed.[42] Besides this he was to judge cases of appeal, and in all the courts his vote would be treated in the same way as that of Athena.[43] The priests and priestesses were instructed, when they offered up prayers for the Roman people and the Senate, to pray for him likewise, and both at public and at private banquets everyone was to pour a libation for him.

20.   These were the decrees passed during that period. When Octavian became consul for the fifth time with Sextus Appuleius, all the measures he had taken were ratified by oath on the first day of January. When Octavian's despatch concerning the Parthians arrived, a further series of measures was approved. The first name of Octavian was to be included in public hymns on the same terms as those of the gods; one of the tribes should be named Julian after his family name; at all the public festivals he should wear the crown which is normally only worn at a triumph; those senators who had been associated with his victory would walk in the triumphal procession dressed in togas bordered with purple; the day on which he entered Rome should be celebrated with sacrifices by the whole population, and should rank as a sacred day for ever after; he was empowered to appoint as many priests as he thought fit beyond the regular number for any occasion that he might choose. This last privilege, which was granted at that date, was later indefinitely extended, so that I need not in future specify the exact number of officials appointed. Octavian accepted all but a few of these tributes, but he expressly asked that the resolution whereby the whole population of Rome was to go out to meet him should not be put into effect. However, the action which gave him more pleasure than all these honours was the formal closing by the Senate of the gates of the temple of Janus, which signified that the Roman people's wars were at an end, and also the taking of the augury for the prosperity of the state, which had not been carried out for years for the reasons I have mentioned.[44] It is true that the Treveri,[45] who had called in the Germans to help them, were still under arms, as also were the Cantabri,[46] the Vaccaei[47] and the Astures[48] – these three were subdued by Statilius Taurus and the Treveri by Nonius Gallus –and there were many other disorders taking place in various regions. But since no consequences of importance resulted from them, the Romans did not consider that they were at war at that period, and for my part I have nothing of note to record about them.

Meanwhile Octavian, besides the other business which he transacted in Asia, granted permission that precincts sacred to Rome and to his father Caesar, whom he named the hero Julius, should be dedicated in Ephesus and in Nicaea. These had become the most important cities in the province of Asia and in Bithynia, respectively, at that time. He laid it down that the Romans who lived in those places should honour the two divinities. At the same time he allowed the aliens, under the name of Hellenes, to consecrate precincts to himself, those of the Asiatic province in Pergamum and those of the Bithynians in Nicomedia. This practice began with Octavian and it has been carried on under other emperors, not only with regard to the Hellenic peoples, but to all others in so far as they acknowledge Roman rule. In Rome itself and in Italy generally, no emperor, however greatly venerated he may have been, has so far ventured to do this. However, even there other divine honours are conferred after their death upon those emperors who have ruled virtuously, and in fact shrines are built in their honour.

21. These events took place during the winter,[49] and during the same period the people of Pergamum were also granted permission to hold the sacred games, as they were named, in honour of Octavian's temple. During that summer Octavian crossed over to Greece and from there returned to Italy.

When he finally entered Rome, not only did all the citizens offer sacrifice, as I have mentioned above, but even the consul, Valerius Potitus. Octavian, it is true, had been consul throughout the year, as he had been for the two years before, but Potitus had succeeded Sextus Appuleius. It was he who in public and in person sacrificed oxen upon Octavian's arrival on behalf of the people of Rome and of the Senate, something which had never been done for any man before.

After this Octavian spoke in praise of his subordinates, and conferred honours upon them as was his custom. To Agrippa, among other distinctions, he also presented a dark blue flag to commemorate his naval victory, and to the soldiers he gave other gifts. The populace were granted four hundred sesterces each, first to the men of adult age and later to the children on account of his nephew Marcellus.[50] Octavian refused to accept from the Italian cities the gold required to make the triumphal crowns they had voted for him, and meanwhile not only paid all the debts which he himself owed, as has already been explained, but did not press others to pay their debts to him. Because of these concessions, the Romans forgot all the hardships they had suffered and accepted his triumph with pleasure, as though the enemies he had conquered had all been foreigners. Indeed the quantity of money which was circulating through all parts of the city alike was so huge that the price of goods increased, and loans for which the borrower had willingly paid twelve per cent could now be obtained for a third of that rate.

In his triumph Octavian celebrated on the first day his victory over the Pannonians[51] and Dalmatians, the Iapydes[52] and their neighbours, and a number of Germans and Gauls. I should explain that Gaius Carrinas had subdued the Morini[53] and other tribes which had risen in rebellion with them, and had driven back the Suebi[54] who had crossed the Rhine to attack the Romans. Accordingly this triumph was celebrated both by Carrinas – in spite of the fact that his father had been executed by Sulla, and that he himself together with others in like case had been debarred from holding office – and by Octavian, who was duly entitled to the credit for the victory by virtue of his position as supreme commander.[55] These were the achievements that were honoured on the first day. On the second the naval victory at Actium, and on the third the subjugation of Egypt were commemorated. All the processions presented a striking appearance on account of the spoils from Egypt – indeed the quantity of plunder from there was enough to decorate all the processions – but the Egyptian spectacle surpassed all the others in luxury and magnificence.

Among the items which were carried along was an effigy of the dead Cleopatra lying on a couch, so that in a sense she too, together with the live captives, who included her children Alexander, named the Sun, and Cleopatra, named the Moon, formed a part of the pageant. After this came Octavian, who rode into the city behind the whole procession. He played his part in all respects according to the usual customs, except that he allowed his fellow consul and the other magistrates, contrary to precedent, to follow him,[56] together with the senators who had taken part in the victory. The normal arrangement was for these officials to lead the procession, and for the senators only to follow it.

22.   After these ceremonies had been completed, Octavian dedicated the temple of Minerva, also known as the Chalcidicum, and the Curia Julia, which had been built in honour of Julius Caesar. In the Curia he erected the statue of Victory, which is still in existence; its purpose, it seems likely,

was to show that it was from this goddess that he had received the empire. The statue had belonged to the people of Tarentum, and it was now brought from that city to Rome, placed in the Senate chamber, and decorated with spoils from Egypt. The same was done in the case of the shrine of Julius Caesar, which was consecrated at this time, for many of the spoils were also lodged in it. Others were dedicated to Jupiter Capitolinus and to Juno and Minerva; this was done after all the objects in those temples which were believed to have been placed there previously as dedications – or which were still there as dedications – had been removed by decree as being defiled. In this way Cleopatra, despite having been defeated and captured, was nevertheless glorified, since her ornaments now rest as dedications in our temples, and she herself appears in gold in the temple of Venus.

On the occasion of the consecration of the shrine to Julius Caesar contests of many kinds took place: the boys of noble ancestry rode in the equestrian formation which is known as 'Troy', and the men of the same rank competed with chargers, pairs and four-horse teams, while a senator named Quintus Vitellius fought as a gladiator. Huge numbers of wild beasts and tame animals were killed, and among them were a rhinoceros and a hippopotamus, which were then seen in Rome for the first time. The characteristic features of the hippopotamus have been described by many people and even more have seen it. The rhinoceros, which is less familiar, resembles the elephant in some respects, but the horn which it carries is actually on its nose, and its name is derived from that feature.

These creatures, then, were introduced into the games, and Dacians[57] and Suebians fought one another in mass combats. The latter tribe are Germans, the former are related to a branch of the Scythians. The Suebi, to be precise, live beyond the Rhine (though many others claim their name), and the Dacians on both sides of the Danube. Those Dacians who inhabit the southern side of the river, near the territory of the Triballi, are classified as belonging to the region of Moesia and are called Moesians. Those on the other side of the river are also called Dacians, and are either a branch of the Getae, or Thracians from the Dacian race, which once inhabited Rhodope. These Dacians had at an earlier date sent envoys to Octavian, but since none of their requests were granted, they went over to Antony. However, strife broke out among them, with the result that they rendered no great service to him. Some of them were later captured and were matched against the Suebi. The whole spectacle lasted for many days, as might be expected, and continued without interruption, even though Octavian fell ill; others presided and the performances were carried on in his absence. On one of the days when these games were in progress, the senators gave banquets in the forecourts of their various homes, but I do not know why this was done, since no explanation has been recorded.

23. These were the main events of that period. In the previous year, while Octavian was still in his fourth consulship, Statilius Taurus[58] built at his own expense an amphitheatre for hunting performances constructed of stone in the Campus Martius, and dedicated it with a gladiatorial contest. For this service the people granted him the right to choose one of the praetors each year.

During the same period Marcus Crassus was sent to Macedonia and Greece, and carried out campaigns against the Dacians and the Bastarnae. I have already explained who the former people are, and why they were at war with Rome. The Bastarnae, on the other hand, who strictly speaking are classed as Scythians, had at this time crossed the Danube and conquered the territory which lay opposite theirs; they went on to subdue the Triballi, whose lands border this region, and the Dardani, who inhabit Triballian territory. So long as they were engaged in these operations, they did not come into conflict with the Romans. However, when they crossed the river Haemus and overran the part of Thrace belonging to the Dentheleti, who have a treaty of alliance with Rome, Crassus went out to meet them. He did this partly to protect Sitas, the king of the Dentheleti, who was blind, but also because he feared that Macedonia might be invaded. His mere arrival in the neighbourhood of the Bastarnae threw them into a panic, and impelled them to withdraw from the country without a battle.

Soon after, he pursued them on their homeward march, occupied the region known as Segetica, invaded Moesia, laid the country waste and attacked one of their fortresses. Here his advanced troops were driven back, because the Moesians believed them to be unsupported and made a sortie. However, when he reinforced them with his main body, he repulsed the enemy, laid siege to the fortress and destroyed it.

24. While he was thus engaged, the Bastarnae paused in their retreat and halted near the river Cedrus, to see what would then happen. After

defeating the Moesians, Crassus next advanced against the Bastarnae, whereupon they sent envoys, urging him not to pursue them, since they had done the Romans no harm. Crassus kept the envoys with him, on the pretext that he would give them his answer on the following day. He treated them hospitably, proceeded to make them drunk, and thus discovered all their plans, for the whole race is insatiably fond of wine, and quickly becomes over-charged with it.

Meanwhile during the night Crassus advanced into a forest and halted there, having first posted look-outs in front of the wood. The Bastarnae, supposing that these scouts were unsupported, ran to attack them and pursued them as they fell back into the depths of the forest; there Crassus killed many of them on the spot and many more in the rout which followed. Not only were the fugitives impeded by their waggons which were stationed behind them, but their desire to save their wives and children also contributed to their undoing. Crassus himself killed their king, Deldo, and would have dedicated to Jupiter Feretrius the king's armour as *spolia opima*,[59] if he had been in supreme command.

This was the course which the battle followed. Of the remainder of the Bastarnae, some lost their lives when they fled into a grove which was set on fire from all sides; others perished when they jumped into the Danube, or as they scattered and fled through the countryside. A small number survived and occupied a strong position, where Crassus besieged them without success for some days. Then he completed their destruction with the help of Roles, the king of a tribe of the Getae. When Roles visited Octavian, he was treated as a friend and ally for the support he had given; those of the Bastarnae who had been taken prisoner were distributed among the Roman soldiers.

25.   After these operations Crassus turned against the Moesians. With some he prevailed by persuasion, others were frightened into submission, and others overcome by force. In the end, at the cost of great hardship and many dangers, he subdued all but a very few. His troops suffered severely from the cold, and still more at the hands of the Thracians, through whose territory he was retreating and whom he believed to be well disposed, but finally – since by then it was winter – he made his way into friendly territory. Because of these difficulties he thought it best to content himself with what he had accomplished. A triumph and the appropriate sacrifices were decreed not only for Octavian but also for

himself. However, he was not granted the title of Imperator, as some sources report: it was Octavian alone who received this.[60]

Meanwhile the Bastarnae were indignant at the defeats they had suffered, and when they discovered that Crassus did not intend to take the field against them, they turned upon the Dentheleti and Sitas, their ruler, whom they considered to be more responsible than anyone else for the ills that had befallen them. So Crassus was obliged, much against his will, to resume the campaign; then, urging his men forward by forced marches, he attacked unexpectedly, overcame the enemy and imposed whatever terms he chose. Now that he had taken up arms again, he felt impelled to punish the Thracians, who had harassed his march during his withdrawal from Moesia, for they were reported at this time to be fortifying positions and to be bent upon war. Some of his opponents, namely the Maedi and the Serdi, were defeated in battle, after which the prisoners had their hands cut off; the fighting was hard, but in the end he subdued them and overran the rest of their territory, with the exception of the lands of the Odrysae. He spared this tribe because they are dedicated to the service of Dionysus, and had come on this occasion to meet him unarmed. He granted them possession of the land in which they worship the god, and took it away from the Bessi who were then occupying it.

26.   While these operations were still proceeding, Roles, who had gone to war with Dapyx, the king of another tribe of the Getae, appealed to Crassus for help. Crassus marched to his assistance and managed to drive the enemy's cavalry back upon their infantry. This success inspired such terror in his adversaries that the action which followed was no longer a battle but a massacre of the fugitives from both parts of the army. After this, finding that Dapyx had taken refuge in a fortress, Crassus cut off his retreat and besieged him there. During the siege one of the beleaguered garrison hailed Crassus from the walls in Greek, contrived a meeting, and arranged to betray the place. When the barbarians were taken, they turned their arms upon one another, and Dapyx was killed together with many of the garrison. Although Crassus captured his brother alive, he not only did him no harm but even let him go.

After completing these operations, Crassus led an expedition against the cave called Ciris. This is very large, and so well situated for defence that, according to legend, the Titans took refuge there after their defeat by the gods. A great multitude of the local inhabitants had occupied the cave, bringing with them all their herds and their most valued possessions. Crassus first reconnoitred all the entrances to the cave, which are tortuous and difficult to discover, then blocked them up, and in this way subdued the inmates by hunger. After this success he gave no respite to the rest of the Getae, even though they were not the subjects of Dapyx. He advanced against Genucla, the most strongly defended fortress of the kingdom of Zyraxes, because he had heard that the legionary standards, which the Bastarnae had captured from Gaius Antonius,[61] were kept there. He attacked the place both from the landward side and from the river Danube, on which the city is built, and in a short while captured it, though not without hard fighting. It seems that the king, as soon as he learned of the Romans' advance, set off with money to visit the Scythians and seek an alliance, but he did not return quickly enough.

27.   These were his achievements among the Getae. Some of the Moesians whom he had previously subdued rose in rebellion, but his subordinates reconquered these. Meanwhile he himself led an expedition against the Artacii and a few other tribes, which had never before been subject to Rome. The former refused to acknowledge his authority and took especial pride in their independence, thus encouraging at once resentment against the Romans and the desire to overthrow their rule among the other peoples. Crassus succeeded in bringing them all to terms, some of them by force after they had caused him no little trouble, others through fear for their fellow countrymen, whom the Romans were now subjugating.

These operations continued for a considerable time, but both the actions which I record and the names correspond to the tradition which has been handed down. In ancient times, it is true, tribesmen of the Moesians and the Getae occupied all the land between the Haemus and the Danube rivers. But as time went on, some of these changed their names, and since then all the tribes living north of Dalmatia, Macedonia and Thrace and separated from Pannonia by the river Sava, a tributary of the Danube, have been included under the name of Moesia. Of the many tribes now to be found among them are the one formerly known as the Triballi, and also the Dardani, who still keep their old name.

BOOK 52

The following is contained in the Fifty-Second Book of Dio's *Rome*:

How Octavian planned to lay aside his sovereignty (chs. 1–40)
How he began to be called emperor (ch. 42)

1.   We have now surveyed the record of events – what the Roman people achieved and what they suffered – under the rule of kings, of the republic and of the war-lords over a period of seven hundred and twenty-five years.[1] After this they began again with what was, strictly speaking, a monarchy, although Octavian intended to lay down his arms and entrust the direction of affairs to the Senate and the people. But before taking this decision he had consulted Agrippa and Maecenas, to whom he was in the habit of confiding all his secret plans. Agrippa was the first to speak, and his advice was as follows.

2.   'You must not be surprised, Caesar, if I try to dissuade you from the idea of making yourself sole ruler, even though I personally should enjoy many advantages if you occupied that position. Now, if this arrangement were to your advantage as well, I should give it my full support. But the effects of monarchy upon those who exercise it are by no means the same at its effects upon their friends. On the contrary, the former are exposed to jealousies and dangers, while the latter reap all the benefits they could desire without running any of these risks. So I have thought it right in this instance, as in all others, to look ahead not only in my interests but in yours and those of the state.

'Let us now consider at leisure all the essential qualities of this mode of government, and be guided in whatever direction our reason may lead us, for I suppose nobody will argue that we are obliged to choose monarchical rule in any event, even if it is to nobody's advantage. If we did this, the world would conclude either that our good fortune had been too much for us, and that our very successes had deprived us of our judgement, or else that your father's name and our devotion to his memory were put forward as a mere screen behind which we were all the time striving for power and that we were using the people and the Senate as a façade, with the aim not of freeing those who plotted against their liberties, but of enslaving them to our rule. In either case, our action would stand condemned. For who will not be angry when he observes that we have said one thing, and then finds that we mean something different? Surely he will hate us more bitterly than if we had revealed our ambitions from the very beginning, and aimed directly at the monarchy.

'It is true that the idea has become accepted that the readiness to resort to violence is deeply ingrained in human nature, however selfish that may appear. Anyone who is pre-eminent in any respect thinks it his due to enjoy more advantages than his inferior, and if he achieves any success, he attributes this to the strength of his own spirit, but if he fails, to the action of some higher power. On the other hand, the man who pursues his ends by means of intrigue and wrongdoing is first of all judged to be cunning, devious, malicious and unprincipled, and this is a verdict which, as I know well, you would not tolerate that anyone should utter, or even contemplate about yourself, even if you could rule the whole world by such methods. Secondly, even if such a man succeeds, his fellows consider that the advantage he has gained is unfair, and if he fails, that his misfortune is well deserved.

3.   'This being so, men would find fault with us just as much if they saw that we now cherished that ambition, even if it had never entered our minds at the start. For it is surely worse for men to let themselves be defeated by circumstances, and then not only fail to restrain themselves, but misuse such opportunities as fortune has given them, than it is to harm others in consequence of failure. In the latter case they are often compelled by the very reverses they have suffered to commit wrongs even against their will, because their own interests demand it, whereas in the former they deliberately throw off all restraint, even when this is contrary to their interests. So in the case of men whose souls lack any upright principle and who cannot use with moderation such blessings as have been bestowed on them, how could one expect them to rule honourably over others, or to conduct themselves well in adversity? We believe that we are free from either of these faults, and have no desire to cast reason aside, but will adopt

whatever course we find best after due deliberation. Let us therefore follow these lines in making our decision. I shall speak quite frankly, for it would be impossible for me to do otherwise, and I know very well that you would take no pleasure in listening to any combination of falsehood and flattery.

4. 'Equality before the law is an auspicious concept and works very justly in practice. Where we have men to whom heredity has allotted the same kind of nature, who belong to the same race as one another, have grown up under the same institutions, have been trained under similar laws, and contribute in equal degree with one another the service of their bodies and minds to their country, is it not just that they should share equally in all other respects as well, and is it not best that they should receive no distinctions save on account of merit? For equality of birth strives for an equal share of privilege, and if it obtains this it rejoices, while if it fails, it is incensed. Moreover the human race all over the world, since it originated from the gods and will return to the gods, turns its eyes upwards and will not consent to be ruled for ever by the same person, nor will it submit to sharing the hardships, the dangers and the sacrifices, while at the same time it is excluded from sharing the advantages. Or, if it is forced to accept such conditions, it will hate the regime which has imposed them, and if it can find the occasion, revenge itself upon what it hates.

'Now all men, of course, claim the right to rule, and for this reason suffer themselves to be ruled in turn. They are unwilling for others to impose upon them, but on this account are themselves obliged not to impose upon others. They take pleasure in those honours which are paid them by their equals, and they approve of the penalties which are inflicted by the laws. If they live under a system of this kind, they regard its advantages and disadvantages as shared by all alike; they desire that no harm should befall any of its citizens, and they offer up their prayers that all its blessings should be enjoyed by the community at large. If any one of them is endowed with any particular excellence, he is most willing to make it public, practises it with enthusiasm and displays it with pleasure. Or if he sees such a quality in one of his fellows, he readily brings it forward, eagerly takes part in fostering it, and honours it most handsomely. On the other hand, if a fellow citizen commits a disgraceful action, he attracts the hatred of all, while if he suffers a misfortune, everyone takes pity on him. In short, each individual regards the resulting disgrace or loss as something experienced by the whole community.

5. 'These are the essential features of a democracy. In a tyranny all the opposite elements prevail. But there is no need for me to recount the details at length. The principal characteristic of the system is that nobody is willing to be believed to know or possess anything of value, because to hold any such advantage generally attracts the utmost hostility from the ruling power. On the contrary, everyone takes the tyrant's character as the standard for his own life; he then pursues whatever aims he may hope to achieve by getting the advantage over others through the tyrant's activities and without risk to himself. Hence the majority exert themselves only in their own interests and hate all their fellow-citizens; they consider the successes obtained by their neighbours as losses to themselves, and the misfortunes of others as their own gains.

'This being so, I do not see what reason could possibly persuade you to desire to become sole ruler. Such a regime is difficult to impose upon democracies in general, and would be far more difficult still for you yourself to operate. Surely you can see how the city of Rome and its affairs are even now in a state of turmoil. It is difficult in the first place to make yourself master of the mass of our citizens who have lived for so many years in freedom, and secondly it is difficult, when we are surrounded by so many enemies, to reduce once more to slavery the allies and the subject nations, bearing in mind that some have been democratically governed for generations, and others we have ourselves set free.

6. 'Let us begin with the least weighty problem. It will be essential for you to raise large sums of money from all sides, for it is impossible to maintain the army at its present strength, not to mention other kinds of expenditure, out of the existing revenues. Now this requirement applies equally to democracies, since no form of government can function without expense. But in democracies many citizens contribute large sums, preferably of their own free will. They pride themselves on doing this out of public spirit, and they obtain suitable honours in return for their generosity. Sometimes compulsory contributions are also levied from the whole citizen body, and in that case they accept them, both because this is done with their consent, and because the taxes they are paying are for their own benefit.

'But in the case of monarchical regimes, all their subjects expect that the government, which they believe disposes of unlimited wealth, should bear the expense alone. They are very ready to investigate the ruler's sources of income, but less so to calculate his outgoings. They do not contribute sums from their private means gladly or even voluntarily, and the public levies which they pay are not supported by their free votes. As far as voluntary contributions are concerned, nobody would offer one, since he would not readily admit that he was rich. Indeed it would not be in the ruler's interest that he should come forward, since he would immediately gain a reputation among the people for his public spirit, form an inflated opinion of himself and incite an uprising.

'On the other hand, a general levy is a great burden to the populace, all the more so since they endure the loss in resources while others enjoy the gain. Of course in democracies the majority of those who contribute the money also serve in the army, so that in a sense they recover their taxes. But in monarchies those who are engaged in agriculture, manufacturing, commerce and politics belong to one sector of society, from which the state's revenues are mainly drawn; it is a different sector which bears arms and receives pay.

7.   'Such is the nature of this one factor, the financial problem, and it will cause you trouble. And there is another one to consider. It is imperative that anyone who from time to time commits a crime should pay the penalty. Most men are not kept within the bounds of moderation by mere admonition, or even by example; it is absolutely necessary to punish them by disfranchisement, by exile, or by death. Moreover such penalties are not infrequent in an empire the size of ours which contains such a vast population, especially at the time of any change of government. Now if you appointed other men to judge the accused, they would vie with one another to acquit them, and especially those whom it might be thought you hated, for judges, of course, create a certain impression of authority whenever they do something which does not conform to the desire of the ruler. Then, if some offenders are convicted, people will conclude that the judges have condemned them deliberately, to give you satisfaction. On the other hand, if you sit in judgement yourself, you will be compelled to punish many of your peers – an unhappy state of affairs – and you will inevitably be believed to be indicting some of them on grounds of personal animosity rather than of justice. No one believes that those who have the

power to use coercion are acting uprightly when they pass judgement. It is always assumed that authority out of shame erects a screen and a false picture of constitutional government to obscure the truth, while behind the legal title of a court of justice it merely gratifies its own desires.

'This, then, is what happens in monarchies. In democracies, on the other hand, if a man is accused of committing a private offence, he is brought before a private court and must answer to a jury of his equals. If he is charged with a public crime, then in this instance too a jury of his peers, who are chosen by lot, judges the case. This makes it easier to accept the verdicts which are reached by these juries, since men recognize that whatever penalty they suffer neither originates from a judge's power nor has been wrung from him as a favour.

8. 'Now apart from those who have actually committed some offence, there are many others who have a high opinion of themselves, some on account of their birth, others of their wealth, or of some other endowment. These are by no means bad men, and yet they are by personal conviction opposed to the monarchical principle. If the ruler allows these men to increase in influence, he cannot live in safety, and yet if he seeks to curb their activity, he cannot do so with justice. What is he to do with these men? How shall he treat them? If you destroy their families, reduce their wealth, and humble the pride, you will lose all the goodwill of your subjects. How could you possibly possess it, if they are denied the right to be born into a noble family, or to make money honestly, or to become strong, or brave, or intelligent? And yet if you allow these various elements in society to flourish, you will not be able to deal with them easily. Of course, if you alone could handle all the business of state, conduct wars successfully, find suitable solutions for every situation, and had no need of a colleague in any of these spheres, the question would be different.

'But as things are, since you would have such an immense empire to govern, it is imperative that you should have many assistants, and it is right that they should be both brave and spirited. Now if you entrust the offices of state and the command of the legions to men of this calibre, both you and your system of government will run the risk of being overthrown. It is impossible for a man of real worth to possess a nature which lacks all spirit, any more than a man who has been reared in a servile state of life can acquire it. On the other hand you can be sure that the man who proves his mettle will always desire liberty and hate despotic authority.

'Yet if you entrust nothing to such citizens and put the management of affairs into the hands of mediocrities and nonentities, you will very soon bring upon yourself the enmity of the former, who will think you have no confidence in them, and likewise very soon fail in the most important undertakings. For what worthwhile results could an ignorant or lowly born person accomplish? Which of our enemies would not look down on him? Which of our allies would obey him? Who even among the private soldiers would not think it demeaning to be commanded by such a man? I need not enlarge to you upon all the harmful consequences which naturally flow from a situation of that sort, for you know them very well. But I shall make this one point, as I am bound to do, that if an official of this kind failed completely to carry out his duty, he would harm you far more than our enemies could. If, on the other hand, he fulfilled any of his functions with success, his lack of education would make him lose his head, and he might prove a serious danger to you.

9. 'This state of affairs does not apply in the democracies. There the greater the number of men who are endowed with wealth and with courage, the more they compete for honour, and thereby strengthen the state. The state for its part exploits their abilities and rejoices in them, unless one of them desires to establish a tyranny, in which case the citizens punish him most severely. The fact that this is so, and that democracies are greatly superior to monarchies, is shown by the example of Greece.[2] So long as the peoples of Greece were subject to monarchies, they achieved nothing of consequence, but once they began to live under popular rule, their fame spread throughout the world. The experience of the other races of mankind bears out the same principle. Those which still live under tyrannies are always in a state of slavery, and always conspiring against their rulers. Those who are governed by leaders elected for a year or longer continue to be both free and independent.

'But why need we refer to the examples set by other peoples, when we have our own at home? We Romans at first lived under a different form of government. Then, after enduring many harsh experiences, we longed to obtain our liberty. After we had won it, we rose to the position of proud authority which we enjoy today, and yet our supremacy depends upon nothing else but the virtues which are bred by democracy. On the strength of these principles, the Senate deliberated, the people confirmed their proposals, the soldiers were fired with ardour and their commanders with ambition. None of these things could be achieved under a tyranny. At any rate, the ancient Romans hated tyranny so passionately for these reasons that they even declared that form of government to be accursed.

10.   'Apart from these considerations, let us also speak of those which affect your personal interests. How could you find the strength to deal with such an immense range of problems, not only by day, but also by night? How could you support such a burden if your health should fail? Which of the accustomed blessings of mankind could you enjoy, and how could you be happy if you were deprived of them? Where could you find genuine pleasure, and when would you not be oppressed by intense pain? It is a hard necessity that the man who wields such immense power should be beset by many anxieties, exposed to many fears, and experience very little enjoyment of the sweets of life, but should at all times and places see and hear and do and suffer only that which is hard to bear. This, I believe, is why some men, Greeks and barbarians alike, have refused royal thrones, even when these were offered to them.

'You will need to anticipate and to take advice on all these problems before you become involved in them. For it is shameful, or rather quite impossible, for a man to draw back once he has cast an eye upon such an office. And you must not be deceived either by the vast scope of its authority, or the magnitude of its possessions, or its host of bodyguards, or its throng of courtiers. For men who take on great power take on many troubles; those who lay up great wealth are required to spend it on the same scale; the host of bodyguards is recruited because of the host of conspirators; and as for the flatterers, they would be more likely to destroy you than to preserve you.

'For all these reasons no man who has given the question due thought would desire to become supreme ruler.

11.   'But if the fact that such rulers can make others rich, or save their lives, or bestow many other blessings upon them – or for that matter insult them and do harm to anyone they please – should lead anyone to believe that tyranny is worth striving for, he is utterly wrong in his conclusion. I need not tell you that a life spent in debauchery or wrong-doing is disgraceful, or beset with dangers, or that it is detested by gods

and men. You are not that kind of man, and no reasons of this sort would ever influence you to become sole ruler. In any case, I have chosen just now to describe only what those who use their power in the best possible way are obliged to do or to suffer: I have said nothing of all the harm that could be done by those who mismanage their task. But as for the argument I have just mentioned, that the supreme ruler has the means to bestow an abundance of benefits, this of course a power worth striving for.³ And yet, however noble, imposing, glorious and secure such a prerogative may be in the hands of a private citizen, this does not outweigh the more harmful consequences of its being exercised by a king. In short, a man should not accept such liabilities for the sake of enjoying that privilege in particular, especially when he is likely to pass on to others the benefits he derives from his position, while he alone incurs the odium that goes with it.

12. 'And secondly, this privilege we have described is not without its contradictions, as people seem to imagine, since no ruler can possibly satisfy all those who apply for his largesse. For those who believe they deserve to receive some mark of favour from him are virtually the whole of mankind, even though nothing may be due to them just then. Every man, naturally, has a high opinion of himself, and wishes to enjoy some benefit from the man who is in a position to grant it. And yet the rewards which can actually be handed out, by which I mean honours, offices and in some instances money, do not take long to enumerate, compared with the huge number of petitioners.

'This being so, more resentment is bound to be felt towards the ruler by those who come away empty-handed than goodwill by those whose requests are fulfilled. The latter regard their rewards as no more than their due, and think there is no special reason to be grateful to the giver, since they are receiving only what they expected. More than this, they positively recoil from showing gratitude, for fear of creating the impression that they are unworthy of the good that has been done them. The others, when their hopes miscarry, feel a grievance for two reasons: first, they consider that they are being deprived of what is rightfully theirs, for men always believe that they already own whatever they yearn for; secondly, they consider that if they resign themselves too easily to their failure to obtain whatever they were expecting, they are acknowledging some shortcoming on their part.

'Behind all this lies the consideration that the ruler who grants such favours wisely makes it his first concern to investigate the merits of each applicant, and hence he honours some and passes over others. As a result of his verdict, those who have been singled out find a further cause for satisfaction, and the others an additional resentment, the feelings of each being intensified by their own consciousness of its correctness.

'On the other hand, if a ruler tries to guard against this outcome and decides to distribute these honours at random, he will fail in every respect. Those who were unworthy in the first place, if they found themselves honoured regardless of their merits, would merely become worse: they would assume that they were either being commended for the good they had done, or at any rate courted for the harm of which they were capable. The virtuous, if they saw that they were by no means being preferred to their inferiors, but merely treated on an equal footing, would be more angry at being brought down to the level of the others than pleased at being actually found worthy of some honour. They would then cease to practise the nobler principles of conduct, and vie with one another in pursuing the baser. So the result of the attempt to distribute honours evenly on this principle would be the following: those who granted them would reap no beneficial effect for society, and those who received them would behave worse than before. Accordingly this prerogative, which some people would regard as an especially attractive feature of monarchical rule, would prove extremely difficult for you to exercise.

13. 'You must consider carefully these factors, and the others I mentioned a little while ago. Then act wisely, while you have the opportunity, and entrust to the people the control of the army, the provinces, the offices of state and the public funds. If you do this now and of your own accord, you will be at once the most famous of men and the most secure. But if you wait until your hand is forced in some way, you are likely to suffer some calamity and lose your reputation as well. Bear in mind the lessons of the past. Marius,[4] Sulla,[5] Metellus[6] and Pompey[7] in his early years, when they took control of affairs, all refused to assume sovereign power, and came to no harm as a result. On the other hand Cinna,[8] the younger Marius,[9] Strabo,[10] Sertorius[11] and Pompey at the end of his career all experienced the desire to assume sovereign power – and perished miserably.

'It would be an immensely hard task to bring this city, which has known democratic government for so many years, and which rules an empire of such a size, to a state of slavery. You know how the people banished Camillus,[12] merely because he used white horses in his triumphal procession, and how they deposed Scipio[13] from power, after condemning him for some overweening action. And you will remember how they treated your own father, Julius Caesar, because of the mere suspicion that he wished to make himself sole ruler. Yet there have been no better men than these.

'Having said this, I do not advise you simply to lay aside the sovereignty. You should first take all those measures which the public interest demands, and settle all outstanding problems by decrees and laws, as was done by Sulla. For even if some of his legislation was later overturned, the greater part of it and the more important measures survived. And do not tell me that even then some men will divide the community into factions. I should only have to repeat the argument that the Romans would find the rule of a monarch far more intolerable than the solution I have mentioned. For if we were to review all the calamities and contingencies which might befall a nation, it would be absurd for us to be more frightened by those dissensions which naturally arise from a democratic system of government than by the tyrannical regimes which are the natural outcome of monarchy. I have not attempted to say anything of the frightful nature of such tyrannies, since I was unwilling merely to criticize in passing something which is so utterly damnable. I hoped rather to prove to you that the nature of monarchy is such that even virtuous men ... (cannot possibly redeem it).'

[The end of Agrippa's speech is missing from the manuscripts, and the same applies to the early part of Maecenas's speech and Dio's introductory passage. Zonaras's synopsis at this point runs as follows:

But Maecenas advised the contrary course. He pointed out that Octavian had already for a long time been directing the monarchy, and that it was inevitable that he should do one of two things, either remain in the same position, or abandon his present course and perish.]

14.   '... And so, if you care at all for your country, for whose sake you have fought so many wars and would gladly lay down your very existence, reform our life and order our affairs in the direction of greater moderation. The question concerns the privilege of doing and saying exactly what one pleases. Now if you examine the matter carefully, this freedom, if it is exercised by men of sound judgement, becomes a source of great benefit

for all, but, if exercised by the misguided, leads to disaster. Accordingly, the man who grants such a licence to the latter is in effect putting a sword into the hand of a child or a madman; if he offers it to the wise, he is not only preserving their other privileges, but saving the incapable even in spite of themselves. So I urge you not to fix your gaze upon the fair-seeming language in which these matters are often presented, and thus be led astray. You should look ahead to the consequences which arise from these, put an end to the unruly behaviour of the populace, and take the direction of affairs into your own hands and into those of the other citizens among us who are best qualified. The business of deliberation can then be dealt with by the wisest heads, that of governing by the best leaders, and the duty of serving in the army for pay by the strongest and the most needy. In this way each class of citizens will carry out with enthusiasm the tasks which rightly fall to them, and will readily perform whatever services they owe to one another. They will not be aware of inequalities between them, if one class suffers some deprivation compared to another, and they will become members of a democracy in its true form, and share a freedom which is secure. The truth is that the supposed freedom of the mob proves in reality to be the bitterest servitude, under which the better elements suffer at the hands of the worse, until in the end both are destroyed. But the freedom which I have described above everywhere singles out for honour the men of wisdom, while it allows equality to all the rest according to their deserts. In this way it ensures happiness impartially to all who possess this kind of liberty.

15. 'You must not suppose that I am urging you to enslave the people and Senate and set up a tyranny. This is a course which I would never suggest to you, nor you venture to put into effect. The course I have in mind would be both honourable and in the best interests of yourself and of the state. This is that you take counsel with the best men in Rome and pass all the appropriate laws without opposition or protest on the part of the masses; that any wars should be conducted according to the plans which you have drawn up; that the rest of the citizens should obey these orders forthwith; that the choice of officials should be made by you and your advisers; and that you and they should also determine honours and punishments.

'The strength of this arrangement would be that whatever decisions you reached in consultation with your peers would at once become law;

that our wars would be declared at an appropriate moment and carried on with secrecy; that those charged with the management of any enterprise would be chosen on grounds of merit, and not by lot or through rivalry; that the good would be rewarded without arousing envy and the bad punished without provoking rebellion. All the business of state would thus stand the best chance of being efficiently handled: it would not be referred to the popular assembly, nor debated in open session, nor entrusted to the representatives of factions, nor exposed to ambitious rivalry. The citizen body could then enjoy the blessings which properly belong to it, instead of taking part in dangerous wars abroad or unholy strife at home.

'Every democracy suffers from these abuses – since the most powerful men compete for the principal offices of state, hire the weaker citizens as their supporters and reduce everything to chaos – but these evils have appeared most frequently in our country, and there is no way of checking them save the one I propose. The proof of my words is the inordinately long period during which we have engaged in civil wars and civil strife. The cause is the immense size of our population and the magnitude of the issues at stake. Our population embraces every variety of mankind in terms both of race and of character; hence both their tempers and their desires are infinitely diverse, and these evils have gone so far that they can only be controlled with great difficulty.

16.   'Our past bears witness to the truth of what I have just said. So long as our numbers were not large and we did not differ in any important respects from our neighbours, our system of government worked well, and we brought almost the whole of Italy under our rule. But ever since we ventured beyond our native soil, crossed the water, set foot on many islands and many continents, and filled the whole sea and the whole earth with our name and power, we have experienced nothing but ill-fortune.

'At first it was only at home and within our own walls that we split into factions and quarrelled with one another, but later we introduced this sickness even into the army. For this reason our city, like a great merchant vessel, manned with a crew of every race but lacking a pilot, has now for many generations continued to roll and plunge as it drifted here and there in a heavy sea, a ship without ballast. Do not, then, allow her to be exposed to the storm any longer, for you can see that she is waterlogged. And do not let her be smashed to pieces on a reef, for her timbers are rotten and she will not be able to hold out much longer. But since the gods have taken pity on her and appointed you as her arbiter and overseer, do not betray her. Act so that with your support she may continue her course in safety for the ages to come.

17.   'I think that you have long ago been convinced that I am advising you well when I press you to make yourself the sole ruler of the people. If this is your view, then you should take up the leadership without hesitation and with full conviction, or rather do not let it slip. The question we are considering is not a matter of seizing hold of something, but of resolving not to lose it and thus expose ourselves to further danger. For you will not be forgiven if you thrust the control of affairs into the hands of the populace, or even if you entrust it to some other man. Remember that many have suffered at your hands, that virtually all of them will lay claim to sovereign power and that none of them will be willing to let you go unpunished for your actions, or survive as a rival.

   'The proof of this is the case of Pompey, who, once he had laid down the supreme power, was despised, became the object of conspiracies and lost his life for this reason, when he was unable to recover his authority. Your father, Julius Caesar, was also destroyed for doing the same thing as you have in mind. And Marius and Sulla would certainly have suffered a similar fate, if they had not died first. And yet according to some accounts Sulla was afraid of precisely this outcome, and forestalled it by taking his own life.[14] At any rate, many of his laws began to be rescinded even while he was still alive. And so you must expect that there will be many who will play the part of Lepidus[15] to you, and many others the part of a Sertorius,[16] a Brutus or a Cassius.

18.   'Now that you have recognized these facts and the other issues involved, surely you will not abandon your own position and your country merely for fear that some people may think you deliberately sought to make yourself ruler. First, even if anyone does suspect this, such an ambition is in no way contrary to human nature, and the risk you run is a noble one. Secondly, everyone knows of the necessity which forced you into your present situation. So if there is any reason to find fault with what you have done, there would be no injustice in laying the blame on your father's murderers. If they had not killed him in so unjust and cruel a fashion, you would not have taken up arms, nor mustered your legions,

nor made your alliance with Antony and with Lepidus, nor would you have been obliged to defend yourself against these very men.

'It is common knowledge that in all these actions you had right and justice on your side. And so even if some small injustice has been committed, we cannot at this point safely undo it. Therefore, for your own sake and for the state's, let us obey Fortune who now gives you the supremacy. And let us show ourselves most grateful to her, since she has not only delivered us from the affliction of civil war, but has entrusted to you the re-organization of the political system. She has enabled you, if you devote yourself to the task as you should, to prove to all mankind that the troubles which were stirred up and the wrongs which were committed were the work of others, but that you are a man of virtue.

'You must not be dismayed at the great size of the empire, for the further it stretches, the more numerous are the redeeming elements it contains, and it is far easier to guard one's possessions than to increase them. One must endure hardship and danger to acquire what belongs to others, but a little care is enough to keep what you already hold. Moreover you can rest assured that you will live safely enough in that position and enjoy all the blessings known to mankind, provided that you are willing to govern the state as I shall advise you. And do not think that I am digressing from the matter in hand, if I now speak at length about the office you are to hold. My purpose in doing so is not to enjoy the sound of my own voice, but to give you a clear demonstration that it is both possible and easy, for a man of good sense at least, to govern well and without danger.

19.   'I advise you then that you must first immediately carry out a review and a careful re-selection of the entire Senate, since as a result of our civil strife a number of men have become senators who are quite unfit for the office. Those who possess true worth you should retain, but the rest you should strike off the roll. Still, you should not dismiss any good man on account of his poverty, but even give him the money he needs. In place of those who have been expelled, bring in men of the noblest descent, the highest qualities and the greatest wealth, and recruit them not only from Italy, but also from our allies and subject states. In this way you will enlist many helpers for yourself, and you will have in safe keeping the leading figures from all the provinces. Because these regions will henceforth be without their recognized leaders, they will not start any rebellions and

their most eminent men will be well disposed towards you, because they will have been made partners in your empire.

'You should apply the same principle to the knights, by enrolling in the equestrian order the men of secondary rank in birth, talent and wealth from the various regions. You can admit to both classes as many new members as you please, and there is no need to be too strict concerning the numbers you accept. The more men of good name you have in your administration, the easier you will find it to conduct all your business in times of emergency. And as far as the people you are governing are concerned, this will make it all the easier to convince them that they are not being treated as slaves or as in any way inferior to us. You will then be seen as sharing with them not only all the other benefits which we enjoy, but also the leadership of the state, and they will come to cherish that position of yours as if it were their own. This is not an exaggerated statement, which I might need to retract. I would go further, and say that all the citizens ought each to be given a share in the governing process: they should see themselves as being on an equal footing with us in this respect too, and so become our faithful allies,[17] living as it were in a single city, our city of Rome. They would then regard this as truly a city, and their own homes, the countryside and villages in relation to it. On this subject I shall consider more carefully in due course what we must do to avoid granting the people every concession at once.

20.   'As regards the age of eligibility for office, we should admit men to the order of knights when they are eighteen years old, for at that age their physical fitness and suitability of temperament shows itself very clearly, but we should not enrol them in the Senate until the age of twenty-five. It is surely blameworthy and indeed risky, seeing that we do not entrust our private affairs to anybody until he has reached that age, to allow men even younger than this to handle public business. After they have served as quaestors, aediles, or tribunes, they may become praetors when they reach the age of thirty.

'My view is that you ought to appoint these magistrates and consuls to hold office only in Rome, and these only out of reverence for our ancestral institutions and to avoid giving the impression that you are completely re-modelling the constitution. But you should yourself choose the men for all these posts and cease to delegate the filling of any of them either to the populace or to the assembly, since they will quarrel over them, or to the Senate, since the senators will exploit this privilege to pursue their personal ambitions.

'Moreover you should not preserve the ancient powers of these offices, for fear that history should repeat itself. Instead, you should retain the honours which are associated with them, but also reduce the influence they can exert, in such a way that without stripping such positions of any of their prestige, you will provide no scope for those who may wish to bring about a revolution. You will achieve your purpose best if you arrange for their holders to occupy posts at home rather than abroad, and if you make sure that they do not command armed forces either during their term of office or immediately afterwards, but only when as much time has elapsed as you consider sufficient in each case. In this way they will not be tempted to stir up a rebellion through holding the command of legions while they are still conscious of the prestige of their office, since they will become less restless after they have returned to civil life for some time. These magistrates should preside over such of the festivals as are properly associated with their position, and should each and all sit as judges in all kinds of cases during their term of office in Rome, excepting cases of homicide. Courts should be set up on which the other senators and knights should also sit as members, but the final authority should rest with the magistrates I have mentioned.

21.   'The prefect of the city[18] should be chosen from men who are leading citizens of Rome, and who have previously served in all the appropriate offices. He should govern the city not only when the consuls are absent, but should be in charge of its affairs at all times. He must also deal with the cases which are referred to him from the other magistrates whom I have mentioned, whether this is a matter of appeal or review, and in addition those which involve the death penalty. His jurisdiction should cover not only those who live in the city, with the exceptions that I shall name separately, but also those who live outside it up to a radius of a hundred miles.

'Another magistrate belonging to the class I have mentioned above should be appointed to acquaint himself with and supervise all matters relating to the property, the families and the conduct of the senators and of the knights, and not only of the men but of their wives and children. He should personally correct behaviour of the kind which does not call for punishment, but which, if overlooked, can produce many great evils for society; however, concerning the most important issues he should consult you. This post should be held by a senator, preferably the best man available after the prefect of the city, rather than by one of the knights.[19] As regards the title of his office it would be most suitable for him to take one which is associated with your functions as censor, for it is entirely fitting that you should preside over the census, so he might be called sub-censor.[20] These two, the prefect of Rome and the sub-censor, should hold office for life, unless one of them deteriorates in some way, or is incapacitated by sickness or old age. There would be no danger in their holding office for life, since the one would have no armed forces under his command, and the other only a few, and would exercise his power for the most part under your eyes. If these men held office only for a year, they would shrink from offending anybody and would be afraid of acting vigorously, since they would constantly be looking ahead to their retirement into private life, and to the time when others would take over their power. They should also draw a salary, both to compensate them for the loss of their leisure and to strengthen the prestige of their appointment.

'That is my advice concerning these two officials. As regards those who have already served as praetors, they should be given some command over the subject nations. Men who have not yet become praetors should not, in my opinion, be given such posts, but should serve for one or two terms as subordinates to the former praetors. After this they should hold office as consuls, assuming that their record has been satisfactory throughout their service, and they should then be appointed to senior governorships.

22.   'I advise you to arrange these appointments as follows. The whole of Italy, that is the whole area beyond a radius of one hundred miles from Rome, and likewise all those territories which acknowledge our rule – the various islands and continents – should be divided into districts, according to their separate races and nations; those cities which are sufficiently strong and independent to be administered by one man with full powers should also be treated as separate entities. You should then station a military force in each district or independent city, and send out as governor one of the former consuls, who will exercise overall authority, and two of the former praetors. One of the praetors, who should have served recently in Rome, should supervise all questions which concern

private affairs and the commissariat of the district, and the other, who will be one of those who have already performed this first sort of duty, will take charge of the public business of the cities and will have the troops under his orders, except in cases which concern disfranchisement or the death sentence. Cases of this kind should be referred exclusively to the former consul who is the governor, except when the persons involved are centurions from the municipal governing class, or distinguished private citizens in their respective communities. In both these instances you should not permit anybody but yourself to punish the accused; otherwise they may feel such fear of one or other of these officials that they might at some time act against you as well as them.

'As for my advice that the second of the former praetors should be given command of the troops, this should take effect as follows. If only a small body of troops is serving in auxiliary garrisons or in a single legion, then my proposal is suitable as it stands. But if two legions composed of Roman citizens are wintering in the same province, and I should advise you not to entrust a larger body to any one commander, it will no doubt be necessary for both the former praetors to take command of this force, each taking one legion: each would also retain his share of authority, as already specified, in other matters which affect public business and private citizens respectively. The former consul should discharge those duties which I have mentioned above, and in addition deal with cases which come up for appeal and those which are referred to him by the praetors for review. You should not be surprised at my proposal to divide Italy as well as the other territories into these administrative regions. The country is so large and its population so numerous that it cannot be administered efficiently by magistrates residing in Rome. A governor ought always to be present in the district which he governs, and as regards the magistrates we should only lay upon them those tasks they can properly perform.

23. 'All the men who are posted to appointments outside Rome should receive salaries, the highest ranks more, the lowest less, the intermediate in proportion. It is impossible for them to live on their private means in a foreign territory, nor should they continue to make an unregulated and unlimited outlay as they do at present. They should hold office for not less than three years, unless they are guilty of misconduct, and for not more than five. If the term of office is only for one year or a shorter period, the holders learn only the bare essentials of their work, and are

then moved on before they can put any of their experience to use. On the other hand the longer terms which last for many years are apt to give many of the officials an exaggerated opinion of themselves and encourage them to rebellion. For this reason I believe that governorships of the more important provinces should never be given consecutively to the same man. If a man holds office for a period longer than is desirable, it makes no difference whether he remains the governor of the same province or serves in several in succession; moreover officials actually improve when some time elapses between their periods of service, during which they return home and resume private life. For the senators, then, I have now described what I consider to be their duties and how they should perform them.

24. 'In the case of the knights, the two best should command your personal bodyguard.[21] It can be dangerous if this post is held by one man, and sure to produce confusion if held by more than two. Choose two prefects for this command, then, so that even if one of them suffers any bodily harm, your security is still maintained. The holders of this post should have seen active service in many campaigns, and also possess plenty of administrative experience. They should have command not only of the Praetorian Guard, but of all the other troops in Italy, and have powers of capital punishment over offenders; the exceptions to this last are the centurions and other officials attached to the staffs of magistrates of senatorial rank. These should be tried by the senatorial magistrates themselves; in this way, because of the authority vested in them to award both punishments and honours, they can be assured of the unquestioning support of their subordinates.

'The prefects just mentioned, with deputy commanders below them, should have authority over all the other troops in Italy and likewise over the Praetorian Guard, both those who are in attendance on you and any other contingents of importance. These are not only their proper functions, but also quite numerous enough: we should not require of these officers more tasks than they can effectively handle, otherwise they may not have time for the essentials, or may find that they cannot efficiently supervise all their duties. These military prefects should be appointed for life, as should the prefect of Rome and the sub-censor.

'Other officials are required to take charge of the night watch,[22] to act as commissioner of grain and supervisor of the market in general. Both should be recruited from the knights; we should find the best men available, after the prefects have been selected. Their appointments should run for a specified term, as is the case with the magistrates elected from the Senate.

25.   'The management of the public funds, and here I am referring both to those of the people and those of the empire, in Rome, in Italy and outside it, should likewise be entirely carried on by the knights. These officials, as well as all the other members of the equestrian order who hold administrative positions, should be paid a salary, which should be of a larger or smaller size according to the dignity and the scope of their duties. The reasons for these separate proposals concerning the knights are as follows. Concerning the second point, it is impossible for them, since they are poorer than the senators, to meet their expenses from their private means, even when they are working in Rome. And concerning the first, it is neither practicable nor in your interest for the same men to be placed in charge both of the armed forces and of the public funds.

'Besides this, there are advantages in having all the business which concerns the empire transacted by a large class of officials. By this means, a great many citizens will at once prosper and gain experience of public affairs; the enjoyment of the shared advantages of the empire will be spread more widely among your subjects, they will become better disposed towards you, and you will greatly increase the total of those who are best fitted at any particular time to supply the needs of government. One official from the equestrian order is sufficient for each department of the fiscal service in the capital and for each province outside. He should be provided with as many subordinates recruited from the knights and from your own freedmen as the needs of the case may demand; it is desirable that assistants of this kind should share the work of the knights, so that your service offers an incentive for merit, and you yourself are provided with sources from whom you can learn the truth – even against their wishes – in case any irregularity is committed.

'If any of the knights, after holding positions in many different parts of the service, distinguishes himself enough to become a senator, his age should be no obstacle to his enrolment. Indeed some knights should be elevated to the Senate even if they have risen no higher than the rank of military tribune in the legions, but not if they have served in the ranks. To include in this category the names of men who have carried loads of firewood and charcoal would be a degradation and a reproach to the senatorial order. But in the case of knights who began their service with the rank of centurion,²³ there should be nothing to prevent the most distinguished of them from rising to a higher order.

26. 'Such is my advice, then, as regards the senators and the knights, but I have a further message concerning both orders. First, while they are still children, they should attend the schools. Next, when they enter adolescence they should turn their attention to riding and to the use of weapons and should have salaried public teachers to instruct them. If this is done, they will have received from their childhood both training and practice in all that will be required of them when they arrive at manhood, and so will be of greater service to you for every task. The best ruler, the one who is of any real value, should not only perform all the duties which fall to his lot, but should provide for the rest of his subjects, so that they can develop their virtues to the full. Now this achievement could be yours, not if you allow them to do whatever they choose, and then condemn those who go astray, but rather if, before any mistakes are made, you instruct them in all those activities which, if practised, will make them more useful both to themselves and to you. At the same time you must allow nobody any excuse, on the ground either of wealth, or nobility of birth, or any other form of excellence, for behaviour which is indolent, or effeminate, or in any other respect a sham.²⁴

'Many people are afraid that, if they display excellence in any form, they may attract envy or danger, and so often do things which are unworthy of themselves, and they imagine that by such behaviour they will live a safer life. The results are twofold. They themselves are regarded as pitiable beings and as the victims of injustice in precisely this respect, that people believe they have forfeited the opportunity to live upright lives. The ruler, for his part, suffers not only a loss, in that he is deprived of men who might have been good citizens, but also ill-fame, because he is blamed for what has happened to them. This is a situation which you should never allow to arise.

'On the other hand you need have no fear that anyone who has been brought up and educated on the lines that I propose will ever dare to attempt to overthrow the state. On the contrary, it is the ignorant and the self-indulgent whom you should suspect. Such people can easily be influenced to do anything, commit the most shameful and atrocious actions, first towards themselves and then towards others. But those who have been well nurtured and educated do not deliberately harm anyone else, least of all the man who has cared for their upbringing and training. If one of these does show himself to be so unprincipled and ungrateful, you should refuse to entrust him with any position in which he can do mischief. If, even so, he rebels, then let him be tried and punished. You need not fear that anyone will blame you for this, provided that you have followed my advice. When you take revenge upon the offender, you will be doing no wrong, any more than the physician who employs cautery or the knife. All men will agree, you may be sure, that the guilty party has been justly punished, because after sharing the same upbringing and education as the rest, he conspired against you. These, then, are the measures you should adopt concerning the senators and the knights.

27.   'We must also maintain a standing army[25] to be recruited from the citizen body, the allies and the subject nations. Its strength in the different provinces will vary according to the demands of the situation, and these troops should always be under arms and continually training for active service. Winter quarters should be built for them in the most suitable places, and the men should serve for a specified term, so that a period of years is allowed for them between their retirement from service and old age. The factors which make a standing army necessary are the following. In Rome we are at a great distance from the frontiers of the empire, but we have enemies living near our border on every side, and in times of emergency we can no longer rely upon forces which have been raised for a particular campaign. On the other hand, if we allow all those of military age to bear arms and train for fighting, rebellions and civil wars will constantly arise from their dissensions. But if we prevent them one and all from becoming soldiers and then afterwards need their aid in war, we shall be in constant danger, since we shall only be able to call upon inexperienced and untrained troops.

'For this reason my opinion is that while the majority of those of military age should spend no part of their lives under arms or in fortified camps, the hardiest among them and those in most need of a livelihood should be enlisted and given a military training. This class will be better soldiers if they spend all their time in this one occupation, while the others will find it easier to pursue their farming, seafaring and other vocations, which belong to times of peace, if they are not obliged to serve on campaigns, but have others to defend them. In this way the most active men in the population, those who are in their physical prime, who are often compelled to win a livelihood by brigandage, will be maintained without harming others, and the rest will live their lives free from danger.

28. 'Where, then, are we to find the money to pay these troops and meet the other necessary military expenditure? I shall deal with this question, but let me first make the point that even under a democracy we should need money in any event. We cannot survive without soldiers, and soldiers will not serve without pay. We need not, therefore, agonize over the idea that the need to raise money is confined to a monarchy, nor be led by such an argument to turn our backs on that system. Rather we should begin from the assumption that, whatever form of government we adopt, we are still obliged to obtain funds.

'I therefore propose that you should first sell the property which belongs to the state – and I notice that in consequence of the wars this has increased to a great size – except for a small residue which may be very useful or necessary to you, and that you lend out all the money obtained from these sales at a moderate rate of interest. In this way not only will the land return to cultivation, as it is transferred to owners who will cultivate it themselves; but they will also in the process acquire a capital and become more prosperous, and the treasury will gain a permanent revenue which will cover its expenditure.

'Next, I advise you to make an estimate of the revenues from this quarter and of all the other revenues which can be relied upon to accrue from the mines or from any other source. You should then draw up and balance against this an estimate of total expenditure. This should cover not only military outgoings but those which concern the well-being of the state, and beyond that those which are required for unforeseen campaigns and all the other contingencies which are likely to arise in an emergency. After this we should cover any deficiency of revenue by imposing a levy upon all property without exception which yields a profit for its owners, and by setting up a system of taxation for all the peoples over whom we rule. For it is only just and proper that no private individual or community should be exempt from these taxes, since they will enjoy the benefits provided by them on the same basis as the rest.

'You should appoint tax collectors to superintend this business in each region, and ensure that they bring in the total sum which falls due from all sources of revenue during the period of their supervision. This arrangement will lighten the process of collection for the officials, and not the least of the beneficiaries will be the tax-payers themselves: by this I mean that they can send in their contributions in the small instalments assessed for them, whereas now, if they delay settlement for even a short period, the whole is grossed up and demanded from them in a single payment.

29.   'I do not ignore the fact that some people will be bitterly aggrieved if this system of assessment and taxes is established. But I also know this, that if they suffer no further abuses and can understand that their payments will contribute to their security and give them peace of mind to enjoy the rest of their property, and furthermore that the greater part of their taxes will revert to themselves as governors, procurators and soldiers, they will feel deeply grateful to you. After all they will only be parting with a small fraction of the resources they enjoy and will not be subject to abuses. They will feel this all the more when they see that you live moderately and do not spend wastefully. Surely anyone who saw that you were sparing in your own expenses on yourself, but open-handed with that which is devoted to the public good, would willingly contribute, since he would conclude that your wealth assured his own security and prosperity.

30.   'So far as the raising of funds is concerned, then, a very large amount would be provided from these sources. There are other spheres of administration which I have not yet mentioned, and for these my advice is as follows. Make this capital beautiful, spare no expense in doing so, and enhance its magnificence with festivals of every kind. It is right for us who rule over so many peoples to excel all others in every field of endeavour, and even display of this kind tends to implant respect for us in our allies and to strike terror into our enemies.

'The affairs of the other territories should be dealt with as follows. In the first place the populace should exercise no powers of decision whatever, nor should they have the right to form an assembly, for nothing good would come out of their proceedings and they would constantly be causing disturbances. On the same principle I believe that even our own populace in Rome should not come together either as a court, or to elect the officers of state, or indeed hold any assembly whose purpose is to transact business.[26] Secondly the cities should limit themselves in erecting public buildings to what is strictly necessary both as regards their number and their size, nor should they waste their resources in providing a large quantity or variety of public games: otherwise they risk dissipating their energies in futile enterprises and falling into quarrels as a result of senseless rivalries.

'Certainly they should hold a number of festivals and spectacles, with the exception of the horse-racing we have here in Rome, but not on such a scale that the public treasury should be impoverished, or the estates of private citizens ruined, or that any stranger resident there should be compelled to contribute to their expense, or that every victor in every contest should be granted free subsistence for life. There is no reason why the well-to-do should be forced to spend their money outside their native land, and as for the competitors, the prizes which are available for each event are sufficient reward, unless a man wins a title in the Olympian or the Pythian games, or at some contest here in Rome. Only in these cases should free subsistence be awarded, and if this rule is observed, the cities will not waste their resources, nor will any athlete embark on training except those who have a prospect of winning: the others will be able to follow some vocation that is more useful to themselves and to the community. This is my view on these subjects.

'As for those horse-races which are not associated with gymnastic contests, I consider that no city other than Rome should be permitted to hold them. The purpose of this regulation is, first, to prevent huge sums of money from being thrown away to no purpose; secondly to discourage the public from becoming demoralized by its obsession with this sport: and above all to keep those who are serving in the army supplied with the best horses. It is with these factors in mind that I would prohibit outright the holding of such races anywhere other than in Rome. In the case of the other games I have proposed that the outlay should be kept within reasonable limits: my purpose here is that each community by observing due restraint in budgeting for its entertainments of eye and ear may live in a more temperate fashion and avoid factious rivalry.

'None of the cities should employ its own coinage or system of weights and measures, but all alike should use ours. Nor should they send an individual embassy to you, unless its mission concerns a judicial decision. Whatever plea they may have to make should first be addressed to the governor, and through him such of their petitions as he may think fit can be forwarded for your attention. Through this procedure they will neither spend money nor resort to any disreputable practices; moreover the answers they receive will be direct and unadulterated: no money will have changed hands and no intermediaries played a part.

31. 'Now let us consider how best to handle other matters. In the first place as regards diplomatic transactions, it seems to me that the best procedure is for you to introduce to the Senate all foreign embassies, whether they come from hostile powers or from nations which are in treaty relations with us, and whether they represent kings or democracies. Among other reasons, the ceremony is in itself imposing, and it is important to emphasize the fact that the Senate is sovereign in all matters, and that those delegations which press their case in a reckless fashion will face a large body of opponents.

'Secondly, all legislation should be enacted through the Senate and no measure should be imposed upon all the people alike except the ordinances of this body. If this principle is observed, the dignity of the empire will be more securely established, and in the eyes of the whole people the judgements handed down in accordance with the laws will be placed beyond any possibility of dispute or uncertainty.

'My third point concerns members of the Roman Senate. If any of them or any of their wives or children should be charged with a serious offence, the penalty for which on conviction would be disfranchisement or exile or even death, you should lay the matter before the Senate without making any previous judgement yourself, and you should entrust the entire decision of the case to the Senate, uninfluenced by your opinion. The object of this procedure is that wrongdoers, since they are being tried by a jury consisting solely of their peers, may be punished without animosity being aroused against you, and that the others, when they see this, may improve their conduct for fear of being publicly disgraced themselves. These proposals relate only to those offences concerning which there are laws in existence and judgements are passed in accordance with them.

'In the event of someone having abused you or used improper language in some other fashion against you, you should neither pay attention to your detractor nor follow up what he has said. It would reflect on you to believe that anybody had wantonly insulted you, if, so far from causing any harm, you are in fact conferring benefits upon all; it is only those whose rule is at fault who act in this way, for their own conscience tells them that the slanders are well founded. Besides this, it is even dangerous to take such vilification in bad part. If what is said is true, it would be better not to be angry at all, and if false, better to conceal one's anger. In the past, many people through losing their composure have caused rumours against themselves to multiply and to prove even harder to endure. That is my opinion concerning those who are accused of traducing you. Your position should be invulnerable to any insolence and too exalted for such conduct to come near you; and you should never allow it to enter your head or allow others to imagine that you can be treated with disrespect. In short, men should regard you just as they do the gods, as surrounded by an inviolable sanctity.

'However, if anyone is accused of conspiring against you –and such an attempt could come about – you should not, even in this case, either judge the charge yourself or pass any verdict beforehand, for it is quite inadmissible that the same man should be at once plaintiff and judge. Instead, you should bring the offender before the Senate, let him defend himself there, and if he is convicted, punish him. But you should moderate his sentence as far as possible, so as to strengthen the belief that he is guilty. I advise this because most men find it very difficult to credit that an unarmed man is conspiring against one who is armed: the only way in which you can convince them will be to show as far as possible that you are neither angry nor implacably bent on revenge when you pass sentence. I make an exception, however, in the case of a general commanding an army who openly rebels against you. It is not fitting for such a man to be tried at all, but he should be punished as a public enemy.

32. 'These issues, then, and those others which are of the highest importance to the state, should be referred to the Senate, on the principle that interests which are common to the whole people should be handled in common. And besides, there is no doubt an instinct naturally inherent in mankind which makes them respond with pleasure to any indication from a superior that they are his equals, with the result that they not only approve of all decisions made by another so long as they themselves were consulted, but even welcome them as though they had originated from their own choice.

'For this reason, then, I advise that such business should be laid before the Senate. In addition, all the senators alike who are present should give their opinions on all other matters with this single exception, which arises when one of their number is on trial. In that event, the vote should not be open to all senators, unless the accused is not yet sitting as a senator, or is still among the ex-quaestors. It would be quite incongruous for a man who has not yet served as a tribune or as an aedile to vote against men who have held these offices, and even more so for one of the latter to vote against former praetors, or for these last to vote against former consuls. Instead, the power to judge all senators should be vested in former consuls alone: the other senators should vote only in those cases which involve their peers and subordinates.

33.   'You yourself, however, should be solely responsible for cases which come to you on appeal or are referred to you by the senior magistrates and the procurators, and likewise by the prefect of the city, the sub-censor, and the prefects in charge of the grain supply and the night watch. None of these should exercise such an absolute jurisdiction or wield an authority so final as to rule out an appeal from his decision. It is for you, therefore, to judge these cases and those which involve knights, centurions from the municipal governing class and leading private citizens who are charged with offences punishable by death or disfranchisement. Such cases ought to be referred to you alone, and, for the reasons I have mentioned, nobody else should have them solely under his jurisdiction.

'As a matter of general principle, you should always in arriving at decisions be brought into consultation with senators and knights of the highest rank, and, as circumstances may demand, by those who have served as consuls and praetors. The object of this practice is twofold. It will help you to form a more precise knowledge of these men's characters, and hence to make the best use of their talents, and it will familiarize them with your habits of mind and your plans before they go out to take up their governorships of the provinces. You should not, however, ask them to express their opinions publicly on any subject which demands particularly careful deliberation: they might, in their desire to conform to the views of their superiors, hesitate to speak frankly. It would be better to have them write down what they think on tablets. You should study these in private, so that they remain entirely confidential, and then have the record erased forthwith. Certainly the best way for you to discover exactly what each man thinks is to give him the assurance that his opinion cannot be identified among all the others.

'To help you carry out your judicial duties, deal with your correspondence, attend to the decrees of states and the petitions of individuals, and all the other business involved in the administration of the empire, you should call upon men selected from the knights to be your assistants and subordinates. In this way the transactions of each department will be kept running more smoothly, and you will not make mistakes through relying on your own judgement, nor wear yourself out by relying on your own efforts. You should accord to everyone who wishes to offer you advice on any subject whatsoever the right to speak frankly and without fear of the consequences. If you are pleased with what he tells you, the result will be of great advantage to you, and if you are not convinced, this will do you no harm. Those who secure your approval for their suggestions you should both praise and honour, since their discoveries will redound to your credit, but you should not disparage nor censure those who fail to satisfy you: you should appreciate their intentions rather than blame their lack of success. You should be on your guard too against making a similar mistake in the military sphere: you should neither be made angry by an unintentional failure, nor jealous by a stroke of good fortune.

'If they are encouraged in this way, all men will gladly and devotedly risk their lives for your sake: they will feel confident that if they make a slip they will not be punished for it, and that if they succeed they will not be victims of intrigue. Certainly many men for fear of jealousy on the part of their superiors have preferred to fail rather than to succeed; in this way they have ensured their own safety and caused the loss to fall upon their masters. And so, since it is you who must accept the major share of either outcome, of the failures as well as the successes, you should never allow yourself to become jealous; such a feeling may appear to be directed against others, but in reality it is levelled at yourself.

34. 'Whatever you wish your subjects to think and to do, you must say and do yourself. You can better educate them in this way, rather than by terrorizing them through the penalties laid down by the laws. The former approach incites emulation, the latter fear, and it is always easier for a man to imitate what is right when he sees it put into practice than to avoid what is wrong when he hears it merely prohibited by edict. You must carry out to the letter everything that you undertake and show no

indulgence towards yourself, for you can be absolutely certain that men will straightaway learn of whatever you say or do. In effect, you will live on a stage with the whole world for your audience, and if you make even the slightest mistake, there is no way in which this will pass unnoticed. In all your actions you will never be alone, but constantly in the company of multitudes. And since the rest of mankind takes the keenest pleasure in prying into the affairs of their rulers, if they should ever discover that you are urging them to follow one course while adopting another yourself, they will not fear your threats, but will imitate your actions.

'You should, of course, supervise the lives of your subjects, but not probe them too strictly. You should judge cases which are referred to you by others, but if no accusation has been made, act as if you knew nothing, except, of course, when an offence against the public interest has been committed. Such matters should be properly investigated, even if no individual brings a charge. In the case of private misdemeanours, you should have sufficient knowledge to safeguard you from the mistake of employing an unsuitable person as your agent on any particular occasion, but you should not pursue those who commit them. Human nature often tempts men to break the law, and if you were to prosecute in every single instance, few, if any, of the accused would be left unpunished; but if you temper the letter of the law with leniency and humanity, you may succeed in bringing the offenders to see reason. You must remember that the law, although it is bound to make penalties drastic, cannot always conquer nature. So there are men who, either because they believe that their misdeeds have escaped notice, or because they have been only mildly censured, do in fact reform themselves. This may be through shame at having been discovered, or because their self-respect prevents them from repeating the lapse; on the other hand if they have been publicly exposed and have lost all sense of shame or been punished too harshly, then they overturn and trample underfoot all the established usages of the law and become completely enslaved by their natural impulses. From this it follows that it is neither easy to punish all offenders without exception, nor is it proper in certain cases to allow them to exult openly in their wrongdoing.

'That is how I advise you to deal with men's offences, with the exception of those who are beyond reform. Their good conduct, on the other hand, you should reward even more highly than the worth of their actions might suggest. You will succeed best at persuading men to refrain from doing wrong by means of kindness, and to aim at better ways by generosity. You need not fear that either money or the other means of remunerating the well-deserving will ever be lacking. I should rather expect that the numbers who will earn such recognition will be far too few, bearing in mind that you rule such vast areas of land and sea. Nor need you be concerned that any of those you have recompensed will ever show you ingratitude, for nothing is more effective in captivating and winning over a man, whether he is a foreigner or even an enemy, than the sense that he is not only protected against wrong but is positively treated with kindness.

35. 'This is how you should treat your subjects, in my opinion. So far as your own position is concerned, you should not allow any exceptional or exaggerated status to be conferred on you either in word or deed, by the Senate or anyone else. For while any distinctions which you grant to others do honour to them, nothing that is voted to you can give you a higher rank than you already possess, and it would be hard to dissociate a suspicion of falsity from the very act of bestowing it. No subject would ever be believed to have proposed any such distinction to his ruler of his own free will, and since all the honours granted to a ruler in fact originate from himself, he not only earns no approval but even attracts ridicule for receiving such tributes. It follows, then, that you must rely on your own good deeds in order to add to your lustre in any way. You should never allow gold or silver images to be made of yourself, for not only are they expensive, but they positively invite conspiracy and last only for a short while. Rather than this, you should build images of yourself in the hearts of your people, and the substance from which these are made should be your own good deeds, which should prove unalloyed and imperishable.

'Equally, you should never allow a temple to be built in your honour, for it is futile to spend huge sums on projects of this kind. There are plenty of urgent needs for which the money can be better used, for genuine wealth is accumulated not by raising large revenues but by effecting large savings. Besides this, the building of temples adds nothing to a man's true fame. It is virtue which raises many men to the level of the gods, and no man ever became a god by vote. It follows that for the good man and the upright ruler the whole earth will be your hallowed precinct, all cities your temples, and all mankind your statues, since you will be enshrined and glorified in their regard.

'As for those who follow a different course in governing their countries, such honours not only fail to make them venerated, even though shrines are set aside for them in all their cities, but in fact harm their reputation by becoming as it were trophies of their baseness and monuments to their injustice. Indeed the longer these temples remain standing, the longer the memory of their ill-fame is preserved.

36.   'So if you desire to become truly immortal, act as I advise: beyond this, you should not only revere the Divine Power everywhere and in every way according to the traditions of our ancestors, but also oblige all others to honour it.

'You should utterly abominate those who seek to pollute our religion with alien rites, and punish them. You should act thus not only for the sake of the gods, since the man who despises these will not reverence anything else, but because men of this kind by introducing new deities in place of the old persuade many people to adopt foreign customs; these in turn generate conspiracies, factions and secret societies, all of which are detrimental to a monarchy.

'You should on no account, therefore, permit anyone to be an atheist or a sorcerer. Soothsaying, it is true, is a necessary art, and you should certainly appoint men to be diviners and augurers, who can be called in by those who wish to consult them. But the practitioners of magic should be forbidden to carry on their craft. For such men, who occasionally speak the truth, but for the most part deal in falsehoods, often incite many of their followers to attempt revolutions. The same also applies to many who claim to be philosophers, and for a similar reason I warn you to be on your guard against them. Because you have had experience of good and honourable men such as Areius and Athenodorus, you should not believe that all the others who profess to be philosophers are like them. There are men who make this vocation a screen, and use it to work untold harm, both upon communities and upon individuals.

37.   'Because of your intelligence and because you have no desire to acquire more than you already possess, you should be strongly disposed towards peace, but in your preparations you should be thoroughly organized for war. Here it is a question of ensuring that no man should either wish or attempt to wrong you, but that, should he do so, he can be easily and promptly punished. For these and other reasons you need people

who will keep their eyes and ears open in all matters touching your leadership of the state, and clearly you must be informed of any situation which may demand preventive or corrective action. But remember that you should not accept uncritically all that they tell you, and sift their reports with great care. There are plenty of men who, either because they hate certain people, or hanker after their possessions, or wish to do a favour to another, or have demanded money from someone and failed to obtain it, lay false information against their victims to the effect that they are plotting revolution, or planning or saying something against the interests of the ruler. So you should not give them immediate or even easy credence, but test all their allegations. If you take your time about giving your trust to any of these men, no great harm will be done, but if you act too swiftly you may make a mistake which proves to be irretrievable.

'Now it is both right and necessary that you should honour those of whom you have a high opinion, both among your freedmen and the rest of your entourage; this habit will do you credit and greatly increase your security. They should not enjoy powers which grow to excess, but should all be subject to strict discipline, so that your reputation should never suffer from their actions. Remember that everything they do, whether for good or ill, will be attributed to you and that your own character will be judged in the light of the conduct which you tolerate in them.

'As regards the men who are in positions of power, you should allow them neither to take advantage of others, nor in their turn to suffer from informers: the fact that a man exercises power should not be held against him as a crime, provided that he commits no offence.

'In the case of the populace, on the other hand, you should defend their interests vigorously when they are wronged, and not listen too readily to their accusations. You should investigate the actions of whoever is accused strictly on their merits, and not be predisposed to suspect whatever is superior or trust whatever is inferior. You should show your admiration for those who are industrious and exercise some valuable skill, and your displeasure at those who are idle or who occupy themselves only with trivialities. This will encourage your subjects to emulate the former mode of life and avoid the latter because of its penalties, and become, as you desire, more successful in their private affairs and more beneficial to the interests of the state.

'It is important to reduce to a minimum the number of disputes between citizens concerning private affairs, and to ensure that these are settled as quickly as possible, but it is even more important to restrain rash initiatives undertaken by communities: if such groups seek to impose their will on others, or to exceed their resources in any enterprise or expenditure, they must be checked, no matter if they send petitions invoking blessings on the empire and praying for your safety and good fortune. It is also important to eliminate their mutual quarrels and rivalries, and not to permit them to adopt empty titles or do anything else which will bring them into collision with other peoples. You will find that all of them, both individuals and communities, will readily obey your decisions in this and every other matter, provided that you never single out any one for an exceptional concession; for to apply the laws inconsistently undermines even those that are firmly established. For this reason you ought not to allow your subjects in the first place even to ask you for what you do not intend to give them, and you should put strong pressure on them at the start to refrain from petitioning for any concessions which are prohibited.

38. 'So much for these matters. I also advise you never to exercise your authority to the full against your subjects as a whole, nor to regard it as in any way diminished if you do not put into practice all the measures you could impose. Instead, the greater your power to carry out all that you desire, the more eager you should be that your desires in all matters should be limited to what is fitting. Always examine your heart in private as to whether in a given situation you are acting rightly or not, and as to what you should do or refrain from doing to earn your subjects' love, so that you may follow the one course and avoid the other. You should not suppose that the world considers you to be doing your duty merely because you hear nobody actually blaming you, nor expect that any man would be so foolhardy as to find fault openly with any of your actions. No one will do this, no matter how gravely he may have been wronged: on the contrary, many people feel obliged actually to praise their persecutors in public, while they struggle to conceal their indignation. The ruler must learn to recognize the state of mind of his subjects not from what they say, but from what it is natural for them to think.

39. 'These are the lines of conduct I should wish you to follow, and others of a similar nature. There are many examples which I must pass

over, since it is impossible to include them all in a single discussion. But there is one general precept which may serve to summarize both what I have said above and what I have left unsaid. If you perform of your own accord all the actions you would wish another man to perform if he were your ruler, you will not go astray, but will succeed in all your endeavours and in consequence lead a life which is filled with happiness and completely free from danger. For how can men fail to regard you with affection as their father and their saviour, when they see that you are both disciplined and principled in your life, formidable in war yet disposed to peace, that you show no arrogance and take no advantage; when you associate with them on a footing of equality, do not enrich yourself in the process of levying tribute, do not live in luxury while imposing hardships on others, and refrain from licentious behaviour while reproving it elsewhere – in short when you lead a life which is in every respect most similar to theirs. You hold in your own hands the most potent guarantee of your security – the fact that you never do wrong to another; and so take heart and believe me when I tell you that you will never become a target for hatred or conspiracy. From this it must follow that you will also lead a happy life, for what is sweeter or more blessed than to enjoy rightfully all the felicities that man can possess, and have the power to bestow these upon others?

40.   'Ponder these thoughts and the rest of the advice I have offered, be persuaded by me, and do not let slip this fortune which has singled you out from all mankind and set you over them as their ruler. For if, in reality, you prefer the fact of monarchical rule yet fear the name of king as accursed, you need not accept that title, but can still rule under the style of Caesar. If you need other titles besides, the people will give you that of Imperator as they did your father Julius, and they will pay homage to your august status by yet another form of address. In this way you can enjoy to the full the reality of kingship without the stigma which attaches to the name.'

41.   With these words Maecenas ended his speech, and Octavian warmly praised both him and Agrippa for the versatility of their thinking, the fullness of their expression and the frankness of their words, but it was the advice of Maecenas that he was inclined to accept. However, he did not immediately attempt to apply all his counsellor's suggestions, since he

feared that he would probably fail at some point if he set out to change the natural proclivities of mankind at a single stroke. Instead, he introduced some reforms straightaway, others later. Others, again, he left to those who would succeed him as emperor, as time might show that a better moment had arrived. Agrippa, for his part, even though he had urged the opposite view concerning these policies, gave Octavian his full support in applying them, just as if he had advocated them himself.

These measures and the others I have described earlier in this account were enacted by Octavian in the year during which he held the consulship for the fifth time, and he also assumed the title of Imperator. I am not speaking here of the title which had been bestowed in accordance with the ancient custom upon various generals on account of their victories: Octavian had received this many times before and did so many times after as a result of his military achievements, so that in all he was awarded it twenty-one times. I use it in its other context, which denotes the possession of the supreme power in the state, in which sense it had been voted to his father, Julius Caesar, and to the latter's children and descendants.[27]

42.   After this he took up the office of censor with Agrippa as his colleague, and besides making other reforms he carried out a purge of the Senate. Because of the civil wars, a large number of knights and persons of still lower status had become members of the Senate without any rightful qualification for being there, so that its membership had increased to one thousand. Although Octavian wished to expel these men, he did not himself strike their names off the roll, but rather urged them in view of what they knew about their families and their lives to make themselves judges of their case. In this way he first persuaded some fifty of them to withdraw voluntarily from the Senate, and then compelled a further hundred and forty to follow their example. Octavian did not disfranchise any of them, but he posted up the names of the second group. He spared those in the first the humiliation of publishing their names, because they had wasted no time but immediately obeyed him. To all appearances, then, these men returned to private life of their own accord. By contrast Quintus Statilius was deposed very much against his will from the tribuneship to which he had been appointed. Octavian also nominated some other men to be senators and he enrolled among the former consuls two men of senatorial rank, Gaius Cluvius and Gaius Furnius; this was because they had been unable to serve as consuls after their election, since

other men had occupied their offices first. At the same time he increased the number of patrician families,[28] supposedly with the consent of the Senate. His reason here was that the majority of the patricians had perished, for no class suffers such heavy losses in our civil wars as the nobility, and also because the patricians are always regarded as indispensable for the preservation of Rome's ancestral institutions.

Apart from these measures, he forbade all the members of the Senate to travel outside Italy, unless he himself should order or give them leave to do so. This regulation is still observed to the present day, for no senator is allowed to leave the country to visit any place except Sicily and Gallia Narbonensis. Because these regions are close to Rome, and their inhabitants are unarmed and peaceable, those who have any property there are allowed to visit them as often as they wish without asking permission.

Octavian further noticed that many of the senators who had supported Antony were still inclined to be suspicious of him. He was also alarmed that they might plot a rebellion, and so he gave it out that all the letters which had been found in Antony's strong boxes had been burned. It is true that he had destroyed some of them, but he was careful to keep the greater number, and later did not shrink from making use of them.

These were Octavian's actions at that period. He re-settled Carthage, because Lepidus had devastated a part of the city, and by this action, it was argued, had annulled the rights of the earlier colonists.[29] He summoned Antiochus, the ruler of Commagene, to Rome; when he was engaged in a quarrel with his brother, the latter had sent an envoy to Rome and Antiochus had had the emissary treacherously murdered. Octavian brought Antiochus before the Senate, and when he was found guilty, had him put to death. He also acquired the island of Capri from the Neapolitans, and gave them other land[30] in exchange. Capri lies not far off the mainland in the neighbourhood of Surrentum. The soil is good for nothing, but the place is still famous, because Tiberius had a residence there.

BOOK 53

The following is contained in the Fifty-Third Book of Dio's *Rome*:

1.   These were the events of that year.[1] In the following year Octavian was consul for the sixth time, and performed all the other duties according to the traditions which have been handed down from the earliest antiquity. In particular he handed over one set of the fasces[2] to Agrippa, his colleague in the consulship, as it was his duty to do, while he himself used the other set. Finally, after having fulfilled his term of office, he took the oath according to ancestral custom.[3] Whether he ever repeated this action[4] I do not know, for he always accorded extraordinary honours to Agrippa. For example he gave him his niece[5] in marriage; whenever they were on active service together, he furnished Agrippa with a tent of the same type

as his own; and the watchword for the day was given out by both of them.

During this year, besides carrying out his other duties as usual, he completed the taking of the census.[6] At this census he was designated *Princeps senatus*, as had been the custom when Rome was a republic in the full sense of the term. In addition he completed and dedicated the temple of Apollo[7] on the Palatine hill, together with the precinct surrounding it and the libraries. He also celebrated with Agrippa the festival which had been decreed in honour of the victory of Actium, and during these ceremonies he arranged for the boys and men of the nobility to participate in chariot-racing. This festival was held for a time[8] every four years and was supervised by each of the four priesthoods in succession, that is the Pontifices, the Augurs, the Septemviri and the Quindecimviri. On this occasion a gymnastic contest was also held, for which a wooden stadium was built in the Campus Martius, and gladiatorial combats between prisoners of war took place. These events lasted for several days and were not interrupted even when Octavian was taken ill. Agrippa continued to officiate and carried out Octavian's duties as well as his own.

2. Octavian paid for these spectacles out of his private means, it was generally supposed. When money was needed for the public treasury, he borrowed the amount and paid it in. For the management of the public funds he ordered two magistrates to be chosen each year from the former praetors. He distributed to the people a fourfold allowance of grain and he gave sums of money to a number of senators.[9] This was because many of them had become so poor as to be unwilling to take on even the office of aedile,[10] because of the large expenditures which were demanded of its holder. Accordingly the other duties of the aedileship, and especially its judicial functions, were transferred to the praetors, as had often happened in the past, the more important of these to the *praetor urbanus*, and the others to the *praetor peregrinus*. In addition to these reforms, Octavian personally appointed the *praetor urbanus*, as he did many times subsequently.[11] At this time too Octavian cancelled all debts owed to the public treasury before the battle of Actium, excepting those which were secured by buildings, and he burned the notes of those who in years past had owed money to the state.

As regards religious matters, he forbade Egyptian rituals to be celebrated within the city limits,[12] but he provided for the maintenance of the

Roman temples. He decreed that those which had been built by private individuals should be repaired at the expense of their sons and daughters, if any survived, and the rest he restored himself. However he did not claim the credit for the construction of these, but allowed it to go to those who had originally erected them.

Then, recognizing that he had caused many unjust and illegal measures to be enacted during the period of strife between political factions and the civil wars, especially at the time when Antony and Lepidus had shared the Triumvirate with him, he rescinded every one of these by means of a single decree. He set the end of his sixth consulship as the date when these laws would cease to have effect.

As these actions earned him much popularity and praise, he was impelled to make another magnanimous gesture. To pursue a policy of this kind would, he hoped, increase the esteem in which he was held, and would result in his rule being supported by the people of their own accord, and dispel any impression that they had been coerced against their will. So after he had explained his intentions to his closest friends among the senators, he entered the Senate in his seventh consulship and read the following speech.

3.   'I know very well, Conscript Fathers, that I shall appear to you to have made an incredible choice. Whatever each one of you in my audience would be unwilling to do himself, he is reluctant to believe when anyone else claims to have done it. This is especially true since every man is jealous of his superiors, and so is the more ready to disbelieve any statement which represents a position beyond his own. I also recognize that those who make statements which lack credibility not only fail to convince others, but create the impression that they themselves are impostors. Now if I were announcing something which I had no intention of carrying out at once, I should have been very unwilling to mention it at all, for fear that I should not earn your gratitude, but some most damning accusation. But as it is, since the action must follow the word this very day, I feel confident that, so far from incurring the dishonour of telling a lie, I shall win such fame as no man can surpass.

4.   'The fact that it is in my power to rule over you for life is evident to you all. Every one of the rival factions has been justly tried and extinguished, or else persuaded to see reason through acts of clemency. Those who took

my side have found their attachment to me strengthened by the rewards bestowed for their services, and cemented by their participation in the government. It follows that none of them is anxious for political change, and if anything of that kind were to take place, those who will support me are even more ready to do so than before. The loyalty and the strength of my army stands at its peak: we have money and we have allies, and, most important of all, the disposition both of yourselves and of the people leaves no doubt that you wish to have me at your head.

'Yet for all that, I shall lead you no longer, and nobody will be able to say that all the actions of my career to date have been undertaken for the sake of winning supreme power. On the contrary, I lay down my office in its entirety and return to you all authority absolutely – authority over the army, the laws and the provinces – not only those territories which you entrusted to me, but those which I later secured for you. Thus my deeds in themselves shall also bear witness to the fact that from the very beginning I had no desire to rule, but in truth wished to avenge my father, who had been atrociously murdered, and to rescue the state from the terrible evils which continuously assailed it.

5.   'Indeed, I could wish that I had not taken command of affairs to the extent that I did – that is I should have preferred that the city had not needed me for any such task, but that we of this generation could have lived out our lives in a state of peace and harmony, as our forefathers once did. But since some destiny,[13] as it seems, brought you to such a pass that you had need even of me, in spite of my youth, and put me to the test, I set my hand to every task with a spirit beyond my years,[14] and accompli- shed them all with the help of a good fortune which far exceeeded my powers, so long as the situation required my help. There was nothing in the world which could deter me from helping you when you were in danger – no hardship, no fear, no threats from your enemies nor entreaties from your friends, neither the multitude of the conspirators nor the desperation of our opponents. I gave myself to you without stint in all the emergencies which have arisen, and what I did and suffered is known to you all. From these efforts I gained nothing for myself, save only that I helped my country to survive; for you the outcome is that you now live safe and sound. Since fortune, working through me, has blessed you by restoring a peace that knows no treachery and a harmony that knows no turmoil, you should receive back your freedom and the republic,[15] take

over the army and the subject provinces, and carry on the government as
was your custom in the past.

6. 'This plan of mine should not surprise you, if you bear in mind my
clemency in other respects, and the fact that I am mild by nature and have
no desire to dominate. Or if you reflect that I have never accepted any
extraordinary status, nor anything in excess of what the majority might
possess, although you have often voted many such privileges to me. And
yet do not condemn me as foolish, because at the moment when it is in
my power to rule over you and to exercise so great a sovereignty over
this vast world, I do not wish it. For if one looks at this situation from the
point of view of justice, I believe it to be most just that you should control
your own affairs; if from the point of view of expediency, most expedient
that I should be freed from the burdens of office and not be exposed to
jealousy and intrigue, and that you should enjoy a government which
combines liberty, moderation and humanity. Lastly, from the point of
view of glory, for whose sake many men are willing to fight and risk their
lives, is it not most glorious on my part to lay down this exalted position
of leadership and retire of my own accord into private life? And so, if any
of you finds it impossible to credit that a man can truly entertain and
proclaim these ideals, at least believe it of me. I could recall many great
benefits conferred on you by my father and myself,[16] which give us a
right to claim your affection and your esteem. But there is nothing that I
would rate above this, nor could I take greater pride in any other action –
that he refused the monarchy when you offered it, and that I, when I hold
it, now lay it down.

7. 'What other achievements can be compared with this? The conquest
of Gaul, the enslavement of Pannonia,[17] the subjugation of Moesia,[18] or
the overthrow of Egypt? The victories over Pharnaces,[19] or Juba,[20] or
Phraates,[21] or the campaign against the Britons,[22] or the crossing of the
Rhine? These are greater achievements than the sum of our forefathers'
exploits throughout the whole of our past. And yet none of them deserves
to be compared to my present action – to say nothing of our civil wars,
the greatest in magnitude and the most varied in their vicissitudes that
have ever taken place. This conflict we fought to a successful conclusion,
and settled on humane terms. We overcame all those who resisted us as
enemies, while we spared as friends all those who yielded. Through this

treatment we set an example, so that if fate should ever cause our city to be plagued with such strife again, one may pray that it should resolve its quarrels in the same way.

'In that struggle we developed so great a strength and advanced our cause to such heights of prowess and good fortune that we could have imposed our autocratic rule upon you, with or without your consent; yet we did not lose our senses nor were carried away by the desire for sole supremacy. Instead, the fact that Julius Caesar put that power aside when it was offered him, and that after it has been given to me, I now return it to you, are actions which transcend the human scale. I say these things not as idle boasts. I should not have mentioned them at all if I intended to get any advantage by doing so. It is rather that I wish you to see that over and above all the services and good offices rendered to the state at large and to individuals of which we might be proud, there is another in which we rejoice most – the fact that the prize which others desire so passionately that they are ready to use violence to win it, we put aside even when it is pressed upon us.

8. 'Who could be found who is more magnanimous than I – not to speak again of my late father – or who more nearly divine? Consider my situation – and let Jupiter and Hercules be my witnesses. I have an army of surpassing strength and quality, both of Roman citizens and of allies, who are devotedly loyal to me. I rule the entire Mediterranean Sea to the Pillars of Hercules, save only for a few tribes. My sway now extends to cities and provinces in every continent: there is no enemy at war with me abroad, and no faction stirs up strife at home. Yet at this time, when all of you live in peace and harmony, and best of all willingly accept my rule, I choose, unprompted and of my own free will, to stand aside from this great empire and renounce these vast possessions. If our ancestors, Horatius,[23] Mucius,[24] Curtius,[25] Regulus[26] and the Decii,[27] were willing to risk their lives or lose them for the glory of having accomplished some great and noble exploit, why should not I desire even more strongly to take this decision, through which I shall, while I am still alive, excel both them and all other men in renown? Let none of you think that it was only the ancient Romans who strove to perform deeds of valour and win fame thereby, but that in our day all manly virtue has vanished from our country. Or, worse still, let no one imagine that I wish to betray you by delivering you into the power of unprincipled men, or into the hands of

the mob, from which not only does no benefit to mankind ever spring, but in all cases the most grievous of ills. No, it is to you, our senators, the best and wisest of our citizens, that I restore the handling of all public concerns. The other choice, that of surrendering power to the unfit, I would never have adopted, even if I had been obliged to die a thousand deaths, or even to assume sole authority myself. The present solution I choose both for Rome's sake and for my own. For I myself have undergone long toil and many adversities and can no longer summon the necessary strength of mind or of body. Besides this, I can foresee the jealousy and the hatred which are generated against even the best of men in the minds of some of their fellows, and the plots to which these give rise. These are the reasons which make me prefer the lot of a private citizen whose name is beyond reproach to that of a ruler who lives in constant peril. And as for the affairs of the community, it would be far better if these were managed in common and by many people rather than depending on the will of one man.

9.   'For these reasons I beg and implore of you to approve my choice and give me your whole-hearted support, remembering the services I have rendered you both in war and in government; you can repay me completely for these by granting me this one favour, to allow me henceforth, at last, to live out my life in peace. If you do this, you will see that I understand not only how to rule but how to be ruled, and that all the commands I have imposed upon others I can accept for myself. Indeed, I expect to live in security and to suffer no harm from any man in word or deed. Such is the confidence in your goodwill which my conscience gives me.

'I may, of course, come to some harm, as many do. It is impossible for a man to please everybody, especially when he has been entrusted with affairs of such importance and has taken part in the greatest of wars, both foreign and civil. In that event, I willingly accept the choice of dying even before my time as a private citizen, rather than becoming immortal as a sole ruler. Indeed this decision in itself will bring me fame – the fact that I did not take another man's life to win supreme power, but even sacrificed my own to avoid being a king. And so the man who dares to kill me will be punished, I do not doubt, by heaven and by yourselves, as happened in the case of my father, Julius Caesar. He was declared to be the equal of the gods and was granted perpetual honours,[28] while those who killed him

were destroyed, wretches who suffered a wretched death. Immortality is
a state which it is not in our power to possess, but by living nobly and
dying nobly we do in a certain measure achieve this condition. And so I,
who have reached the one objective and hope to attain the other, give
back into your hands the army, the provinces, the revenues and the laws.
I add only a few words of advice so that you may not be dismayed by the
difficult nature of the affairs you have to handle and the sheer size of the
task, and so lose heart, or on the other hand belittle its importance, imagine
it can easily be managed, and so neglect it.

10. 'And yet, I should not hesitate to offer you at least an outline
of what needs to be done in each of the principal departments of
administration. What does this consist of? First, you should resolutely
defend the established laws and change none of them, for what remains
in its accustomed place, even if inferior, is of more use than what is
constantly subject to change, even though the latter may seem to be
superior. Next, you must carry out meticulously what these laws require
you to do, refrain from doing what they forbid, and apply this principle
not only in word but in deed, in public no less than in private, so that you
may earn commendation and not condemnation. You should entrust the
public offices, both for civil and for military affairs, to those who excel
in virtue and in wisdom. Let no man be the object of your jealousy, and
when you compete with one another let it not be for the personal
advantage of this man or that, but to ensure the safety and prosperity of
the city. You should honour men who uphold such principles, but punish
those who show a different spirit in public life. Treat your private means
as if they were the property of the state, but keep your hands off public
funds as you would from your neighbour's goods. Guard vigilantly what
you already have, but never covet what does not belong to you. Do not
treat the allies or subject nations arrogantly, or exploit them for your
gain, and in your dealings with hostile states neither wrong them nor fear
them. Keep your weapons always ready to hand, but do not use them
either against one another or against those who are at peace. Make sure
that the troops are properly provided for, so that they never hanker after
what belongs to others through want of their own. Keep them in hand
and well disciplined, so that they may never become insolent and do
harm.

   'But there is no need for me to make a long speech, spelling out every detail which it is your duty to observe, since you can easily conclude from these general remarks how individual matters should be dealt with. I shall end with one more observation, namely that, if you conduct the affairs of state on these lines, you will enjoy prosperity yourselves and give great satisfaction to me, who found you beset with the storms of civil war and brought you safely to your present state. But if there is any part of the plan I have put before you which you are unable to carry out, you will cause me to regret my action, and you will cast the city once more into the midst of many conflicts and great dangers.'

11.   While Octavian was reading this speech, the senators were gripped by a variety of conflicting emotions. There were a few who knew his intention and so continued to applaud him enthusiastically throughout. Of the rest, some listened to his words with suspicion, while others believed them; both were equally astonished, the one at his astuteness and the other at his decision, and both displeased, the former at his scheming, and the latter at his change of mind.

There were already a number of senators who detested the republican constitution as a cause of internal dissension, who had been pleased at the change in government and who warmly supported Octavian. Thus, although his speech inspired different feelings in them, yet their conclusions were the same. Those who believed he had spoken the truth could not openly show their pleasure: those who were in favour of his decision were prevented by their fears, and the others by their disappointed hopes. On the other hand, those who were unconvinced did not dare to attack what he had said or to challenge his sincerity, some because they were afraid and others because they had no wish to do so. And so his audience, taken as a whole, were compelled either to believe him or else pretend that they did. As for praising him, some lacked the courage and others the desire to do so. On the contrary, both while he was reading his speech and afterwards they frequently broke in with shouts, pleading for monarchical government and bringing forward every argument in its favour, until finally they compelled him, as it seemed, to accept autocratic powers. Then the first action he took was to have a decree passed granting to the members of his future bodyguard twice the rate of pay which was received by the rest of the army, to ensure that he was strictly guarded. So genuine was his desire to lay down absolute power.

12. In this way Octavian's leadership was confirmed both by the Senate and by the people. Even so, he still wished to be regarded as a representative of the people, and hence while he undertook the whole care and supervision of public business on the ground that it demanded a special degree of attention, he announced that he would not personally govern all the provinces, and that those which he did take on, he would not continue to govern permanently. In the event, he handed over the weaker[29] provinces to the Senate, on the ground that they were at peace and free from war, but he kept the stronger under his authority, arguing that they were insecure and exposed to danger and either had enemies near their frontiers or were capable of starting a serious rebellion on their own initiative. The purpose of this decision, as he explained it, was that the Senate should enjoy without anxiety the fairest territories in the empire, while he should confront the hardships and the dangers. But the real object of this arrangement was that the senators should be unarmed and unprepared for war, while he possessed arms and controlled the troops.

Thus it was held that Africa, Numidia, Asia, Greece (including Epirus), the regions of Dalmatia and Macedonia, Crete and the Cyrenaic portion of Libya,[30] Bithynia and the adjoining territory of Pontus,[31] Sardinia and the Spanish province of Baetica should be placed under the control of the Senate and the people. Octavian took charge of the rest of Iberia, that is the regions of Tarraco and Lusitania, and all the Gauls – Gallia Narbonensis, Gallia Lugdunensis, Aquitania and Belgica – both the native inhabitants and the foreign tribes which dwelt among them. I should explain that some of the Celts, whom we call Germans, had occupied all the Belgic territory which borders the Rhine and named it Germany.[32] The southern portion of this region extends to the sources of the Rhine and the northern to the British Ocean. The above provinces, together with those of Coele Syria,[33] Phoenicia, Cilicia, Cyprus and Egypt, were allotted at that same time to Octavian. At a later date he returned Cyprus and Gallia Narbonensis to the people and took Dalmatia[34] for himself. A similar arrangement was adopted later for the other provinces, as my narrative will show in due course. I have specified these provinces in this way because at the present day each of them is governed separately, whereas originally and for many years they were administered in groups of two or three together. I have not mentioned the others, because some of these were acquired at a later date, and the rest, even if they had already been subdued, were not under the authority of a Roman governor, but had either been left autonomous[35] or entrusted to the rule of one kingdom or another. All those territories which came under the authority of the Romans after this period were added to the provinces administered by the emperor who was ruling at the time.

13. This was how the provinces were allotted. And since Octavian wished even then to impress upon the Romans that his mode of government was far removed from monarchical rule, he undertook to limit his administration of the provinces assigned to him to a period of ten years. He promised that he would establish order there within that period, and added with a touch of boasting that, if they were pacified more quickly, he would return them all the sooner to the Senate. Then he first appointed the senators themselves to govern both types of province,[36] with the exception of Egypt. For this people alone he appointed a knight, whom I have already mentioned, for the reasons given at that point in my narrative.[37]

Next he decreed that the senatorial provinces should be governed by magistrates chosen annually by lot, except in a case where a senator was entitled to special privileges because of the number of his children or because of his marriage.[38] These governors were to be sent out by a vote of the Senate taken in public session; they were not to carry a sword in their belt, nor to wear military uniform; the title of proconsul was conferred not only upon the two ex-consuls, but extended to other governors who had served only as praetors, or at any rate held the rank of ex-praetors; both classes of governor were to be attended by as many lictors as was the custom in Rome[39]; officials were to put on the insignia of their office immediately upon leaving the city limits, and to wear them continually until they returned.

The other governors, those who were to serve in the imperial provinces, were to be appointed by the emperor and to be called his envoys, and pro-praetors,[40] even if they were from the ranks of the ex-consuls. Thus of the two titles which had flourished for so long under the republic, Octavian gave that of praetor[41] to the men of his choice on the ground that from very early times it had been associated with warfare, and named them pro-praetors. The title of consul he gave to the senatorial nominees, on the ground that their duties were more peaceful, and called them proconsuls. He kept the full titles of consul and praetor for magistrates holding office in Italy, and referred to all the governors outside Italy as ruling in their stead.

Accordingly the governors whom the emperor had appointed were to be known as pro-praetors and to hold office for as much longer than a year as he thought fit. They were also to wear military uniform and carry a sword, with which they have authority to execute even soldiers. No one else, it should be noted, whether proconsul, pro-praetor or procurator, who is not empowered to put a soldier to death, has been granted the right of wearing a sword, and this power has been conferred not only upon the senators but also upon those knights who are entitled to wear a sword.[42]

So much for these details. All the pro-praetors alike are attended by five lictors, and in fact all of them except those who were ex-consuls when they were appointed to their governorships are styled on account of this number of five.[43] Both these classes of official assume the insignia of their position of authority when they enter their allotted province, and lay them down immediately after concluding their term of office.

14. It was in this manner and on these conditions that the practice was established of sending out ex-consuls and ex-praetors as governors of the two classes of province. In the one category the emperor would post the governor of his choice to whichever province and at whatever time he wished, and many men obtained provincial appointments while they were still serving as praetors or consuls, as sometimes occurs even at the present time. In the case of the senatorial provinces Octavian by his own decision allotted Asia and Africa to ex-consuls and all the other provinces to ex-praetors, but he forbade any of them to govern such a province until five years after the date at which he had last held a public office in Rome. For a time all the senatorial candidates, even if there were more of them than the number of provinces, were appointed to such governorships by lot.[44] But later, since some of them did not govern well, the appointment of these officials too was transferred to the emperor. Because of this procedure it is the emperor who in a manner of speaking also appoints the governors of the senatorial provinces to their posts, for in practice he draws up a list of the number of candidates to correspond to the number of provinces and orders lots to be drawn for the names he has chosen. Some emperors have also sent to the senatorial provinces men whom they have personally selected and allowed them to hold office for

more than a year, and some have allotted certain provinces to knights instead of to senators.

These were the arrangements laid down at that time concerning those senators who possessed authority to inflict the death sentence upon the inhabitants of the provinces they governed.[45] I should explain that there is also a class of senators who are not so authorized, namely those who are sent to the provinces known as 'the provinces of the Senate and the people', and who serve there either as quaestors, who are chosen by lot, or as deputies to those senators who hold the power of life and death. This would be the correct designation for these functionaries if we are thinking not of their official title, but of their actual duties as I have just described them: they are also referred to as 'envoys' if the Greek equivalent of their title is used.[46] At any rate this appellation has been closely enough defined in what has been written above. In the case of the deputies in general, each governor chooses his own. The ex-praetors nominate one from their colleagues or even from their juniors, and the ex-consuls three from among those of equal rank, subject to the emperor's approval. A change was made in respect of the selection of these men too, but the new arrangement was soon discontinued, and it will be enough to mention it at the proper time.

15.   This then is the procedure for making appointments to the provinces of the Senate and the people.

As to the others – the imperial provinces which contain more than one legion – the officials posted to them are intended to govern them as deputies of the emperor: they are chosen by the emperor himself, generally from the ranks of the ex-praetors, though sometimes also from the ex-quaestors, or from those who have held some office between the praetorship and the quaestorship. These, then, are the posts for which senatorial rank is required.

In the case of the knights, the emperor himself selects men from this order to serve abroad as military tribunes, both those who are prospective candidates for the Senate and others. I have touched on their differences in rank in an earlier chapter. Some of these are posted to purely legionary garrisons, others to command auxiliary troops as well. Here the emperor follows the practice which was initiated by Augustus.

The procurators, the officials who collect the public revenues and authorize expenditure according to the instructions given them, are sent out to all regions alike, both to the people's provinces and to those administered by the emperor. These positions are held by knights and sometimes even by freedmen; however, the proconsuls levy tribute from the peoples they govern. The emperor issues instructions to the procurators, the proconsuls and the pro-praetors, so that they go out to their provinces in possession of clearly defined orders. Both this practice and the award of salaries to these and other officials were established in Augustus's time. At an earlier date a system had existed whereby contractors farmed the taxes from the public treasury and provided the officials with such funds as they needed to carry on their work. Under Octavian, however, these officials began to receive a fixed salary for the first time. This was not paid to them all on an equal scale, but roughly according to their needs, and the procurators in fact derive the title of their rank from the size of the salary allotted to them.

A number of regulations were laid down for all these officials alike. They were not empowered to conscript soldiers, nor to demand taxes beyond the amount specified, unless the Senate should pass a decree or the emperor issue an order. As soon as their successor arrived they were to leave the province forthwith, and not delay on the homeward journey but return to Rome within three months.

16.   This was how the regulations were laid down, more or less, at that time. As events turned out, Augustus was to exercise complete and permanent authority over all these matters. This was because he not only had control of the funds, but also commanded the army: nominally the public revenues had been separated from his own, but in practice the former, too, were spent as he saw fit.[47] At any rate, when his ten-year period of office expired,[48] another five years was voted to him, then another five, after that ten, and then ten for the fifth time. Thus through this succession of ten-year periods he remained sole ruler for life. It was for this reason that later emperors, although they were no longer appointed for a limited period but for their entire lives – once and for all – nevertheless always celebrated their reign every ten years, as if they were once more renewing their sovereignty, and this practice continues to the present day.[49]

Octavian had even before received many honours when the questions of declining the sovereignty and of allotting the provinces were being discussed. At that time the privilege of placing the laurel trees in front of the royal residence,[50] and of hanging the wreath of oak leaves above them, was voted in his honour to recognize in perpetuity his status as victor over his enemies and the saviour of the citizens. The royal residence is known as the Palatium, not because it was ever decreed that it should be so called, but because Octavian lived on the Palatine hill and had his military headquarters there. The house also gained some measure of renown from the Palatine hill as a whole, because Romulus had once resided there. Accordingly, even if the emperor actually lives somewhere else, his residence keeps the name of Palatium.

When Octavian had finally put his plans into effect, the name Augustus was conferred on him by the Senate and the people. At the time when they wished to give him some title of special eminence, and some people were proposing one title and some another and pressing for its adoption, Octavian had set his heart strongly on being named Romulus. But when he understood that this aroused suspicions that he desired the kingship, he abandoned his efforts to obtain it and adopted the title of Augustus, as signifying that he was something more than human, since indeed all the most precious and sacred objects are referred to as *augusta*. For this reason when he was addressed in Greek he was named *Sebastos*, meaning an august individual: the word is derived from the passive form of the verb *sebazo*, I revere.

17.   Through this process the power both of the people and of the Senate was wholly transferred into the hands of Augustus, and it was from this time that a monarchy, strictly speaking, was established. It would certainly be most truthful to describe it as a monarchy, even if at a later date two or three men held the supreme power at the same time. It is true that the Romans hated the actual name of monarch so vehemently that they did not refer to their emperors either as dictators or kings or anything similar.[51] But since the final decision in the governing process is referred to them, it is impossible that they should be anything other than kings. Certainly the offices of state which in general owed their existence to the laws are, it is true, kept in being even now, except for that of censor, but the entire conduct and direction of affairs depend upon the wishes of the one man who holds power at the time. And yet in order to maintain the impression that this authority is derived from the laws and not from their own supremacy, the emperors have arrogated to themselves all the functions, together with their actual titles, attached to those offices in

which power resided and which were held with the free consent of the people, with the single exception of the dictatorship.

Thus, for example, the emperors are very often created consuls, and they are referred to as proconsuls whenever they are outside the city limits. They adopt the style of Imperator for life – not only those who have won victories in the field, but all the others besides, to indicate their independent authority – and they use this title instead of those of king or dictator. The emperors have never used these last since they first fell out of use in the conduct of government, but they secure for themselves the prerogatives of these positions through the title of Imperator. This designation empowers them to raise troops, collect funds, declare war, conclude peace, rule foreigners and citizens alike, at all times and in all places, and even to put to death both knights and senators within the city limits, and to act in all the other capacities once entrusted to the consuls and the other officials who possessed *imperium*.[52]

Similarly, by virtue of holding the censorship[53] they scrutinize our lives and morals as well as conducting the census; they add some names to the orders of knights and senators and strike out others as they see fit. Then by virtue of being consecrated in all the priesthoods, and of being entitled to confer most of these offices upon others, and because of the fact that, even if two or three persons share the imperial power at the same time, one of them is Pontifex Maximus, they exercise supreme jurisdiction in all matters both profane and sacred.

The so-called tribunician power, which was once held only by men whose influence was rapidly beginning to climb, gives them the right to veto the consequences of any measure taken by any other official, should they disapprove of any such, and protects them against insult or abuse. Moreover, if they appear to have suffered, even to the most trivial extent, not only by deed, but even by word, they may destroy the perpetrator as one guilty of sacrilege, without a trial. The emperors, it should be explained, do not see fit to become tribunes, since they belong entirely to the patrician class.[54] But they assume tribunician power to the full as this existed when the office was at the height of its political influence, and they use it to number the years of their own rule, the principle being that they receive the power each year together with those who are regularly appointed tribunes. These then are the offices which they have arrogated to themselves from the republic. They have preserved the form in which each of them was instituted, and retained the same titles for them. Their object has been to create the impression that they hold no power without a gift having been made of it to them.

18.   But besides this status they have acquired another, which was granted to none of the ancient Romans outright and absolutely, and the possession of this alone would enable them to exercise the powers I have mentioned above and the others as well. They have been set free from the laws,[55] as the very words in Latin express it: that is, they are exempted from all binding tradition, and are not liable to any of the written provisions of the laws. Thus, by means of these democratic titles, they have vested in themselves all the authority of the government to such an extent that they actually possess everything that kings possessed except their paltry title. To be addressed as Caesar or Augustus does not impute any power which is peculiar to them, but merely shows that in the first case they are the heirs of the family to which they belong, and in the second the illustrious nature of their official position. The term Father perhaps confers a certain authority upon them, such as fathers once possessed over their children. However, this was not its meaning when it was first bestowed upon the emperors.[56] It was intended rather as an honour and also an exhortation both to them that they should love their subjects as they would their children, and to their subjects that they should revere them as they would their fathers.

I have described the various titles used by the holders of the imperial power in accordance with the laws and with what has now become tradition, and I have also described their nature. In our day they are all, generally speaking, conferred upon the emperors at the same time, except for that of censor, but to the earlier emperors each was voted at different times. In the case of the censorship some of the emperors took the office according to the traditional practice, and Domitian took it for life, but this is no longer the custom today. Now they enjoy the powers of this office, but are not elected to hold it and do not use the title except in taking the census.

19.   Thus the constitution was reformed at that time, as I have explained, for the better, and greater security was thereby achieved: it would indeed have been impossible for the people to have lived in safety under a republic. However, the events which followed that period cannot be told in the same way as those of earlier times. In the past all matters were

brought before the Senate and the people, even if they took place at a distance from Rome: in consequence everybody learned of them and many people recorded them, and so the true version of events, even if considerably influenced by fear, or favour, or friendship, or enmity in the accounts given by certain authors, was still to a significant extent available in the writings of the others who reported the same happenings, and in the public records.[57]

But in later times most events began to be kept secret and were denied to common knowledge, and even though it may happen that some matters are made public, the reports are discredited because they cannot be investigated, and the suspicion grows that everything is said and done according to the wishes of the men in power at the time and their associates.[58] In consequence much that never materializes becomes common talk, while much that has undoubtedly come to pass remains unknown, and in pretty well every instance the report which is spread abroad does not correspond to what actually happened. Besides this, the very size of the empire and the multitude of events which take place simultaneously make it very difficult to report them accurately. In Rome, for example, and in the subject territories events crowd upon one another, and in the countries of our enemies there is something happening all the time, indeed every day. Concerning these matters nobody other than those directly involved can easily obtain clear information, and many people never even hear in the first instance of what has occurred. So in my own account of later events, so far as these need be mentioned at all, everything I shall say will follow the version that has been made public, whether this is really the truth or otherwise. But in addition to these reports, I shall give my own opinion, as far as possible, on such occasions as I have been able – relying on the many details I have gathered from my reading, or from hearsay, or from what I have seen – to form a judgement which tells us something more than the common report.

20.   Octavian, as I have mentioned, was given the name of Augustus, and straightaway on the very same night a portent occurred which made no small impression on him. The Tiber overflowed its banks and flooded all the low-lying districts of Rome, so that these became navigable to boats. From this sign the soothsayers prophesied that he would attain great power and hold the whole city under his sway. At this, various people began to vie with one another in uttering extravagant flatteries,

but a certain Sextus Pacuvius – or as others say Apudius – excelled them all. In a session of the Senate he proclaimed himself dedicated to the emperor, following the custom of the Spaniards,[59] and urged others to do the same. When Augustus checked him, he rushed out to the crowd which was standing close at hand, and, as he was tribune, compelled first the bystanders and then the rest of the populace, as he traversed the streets and lanes, to declare themselves likewise dedicated to Augustus. From this episode originated the practice of saying, as we do to this day when appealing to the sovereign, 'We have dedicated ourselves to you.'

Pacuvius ordered everyone to offer sacrifice on account of this portent, and in the presence of the crowd he declared that he intended to make Augustus his heir on the same terms as his own son – not that he possessed much to bequeath, but because he hoped to receive even more, and so it turned out.

21.   Augustus dealt with all the business concerning the empire even more conscientiously than before, to give the impression that he had accepted the task in accordance with the wishes of all, and he passed many laws. I need not describe all these minutely in each instance, but only those which are relevant to my history. I shall follow the same procedure in dealing with later events. In this way I hope not to weary my readers by introducing a mass of detail, such as even those who make a speciality of such studies do not master so thoroughly.

However, in introducing these laws Augustus did not rely wholly upon his own judgement. Some of them he laid before the popular assembly in advance, so that if anything caused displeasure, he would have time to discover and correct it. He encouraged all comers to offer suggestions, in case anybody could think of some improvement, and he allowed them complete freedom of speech; indeed he even changed certain provisions in the proposed laws. Most important of all, he called in the consuls – or the other consul if he himself held the office – to advise him for periods of six months, together with one of the holders of each of the other offices of state, and fifteen men chosen by lot from the rest of the Senate. In consequence it became a practice that all legislation put forward by the emperors is communicated after a fashion through these advisers to all the other senators. Augustus would still bring certain matters before a full session of the Senate, but he generally followed the plan just described, preferring to consider most business and especially the most important items in a quiet preliminary consultation with a few advisers, and sometimes he even sat with these men when he was trying cases.

The Senate as a whole continued to sit in judgement on its own, as it had done before,[60] and on certain occasions conducted negotiations with delegations and heralds from both peoples and kings. Besides this the people and the plebs continued to meet for the elections, but nothing was done that did not meet with Augustus's approval. It was he, at any rate, who selected and put forward for nomination some of the candidates for office, though for some others he observed the traditional custom and left the election to the vote of the popular and the tribal assembly.[61] But he also made sure that no candidates should be appointed who were unfit or who owed their election to partisan intrigue or to bribery.

22.   In general terms, this is how Augustus managed the empire. I shall now mention each of his actions which it is necessary to record, together with the names of the consuls under whom they were put into effect. In the year already referred to,[62] Augustus had noticed that the roads outside the city walls had been so neglected that it had become difficult to travel along them. He therefore ordered some of the senators to have the other roads repaired at their expense, while he himself dealt with the Via Flaminia, since he intended to lead out an army along it. The work was completed without delay, and accordingly statues of Augustus were erected on arches placed on the bridge over the Tiber[63] and at Ariminum.[64] The other roads were repaired later, either at public expense or at that of Augustus – according as to how one chooses to pur it – for none of the senators would willingly spend money on this project. I find it impossible to distinguish between the two funds, even though Augustus frequently converted into currency silver statues of himself which had been erected by some of his friends and some of the subject peoples; his object in doing this was to make it appear that all the expenditure which he said he was undertaking came out of his own pocket. For this reason I have no opinion to offer as to whether any emperor on a given occasion took the money from the public funds or paid it out himself. Both procedures were frequently adopted, and there seems no reason to classify such expenditure as loans or gifts respectively, when the emperor and the people repeatedly resorted to both without distinction.

These were the actions he carried out at that time. Augustus also set out with the intention of making an expedition to Britain,[65] but when he arrived in the provinces of Gaul he spent the time there. There were signs that the Britons would come to terms with him and the affairs of the Gauls were still in turmoil, since no sooner had they been subjugated by Julius Caesar than the civil wars had begun. Augustus took a census of the inhabitants and brought the benefits of order to their life and government. From Gaul he travelled to Spain and established order in that province too.

23.   After this he became consul for the eighth time,[66] together with Statilius Taurus.[67] In this year too Agrippa dedicated the precinct known as the Saepta.[68] He had not undertaken to repair a road, but instead he had decorated with marble tablets and paintings this enclosure which is surrounded by porticoes and had been constructed by Lepidus in the Campus Martius for meetings of the Comitia Tributa. Agrippa named it the Saepta Julia in honour of Augustus, and so far from incurring any jealousy through his action he was signally honoured both by Augustus himself and by the rest of the people. The reason was that he gave Augustus advice on the most humane, the most ambitious and the most advantageous projects, but did not claim even the smallest share in the glory which they earned. Instead he used the honours which Augustus conferred upon him not for his personal gain or enjoyment but for the benefit of the emperor himself and the public at large.

By contrast Cornelius Gallus[69] behaved with great arrogance in consequence of the honour he had received. He circulated much disparaging gossip concerning Augustus and committed many other indefensible actions besides. Not only did he set up statues of himself throughout Egypt, but he also caused a list of his achievements to be inscribed upon the pyramids. His associate and close friend Valerius Largus lodged an accusation against him for this action, and he was stripped of his honours by Augustus and even barred from residing in any of the imperial provinces. After this, many others denounced him and brought a multitude of charges against him. The Senate passed a unanimous vote that he should be convicted in the courts, exiled, stripped of his property, which should be handed over to Augustus, and that the Senate itself should offer up sacrifices.

24.   Gallus's spirit was broken by this treatment, and he took his own life before the decrees came into effect. His case provides another proof of the dishonest nature of mankind. They now treated the man whom they had

formerly flattered in such a way as to compel him to die by his own hand. They then veered round in favour of Largus because his star was beginning to rise, but with every intention of voting in the same fashion against him if he were to suffer a similar fate.

However, Proculeius's opinion of Largus was such that once, on meeting him, he covered his own nose and mouth with his hand, thus indicating to the bystanders that it was not safe even to breathe in his presence. Another man whom Largus did not know approached him, attended by witnesses, and asked whether Largus knew him. Receiving a negative answer, he wrote it down, as though this would hinder such a scoundrel from informing even against a man he had not previously known.

But we have an example in the behaviour of Marcus Egnatius Rufus of how most men seek to rival the deeds of others, even when they are wrongful ones, rather than guard against the fateful consequences for themselves. Rufus had held the office of aedile.[70] He had carried out his duties well in many respects, and in particular he had helped with his own slaves and other men hired for the purpose to save those houses which had caught fire during his year of office. In return for these efforts he had been reimbursed from public funds for the sums he had spent in the discharge of his duties, and had then been elected praetor – contrary to the law. These successes aroused in him so great a sense of his own importance and of contempt for Augustus that he published an announcement to the effect that he had handed over the city unimpaired and in perfect condition to his successor. All the other leading men in Rome were incensed at this, Augustus most of all, and before long he was to teach Rufus a lesson not to give himself airs above the majority. For the present he ordered the aediles to take precautions that no building should catch fire, and that if any conflagration started to have it put out.

25. In the same year Polemon,[71] the king of Pontus, was admitted to the number of friends and allies of the Roman people, and senators were accorded the privilege of occupying front seats in all the theatres of his kingdom. Augustus was planning an expedition to invade Britain, since the inhabitants were unwilling to come to terms, but his scheme was checked by the revolt of the Salassi,[72] and by an outbreak of hostilities in the territories of the Cantabri and the Astures. The Salassi live at the foot of the Alps, as I have mentioned earlier; the two other tribes inhabit the

most impregnable region on the Iberian side of the Pyrenees and also the plain which lies below. These events caused Augustus, who was now serving as consul for the ninth time[73] with Marcus Silanus as his colleague, to dispatch Terentius Varro against the Salassi. Varro launched his invasion from a number of directions at once to prevent his opponents from concentrating their forces, which would have made them more difficult to subdue, and he overcame their resistance easily enough since they attacked his forces only in small groups. Having forced them to surrender, he first demanded a fixed indemnity, as though he had intended to impose no other punishment. Then he dispatched soldiers all over the country apparently to collect the money, but he also arrested all the men of military age; these were sold into slavery on the understanding that none of them should be set free within twenty years. The best of their land was given to some of the Praetorian Guard, and later the city called Augusta Praetoria[74] was built there.

Augustus opened hostilities against the Astures and the Cantabri simultaneously and led the campaign himself. However, these tribes would neither surrender, because they felt confidence in the strength of their mountain fastnesses, nor would they come to close quarters, since they were outnumbered by the Romans and most of their troops were javelin-throwers. Their tactics caused Augustus many difficulties, since whenever he moved his troops in any direction, they continually forestalled him by occupying the higher ground in advance and ambushing his troops in the valleys and woods, and in this way they reduced the campaign to an impasse. Augustus fell ill from the fatigue and anxiety caused by these conditions and retired to Tarraco, where he remained in weak health. Gaius Antistius took charge of the operations and scored many successes. This was not because he was a better general than Augustus, but because the barbarians despised him, and so engaged in pitched battles with the Romans and were defeated. In this way Antistius captured a number of places, and later Titus Carisius occupied Lancia, the principal fortress of the Astures, after it had been abandoned, and captured many others.

26.   When this campaign had been ended, Augustus discharged the older age groups in his army, and enabled them to build a city in Lusitania, which was named Augusta Emerita. For the troops who were still of an age to continue active service he arranged for a number of spectacles to

be held within the military camps, and these were organized by Tiberius[75] and Marcellus, who were the aediles for the year.

At this time he also granted to Juba[76] the territory of the Gaetulians and the possessions of Bocchus[77] and of Bogud; these gifts were made in return for the Prince's hereditary lands, most of the inhabitants of which had become enrolled under Roman authority.

When king Amyntas[78] died, Augustus did not allow the kingdom to pass to his sons, but made it part of a subject territory. Thus Galatia together with Lycaonia were placed under a Roman governor, and the parts of Pamphylia which had formerly been allotted to Amyntas were re-united with their own region.

At about the same time Marcus Vinicius led a punitive expedition against some of the Germans,[79] because they had arrested and killed a number of Roman citizens who had entered their country to trade with them, and this exploit caused the title of Imperator to be bestowed upon Augustus.[80] Because of this expedition and Augustus's other achievements during this period a triumph was decreed to him as well as the title. However, as he chose not to celebrate this, a triumphal arch was erected in the Alps in his honour, and he was accorded the right always to wear both the victor's crown and the triumphal costume on the first day of the year.

27.   After these military successes Augustus closed the precinct of Janus,[81] which had been opened on account of the beginning of hostilities. Meanwhile Agrippa proceeded to embellish the city at his own expense. First he completed the edifice known as the Basilica of Neptune to commemorate the naval victories of Naulochus and Actium and enhanced its beauty with the painting which depicts the Argonauts, and after this he erected the Laconian *sudatorium*.[82] He named the gymnasium Laconian because the Lacedaemonians were particularly celebrated at this time for stripping and exercising after anointing themselves with oil. He also completed the building known as the Pantheon. This name may originate from the fact that among the multitude of images which adorn it are the statues of many gods, including those of Mars[83] and Venus. However, in my own opinion it is so called because, being circular, it resembles the shape of the heavens.[84] Agrippa wished to place a statue of Augustus there as well and to honour him further by giving his name to the building, but when the emperor would not accept either tribute, Agrippa had a statue

of Julius Caesar placed within the temple and others of Augustus and himself in the ante-chamber.[85] These actions were carried out not through any ambition on Agrippa's part to make himself a rival to Augustus, but from his genuine goodwill towards the emperor and his constant devotion to the public good; the result was that Augustus, so far from finding any cause for censure, honoured him all the more.

Thus, for example, when the marriage of his daughter Julia was taking place in Rome and Augustus was unable through illness to attend at that time, he deputed Agrippa to conduct the celebrations in his absence. Later, when the house on the Palatine hill, which had formerly belonged to Antony and had subsequently been given to Agrippa and Messalla,[86] was burned down, Augustus gave money to Messalla, but arranged for Agrippa to share his own dwelling. Agrippa not unnaturally took great pride in these marks of esteem. In the same way a certain Gaius Toranius earned general approval because when he was tribune he brought his father into the theatre and made him sit beside him on the tribunes' bench. Publius Servilius also made a name for himself because during his term as praetor he arranged a festival during which three hundred bears and the same number of African wild beasts were killed in the arena.

28.   Augustus now held the consulship for the tenth time with Gaius Norbanus as his colleague, and on the first day of the year the Senate confirmed his acts by taking their oaths.[87] The news arrived that Augustus was approaching the city, his return having been delayed by his illness, and he undertook to make a gift to the people of four hundred sesterces each, though he forbade that the edict announcing this bounty should be displayed until the Senate had approved the measure. Thereupon the Senate declared him released from all obligation to the laws. Their purpose, as I have explained above, was that he should be in practice independent and master both of himself and of the laws, and hence might do anything that he wished and refrain from anything he did not wish. These rights were voted to him while he was still outside the city; then, as soon as he entered Rome, various other privileges were granted him in honour of his restoration to good health and his return. Marcellus was given the right to sit in the Senate among the former praetors, and the right to stand for the consulship ten years earlier than the normal age,[88] and Tiberius the right to stand for each office five years before the normal age; the former was at once elected aedile and the latter quaestor. When

there were not enough candidates for the quaestorship to fill the vacancies in the provinces, all those who had held the quaestorship during the last ten years without having been posted to any province were allowed to draw lots for the vacant posts.

29. These were the events of note which took place in the city at that time. As soon as Augustus had quitted Spain, where he had left behind Lucius Aemilius[89] as governor, the Cantabri and the Astures rose in rebellion. They sent a message to Aemilius declaring that they wished to make a present of grain and other commodities, before the least sign of their intention had become apparent. Then, after they had brought together a large number of Roman soldiers, supposedly to transport the presents, they led them to places they had chosen for their plot and massacred them. However, they did not rejoice for long, for their country was ravaged, some of their forts were burned and, worse still, the hands of all who were taken prisoner were cut off, and so they were quickly subdued.

While these events were in train, another new campaign began and ended in a short time. The expedition was led by Aelius Gallus, the governor of Egypt, against the country known as Arabia Felix,[90] ruled by a king named Sabos. At first Gallus's expedition could find no human being in sight, and yet their advance was by no means easy. His men suffered great hardship from the desert, the sun and the water, which contained some strange property, so that the greater part of the army perished. The disease which attacked them proved to be unlike any of the familiar ailments. First of all it affected the head, causing it to become parched, and most of the victims died from this affliction immediately. For those who survived this stage, the symptoms passed by the intermediate parts of the body and descended to the legs, causing great pain in them. There was no remedy for it except a mixture of olive oil and wine, which was both drunk and used on the skin. But this was available to only a few of the men, since the country produces neither of these commodities, and the troops had not laid in any large supply beforehand. In the midst of these hardships the barbarians also attacked them. Up to then they had been defeated whenever they had come to close quarters, and had even abandoned a number of villages. But now with the disease as their ally they recovered their territory and drove the survivors of the expedition out of their country. These were certainly the first of the Romans – and

I believe the only ones – to penetrate so far into Arabia in order to make war, for they advanced as far as the place called Athloula,[91] a name which is well known.

30.   Augustus became consul for the eleventh time with Calpurnius Piso as his colleague,[92] and was then again taken ill, this time so seriously that there appeared to be no hope of his recovery. At any rate, he arranged all his affairs as if he were at the point of death, and gathered around him the officers of state and the most prominent senators and knights. He did not indicate any successor,[93] although everybody was expecting that Marcellus would be the first choice for this position. However, he spoke to the company for a while about matters of public policy, delivered to Piso the list of the forces and the records of the public revenues written in a book,[94] and handled his ring to Agrippa. He had become too weak to deal with even the most urgent matters, but a certain Antonius Musa restored him to health by means of cold baths and cold potions. In return for this service Musa was paid large sums both by Augustus and by the Senate, and was also given the right to wear gold rings,[95] for he was a freedman. He was also granted exemption from taxes both for himself and for the other members of his profession, not only his contemporaries, but even future generations. However, fate decreed that the man who had taken into his own hands the functions both of Fortune and of Destiny should himself become ensnared. For while Augustus's life was saved in this way, Marcellus, when he fell ill not long afterwards,[96] received the same treatment from Musa, but died. Augustus delivered a eulogy in the traditional manner, gave him a public burial and placed his body in the tomb which he was building. He also completed as a memorial to the young man the theatre whose foundations had already been laid by Julius Caesar and which was now named the theatre of Marcellus in his honour. He also gave orders that a golden image, a golden crown and a curule chair should be carried into the theatre at the festival of the Roman Games,[97] and should be placed in the midst of the magistrates who officiate at these.

31.   These actions were carried out later. At the time when Augustus had recovered his health, he brought his will into the Senate with the intention of reading it aloud, so as to inform the world that he had left no successor to the empire.[98] However, this reading never took place, for no

one would consent to it,[99] but what caused universal astonishment was his attitude towards Marcellus. He had shown his love for Marcellus both as a son-in-law and as a nephew, and besides conferring other honours upon him had gone out of his way to help the young man make a brilliant success of the games which he was supervising as aedile. Thus throughout the whole summer the Forum had been sheltered by means of a canopy stretched overhead; a dancer, who was a knight, and a woman of noble birth had been persuaded to take part in the stage performances, and yet Augustus had not entrusted the monarchy to him, and had given his preference to Agrippa. From this it would appear that he did not yet possess confidence in the young man's judgement, and that he either wished the people to recover their liberty or Agrippa to be given the leadership by them. Certainly he understood that Agrippa was much beloved by the people, and he wished to avoid the impression that the supreme power was being entrusted to him by Augustus's decision alone.

32. So when he regained his health and discovered that Marcellus was not well disposed towards Agrippa because of what had happened, he immediately sent the latter to Syria,[100] so that no occasion for friction or quarrelling might arise through their being in one another's company. Agrippa immediately left Rome, but did not travel as far as Syria; instead he acted with even more than his accustomed tact, sent his subordinates there, and himself waited in Lesbos.

These were the actions taken by Augustus in the manner I have described. The number of praetors appointed was ten, since he considered that no more than these were required, and this figure was maintained for several years.[101] His intention was that most of them should perform the same duties as before, but that two should be in charge of financial administration each year. After he had given detailed instructions on these matters, he went to the Alban Mount[102] and formally laid down the consulship. Ever since the conduct of affairs of state had been regularized, both he himself and most of his colleagues had held the office for a full year. He now wished to suspend this practice, so that as many men as possible might serve as consuls,[103] and he arranged for his resignation to take place outside the city so that he should not be hindered in his purpose. He was praised both for his action in itself and because he chose Lucius Sestius to replace him. This man had always been an ardent supporter of

Brutus, had fought with him in all his campaigns and even at this time cherished his memory, possessed statues of him and delivered eulogies on him. It seems that Augustus, far from disapproving of Sestius's loyalty and attachment to his friend, honoured him for that reason. Because of this the Senate passed a resolution that Augustus should be a tribune for life[104] and gave him the privilege of introducing before the Senate at each session any one subject at whatever time he chose,[105] even if he were not then consul. They also voted that he should hold once and for all and for life the office of proconsul, so that he was not obliged either to lay it down on entering the city limits or to have it renewed when he left them,[106] and for the subject territories they granted him authority superior to that of governor in each locality.[107] In consequence both he and the succeeding emperors acquired a certain legal right to employ the tribunician power in addition to their other powers, for neither Augustus nor any other emperor used the title of tribune.

33.   I believe that Augustus was granted these privileges at that time not as a result of flattery, but because he was genuinely being honoured, for he treated the Romans in most respects as if they were free citizens.[108] Thus when Tiridates[109] came to Rome in person together with a delegation from Phraates to argue out the quarrel between them, Augustus brought them before the Senate, and when it referred the decision of the dispute to him, he did not hand over Tiridates to Phraates; instead he returned to Phraates the son whom the king had once sent him and whom Augustus had been holding as a hostage, on condition that the prisoners of war and the legionary standards which had been captured when Crassus and later Antony had suffered defeat should be returned.[110]

During the same year one of the junior aediles died and Gaius Calpurnius succeeded him, even though he had served previously as a senior aedile. No instance has been recorded of this having happened before.[111] During the Feriae Latinae two prefects of the city[112] officiated for each day, and one of them held this position though he had not yet reached the age even of adolescence.

At this time the accusation was current that Livia had had a hand in the death of Marcellus, because he had been preferred for the succession before her sons. This suspicion was much disputed because of the climatic nature both of that year and of the one that followed, which proved so unhealthy that there was a high rate of mortality in both. And just as it often happens that some sign is noticed before such events take place, so on this occasion a wolf was caught in the city, and fire and storm damaged many buildings. Besides this the Tiber rose and carried away the wooden bridge,[113] and made the city navigable for boats for three days.

BOOK 54

The following is contained in the Fifty-Fourth Book of Dio's *Rome*:

1.   During the following year,[1] when Marcus Marcellus and Lucius Arruntius were consuls, the city was again flooded by the overflowing of the river and many objects were struck by thunderbolts, in particular the statues in the Pantheon, so that the spear even fell from the hand of Augustus. The people suffered both from sickness and from famine, for the plague affected the whole of Italy and nobody tilled the land, and I suppose that the same afflictions also prevailed abroad. The Romans concluded that these disasters had befallen them for no other reason than that they did not have Augustus serving as consul at that time, and they therefore wished to appoint him dictator. They shut up the senators in their chamber and compelled them to pass this measure, threatening that they would burn down the building with the members inside it. Then they took the twenty-four fasces, went to Augustus and implored him to agree to be named as dictator and become commissioner for the corn

supply, as Pompey had once been. He accepted the latter post under
duress, and ordered that two men should be selected annually to supervise
the distribution of grain; these were to be drawn from men who had
served as praetors not less than five years previously. As for the dictatorship
he refused to let himself be named, and even rent his clothes when he
found that he could not curb the people's desire for his appointment in
any other way, either by reasoning or by entreaty. He knew that the
authority and the honour he already possessed raised him above the
position of past dictators, and he was rightly on his guard against the
jealousy and hatred which the title would provoke.[2]

2. He acted in the same way too when the people sought to appoint him
censor for life. He refused to take on the office himself, and at once
appointed others to hold it, namely Paulus Aemilius Lepidus and Lucius
Munatius Plancus.[3] The latter was a brother of the Plancus who had been
proscribed, while Lepidus had himself been condemned to death at that
period. These were the last two private citizens to hold the office at the
same time, and this no doubt had its relevance to the sign which they
immediately witnessed. On the very first day of their appointment the
platform on which they were to carry out their duties collapsed as they
mounted it and was smashed to pieces; thereafter no others of similar rank
to these men have ever became censors together. But even at this time,
and in spite of the appointment of these two, Augustus carried out many
of the duties which belonged to them.

As regards the public banquets, he abolished some altogether and
reduced others to a more modest scale; he entrusted the supervision of all
festivals to the praetors and ordered provision to be made for these from
the public treasury; he also forbade any praetor to spend more than his
colleagues from his own means on any of these events, or to put on a
gladiatorial combat unless the Senate decreed it, or to arrange such events
more than twice a year, or to employ more than a hundred and twenty
fighters; the curule aediles were given the responsibility of putting out
fires, for which service he gave them six hundred slaves as their assistants.
By this time even knights and women of rank had given performances
on the stage, and so the sons of senators had already been debarred from
such activities: Augustus now extended this prohibition to their grandsons, in so far as any of these belonged to the equestrian order.

3.   In making these regulations he showed himself in practice as well as in name both a lawgiver and an absolute ruler. But in other respects he behaved with moderation, so much so that he even gave his support to some of his friends when their actions came under public scrutiny. A certain Marcus Primus was accused of having made war upon the tribe of the Odrysae when he was governor of Macedonia. At his trial he pleaded at one point that he had acted with the approval of Augustus and at another with that of Marcellus. Augustus went to the court-room of his own accord, and when he was asked by the praetor whether he had given the man orders to make war, said that he had not.[4] Licinius Murena, who was defending Primus, uttered some rather disrespectful remarks to Augustus, and actually asked him, 'What are you doing here, and who sent for you?' Augustus merely replied, 'The public interest.' For this response he was praised by people of sound sense and was even given the right to summon the Senate as often as he saw fit. But some of the others thought the worse of him.

At any rate there were not a few who voted for Primus's acquittal, and others joined in a plot against Augustus. The leader was Fannius Caepio, but a number of others gave him their support. Even Murena[5] was said to have been implicated in the conspiracy: the charge may have been true or false, since he was notoriously rough-tongued and headstrong in his manner of address towards all alike. These men were not brought to trial, but were convicted by default on the assumption that they intended to escape, and were executed soon afterwards. Nothing could avail to save Murena, neither Proculeius his brother, nor Maecenas his sister's[6] husband, even though both these men were held in the highest honour by Augustus. Indeed, since some of the jurymen cast their votes to acquit even these conspirators, the emperor had a law passed that in trials where the defendant was not present the vote should not be secret and the accused should be convicted only if it were unanimous. At any rate Augustus gave a decisive proof that in passing these measures he had acted not out of anger, but for the public good. There were two slaves who had accompanied Caepio in his flight. One of these had wished to defend his young master when he met his death, and this man Caepio's father freed. The second had deserted the young man; Caepio's father had him led through the Forum carrying an inscription to explain the reason why he was to be put to death, and later crucified him; the emperor showed no disapproval of either of these actions. Indeed he would have disarmed all the criticism of those who were displeased with what the had done, if he had not actually allowed sacrifices to be voted and offered up, as if it were for a victory.

4. It was in this year too that he gave back to the people the provinces both of Cyprus and of Gallia Narbonensis, as regions which no longer required the presence of troops under his command, and accordingly proconsuls now began to be sent to these peoples too. He also dedicated the temple of Jupiter the Thunderer. Two stories have been handed down concerning this temple. The first relates that on that occasion peals of thunder were heard while the ceremony was being performed. Then at a later date Augustus experienced the following dream. It seemed to him that the people approached and did reverence to Jupiter the Thunderer. They acted thus partly because of the unfamiliarity both of the name and of the shape of the statue, and partly because it had been erected by Augustus, but chiefly because they came to it first as they climbed the Capitoline hill. At this the statue of Jupiter in the great temple on the Capitol became angry, because he was now reduced to second place in worship. In the dream Augustus remarked to the Capitoline Jupiter that he had the Thunderer as his sentinel. Then, when it was day, he fastened a bell to the statue to confirm the vision he had seen. He did this because those who guard blocks of houses at night carry a bell, in order to warn the inhabitants whenever they need to do so.

5. These were the events which took place in Rome. In the same year war again broke out with the Cantabri and the Astures.[7] The Astures rose in revolt because of the luxurious habits and the cruelty practised by Carisius, and the Cantabri because they found that their neighbours had rebelled and because they despised their own governor, Gaius Furnius. This official had only recently arrived and they supposed that he was unfamiliar with local conditions. However, he made a different impression on them in action, for he defeated them and reduced them to slavery; then, coming to the aid of Carisius, he did the same to the Astures. Not many of the Cantabri were taken prisoner, for when they saw they had lost all hope of freedom, they lost all desire to preserve their lives either. Some set fire to their forts and cut their own throats, others willingly

remained with their companions and died in the flames, while others took poison in the sight of all. In this way the great majority and the fiercest among the tribesmen were wiped out. In the case of the Astures, once they had been driven off from the siege of a stronghold and had later been conquered in battle, they abandoned resistance and were quickly overcome.

At about the same time the Ethiopians, who inhabit a territory south of Egypt, advanced as far as the city named Elephantine[8]; they were led by their queen, Candace, and devastated the whole country as they went. However, when they reached the city and learned that Gaius Petronius, the governor of Egypt, was approaching, they withdrew, hoping that they could get away before he arrived. But they were overtaken by Petronius on the road and defeated, and so, falling back before him, they drew him on into their own territory. He proceeded to lead a successful campaign there and captured several cities, including their capital, Napata.[9] This place was razed to the ground and a garrison established elsewhere in the territory. Meanwhile Petronius had found that he could neither advance further on account of the sand and the heat, nor usefully maintain his whole army where it was, and so he retired, taking the greater part of his troops with him. At this the Ethiopians attacked the garrisons, but Petronius once more marched against them, relieved his own men, and compelled Candace to come to terms.

6.   While these events were in progress, Augustus visited Sicily to settle affairs in that island and in other territories, and travelled as far as Syria. While he was still there the people of Rome plunged into bitter strife concerning the election of the consuls. This episode made it clear that it was impossible for a democratic system of government to be carried on among them, for even though they possessed little power either in the electoral process or in the conduct of the offices of state, they fell to rioting. One of the consulships, it appears, was being reserved for Augustus, and so at the beginning of the year[10] Marcus Lollius alone took up the office. Then, when Augustus refused to assume the other consulship, Quintus Lepidus and Lucius Silvanus contested the election, and their rivalry created such a state of turmoil that those who kept their heads appealed to Augustus to come home. But he refused to move, and when the two candidates came to visit him, he reprimanded them, dismissed them and sent instructions that the vote should be taken while both men

were away. However, this failed to calm the situation, and the people remained as bitterly divided as ever, so that it was a long time before Lepidus was elected. Augustus was angry at these events, for neither could he devote all his time exclusively to Rome,[11] nor did he dare to leave the city without a head. He cast around for a man to put in charge of affairs, and considered Agrippa to be the best choice. As he wished to endow him with a prestige above the ordinary to help him govern the people more easily, he sent for him and obliged him to divorce his wife, even though she was Augustus's own niece, and to marry Julia.[12] Agrippa was at once despatched to Rome to proceed with the wedding and take control of the affairs of the capital. This solution is said to have been adopted partly on the advice of Maecenas, who, when he was deliberating with him on these problems, remarked, 'You have made him so powerful that he must either become your son-in-law, or be killed.' Agrippa then brought under control the various disorders which he found still festering, and in particular he curtailed the celebration of Egyptian rites,[13] which were again creeping into the city: he forbade anyone to practise these, even in the suburbs up to a radius of one mile. When a riot broke out over the election of the prefect of the city, the official elected on account of the national holiday, the Feriae,[14] he was unable to quell it, so that the citizens spent the year without this post being filled.

7.   While Agrippa was dealing with these problems, Augustus, after settling various matters in Sicily and establishing Roman colonies in Syracuse and certain other cities, crossed over to Greece. He paid honour to the Spartans by giving them the island of Cythera, and attending their mess-room. He did this because Livia, when she had fled from Italy[15] with her husband and son, had stayed in Sparta for some time. But he deprived the Athenians of Aegina and Eretria, from which they received tribute, because they had taken the side of Antony, according to some accounts, and besides this he forbade them to sell the status of a citizen for money. The Athenians believed that their misfortune was due to what had happened to the statue of Athena: this effigy, which stood on the Acropolis and had been sited so as to face the east, had turned round to the west, and blood had issued from its mouth.

After Augustus had despatched his business in Greece, he sailed to Samos, where he spent the winter. Then, in the spring of the year in which Marcus Appuleius and Publius Silius[16] took up the consulship, he proceeded to Asia and settled all outstanding matters there and in Bithynia. Although these provinces were considered to belong to the people, besides those mentioned earlier, Augustus did not neglect them for that reason, but supervised the affairs of all of them with the greatest care, as though they were his own. He introduced various reforms, in so far as these seemed appropriate, bestowed grants of money upon some, and imposed a surcharge, over and above the normal tribute, for others. He reduced the people of Cyzicus to slavery, because in the course of some local disturbance they had scourged and put to death some Roman citizens. When he arrived in Syria he dealt out the same punishment to the inhabitants of Tyre and Sidon, because of the disorders their quarrels had provoked.

8.   Meanwhile Phraates had become anxious that Augustus might lead an expedition against him, because he had not yet fulfilled any of the agreements concluded earlier with Rome. So he now returned the standards and all the prisoners of war,[17] except for a few who had taken their own lives out of shame, or else had managed to escape detection and had hidden in the country. Augustus received the standards and the prisoners as though he had defeated the Parthians in a campaign; he took great pride in the settlement, and declared that he had won back without striking a blow what had earlier been lost in battle. Indeed, he gave orders that sacrifices should be voted in honour of his success and that a temple for Mars Ultor, in which the standards were to be dedicated, should be built on the Capitol in imitation of that of Jupiter Feretrius,[18] and he himself carried out both decrees. Besides this he rode into the capital on horseback,[19] and was honoured with a triumphal arch. All these things were done later to commemorate the event. At the time of which we are now speaking he was chosen to be the commissioner for all the highways in the neighbourhood of Rome, and in this capacity he set up the so-called golden milestone.[20] The actual construction of the roads was supervised by officials whom he appointed from the ranks of the praetors, each attended by two lictors. In this year too Julia gave birth to a boy, who was named Gaius, and a permanent sacrifice was authorized, to take place each year on his birthday. This measure, like all the others mentioned above, was carried out in fulfilment of a decree. However, the aediles, on their own initiative, presented horse-racing contests in the Circus and a slaughter of wild beasts on Augustus's birthday.

9. These were the events which took place in the capital. Abroad Augustus governed in conformity with Roman custom those territories which were subject to direct rule, but he allowed the allied nations to manage their affairs according to their ancestral traditions. He was not in favour of adding any new territories to the former category, or of extending the latter by forming new alliances. He judged that the existing number was exactly sufficient, and he impressed this view upon the Senate in writing. Accordingly he did not embark on any campaign – at least for the time being – but actually handed over certain sovereignties. Thus he restored to Iamblichus,[21] the son of Iamblichus, his ancestral kingdom among the Arabians, and to Tarcondimotus,[22] the son of Tarcondimotus, the kingdom of Cilicia, which had been governed by his father, with the exception of a few districts on the coast. These last, together with the kingdom of Lesser Armenia, he handed over to Archelaus, because the Median prince who had previously ruled there had died. He transferred to Herod[23] the tetrarchy of one Zenodorus, and he restored to a certain Mithridates, although he was only a boy, the kingdom of Commagene, for the reason that its king had put the boy's father to death. Then, since the other Armenians had lodged accusations against Artaxes and had invited his brother Tigranes, who was in Rome, the emperor despatched Tiberius[24] to expel Artaxes from the kingdom and restore Tigranes.

In the event Tiberius achieved nothing that was worthy of the scale of his preparations, since the Armenians killed Artaxes before the Roman expedition could arrive. Still, he put on a lordly air, especially after sacrifices had been offered up to commemorate the event, as though he had accomplished something by martial prowess. Indeed, the prospect of imperial rule was already in his thoughts, since when he was approaching Philippi, sounds of a commotion were heard from the field of battle, as if they originated from an army, and fire blazed up of its own accord from the altars which Antony had built in the entrenched camp. And so Tiberius felt uplifted in spirit by these occurrences.

For his part Augustus returned to Samos and spent the winter there. He granted the islanders their freedom as a recompense for his stay and he dealt with not a few matters of business. Many delegations visited him, and the people of India, who had earlier announced their intention of seeking a treaty of friendship, now concluded it. Among other gifts they presented him with some tigers, which were then seen by the Romans for the first time, and likewise, I believe, by the Greeks. They also gave him a boy, who, as we see in the statues of Hermes, had neither shoulders nor arms. Yet in spite of being born with these defects, he could use his feet for every purpose as though they were hands; by this means he could draw a bow, shoot arrows and sound a trumpet. How he managed this, I do not know; I only state what was then reported. One of the Indians, named Zarmarus, wished for some reason to end his life. This may have been through ambition, since he belonged to their caste of wise men, or, in accordance with the traditional custom of the Indians, because of old age, or because he wished to make a public gesture for the benefit of Augustus and of the Athenians (for the emperor had by then arrived in Athens). At any rate he was initiated into the mysteries of the two goddesses[25] – which were specially celebrated out of their normal season, on account of Augustus's presence, so it is said – and the man then threw himself alive into the flames.

10.   The consul for that year was Gaius Sentius Saturninus,[26] but Augustus again declined to take up the office after it had been kept open for him. When it became necessary to select a colleague, the city was again divided by factions, disorders broke out and murders were committed, and so the senators decreed that a bodyguard should be appointed for Sentius. Then, when he refused to use it, they sent envoys to Augustus in Athens, each attended by two lictors. When the emperor learned of these events, he understood that the trouble might well continue indefinitely. Accordingly he did not apply the same solution as before, but appointed one of the envoys, Quintus Lucretius, to the consulship, even though this man had earlier been included in the list of the proscribed; then Augustus himself made haste to return to Rome.

For this action and for the other measures he had taken during his absence abroad, many honours of different kinds were voted for him. He declined to accept any of them, except the founding of an altar to Fortuna Redux, for this was the name they gave the goddess, and the decree that the day on which he had returned to Rome should be added to the public holidays, and be called Augustalia. Since even on this occasion the magistrates and the rest had prepared to go out to meet him, he entered the city by night. On the next day he conferred on Tiberius the rank of a former praetor, and permitted Drusus[27] to stand for the various offices of state five years before the normal age. And since the people behaved in a completely different way during his absence from Rome, when they quarrelled, and during his presence there, when they were cowed, he agreed to be elected at their invitation to the position of overseer of morals for five years. He also accepted the authority of censor for the same period, and that of consul for life,[28] to the extent that he even gained the right to be attended by twelve lictors at all times and places, and to sit in the curule chair between the two men who were then serving as consuls.

When they had voted these measures, they appealed to him to take the whole situation in hand, and to pass whatever laws he wished. The laws which were to be proposed by him they named Augustan laws from that date, and were anxious to take an oath that they would observe them. Augustus accepted all the other proposals as necessary, but released them from the obligation of taking an oath. He knew very well that whatever measure they might decree they would observe, if it conformed to their own convictions, even without taking an oath, while if it did not, they would disregard it even if they offered ten thousand pledges.

11.   Augustus, then, occupied himself with these matters. At this time, too, one of the aediles voluntarily resigned his office because of poverty. As for Agrippa, who had been sent from Sicily, as I have mentioned earlier,[29] as soon as he had dealt with the most pressing business in Rome, he was next posted to the provinces of Gaul. There the inhabitants were not only quarrelling among themselves, but were being harassed by the Germans. When he had restored these situations to order, he travelled to Spain.

In that province it appears that the Cantabri, who had been captured in the recent campaign and sold into slavery, had in every instance killed their masters, returned home and persuaded many of their compatriots to join their uprising. With the help of these they had seized a number of positions and fortified them, and were making plans to attack the Roman garrisons. Agrippa took the field against these rebels, but he also had to overcome some difficulties with his own troops. Not a few of them were well on in years and had been worn out by continuous active service; they feared that the Cantabri would prove a difficult enemy to subdue, and were unwilling to follow Agrippa's orders. However, partly by remonstrating with them, partly by encouraging them, and partly by giving them fresh hopes, he soon succeeded in winning their obedience. But in spite of this he suffered many reverses in his operations against the Cantabri. Not only had his opponents gained much practical experience

through having been enslaved by the Romans, but they had also abandoned any hope that their lives would be spared if they were captured.
However, in the end Agrippa prevailed. He lost many of his men, and
degraded many more because of the defeats they suffered: for example he
gave orders that the entire legion which had been known as the Augustan
should be deprived of its name. But he killed almost all of the enemy who
were of military age, disarmed the others, and compelled them to come
down from their fortresses and live in the plains. Yet he sent no report
concerning the Cantabri to the Senate, nor did he accept a triumph, even
though one was voted on Augustus's orders. He behaved with moderation
in these matters, as was his custom, and once, when he was asked by the
consul for his opinion concerning the latter's brother, he declined to give
it.

He provided the city at his own expense with the water supply which
is known as the Aqua Virgo, and gave it the name Augusta. This gave the
emperor so much pleasure that once, when there was a great shortage of
wine and the people complained bitterly, he declared that Agrippa had
taken the most effective steps to ensure that they should never die of thirst.

12. Such was the character of this man. Others laboured to secure
triumphs and celebrated them, not for feats of arms that could be compared to his, but merely for arresting outlaws or pacifying cities that
were at strife with one another. This was because Augustus, at least in his
early years, was lavish in awarding these marks of esteem, and honoured
a great many men with public funerals. But while these people added to
their fame through such distinctions, Agrippa, it might be said, was
advanced by Augustus to the supreme position. Augustus acted in the
knowledge that the public business demanded most careful attention,
and he feared that he himself, as often happens to men in his position,
might become the object of a plot. He often wore a breast-plate beneath
his tunic, even when he entered the Senate, but he believed that it would
only give him very slight protection.

Accordingly he first added five years to his term of office as *princeps*,
since his ten-year period was about to expire – this date fell during the
consulship of Publius and Gnaeus Lentulus[30] – and then he conferred
upon Agrippa a number of privileges which were almost equal to his
own, in particular the tribunician power for the same period. That number
of years would be sufficient for them, he declared at the time, but not

long after he added the other five years of his imperial power, so that the total number was once more ten.

13.   After attending to these matters, he again carried out a review of the Senate. He thought its numbers were too large, and he could see no merit in a multitude of senators. Besides this, he detested those who were notorious for some vice, but also those who called attention to themselves through their flattery. But, as on an earlier occasion,[31] nobody would volunteer to resign, while Augustus was unwilling to let the odium for the reform fall once more upon himself alone. He therefore personally selected the thirty best men, and later confirmed his action by an oath; he then ordered the thirty, after taking the same oath, to choose five men each, excluding relatives, and to write their names on tablets. Next he had the groups of five cast lots, so that the man in each group who drew the lot should become a senator himself and should write down five more names on the same plan. It was necessary, of course, that the first thirty chosen should be among the names which were being chosen by the second thirty and be included among those for whom lots were drawn. Some of those selected were absent from Rome, and in this case lots were drawn for others to replace them, and these men carried out the duties of the absentees. At first this procedure was followed for several days, as I have described. But later, after various malpractices developed, Augustus ceased to pass the lists of candidates to the quaestors, and abolished the selection of groups of five by lot. Instead, he himself made the selection and nominated the senators who were required to bring up the total to six hundred.

14.   He had originally envisaged a total of three hundred, which was the number elected in early times, and indeed he had expected that he would be quite satisfied if that number of men could be found who were truly worthy of membership. But in the event, all the senators alike were displeased with this plan. Because of the fact that those about to be struck off would far outnumber those who remained, the existing senators were more fearful of being returned to private life than hopeful of serving in the new Senate, and so in the end he enrolled six hundred. He did not stop even there, but instituted further changes. Certain men who were unsuitable turned out to have been admitted even under the new procedure. One Licinius Regulus was enraged because his name had been struck

off, while his son and several other candidates to whom he believed himself superior had been elected by lot; he tore open his clothing in the very chamber, stripped his body, listed the campaigns in which he had taken part and showed the assembly his scars. At the same time Articuleius Paetus, one of those selected to remain a senator, pleaded that he should withdraw and that his father, who had been rejected, should be reinstated in his place.

In consequence Augustus carried out a further review, removed some members and chose others to take their place. Even then a great many senators had lost their seats, and some of these, as often happens in such a case, blamed Augustus on the ground that they had been unjustly expelled. He therefore granted these men the right to attend public spectacles and celebrate festivals together with the full senators; they could also wear the same dress, and for the future he allowed them to stand for the various offices of state. The majority of these in due course returned to the Senate, but a few were left in an intermediate situation, where they found themselves regarded as belonging neither to the Senate nor the people.

15.   After these events many people were accused at the time, and many later, of plotting against both Augustus and Agrippa. The charges may be true or false, for it is impossible for those who remain outside such matters to obtain an accurate knowledge of them. Much of what a ruler does to punish men for alleged conspiracy against him, whether he takes action personally or through the Senate, is suspected to have been prompted by spite, however well justified it may have been. For this reason, I intend to record only what has been reported in all such cases, and not to be inquisitive or speculate about anything except obvious facts, beyond the published version, neither as to whether the action taken was just or unjust, nor whether the report was true or false. This statement of my intention is to be applied to everything I shall write hereafter.

At the time of which we are speaking Augustus had a few men executed. But in the case of Lepidus,[32] although he hated the man – amongst other reasons because his son had been discovered to be plotting against the emperor[33] and had been punished – yet he was reluctant to put the father to death; instead he continued from time to time to find various ways of humiliating him. For example, he would recall him to Rome, even when Lepidus was unwilling to leave his country estate,[34] and would always take him to meetings of the Senate to ensure that he should suffer the maximum of insults and derision, and to remind him of the loss of his power and position. In other respects, too, he treated Lepidus as unworthy of any consideration on his part, and when the Senate was in session called upon him last of all the former consuls to give his vote. It was Augustus's custom to use the regular order of precedence when he invited the other senators to vote, but in the case of the former consuls, he would call upon one first, another second and others third or fourth just as he thought fit, and the officiating consuls followed the same procedure. This was how he used to treat Lepidus. Then, when Antistius Labeo[35] wrote down the name of Lepidus as a candidate for the reconstituted Senate, at the time when the process of selection which I have described was being followed, Augustus first declared that Antistius had perjured[36] himself, and threatened to punish him. At this Labeo replied, 'And what harm have I done by keeping in the Senate a man whom you allow even now to be high priest?' At this Augustus restrained his anger, for although he had often been asked both privately and in public to assume the office of high priest himself, he did not consider it right to do so while Lepidus was still alive. This reply of Antistius was felt to have been most opportune, as was another remark which he made in the chamber, when it was proposed that the senators should take turns in guarding Augustus. Antistius did not dare to oppose the motion, but neither did he wish to support it, and so commented, 'As for me I snore, and so I cannot sleep by the door of his bedroom.'

16.   One of the laws which Augustus enacted laid it down that those who had resorted to bribery in order to obtain an office should be debarred from holding any for five years. He imposed heavier penalties upon unmarried men and women,[37] and on the other hand offered rewards for marriage and the procreation of children. And since the free-born population contained far more males than females, he allowed all those who so desired – with the exception of senators – to marry freedwomen, and directed that their offspring should be regarded as legitimate.

Meanwhile there was an outcry in the Senate concerning the unseemly behaviour both of the women and of the young men; this conduct was cited as a reason for their unwillingness to accept the marriage bond. When the senators urged Augustus to correct this abuse too, and hinted mockingly at his own relations with a large number of women, he began by replying that the essential prohibitions had already been laid down, and that it was impossible to regulate people's conduct further by bringing in more legislation of this kind. Then, when he was forced to reply, he retorted, 'You yourselves should guide and command your wives as you see fit; that is what I do with mine.' When they heard this, they pressed Augustus still more eagerly, since they desired to learn what guidance he professed to give to Livia. Augustus uttered a few words very unwillingly about women's dress, their other ornaments, their going out and their modesty; he appeared quite untroubled by the fact that his words by no means conformed to his actions. He gave another example of the same inconsistency when he was censor. Someone brought before him a young man who had taken to wife a married woman with whom he had previously committed adultery. The accuser laid many charges against the man, and Augustus was in a dilemma as to how he should act, since he did not dare to overlook the affair, nor yet to reprimand him.[38] In the end he recovered his composure with some difficulty, and remarked, 'The feuds which have divided us have brought terrible consequences; let us forget these and turn our minds to the future, so that nothing of this kind may occur again.'

At this time, too, some men were becoming betrothed to infant girls, and in this way enjoying the privileges to which married men were entitled, but without fulfilling their duties. Augustus made an order that no betrothal should be valid unless the man married within two years of giving his word. In other words, the girl must be at least ten years old at the time of the betrothal, if the man were to profit in any way from the engagement. This was because girls are considered, as I have mentioned, to have reached marriageable age on the completion of their twelfth year.

17.   Besides passing each of these laws, Augustus also turned his attention to the distribution of grain. He arranged that each of the serving magistrates should nominate one candidate, who must have served as praetor three years before, and from these nominees four men should be chosen by lot to serve successively as distributors of grain.[39] He also laid it down that one man should always be elected to fill the post of prefect of the city, who was chosen for the Feriae.[40] Besides this he directed that the Sibylline verses,[41] which had become indistinct in the course of time, should be copied from the books by the priests in their own handwriting, so that no one else should read them. He permitted all those who possessed

property to the value of 400,000 sesterces to hold office, provided that they were legally eligible to stand as candidates. This was the sum which he first laid down as the property qualification for the Senate, but later he raised this to 1,000,000 sesterces. To some of those who lived upright lives, but possessed less than the 400,000 at the earlier period, or 1,000,000 later, he presented the balance. For this reason he gave permission to those of the praetors who so desired to spend on the public festivals three times the amount authorized by the treasury. Because of this action – and because he gave leave to a dancer named Pylades who had been banished for sedition to return to Rome – even if some people were angered by the strictness of his other regulations, the majority forgot their grievances. In this context Pylades is said to have given an apt reply, when the emperor reprimanded him for having quarrelled with Bathyllus, a fellow-artist and a protégé of Maecenas: 'If the people spend their time upon us,' he said, 'it is you, Caesar, who are the gainer.'

18.   These were the events of that year. During the consulship of Gaius Furnius and Gaius Silanus,[42] Agrippa again acknowledged the birth of a son, who was named Lucius, and Augustus immediately adopted him together with his brother Gaius. He did not wait for them to attain manhood,[43] but straightaway appointed them as his successors in authority to discourage plotters from conspiring against him. He transferred the festivals of the deities Honor and Virtus so as to take place on the days which now belong to them, directed that those commanders who celebrated a triumph should erect out of the spoils a public monument to record their exploits, and held the fifth celebration of the Ludi Saeculares.[44] He also decreed that the advocates should give their services without pay, on pain of a fine of four times the fee they had received, and he forbade those who were periodically drawn by lot to serve as jurymen to enter any person's house during their year of service. Moreover, since the members of the Senate had become lax in their attendance at its sessions, he increased the fines imposed on those who arrived late, unless they had a good reason.

19.   In the following year during the consulship of Lucius Domitius[45] and Publius Scipio he left for Gaul, giving out that the fighting which had broken out in the province was the reason for his departure. The fact was that he had become unpopular with many people as a result of his

long stay in the capital; he was also making many enemies through the penalties he inflicted on those who broke any of his laws, and at the same time, by sparing many others, he was obliged to violate the very ordinances he had made himself; and so, rather in the manner of Solon,[46] he decided to distance himself from his country. There were some who even suspected that he left on account of Terentia, the wife of Maecenas, and that since Rome was full of rumours concerning their relationship, he had planned to join her abroad beyond the reach of such gossip. It was said that his desire for her was so great that he had once made her take part in a contest of beauty against Livia. Before leaving Rome, he dedicated the temple of Quirinus,[47] which he had rebuilt. I mention this because he had adorned the building with seventy-six columns, which was exactly the number of years of his lifetime, and this made some people put out the report that he had chosen the number intentionally and not by chance. At any rate he dedicated the temple at this time, and he also staged some gladiatorial combats. Tiberius and Drusus presented these on his behalf, after the Senate had given them permission.

He then placed Statilius Taurus[48] in charge of the affairs of the city and of the rest of Italy besides, for he had once more dispatched Agrippa to Syria, and he no longer treated Maecenas with as much favour as before on account of the latter's wife. Then he set out on his journey, taking Tiberius with him, even though the young man was then serving as a praetor. Tiberius, it seems, had taken up the office in spite of the fact that he already held the honorary rank; meanwhile a decree had been passed which enabled Drusus to perform the duties of the post.

The night after their departure the temple of Juventus was burned to the ground, and there were other portents at the same time. A wolf rushed into the Forum by the Sacred Way and killed several people; not far from the Forum a great swarm of ants was observed, and a flame in the form of a torch flared from the south to the north all through the night. On account of these signs prayers were offered up for Augustus's safe return. Meanwhile the four-yearly celebration of his sovereignty was held. This was carried out at the expense of Agrippa, who in his absence was represented by his fellow priests. He was one of the Quindecimviri, who were responsible in regular succession for conducting the festival.[49]

20.   That period was marked by a number of other disturbances.[50] Two Alpine tribes, the Camunni and the Vennii, took up arms against the

Romans, but they were defeated and the revolt quelled by Publius Silius. The Pannonians together with the Norici overran Istria: the former tribe were defeated by Silius and his subordinates, after which the Pannonians again came to terms and caused the Norici to be enslaved in similar fashion. The uprisings in Dalmatia and in Spain were quickly put down. Macedonia was ravaged by the Dentheleti and the Scordisci. In Thrace, Marcus Lollius had marched to the aid of Rhoemetalces, the uncle and guardian of the sons of Cotys, and had also subjugated the Bessi. Later Lucius Gaius,[51] also acting in support of Rhoemetalces, overcame the Sarmatians and drove them back across the Ister. However, the most important of the wars in which the Romans were involved at this time, and no doubt the one which persuaded Augustus to leave the capital, was the campaign against the Germans.

The Sugambri, Usipetes and Tencteri had first arrested a number of Romans in their own territory and crucified them; later they had crossed the Rhine and plundered Germany[52] and Gaul. When a force of Roman cavalry approached, they ambushed them; then in their pursuit of the fugitives they unexpectedly encountered Lollius, the governor of the province, and defeated him too. When Augustus learned the news he set out against them, but found no military task to engage him; for the barbarians, on discovering that Lollius was preparing an expedition and that Augustus was also taking the field, withdrew into their own territory, made peace and gave hostages.

21.. For these reasons Augustus did not need to resort to arms, but it took him the whole of the year in which he had left Rome, as well as the next in which Marcus Libo and Calpurnius Piso were consuls, to settle other problems in this region. For not only had the Gauls been caused great sufferings by the Germans: they had also endured many others through a certain Licinus. Of these I believe there had been a special warning in the form of a sea-monster. This creature, whose body was twenty feet broad and three times as long and resembled that of a woman, except for the shape of its head, had swum in from the ocean and become stranded on the shore.

Licinus was by birth a Gaul, had been captured by the Romans, become a slave of Julius Caesar's and later been freed by him, and finally been appointed procurator of Gaul by Augustus. This man, whose behaviour combined the greed of the barbarian with something of the dignity of the

Roman, tried to pull down anyone who was ever regarded as superior to him, and to eliminate everyone who for the time being showed strength. He provided himself with ample funds for the office to which he had been appointed, and also secured large sums for himself and for his friends. His unscrupulous methods went so far that in some cases where people had paid their taxes by the month he represented the months in the year as totalling fourteen; thus he claimed that December was really the tenth month, and that for this reason they must reckon two more (which he called the eleventh and twelfth respectively) as the last, and pay in the money that was due for these months. It was these sharp practices which endangered his position, for the Gauls managed to gain the ear of Augustus and protested strongly to him. When this happened the emperor shared their indignation in certain matters, while in others he was inclined to excuse Licinus. He said that he knew nothing of some of his alleged misdeeds and affected not to believe others, while some of his practices he actually concealed, out of a sense of shame at having employed such a procurator. For his part, Licinus thought up another scheme and ridiculed all his accusers. When he saw that he had aroused Augustus's anger and was likely to be punished, he took the emperor to his house. There he showed him large quantities of treasure in silver and gold, and many other precious objects piled up in heaps. He then told Augustus, 'All this I have brought together on purpose, master, for you and for the rest of the Romans, so as to prevent the native inhabitants, if they were in possession of so much money, from starting a rebellion. At any rate, I have kept all this for you, and now hand it over to you.' In this way Licinus saved his skin by pretending that he had weakened the resources of the barbarians in order to benefit Augustus.

22. In the meanwhile Drusus and Tiberius were engaged in the following operations. The Rhaetians, who inhabit a territory between Noricum and Gaul north of the Alps, which overlooks Tridentum and borders upon Italy, were overrunning a large area of Gaul to the west of their frontier and carrying off plunder even from Italy. They were also harassing any Roman citizens and allies of Rome who travelled through their country. These actions were familiar enough when committed by nations which had never accepted terms of peace from Rome. But the Rhaetians went further and killed all the males among their prisoners, not only those who had already come into the world, but even those who were still in

their mothers' wombs, whose sex they discovered by some process of divination.

Because of these outrages, then, Augustus first dispatched Drusus against them. He soon routed a body of Rhaetians which had advanced to meet him near the Tridentine mountains, and because of this success was granted the rank of praetor. Some while later, when the Rhaetians had been driven out of Italy but were still harassing Gaul, Augustus also sent out Tiberius. Both commanders then invaded Rhaetia from several directions simultaneously; they led the offensive both in person and through their subordinates, and Tiberius even sailed across the lake.[53] In this way by attacking in separate columns they struck terror into the enemy, and not only easily overcame all those they encountered from time to time in hand to hand combat – since the barbarians were fighting with scattered forces – but also captured the rest, who for this reason resisted less strongly and lost their martial spirit. Because this territory contained a large male population, which might well rise in revolt, the Romans deported most of the men of military age who were in their prime and left behind only enough to keep the country inhabited, but too few to launch an uprising.

23. In the same year Vedius Pollio died. This man had achieved nothing worthy of record, since he was born of a freedman, belonged to the equestrian order and had never performed any action of renown. He had, however, become very well known for two reasons, his wealth and his cruelty, so that he has even found a place in history. Most of his actions are too insignificant to report, but I may mention that he kept in tanks giant eels which had been trained to devour men, and he was in the habit of throwing to them those of his slaves whom he wished to put to death. Once, when he was entertaining Augustus, his cup-bearer broke a crystal goblet. Thereupon Pollio, paying no attention to his guest, ordered the slave to be thrown to the eels. The boy fell on his knees before Augustus and implored his protection, and the emperor at first tried to persuade Pollio not to commit so appalling an action. When Pollio paid no heed, Augustus said, 'Bring all your other drinking vessels like this one, or any others of value that you possess for me to use.' When these were brought, he ordered them to be smashed. Pollio was naturally vexed at the sight; but since he could no longer be angry about the one goblet in view of the multitude of others that had been destroyed, and could not punish his

servant for an act which Augustus had repeated, he restrained himself and said nothing. This is the kind of man that Pollio was; he died in that year, as I have mentioned.

He left many bequests to many people, and to Augustus he gave a large share of his estate, together with Pausilypon,[54] a stretch of land between Neapolis and Puteoli, with the instruction that some work of outstanding beauty should be erected for the people. On the pretext of putting up such a monument, Augustus had his house razed to the ground, but his real intention was that Pollio should have no monument in the city; instead he built a colonnade and had inscribed on it the name not of Pollio but of Livia.

These actions were taken later.[55] At the time we are now considering Augustus established colonies of Roman settlers in many cities in Gaul and in Spain, gave back their freedom to the people of Cyzicus,[56] made a grant of money to the Paphians, who had suffered an earthquake, and also passed a decree permitting them to name their city Augusta. I should explain that Augustus and the senators too aided many cities which had suffered disasters of this kind both before and after this occasion. Indeed if one mentioned every instance, the task of compiling such a record would be endless. But I mention this episode to show that the Senate actually allotted names to cities as a mark of honour, and that the inhabitants did not at that time follow the present custom of making out for themselves lists of names according to their own inclination.

24.   The next year[57] Marcus Licinius Crassus and Gnaeus Cornelius were the consuls. The curule aediles resigned their appointments because they had been elected under unfavourable auspices; later, however, at another meeting of the assembly they took them up, contrary to precedent.
The Basilica of Paullus was burned and the fire spread to the temple of Vesta, so that the sacred objects belonging to the latter were carried up the Palatine hill by the Vestal Virgins – except for the eldest who had become blind – and were placed in the house of the priest of Jupiter. The Basilica was later rebuilt, nominally by Aemilius, who belonged to the family of the man who had erected it in the first place, but in reality by Augustus and by some of Aemilius's friends.

At this time the Pannonians once more rose in rebellion and were subdued, and the region of the Maritime Alps, which is inhabited by a tribe of the Ligurians known as Comati, and which was still free, was reduced to slavery. Elsewhere the revolt of the tribes of the Cimmerian Bosporus[58] was put down. A certain Scribonius claimed to be the grandson of Mithridates and to have succeeded to the kingdom, after the death of Asander, with the approval of Augustus. He had married the wife of Asander who was named Dynamis. This woman was really the daughter of Pharnaces, the former king of Pontus, and the grand-daughter of Mithridates, and had been entrusted with the sovereignty of the province by her previous husband; hence Scribonius was holding the Cimmerian Bosporus under his control. When Agrippa had acquainted himself with the situation, he sent Polemon, the king of that part of Pontus which borders on Cappadocia, to invade the territory. Polemon found that Scribonius had already been killed, for the people of Bosporus, learning that Polemon was about to invade them, had put him to death. However, when they opposed his approach for fear that he might be given sovereignty over them, Polemon engaged them in battle.

But although he gained a victory, he did not succeed in subduing them until Agrippa arrived in Sinope to lead an expedition against them. Once they discovered this, they laid down their arms and surrendered to Polemon. Dynamis then married Polemon, when it was known that Augustus approved of the union. Sacrifices were offered in Agrippa's name on the occasion of these successes, but although a triumph was voted for him, this was not celebrated. In fact he did not even send a dispatch to the Senate to inform them of what had been accomplished, and thereafter other victorious generals, treating his action as a precedent, also abandoned the practice of sending reports to the public. Agrippa formally declined to celebrate the triumph which had been voted. This was why, as I understand it, no other generals of comparable rank were permitted to celebrate a triumph in future: they merely enjoyed the prestige of having triumphal honours voted.

25. All this time Augustus had been dealing with the multitude of problems which faced him in the various provinces of Gaul, Germany and Spain. He had spent large sums in certain districts and received large revenues from others, bestowed freedom and citizenship upon some communities and taken these privileges away in other cases. At length he left Drusus in Germany and himself returned to Rome during the consulship of Tiberius and Quintilius Varus.[59] It so happened that the

news of his approach was received in the city during those days when Cornelius Balbus[60] was mounting various spectacles to celebrate the dedication of the theatre which even to this day bears his name. Balbus accordingly began to put on airs, as though he himself was going to conduct Augustus back into the capital, although in fact he was unable even to enter his theatre except by boat on account of the floods caused by the Tiber, which had overflowed its banks. A meeting of the Senate had been summoned, and to honour Balbus for his construction of the theatre Tiberius called upon him first for his vote. The decrees which were passed included one to place an altar in the Senate-house itself to commemorate Augustus's return, and another to ensure that those who approached him as suppliants while he was within the city limits should not be punished.

However, Augustus did not accept either of these honours, and even avoided any encounter with the people on this occasion too, for he entered the city by night. This was almost always his custom, whenever he made a visit either to the suburbs or to anywhere else, both on his way out and on his return, so as to avoid inconveniencing the citizens. The next day he greeted the people on the Palatine, and then climbed the Capitol, took the laurel wreath from around the fasces and laid it upon the knees of Jupiter. He also arranged for baths and barbers to be placed at the disposal of the people for that day without charge.

After this he summoned the Senate. Because he was suffering from hoarseness, he did not address them himself, but handed his text to the quaestor to read. In this way he presented an account of what he had achieved, and announced regulations concerning the number of years the citizens should serve in the army and the sum of money they should receive on discharge, instead of the land which they were always demanding. The purpose of this declaration was that the soldiers, being henceforth enlisted on stated terms, would have no excuse, at least on this score, for mutinous behaviour. The term of service was twelve years for the Praetorian Guard and sixteen for the legions, and the bounty to be paid would be larger in some cases and smaller in others. These announcements did not inspire either rejoicing or anger among the soldiers, at least for the present, since they had neither obtained all that they wanted, nor yet been disappointed in every respect. For the rest of the population they seemed to hold out good hopes that they would not in future be robbed of their possessions through their land being given to the veterans.

26.   After this Augustus dedicated the theatre which had been named after Marcellus. During the festival which was held for this ceremony the boys of the patrician families, including Augustus's grandson Gaius, performed the equestrian exercise known as 'Troy',[61] and six hundred wild beasts brought from Africa were killed in the arena. To celebrate the birthday of Augustus, Iullus, the son of Mark Antony, who was a praetor, presented games in the Circus and a slaughter of wild beasts, and entertained both the emperor and the Senate in the Capitol; this was to fulfil a decree passed by the latter.

In the same year another revision of the Senate was carried out. Some while before, as we have seen, the property qualification for senators had been set at 400,000 sesterces, because many of them had been deprived of their ancestral estates through the civil wars. Then, as time passed and men acquired wealth, it was raised to 1,000,000 sesterces. The result was that nobody could any longer be found who was willing to become a senator. On the contrary, the sons and grandsons of senators, some of whom were genuinely poor, while others had been reduced to a lowly status through the misfortunes of their ancestors, not only declined to claim their senatorial rank, but even swore that they were ineligible when their names had already been included in the lists. For this reason at an earlier date, while Augustus was still abroad, a decree had been passed that the officials known as the Vigintiviri should be appointed from the knights. Accordingly none of the men who were potential candidates for the Senate was any longer enrolled without having previously held one of the offices which lead to senatorial rank.

These Vigintiviri (twenty men) are what is left of the original Vigintisexviri (twenty-six men). Three of the twenty are in charge of cases carrying the death penalty; three supervise the coinage; four are concerned with the streets of the city; and ten are appointed to the courts which are assigned by lot to the Centumviri (one hundred men). Of the remaining six posts, two dealt with the supervision of the roads outside the walls, and four were formerly sent to Campania; all these posts have been abolished. This decree was passed during Augustus's absence. There was also another which directed that since nobody was any longer willing to stand for the tribuneship, the posts should be filled through the appointment by lot of some of the former quaestors who had not yet reached the age of forty.

This time, however, Augustus himself reviewed the entire membership of the Senate. In the case of those who were over thirty-five he did not intervene, but those who were younger and possessed the necessary property qualification he compelled to become senators, unless any of them were disqualified on grounds of health. He examined their physical condition himself, but for the property qualification he accepted sworn statements: in such instances the men themselves took an oath which was witnessed by others and gave an account of their poverty and of their general mode of life.

27.   While Augustus paid this strict attention to public business, he did not neglect his private affairs. For example he reprimanded Tiberius, because at the festival which was supervised by the latter in compliance with a vow given for the emperor's return, he had seated Gaius at Augustus's side, and he showed his displeasure to the people because they honoured Gaius with applause and shouts of praise. When Lepidus died,[62] Augustus was appointed high priest and the Senate wished on this account to vote him other honours, but he replied that he would accept none of them; when the senators pressed him, he rose and left the chamber. The motion proposing additional honours, then, was not passed, and Augustus did not receive an official residence. However, as it was unavoidable that the high priest should live in a public residence, he made a part of his own house public property. He gave the house of the *rex sacrificulus*[63] to the Vestal Virgins because it shared a party wall with their own quarters.

The senator Cornelius Sisenna was censured for the conduct of his wife, whereupon he told the Senate that he had married her on the advice and with the knowledge of the emperor. Augustus was furious. He did not, it is true, permit himself any violent words or actions, but he hurried out of the Senate-house, and then returned a little later. He chose to behave in this way, as he explained to his friends, even though it was not the correct course to take, rather than remain in his seat and be driven to act in some way that would cause harm.

28.   Meanwhile he enlarged the powers of Agrippa, who had returned from Syria, by conferring tribunician authority upon him for a further five years. He then sent him to Pannonia,[64] which was on the brink of an uprising, and entrusted him with a greater measure of authority than officials outside Italy normally possessed. This was the year in which Marcus Valerius and Publius Sulpicius were the consuls, and Agrippa

embarked on his campaign even though winter had already begun. His approach struck terror into the Pannonians and they abandoned all their plans for rebellion. Agrippa therefore returned, but when he arrived in Campania he fell sick.

It so happened that Augustus was presenting some gladiatorial contests at the festival called Quinquatrus,[65] in the name of his sons, and as soon as he learned of Agrippa's illness he set out from Rome. But Agrippa was already dead when he arrived. Augustus conveyed the body to Rome and arranged for it to lie in state in the Forum. He also delivered the funeral speech over the dead man, after first having a curtain stretched in front of the body. Why he did this, I do not know. According to some accounts, it was because Augustus was high priest, while others say that it was because he was performing the duties of censor. However, both these explanations are incorrect, since the high priest is not forbidden to look upon a corpse and neither is the censor, except when he is about to finish the census; if he looks upon a corpse at that point, before his purification, then all his work must be repeated. Now Augustus not only made the arrangements I have described, but he also had Agrippa's funeral procession carried out in the same manner as was later used for his own: he buried Agrippa in his own tomb, although the latter had chosen one for himself in the Campus Martius.

29. So Agrippa ended his life. He had in general proved himself beyond doubt the noblest of all the men of his time, and he had treated Augustus's friendship in such a way as to bring the greatest benefit both to the emperor and to the state. The more he surpassed others in excellence, the more he willingly subordinated himself to Augustus, and while he applied all the wisdom and courage he possessed to furthering the interests of the emperor, he unsparingly devoted all the honour and power he received from him to ensure the well-being of others. It was for this reason in particular that he was never a cause of disquiet to Augustus, nor of envy to his fellow-citizens. On the contrary, he supported his friend in establishing the monarchy as though he himself were a champion of autocratic rule, and he won the hearts of the people through his benefactions as if he were an ardent supporter of popular government. At any rate at his death he left the gardens and the baths named after him for them to enjoy without charge, and for this purpose[66] he gave to Augustus some of his estates.

The emperor not only made these public property, but also distributed to the populace the sum of four hundred sesterces each and gave it out that Agrippa had requested this. Augustus was in fact left most of Agrippa's property, including the territory of the Chersonese on the Hellespont. I do not know how this land had come into Agrippa's possession. Augustus felt his loss for a long time, and for this reason caused his memory to be honoured among the people; he named the son whom Julia bore him after his death Agrippa.[67] However, even though none of the most prominent men wished to attend the public festivals at this time,[68] Augustus did not allow the people at large to neglect the traditional celebrations, and he personally supervised the gladiatorial combats, although many of these were held without his attendance. Agrippa's death was felt not only as a private bereavement for his family: it was regarded as so much of a public loss to the whole Roman people that portents were noticed at that time in such numbers as normally only occur when the greatest calamities threaten the state.

Thus many owls winged their way about the streets, and the house on the Alban Mount, where the consuls stay while the sacred ceremonies are performed at the Feriae Latinae, was struck by lightning. The star known as the comet[69] hung for several days over the capital, and finally dissolved into flashes of light resembling torches. Many buildings in the city were burned down, including the hut of Romulus: this was set on fire by flaming fragments of meat dropped on it after being snatched from some altar by crows. These were the events relating to Agrippa's death.

30.   After this Augustus was chosen as supervisor and reformer of morals for a further five years[70]; he assumed this office too for fixed periods, as he did the supreme power. He ordered the senators to burn incense in the chamber whenever a session took place, and not to make their accustomed visit to his house; his object here was that the senators should show reverence to the gods and that their meetings should take place without hindrance. Besides this, since very few candidates stood at that time for the office of tribune on account of the disappearance of its powers, he enacted a law which required the magistrates in office each to nominate one of the knights who possessed a property of not less than one million sesterces; from these candidates the people should then fill any vacancies in the tribunate, on the understanding that if these men wished to become

senators later, they should be entitled to do so; if not, to revert to equestrian rank.

When the province of Asia badly needed relief because of the earth-quake which had taken place there, Augustus presented to the treasury from his own funds a sum equivalent to the annual tribute, and he arranged for a period of two years that a governor should be appointed and not chosen by lot.[71]

On one occasion when a case of adultery was being tried in court, and Appuleius and Maecenas were being vilified, not because they had committed any misconduct themselves, but because they were giving strong support to the defendant, Augustus entered the court-room and seated himself in the praetor's chair. He did nothing to upset the procedure, but forbade the accuser to insult either his relatives or his friends, and then stood up and left the room. Because of this action and others, the senators honoured him by erecting statues which were paid for by private subscription, and also by giving bachelors and spinsters the right to watch public shows and attend banquets with other citizens on the emperor's birthday; neither of these concessions had been granted in the past.

31. Now that Agrippa was dead, a man whom Augustus loved for his virtue and not through any necessity, he felt the need for a right-hand man in the handling of public affairs, one who would be far superior to other colleagues in power and influence, and thus be enabled to deal with all business promptly and stand beyond the reach of envy and intrigue. With some reluctance he chose Tiberius, since at this date his own grandsons were still boys. Just as he had done with Agrippa, he first compelled Tiberius to divorce his wife, Vipsania, even though she was the daughter of Agrippa by another marriage, was bringing up one child and was shortly expecting another.[72] Then, after arranging for Julia to be betrothed to Tiberius, he despatched him to fight the Pannonians.

This people had remained at peace for a time because of their fear of Agrippa, but after his death they rose in rebellion. It was not until he had devastated much of their country and caused great suffering to the people that Tiberius finally overcame them; in his campaign he made all the use he could of his allies, the Scordisci, who were neighbours of the Pannonians and used similar weapons. He disarmed the rebels, sold most of the men of military age into slavery and deported them from their homeland. In recognition of these operations the Senate voted him a triumph; Augustus did not allow him to celebrate this with a procession, but awarded him triumphal honours instead.

32.   Drusus experienced a similar sequence of events. Because of Augustus's absence and the fact that the Gauls had become discontented at their subjection, the Sugambri and their allies had taken up arms against the Romans. Drusus managed to forestall their action. Using as a pretext the festival which they celebrate to this day around the altar of Augustus at Lugdunum, he summoned their leading men and seized the subject territory of the Gauls before the Sugambri could act. After this he waited for the latter to cross the Rhine, and then drove them back. Next he crossed the river, entered the territory of the Usipetes, passed along the island of the Batavi and from there marched southward parallel with the Rhine to the territory of the Sugambri, most of which he laid waste. He then sailed northward down the Rhine to the Ocean, secured the alliance of the Frisians, crossed the lake[73] and invaded the country of the Chauci. Here he found himself in great danger, as his ships were left stranded by the fall of the tide. On this occasion he was rescued by the Frisians, who had reinforced his expedition with their infantry, and made good his retreat, since by this time winter had set in. Although he already held the rank of praetor, on his return to Rome he was appointed *praetor urbanus*, Quintus Aelius and Paulus Fabius having just become consuls.[74]

33.   As soon as spring arrived, he set out once more for the war, crossed the Rhine and subdued the Usipetes. He built a bridge over the Lupia,[75] entered the territory of the Sugambri, and marched through it into the country of the Cherusci as far as the river Visurgis.[76] He was able to advance thus far because the Sugambri had fallen out with the Chatti, the only tribe of all their neighbours which had refused to fight on their side, and had mobilized their whole population to attack the latter; so Drusus, seizing his opportunity, passed through their territory unnoticed. He would have gone further and crossed the Visurgis, but was prevented both by his inability to obtain provisions and by the onset of winter. Besides this a swarm of bees had been seen in his camp. Drusus therefore halted his advance at this point, and withdrew to friendly territory, but he encountered some fearful dangers on the way. The enemy harassed him with ambushes throughout his march, and once they trapped him in a narrow pass and came near to overwhelming his army; indeed, they

would have annihilated it had not the tribesmen felt seized with contempt for the Romans, regarding them as already captured and only awaiting the finishing stroke; this led them to abandon their formation when they came to close quarters and brought about their defeat. After this reverse, they no longer showed so much confidence, but merely skirmished with the Romans from a distance and took care to come no closer. This emboldened Drusus to look down upon the enemy in his turn, and he built two fortresses against them, one at the junction of the rivers Lupia and Eliso,[77] and the other on the Rhine in the territory of the Chatti. For these achievements Drusus was awarded triumphal honours. These consisted of the right to enter the capital on horseback, and to assume the powers of a proconsul at the end of his term as praetor. Indeed, his soldiers had awarded him the title of Imperator by acclamation, as it had also been awarded to Tiberius at an earlier date. However, this distinction was not conferred upon Drusus by Augustus, although the emperor had himself received it on several occasions on account of the exploits of these two men.

34. While Drusus was engaged in these campaigns, the festival which fell due during his praetorship was celebrated at great expense, and Augustus's birthday was commemorated by the slaughter of wild beasts both in the Circus and in many other parts of the city. These celebrations were organized almost every year by one of the praetors then in office, even if it had not been required by a decree; the Augustalia, which are still commemorated to this day, were in that year celebrated for the first time in conformity with a decree.

In the same year Tiberius subdued the Dalmatians, who had risen in revolt,[78] and later he again conquered the Pannonians, who had likewise taken up arms, seizing their opportunity when he and the greater part of his army were absent from the province. He carried on a campaign against both tribes at once, switching the offensive from one front to the other. He was rewarded for his successes with the same honours as Drusus. After this Dalmatia was placed under the authority of Augustus; it was considered that armed forces would always need to be stationed there, to control not only the Dalmatians but their neighbours the Pannonians.

Such were the operations of these two generals. At the same period a Bessian from Thrace named Vologaesus, a priest of the god Dionysus who is worshipped by that tribe, attracted some supporters through the many prophecies he uttered, and led these people in an uprising. He defeated and killed Rhascyporis, the son of Cotys, and with the help of his supposed supernatural powers persuaded the forces of Rhoemetalces, the uncle of Rhascyporis, to come over to him without fighting and drove his opponent into flight. In pursuit of Rhoemetalces he invaded the Chersonese and devastated the territory.

In consequence of Vologaesus's successes and also of the raids carried out in Macedonia by the Scaletae, Lucius Piso was ordered to lead a force against them from Pamphylia, where he was governor. When the Bessi learned of his approach, they returned to their own territory, moving ahead of him. He proceeded to invade their country, and although he suffered an initial defeat, he overcame the Bessi and laid waste not only their lands but those of the neighbouring tribes, which had joined in the rebellion. In this campaign he subdued the whole region; some of the tribes willingly accepted his authority, others were frightened into reluctant surrender, others sued for peace after being defeated in battle, while others, when they rebelled at a later date, were again reduced to slavery. These achievements earned Piso thanksgivings and triumphal honours.

35. While these campaigns were in progress, Augustus carried out a census, during which he drew up a schedule of the whole of his own property like any private citizen, and he also compiled a roster of the Senate. He noticed that sometimes the attendance was very small, and so he directed that its decrees should be passed even if there were less than four hundred members present; up till then no decree was valid if it was passed by a smaller number.

When the Senate and the people once more subscribed money to commission statues of Augustus, he refused to have any statue of himself set up, but instead created statues of Salus Publica, Concordia and Pax. The citizens, it seems, made a practice on every possible occasion and on any pretext of collecting money for this purpose, but at last they ceased to pay it in privately as before, so to speak. Instead, they would come to him on the first day of the year and place their contribution in his hands, some giving more, some less. Augustus, after adding as much or more again from his own pocket, would repay it not only to the senators but to the rest of the populace. I have also heard the story that on one day of the year, in obedience to some oracle or dream, he would dress himself as a beggar and accept money from those who approached him. This at least is how the story has been handed down, if one can believe it.

In that year Augustus gave Julia in marriage to Tiberius. When his sister Octavia died, he arranged for her body to lie in state in the shrine of Julius Caesar, and on this occasion too a curtain was placed in front of the corpse. Augustus himself pronounced the funeral oration, while Drusus delivered one from the Rostra. Octavia's death was honoured by public mourning and the senators changed their dress. Her body was borne in the procession by her sons-in-law,[79] but Augustus did not accept all the honours voted for her.

36.   At this time too the priest of Jupiter was appointed for the first time since Merula,[80] and the quaestors were ordered to place each decree on record after its passage; this task, which had previously been entrusted to the tribunes and aediles, had been delegated to their assistants, and for this reason mistakes had been made and confusion had arisen.

A decree was also passed that the temple of Janus Geminus, which had been opened, should now be closed on the grounds that the wars had ceased. It was not closed, however, for the Dacians crossed the Ister on the ice and carried away plunder from Pannonia, while the Dalmatians rose in rebellion against the tribute which had been demanded from them. Tiberius was sent from Gaul, where he had travelled with Augustus, to take command against these tribes, and he recovered control of the territory. Meanwhile the Germans, especially the tribes of the Chatti, were in some cases harassed, in others reduced to submission by Drusus.[81] The Chatti, it seems, had quitted the lands the Romans had given them to live in, and had migrated to join the Sugambri. Later Tiberius and Drusus returned to Rome with Augustus, who had stayed in Lugdunum for most of this period to keep watch on the Germans from close at hand. These two took part in the ceremonies which had been voted in honour of their victories, and performed whatever duties were required of them.

BOOK 55

The following is contained in the Fifty-Fifth Book of Dio's *Rome*:

1.   The events described above took place during the consulship[1] of Iullus Antonius[2] and Fabius Maximus. In the following year Drusus became consul together with Titus Crispinus, and various portents which were by no means auspicious for the former were witnessed. Many buildings, some of them temples, were destroyed by storms and by thunderbolts, and even the temple of Jupiter Capitolinus and the gods who share it with him[3] suffered damage. However, Drusus disregarded these events. He proceeded to invade the lands of the Chatti, and pressed on as far as those of the Suebi. But he met strong resistance as he advanced, and it was only after heavy fighting that he overcame the tribes he encountered. From there he marched on to the territory of the Cherusci, crossed the river Visurgis and advanced as far as the Albis,[4] pillaging everything as he went.

The Albis rises in the Vandalic mountains[5] and flows out, by then a river of great breadth, into the northern ocean. Drusus set out to cross it, but failed in the attempt; he then set up trophies and retired. This was because a woman of superhuman stature met him and said, 'Whither are you bound in such haste, insatiable Drusus? It is not in your destiny to look upon all these lands. Take your leave now, for the end of your labours and of your life is already at hand.' It is a matter for amazement that a voice such as this should come to any man from the divine power, and yet I cannot disbelieve this account, for Drusus immediately left the place, and as he was returning with all speed, fell victim to some disease, and died before he reached the Rhine. And I find further support for the story in the following events. Just before his death wolves prowled around the camp howling; two youths were seen riding through the midst of the entrenchments; the sound of women uttering cries of lamentation was heard, and shooting stars appeared in the sky. So much for these happenings.

2.   Augustus received news that Drusus was sick when the disease was still in its early stages, for he was not far away, and sent Tiberius to him with all speed. Tiberius found him still breathing, and after his death conveyed the body to Rome. He had it carried by centurions and military tribunes on the first stage of the journey, as far as the Roman army's winter quarters; after that it was taken up by the leading men of each city *en route*. When the body had been laid out in state in the Forum, two funeral orations were pronounced over it. Tiberius delivered a eulogy in the Forum, Augustus one in the Circus Flaminius. The emperor, it must be noted, had been absent from Rome on a campaign, and he would have been bound to perform the customary ceremonies in honour of his achievements, if he came within the city limits.[6] The body was carried to the Campus Martius by the knights, both those who were only members of the equestrian order and those belonging to a senatorial family. It was then consigned to the flames and the ashes were laid in the tomb of Augustus. The title of Germanicus was conferred upon Drusus and his two sons, and he was further honoured by the erection of statues, an arch, and a cenotaph on the bank of the Rhine itself.

In the same year and while Drusus was still alive, Tiberius had conquered the Dalmatians and the Pannonians, who had once again risen in revolt. After this he had celebrated a minor triumph[7] and given banquets for the people, some on the Capitol and others in many different places. At the same time Livia, together with Julia, had given a banquet to the women of Rome. The same celebrations were being made ready for Drusus and even the Feriae were to be repeated on his account, so that his triumph could be celebrated during the national holiday, but his sudden death took place before these plans could be put into effect. As a consolation for Livia, statues of herself were voted and her name was inscribed upon the list of mothers who had borne three children.[8] There are a number of exceptional cases in which the law confers the privileges belonging to parents of three children upon men and women to whom the gods have not granted that number. This status was originally accorded through the authority of the Senate, but now through that of the emperor; those who enjoy it are exempt from the penalties imposed for childlessness and are entitled to all but a few of the rewards given to those who bear large families. Not only men but also gods may benefit from these privileges: the purpose is that if anyone bequeaths them a legacy they may accept it.

3.   So much for this topic. Meanwhile Augustus made an order that sessions of the Senate should be held on a specified day. It seems that in the past there had been no precise ordinance on this matter, and for this reason some members often failed to attend. Accordingly Augustus appointed two regular meetings in each month, at which attendance was obligatory, at least for those who were summoned by law, and to ensure that they might have no other pretext for absence, he directed that no court or other institution which required their presence should sit at that time. He also specified by law the number of senators required for the passing of decrees according to the various kinds of decree – to summarize the main heads of his regulation – and he increased the fines imposed on those who absented themselves from the sessions without good reason. Many lapses of this kind had customarily gone unpunished on account of the large numbers of the offenders, and so he directed that if there were many defaulters, they should draw lots and that one out of five, as the lot fell, should pay the fine.

He arranged that the names of all the senators should be inscribed on a white tablet[9] and posted up, and this practice which he initiated is still observed each year. These were the measures he enacted to enforce the senators' attendance. In the event of an emergency, he also provided for the contingency of a smaller attendance than the occasion required. For every session, except those at which the emperor himself was present, the number of senators in attendance was accurately checked, both in Augustus's time and later, for virtually every matter of business. If the attendance was below the legal minimum, the senators would proceed with their debate and the verdict would be recorded, but it would not take effect as it would have done if passed with the house at its proper strength. Instead, the decision would be termed *auctoritas*, the purpose of which was to declare the will of the house. That is the general force of this word; it is impossible to find a word in Greek which will have an equivalent meaning in every context.

The same practice was adopted if the Senate ever met in haste in any place other than the normal one, or on any day other than the one appointed, or without being legally convened, or in the event of a decree being blocked though the opposition of the tribunes – and the house none the less desired its opinion to be known. In that event, the verdict would later be ratified according to established precedent and would bear the name of a decree.[10] This practice, which had been strictly observed for a great many years in bygone times, has in a sense already passed out of use, in the same way as has the special prerogative of the praetors. They had been vexed by the fact that although they were senior in rank to the tribunes, they never introduced any proposal to the Senate. Augustus granted them the right to do so, but at a later date they were deprived of it.[11]

4.   Augustus arranged for these laws, and the others which he had passed at this time, to be written upon tablets and posted in the Senate before he introduced them for deliberation, and he allowed the senators to enter the chamber in twos and threes and read the texts, so that if they were dissatisfied with any clause or had anything better to propose, they could give their view. The following incidents will show how important he considered it to be to some extent democratic. Once, when a former comrade asked Augustus to help him present his case, he at first made out that he was busy and told one of his friends to speak on the man's behalf; however, when the applicant became angry and said, 'But whenever you needed my help, I did not send somebody else to act in my place, I came myself and faced the danger, wherever it was, for your sake,' then the

emperor came to the court-room and pleaded the man's case. On another occasion, when a friend of his was facing a charge, Augustus came to his support, after first declaring his intention to the Senate; yet although he saved his friend, he was by no means angry with the plaintiff. This man had put his case in a most outspoken fashion, but later on, when he appeared before Augustus, who in his capacity as censor was investigating the other's moral conduct, the emperor acquitted him and declared that frankness such as he had shown was indispensable for the Romans because of the baseness of the great majority. Nevertheless he punished others who were reported to be conspiring against him. He also directed that quaestors should serve in the coastal areas near Rome and in various other parts of Italy, and this practice remained in force for many years.

5.   At the time of which we are speaking,[12] he declined, as I have mentioned, to enter the city on account of Drusus's death, but in the following year, when Asinius Gallus and Gaius Marcius were consuls, he made his ceremonial entry, and contrary to the usual custom, he carried the laurel wreath into the temple of Jupiter Feretrius.[13] Augustus did not himself conduct any celebration in honour of the military successes of that year, since he felt that he had lost far more through Drusus's death than he had gained from his victories. However, the consuls supervised the ceremonies which normally take place on such occasions, and among others they presented gladiatorial combats between some of the prisoners of war. Later, when both they and the other officials were accused of having used bribery to procure their election, Augustus took no steps to investigate the charge, and indeed pretended to know nothing about it: he did not wish either to punish any of those involved, or to pardon them if they were convicted. However, in the case of candidates for the offices of state, he now demanded that they should pay a deposit before the elections, on pain of forfeiting this should they resort to any illicit practices. This regulation won the approval of all, but another of his measures provoked a very different response.

Since it was forbidden by law for a slave to be tortured to produce evidence against his master, Augustus directed that whenever such a need arose, the slave should be sold either to the state or to him, so that he could be examined as a witness who was no longer the property of the accused. Some people criticized this principle, arguing that the change of master would in effect cancel out the purpose of the law; others maintained that it was necessary, since because of this inconsistency in the law, many people were conspiring against the emperor himself and the officers of state.

6.   After these events Augustus, although he had laid down supreme power now that his second period of ten years had expired, once more consented to renew it, albeit with a show of reluctance, and he then launched an expedition against the Germans. He himself stayed behind in Roman territory, while Tiberius crossed the Rhine. All the barbarians were alarmed at this move and sent envoys to declare their peaceful intentions, except only the Sugambri. The others, however, gained no advantage either at that time or later, for Augustus refused to make a truce with them unless the Sugambri also took part. The Sugambri did indeed send a delegation, but they failed so completely to reach any settlement that every one of their envoys – and they were many and distinguished – lost their lives as well. Augustus arrested them and kept them in various cities, and this outcome disheartened them so deeply that they took their own lives. After this the Sugambri remained at peace for a time, but later they repaid the Romans in full for what they had suffered.

    Besides dealing with these matters Augustus distributed a bounty to the soldiers, not for having won a victory, although he himself had taken the title of Imperator and conferred it on Tiberius, but because in that year they had Gaius posted to them for the first time to take part in their exercises. Accordingly he promoted Tiberius to the position of commanding general in place of Drusus, and besides increasing his prestige with the title of Imperator, again appointed him consul; on this occasion too, he instructed him to observe the ancient practice of having a proclamation posted in public before taking up his office. He also granted Tiberius the honour of a triumph; he did not wish to celebrate one himself, but he accepted the tribute of having his birthday permanently commemorated by a horse-racing contest in the Circus Maximus. He extended the city limits and changed the name of the month which had hitherto been named Sextilis to August. The people wanted this name to be given to September, because he had been born in that month, but he preferred the other, because in it he had first been elected consul and had won many great battles.[14]

7.   In these measures and distinctions he took pride, but at the same time

he was deeply distressed at the death of Maecenas.[15] This man had rendered him many services, and it was for this reason that he had placed him in charge of the capital for a long time, even though he only held the rank of knight; above all, Maecenas had proved himself to be of the greatest value to Augustus when the latter's temper had been uncontrollable. On such occasions his friend could always dissolve his anger and return him to a calmer state of mind. I will give one example. Maecenas once arrived at a moment when Augustus was judging cases, and when he saw that the emperor was about to condemn many men to death, he tried to force his way through the bystanders and reach his side. When he found himself unable to get near, he wrote on a tablet the words, 'Now rise, at last, executioner!' and threw it, as if it concerned some different matter, into Augustus's lap. At this the emperor passed no death sentences, but rose to his feet and left.

Augustus was by no means offended at such actions, but even welcomed them, because whenever his natural disposition or the pressure of events led him to give way to some excess of anger, this was corrected by the candid advice of his friends.

The proof of Maecenas's goodness was nowhere more evident than in this fact, that he not only endeared himself to Augustus, even though he resisted the latter's most impulsive actions, but also won the affection of everyone else; moreover, although he wielded an influence with the emperor which enabled him to bestow offices and honours upon many men, yet he was never carried away by ambition and remained all his life a member of the equestrian order. And so Augustus felt his loss keenly, not only for the reasons I have mentioned, but because Maecenas, although he was unhappy at the emperor's intrigue with his wife, still made him his heir, and left him free to dispose of all his property with scarcely any reservations, to give to any of his friends, or not, as he saw fit.

Such was the character of Maecenas, and this was how he behaved towards Augustus. He was the first to build a heated swimming pool in the capital, and also the first to invent a series of short-hand symbols to achieve a faster rate of writing; he employed a freedman named Aquila to teach many people how to use this system.

8.   On the first day of the year in which Tiberius became consul together with Gnaeus Piso,[16] he summoned a meeting of the Senate in the Curia Octaviae,[17] because it was situated outside the city limits. He reserved for

himself the duty of repairing the temple of Concord, so that he could have his own name and that of Drusus inscribed there. Then he celebrated his triumph, and together with his mother dedicated the precinct which is known as the precinct of Livia.[18] He also entertained the Senate to a banquet on the Capitol, and Livia gave one for the women of Rome in another place.

A little later disorders broke out in the province of Germany, and Tiberius took the field. The festival which was held to mark the return of Augustus was supervised by Gaius in the absence of Tiberius, but with some help from Piso. The Campus of Agrippa, except for the portico and the Diribitorium, were presented to the state by Augustus himself. The Diribitorium[19] was the largest building ever erected under a single roof; now that the whole covering has been destroyed, the structure is wide open to the sky, since it was impossible to join the roof together again. It was still under construction in Agrippa's lifetime, and in this year it was completed. The portico in the Campus of Agrippa, which was being built by Polla, Agrippa's sister, who also embellished the race-course, was not yet finished.

Meanwhile gladiatorial combats to commemorate Agrippa's funeral were presented; all those who attended, except for Augustus, wore black clothing, and even Agrippa's sons did the same. The fights took place not only between single combatants, but also between opposing groups of equal numbers. They were held in the Saepta,[20] both in honour of Agrippa and also because many of the buildings surrounding the Forum had been burned down. The responsibility for the fire was attributed to those who were deeply in debt: it was believed that they had caused it deliberately in the hope that part of their debts might be remitted if they appeared to have suffered heavy losses. In the event these people gained nothing from the fire, but the streets of the city benefited, since they were henceforth supervised by officials chosen from the people, whom we call street commissioners. These men were entitled to wear official dress and to be attended by two lictors, but only on certain days and in those quarters of the city in which they held authority; they were put in charge of the corps of slaves, which had formerly been under the orders of the aediles, with the task of saving buildings which had caught fire. The aediles together with the praetors and the tribunes were still entrusted with the supervision of the whole city, which was divided into fourteen districts[21] assigned to these officials by lot. This system is still in force at the present time.

9.   These events all took place in that year; nothing that is worthy of mention happened in Germany during the same period. In the following year Gaius Antistius and Laelius Balbus served as consuls.[22] Augustus was displeased at this time, when he perceived that his grandsons Gaius and Lucius showed little inclination to model their behaviour on his own, as would have befitted youths who were being brought up as members of the imperial family. They not only lived in an excessively luxurious style, but also offended against decorum – for example Lucius on one occasion entered the theatre unattended. Virtually the whole population of Rome joined in flattering the two, some out of conviction, others merely to win favour, and in consequence the boys were becoming more and more spoiled; to give one example out of many, the people had elected Gaius consul before he had yet attained military age. These developments angered Augustus, and he even offered up a prayer that no emergency might arise, such as had actually befallen[23] him, which would require a man less than twenty years old to become consul. When the populace even then insisted on their choice, he declared that a man should not take up the office until he had become capable not only of avoiding error himself, but of withstanding the caprices of the people.

After this Augustus conferred a priesthood upon Gaius, and also the right to attend the meetings of the Senate, and to watch public spectacles and take part in banquets in the company of the senators. But as he also wished to give some [sharper warning to Gaius and Lucius to moderate their behaviour, he conferred tribunician power on Tiberius for a period of five years, and placed him in charge of the province of Armenia, which had shown hostility to Rome ever since the death of Tigranes.[24] But this action only caused needless offence both to Augustus's grandsons and to Tiberius: the former considered that they had been slighted and the latter was afraid of their resentment.

At any rate Tiberius set out for Rhodes on the pretext that he needed to inform himself before proceeding to Armenia, and he did not take even his whole retinue with him, let alone any friends; his object was to keep himself and his activities out of sight and mind of Gaius and Lucius. He travelled to Rhodes as a private citizen, although he used his authority to the extent of compelling the Parians to sell him the statue of Vesta with the object of placing it in the temple of Concord. When he reached Rhodes, however, he was careful to avoid any arrogant behaviour in word or action.

This is the truest explanation of his journey abroad, though there is a story that he travelled on account of the behaviour of his wife Julia, because he could no longer endure her company; at any rate he left her behind in Rome. Others say that he was indignant because he had not been named as Caesar,[25] and others again that Augustus had exiled him on the ground that he was plotting against the young men. However, it later became clear that he had not gone abroad either to gather information or because he was vexed at the decrees which had been passed. This was revealed by his subsequent actions and by the fact that at that time he immediately opened his will and read it out to his mother and to Augustus. At any rate every possible speculation was current concerning his behaviour.

In the following year Augustus served his twelfth consulship, and at this time he enrolled Gaius among the young men of military age.[26] He also introduced him into the Senate, designated him as *princeps iuventutis*,[27] and entrusted him with the command of a troop of cavalry . . .

A year later[28] Lucius also received the honours which had been bestowed upon his brother Gaius. On one occasion at this time, when the people had assembled and were pressing for certain reforms to be introduced and had sent the tribunes to Augustus to plead the case, the emperor came and discussed their demands with them. This action was welcomed by all.

10.   At this time Augustus restricted the total number of people who were entitled to be provided with free corn to 200,000: no limit had been set before. Some also say that he distributed a largesse of sixty denarii to each citizen.[29]

(How the Forum of Augustus was dedicated)

(How the temple of Mars in it was dedicated) . . .]

[In the preparations for the dedication of the new Forum and the temple of Mars, it was voted that] Augustus and his descendants should go there as often as they wished, while those who were leaving the age-group of boys and being enrolled among the youths of military age should on that occasion invariably present themselves there; that those who were being posted to commands abroad should ceremonially start from it; that the Senate should pass its decrees there in respect of the granting of triumphs; and that the victors, after celebrating these, should dedicate to this god Mars their sceptre and their crown; that those victors and all others who received triumphal honours should have their statues in bronze erected in this Forum; that if ever military standards captured by the enemy were recovered, they should be placed in the temple; that a festival should be celebrated beside the steps of the temple by the cavalry commanders of each year; that a nail should be driven into the wall of the temple[30] by the censors at the end of their term of office; and that even senators should have the right of contracting to supply the horses which were to compete in the associated horse-races, as well as taking general charge of the temple:[31] the same provision had been made by law in the case of the temples of Apollo and of Jupiter Capitolinus.

When these matters had been decided, Augustus dedicated this temple of Mars. Before this, however, he had conferred upon Gaius and Lucius once and for all the right to officiate at all similar consecrations of buildings, by virtue of a kind of consular power which they exercised according to established tradition. And indeed on this occasion they supervised the horse-races, while their brother Agrippa Postumus,[32] together with the boys of the leading families, took part in the equestrian exercise known as 'Troy'. Two hundred and sixty lions were killed in the arena. There was a gladiatorial contest in the Saepta, and a naval battle between 'Persians' and 'Athenians' was presented at the place where even today some relics of it are still on show.[33] These, of course, were the names given to the combatants, and on this occasion, as originally, the Athenians were the victors. Afterwards water was let into the Circus Flaminius, and thirty-six crocodiles were killed there. Augustus did not officiate as consul during the days when these celebrations were taking place: after holding office for only a short period, he transferred the title of consul to another man.

These were the ceremonies held in honour of Mars. A sacred contest was voted in honour of Augustus himself at the city of Naples in Campania. This event was proposed ostensibly because the emperor had restored the place when it was devastated by earthquake and fire, but in reality because its inhabitants, alone among the Campanians, aspired to emulate the customs of the Greeks. The Romans also formally conferred the title of Father upon the emperor: until then he had only been so addressed, without the title having been established by decree.

Augustus then for the first time appointed two prefects to command the Praetorian Guard, Quintus Ostorius Scapula and Publius Salvius Aper:

I call only these men 'prefect' out of all those who hold a similar office, since this has become the common usage.

In the same year Pylades, the dancer, presented a festival, although he did not give any of the performances himself, since he was by then very old: he merely wore the insignia of office and met the cost of the entertainment. The praetor Quintus Crispinus also presented a festival. I mention this event only because it was on this occasion that knights and women of distinction were introduced on to the stage. Augustus at first attached no importance to this. But when he discovered that his daughter Julia had so far abandoned any restraint in her conduct that she took part in revels and drinking parties by night in the Forum and even upon the Rostra,[34] he was filled with rage. Even before this he had suspected that she had not been leading a decorous life, but had refused to believe it. It seems that those who exercise supreme power know more about everything else than they do about their own affairs, and although their associates have the fullest knowledge of their superiors' actions, the latter possess no accurate information in return. So when Augustus learned what had been happening, he was overcome by a passion so violent that he could not keep the matter to himself, but actually spoke of it to the Senate. In consequence Julia was banished to the island of Pandateria. It lies off the coast of Campania, and her mother Scribonia accompanied her of her own accord. Of those who had committed adultery with her, Iullus Antonius [died together with other prominent men – on the ground that his action was part of a plot against the monarchy – while the rest were banished to islands. Among their number was a tribune; he was not tried until he had completed his term of office.

In consequence of this affair many other women were accused of similar conduct, but the emperor refused to act on all the charges. Instead, he named a specific date as a time limit, and forbade all further prying into what had happened earlier. In the case of his daughter he would not relent in any way, and declared that he would rather have been Phoebe's father than hers; still, he was inclined to spare the others. The Phoebe whom he mentioned, a freedwoman of Julia's, had been her accomplice, but had committed suicide of her own free will before she could be punished. This was why Augustus praised her ...

Gaius took charge of the legions on the Danube,[35] and his service there was peaceful. He took no part in any campaign, not because there was no fighting in progress, but because he was learning to hold command in conditions of quiet and safety, while any operations involving danger were undertaken by others ...

When the Armenians rose in revolt[36] and were joined by the Parthians, Augustus was distressed and was at a loss as to what he should do. He was too old for active service; Tiberius, as I mentioned earlier, had retired to Rhodes, and he did not dare to send any of the prominent men in Rome, while Gaius and Lucius were still young and inexperienced in affairs. At length, driven by sheer necessity, he chose Gaius, conferred proconsular powers on him, gave him a wife[37] so that he might enjoy the additional dignity possessed by a married man, and also appointed advisers for him. Gaius then set out, and was received by everyone with the honours due to the emperor's grandson, or was even by some regarded as his son. Even Tiberius visited Chios and paid his respects in an effort to clear himself of the suspicion of having plotted against him; indeed, he humbled himself to the extent of throwing himself at the feet not only of Gaius, but of his whole retinue ...

When the Asians received news of Gaius's expedition, Phrataces sent a delegation to Augustus to explain what had occurred and demanded the return of his brothers as a condition of peace being restored.[38] In reply Augustus sent him a letter addressed simply to Phrataces and without the designation of king. In it he told him to cease to use that title and to retire from Armenia. At this the Parthian was by no means overawed, but wrote back in a generally arrogant tone, referring to himself as King of Kings and to Augustus merely as Caesar. Tigranes did not immediately send envoys, but when Artabazus[39] later fell ill and died, he chose this moment, since his rival had been eliminated, to send gifts to Augustus, not using the title of king in his letter, and he did in fact solicit the kingdom from Augustus. The emperor took these facts into account, and since at this moment he feared the prospect of war with the Parthians, he accepted the gifts and instructed Tigranes to visit Gaius in Syria, hinting that he could hope for the best ...]

10A. [These people defied] others who marched against them from Egypt, and did not submit until a tribune from the Praetorian Guard was sent against them. This man in due course checked their incursions, with the consequence that for a long while no senator governed the cities of this region.[40]

At the same time as these events new disturbances broke out among the Germans. Some years before, Domitius,[41] while he was serving as governor of the regions bordering the Ister, had checked an incursion of the Hermunduri, a tribe which for some reason had migrated from its own lands and was wandering in search of others. He had settled them in a part of the territory of the Marcomanni, and after crossing the Elbe, where he met no opposition, he had formed a pact of friendship with the barbarians on the other side, and set up an altar to Augustus on the bank of the river. Later he had moved his headquarters to the Rhine. He was anxious to secure the return of a number of men who had been exiled by the Cherusci, but his efforts to negotiate this through other intermediaries had been defeated, and this failure had provoked a feeling of contempt for the Romans among the other barbarian tribes. This was the only enterprise, however, which Ahenobarbus attempted in that year, since the probability of a war against the Parthians meant that no expedition was launched against the Germans.

In the event no war took place against the Parthians either. Phrataces had learned that Gaius was in Syria with proconsular powers, and he also had misgivings concerning his own people, who even before this had shown that he could not count on their loyalty. He therefore anticipated any such defection by making an agreement with the Romans, on the understanding that he should renounce his claim to rule Armenia and that his brothers should remain across the sea in Rome. Nevertheless the Armenians went to war with Rome in spite of the fact that Tigranes[42] had meanwhile lost his life in a war against the barbarians, and Erato, the Armenian queen, had renounced her throne. They took up arms because they were being handed over to the rule of a Mede, one Ariobarzanes, who at an earlier date had approached the Romans in Syria together with Tiridates.[43]

These events took place in the following year, when Publius Vinicius and Publius Varus were consuls.[44] The Armenians accomplished no successes of any consequence against the Romans. But a certain Addon, who was holding the town of Artagira, persuaded Gaius to venture near the walls on the pretext that he would disclose to him secret intelligence concerning the Parthian king, and then contrived to wound him. The Romans thereupon besieged Addon, but he held out for a long time; when he was finally captured, not only Augustus but also Gaius assumed the title of Imperator. Augustus and the Senate handed over Armenia first to Ariobarzanes, and then when he died soon afterwards, to his son Artabazus.⁴⁵

Gaius fell sick as a result of his wound. Since he did not enjoy strong health in the first place, his general condition had already affected his mental activity, and this illness weakened his faculties still further. In the end he begged for leave to retire into private life, and it was his intention to settle somewhere in Syria. Augustus, although much distressed at the news, informed the Senate of the young man's wish, but urged him at least to return to Italy, and then do as he chose. So Gaius immediately resigned all his duties, sailed in a cargo vessel to Lycia, and there died in the town of Limyra. But even before this happened, the spark of Lucius's life had also been extinguished at Massilia.⁴⁶ Like Gaius he was also being trained for high office by being posted to many places on various missions, and he had made a practice of reading out the letters of Gaius personally in the Senate whenever he attended a session. He died of a sudden illness, and so suspicion fell upon Livia of having been involved in the deaths of both men, particularly because it was just at this time that Tiberius returned to Rome from Rhodes.

11. It seems that Tiberius possessed much experience of the art of divination by means of the stars, and had with him Thrasyllus, an expert in all aspects of astrology; he was thus very accurately informed as to what fate held in store both for himself and for Gaius and Lucius. The story goes that on one occasion in Rhodes he was minded to push Thrasyllus over the walls, because the latter was the only man who knew all Tiberius's thoughts; he did not follow up his intention when he noticed that the astrologer's features were gloomy, not indeed because his spirits were low, but because, when he was asked why his expression was melancholy, Thrasyllus replied that he had a premonition that some danger threatened him. Tiberius was greatly impressed that the other could foresee his intended action, [and so he determined to keep Thrasyllus for his own purposes because of his hopes for the future . . .

Thrasyllus possessed so clear a vision of all affairs that when he first caught sight in the distance of the ship which was bringing the message from Augustus and Livia inviting Tiberius to return to Rome, he foretold to his master what news it would deliver.

12. The bodies of Lucius and Gaius were brought to Rome by the

military tribunes and by the most prominent men of each city. Besides this, the golden shields and spears with which the young men had been presented by the equestrian order, when they had been enrolled in the class of military age, were set up in the Senate-house ...

On one occasion when Augustus was hailed as 'master' by the people he not only forbade anybody ever to use this designation for him, but also took steps to enforce this prohibition in every way. After the completion of his third ten-year period of office, he accepted supreme power for the fourth time, although to all appearances only under compulsion. Age had mellowed him and made him reluctant to antagonize the senators, and so he was now unwilling to risk a clash with any of them ...

He arranged an interest-free loan of 60,000,000 sesterces for three years to those who needed it, and for this action he was praised and revered by all ...

On another occasion when fire destroyed the palace and many people offered him large sums of money, he accepted nothing more than a gold piece from whole communities and a denarius from individuals. I use here the words 'gold piece' (*aureus*) for the coin which is worth 25 denarii. Some of the Greek writers, whose books we read in order to acquire a pure Attic style, have also given it this name.

When Augustus had rebuilt his house, he declared the whole of it to be public property; this decision may have been influenced either by the contributions made by the people, or by the fact that, as high priest, he wished to live in a residence that was at once public and private.

13.   The people pressed Augustus strongly to recall his daughter from exile, but he retorted that fire should sooner mix with water than that she should be allowed to return. Thereupon the people threw many firebrands into the Tiber; at the time this produced no effect upon the emperor, but later they urged him so insistently that she was at last brought from the island to the Italian mainland ...

At a later date when war had broken out with the Germans and Augustus had reached a state of exhaustion through old age and sickness and was incapable of campaigning, he was persuaded to make a change of plan, partly through force of circumstances and partly persuaded because of Julia, who had by then been recalled from exile.] Augustus then not only adopted Tiberius, but also sent him out to take command against the Germans[47] and conferred upon him tribunician power for ten years.

However, since he suspected that Tiberius's judgement might somehow desert him and feared that he might make a bid for power, he obliged him to adopt his nephew Germanicus, even though Tiberius had a son of his own. After taking these decisions, the feeling that he now possessed successors and supporters gave him fresh heart, and he reviewed once again the composition of the Senate. He nominated the ten senators whom he held in the highest regard, and after three had been selected by lot, he appointed these to examine the qualifications of the senators. However, in the event there were not many who judged it best to declare themselves disqualified when they were given leave to do so, as on the previous occasion,[48] or whose names were struck off against their will.

Augustus performed this review with the help of others, but he himself carried out a census. However, this only affected those inhabitants of Italy who possessed property worth at least 200,000 sesterces. He did not include the poorer citizens, nor those living outside Italy, since he feared that if they were provoked by this measure, they might rise in rebellion. He did not wish to appear to be wielding the powers of the censor, for the reason I have given before,[49] and so he assumed the authority of the proconsul for the purpose of completing the census and carrying out the purification ceremony.

At this time many of the young men both of the senatorial class and of the equestrian order had become poor through no fault of their own. Augustus gave most of them the sum needed for the property qualification, and for some eighty men he increased it to 1,200,000 sesterces.

Also, since many people were using little judgement in granting freedom to their slaves, he laid down an age which both the master and the slave to be freed must have reached, and also the legal considerations which should be applied to the relations towards freedmen, both of citizens in general and of their former masters.[50]

14.   While Augustus was dealing with these problems, various men took part in conspiracies against him, in particular Gnaeus Cornelius,[51] a son of the daughter of Pompey the Great. For a time Augustus found himself caught in a serious dilemma: he was unwilling to put the conspirators to death, since he recognized that their execution would contribute nothing to his safety, or to let them go, in case this should encourage others to plot against him. While he was at a loss as to what to do and could find no respite from his anxieties by day or from his fears by night, Livia one day

asked him, 'What is it that troubles you, husband? Why do you not sleep?'

Augustus replied, 'What man can rid himself of his cares even for a moment when he is beset at all times by so many enemies and is continually the object of plots by one group or another? Can you not see how many there are who never cease to contrive against me and our sovereignty? And nothing restrains these men – not even the punishment of those who are brought to justice; on the contrary, the rest work all the harder to destroy themselves, as if they were striving after some ideal.'

When Livia heard this, she said, 'There is nothing extraordinary or contrary to human nature in the fact that you should be the object of conspiracies. Since you possess an empire of such a size, many of the actions you take create grievances for large numbers of people. It is impossible, of course, for a ruler to please everybody, and even the most upright of kings cannot avoid antagonizing many people. The truth is that those who wish to do wrong are far more numerous than those who do right, and it is impossible to satisfy the desires of the former. Even among those who possess a certain degree of virtue, some hanker after many great rewards which are beyond their reach, and some feel aggrieved because they receive fewer honours than others, and so both blame the ruler. The result is that it is impossible to escape harm either at the hands of men such as these or, apart from them, of the others who are opposed not to you personally but to the monarchy. If you were a private citizen, nobody would willingly have done you injury, unless he had suffered some wrong, but all men long for the position of ruler and for the privileges it affords, and those who are already in a position of some power are far more covetous than those who enjoy none. It is typical of men who possess no principles and little intelligence to behave in this way; this attitude indeed is ingrained in their nature like any other instinct, and it is impossible either by persuasion or by force to root out such a bent in some of them, for there is no law and no fear stronger than those instincts which are implanted by nature. Bear this in mind, then, and do not let the shortcomings of others disturb you, but rather take every precaution to guard your own person and your supremacy. We should keep a sure hold upon our throne not through the severity of the punishments you inflict upon individuals, but through the strictness of the measures by which you protect it.'

15.   Augustus told her, 'Yes, I know very well that no position of great

authority is ever immune from envy and intrigue, and least of all a monarchy. If we were not subject to troubles and anxieties which are above the heads of all those in private life, we should be the equals of the gods. But this is exactly the cause of my distress – that the situation is inevitable and that it is impossible for any remedy to be found.'

'In that case,' said Livia, 'since the character of some men is such that they are set upon doing wrong in any event, let us protect ourselves against them. We have many soldiers to defend us: some are deployed against foreign enemies, others are posted around your person, and we have a large retinue besides. With all these we should be able to live in security, at home and abroad.'

'There is no need for me to tell you,' Augustus replied, 'that many men have lost their lives at the hands of those who were closest to them. The truth is that monarchies suffer from this especial weakness in addition to the rest, that we have to fear not only our enemies like other men, but also our friends. Far more rulers have been the victims of plots contrived by their intimates than by people who have no connection with them at all. This is because a ruler's friends are in his company day and night, when he exercises, when he sleeps, and when he takes the food and drink they have prepared. The ruler is vulnerable in this peculiar sense: I mean that although he can rally his friends against his known enemies, there is no other ally he can call upon to protect him against his friends. And so we rulers are for ever faced with the fact that while solitude is to be dreaded, so too is company; that while it is frightening to be unprotected, the men who protect us are still more frightening, and that while our enemies create difficulties for us, our friends create even more. I use the word friends, for this is what they must all be called, even if they are not really so. And even if one were to find genuine friends, it would still be impossible to trust them so unreservedly that one could mingle with them at all times with a clear, carefree and unsuspecting heart. These factors, then, and the necessity of ensuring our protection against the other kind of conspirator, create for us a life which is truly appalling. For to labour at all times under the necessity of taking vengeance and inflicting punishments is a very painful position, at least for any honourable man to be in.'

16. 'You are quite right, of course,' Livia told him, 'and I have a piece of advice to offer you – that is if you are willing to accept it and will not

blame me for daring, although a woman, to make a suggestion which nobody else, even of your closest friends, would venture to put forward. This is not because they do not know of it, but because they are not bold enough to speak out.'

'Tell me then,' replied Augustus, 'whatever it is.'

'I will tell you,' answered Livia, 'without hesitation. This is because I have an equal share in whatever happens to you, good or bad: so long as you are safe, I also take my part in reigning, while if you come to any harm, which heaven forbid, that is the end of me too.

'Let us suppose, then, that human nature impels some people to do wrong under any circumstances, and that it is impossible to restrain this impulse once a man has chosen a certain course of action. Suppose again that qualities which some men regard as estimable – I am not speaking here of the vices of the majority – in effect lead them into wrongdoing: for example, the boasting that springs from noble birth or wealth, the high-handed behaviour that is generated by honours received, the arrogance that is bred from courage, the insolence that arises from power, all of which bring many men to grief. Let us grant too that it is impossible to transform the noble disposition into the ignoble, the brave into the cowardly, the prudent into the foolish, and again that one ought not to cut down the wealth of others, or put down their ambitions so long as they are guilty of no offence, for that would be unjust; and suppose lastly that the practice of defending oneself and trying to forestall attack inevitably provokes others and harms our reputation. If all this is the case, well then, let us try a different policy and spare the conspirators. I believe that far more wrongs are put right by kindness than by harshness. Those who forgive are loved not only by those to whom they have shown mercy – and these men will even strive to return the kindness – but they are also respected and revered by all the rest, who will not lightly venture to harm them. On the other hand those who are relentless in their anger are not only hated by the men who have something to fear, but all the rest likewise feel animosity against them and so fall to plotting, if only in self-defence to forestall their own destruction.

17. 'Do you not notice that physicians only very rarely resort to surgery and cautery? This is because they are anxious not to exacerbate their patients' ailments, and most often seek to relieve the malady by applying fomentations and the milder drugs. And do not imagine that just because

afflictions of this kind affect the body, whereas those that concern us affect the soul, there is any difference between them. The truth is that there are many ailments which affect both men's minds – however disembodied they may be – and their bodies, and that these often possess elements in common. Thus the mind may experience a sense of contraction through fear, and of excessive swelling through passion: pain may on occasion make it seem to shrivel up, and arrogance make it grow with conceit.

'And so, since the divergence of experience between minds and bodies is comparatively small, they require treatment of a similar kind. Thus a mild speech, for example, may completely mollify a man who is beside himself with rage, just as a harsh word will rouse to fury another who has been thoroughly composed, while the granting of forgiveness will cause the most arrogant temper to melt, just as punishment will incense the most easy-going of men. Acts of violence, however strongly justified, will always provoke men, while considerate treatment will calm them. This is why a man will find it easier to endure the most painful hardships – and willingly too – if he has been persuaded rather than placed under duress. In fact each of these patterns of behaviour follows a compelling law of nature; thus we see that even among the irrational animals, which possess no intelligence, many of the strongest and fiercest are tamed by petting and brought to heel by allurements, while many even of the weakest and most cowardly are provoked to fury by acts of cruelty which inspire fear in them.

18.   'I do not mean by this that we should spare all wrongdoers indiscriminately, but that we must cut off the headstrong man, the intriguer, the doer of malice, and troublemaker, and the man who possesses an incurably and consistently vicious disposition, just as we treat those members of the body which are infected to a degree which defies healing. As for the rest, whose offences whether wilfully committed or otherwise are due to youth, or ignorance, or misapprehension, or some other combination of chances, we should in some instances merely admonish them with words, in others make them see reason by means of threats, and in others again employ some other moderate method of correction. Here the situation is similar to that of slaves, who commit offences of varying degrees of seriousness to which all men respond by dealing out lighter penalties to some and heavier to others. Accordingly, as far as these political offenders are concerned, you will not be risking anything if you treat them leniently.

Some may be sentenced to exile, others to disfranchisement, others to a fine, others to detention in the country and others in certain cities.

'Some men have even been brought to see reason through failing to obtain what they had hoped for, and being disappointed in their ambitions. Many have actually benefited by being placed elsewhere than in the seats of honour in the public theatres, or being assigned to a post which is humiliating because of its mediocrity, or again by being mortified or intimidated in advance; and yet a man of noble birth and high spirit would rather die than suffer such dishonour. Measures such as these would make it more difficult rather than easy for men to obtain their revenge, while for our part we would escape reproach and live in security.

'In the present situation it is believed that we kill many people out of anger, many others out of greed for their money, others through fear of their courage, and others actually through envy of their virtue. Nobody can easily credit that a ruler who possesses such great authority and power can be plotted against by a private citizen who is unarmed.

'And so some people invent stories of the kind I have mentioned, others spread the notion that many false accusations reach us and that we give credit to many unfounded rumours as if they were true. Spies and eavesdroppers are said to collect such fabrications, sometimes out of personal dislike, sometimes out of resentment, or because they have been bribed by their victims' enemies, or been refused money by the victims themselves. At any rate they concoct many falsehoods, alleging that certain persons have committed some outrage or intend to commit it, or even that when so-and-so uttered such and such words, another heard them and said nothing, a second one laughed, and a third burst into tears.

19. 'I could give you endless examples of this kind, but regardless of how true they may be, these are not matters in which free men should involve themselves, or which should be reported to you.

'You would lose nothing by ignoring such rumours, but if you listened to them they would arouse your anger even against your will, and that is a situation especially to be avoided, above all for one who rules over others. At any rate it is widely believed that because feelings of this kind are aroused, many men are unjustly put to death, some without a trial at all, others through a conviction fabricated by the court. Public opinion does not regard the statements of witnesses, or the depositions extracted under torture, or any other evidence of that kind as providing sufficient proof to condemn the victims. But these are the kind of reports which, even if sometimes unfair, are nevertheless current concerning virtually all those who are put to death in this way. And you, Augustus, must not only avoid committing any injustice, but even appearing to commit any. For although it is enough for a person in private life to keep himself innocent of any offences, it is the duty of a ruler to keep himself clear even of the least suspicion of one. It is human beings, not wild beasts whom you govern, and you will only make them truly well disposed towards you if you can convince them by every means and on every occasion consistently that you will wrong no man, either deliberately or unwittingly. A man can be compelled to fear another, but he ought to be persuaded to love him; and he is persuaded not only by the kindness with which he himself is treated, but also by the benevolence he sees extended to others.

'On the other hand the man who suspects that someone has been put to death unjustly not only fears that he may one day suffer a similar fate: he is also compelled to hate the perpetrator of the deed. To be hated by one's subjects, besides having nothing to recommend it in itself, is also thoroughly unprofitable. Men in general, it is felt, are obliged to defend themselves against all those who wrong them in any way, or else let themselves be despised and so become the prey of others, but rulers should prosecute only those who wrong the state, and should tolerate the existence of those who are alleged to be harming them as private persons. Rulers, so the argument runs, cannot be harmed by insult or direct attack, since there are so many agencies which protect them from both eventualities.

20.   'So when I hear such arguments and reflect upon them, I would urge you to cease to inflict the death penalty upon anyone for reasons of this kind. The position of ruler has been created to ensure the safety of those he rules – to protect them against injury either from one another or at the hands of foreign peoples – but certainly not for rulers to cause harm to their subjects; the most glorious of their achievements is not to put large numbers of citizens to death, but to extend that safety to all, if this is possible.

'We must educate the citizens by means of laws and benefits and warnings to ensure that they act with moderation; besides this we must be vigilant and take due precautions, so that even if they wish to cause harm, they should not have the power to do so. If any sign of disease shows itself in the body politic, we must find some way to treat it and restore it to health, to prevent the ailing member from being completely destroyed. To tolerate the offences of the great mass of citizens is a task which demands great prudence and great power, but if anyone were to punish them all indiscriminately as they deserve, he would destroy before he knew it the greater part of mankind.

'For these reasons, then, I give you my opinion that you should not inflict the death penalty upon anyone for offences of this kind, but find some other means of correcting their behaviour so that they will not commit any crime in future. What offence in any case could a man commit if he is confined to an island, or in the country, or in some city, and is not only deprived of a retinue of servants and of his money but is living under guard, if these restrictions prove to be necessary? Of course if there were nations hostile to us anywhere near, or if some part of our sea belonged to a foreign power, so that one or other of the prisoners might escape to them and do us some harm, or if there were strong cities in Italy possessing fortifications and armed forces which would enable a man who seized them to threaten our position, this would be a different matter. But in fact all the cities in this country are unarmed and possess no fortifications of any military value, and our enemies live at an immense distance from them: great tracts of sea and of land including mountains and rivers which are difficult to cross lie between them and us. What is there to fear, then, from this man or that, defenceless individuals in private positions, who live in the middle of your empire surrounded by your armed forces? For my part I do not believe that anyone could devise a plot in such circumstances, or if he were so mad as to make the attempt, that he could achieve anything by it.

21.   'Let us therefore try the experiment, beginning with these very men who are now accused. Perhaps they may not only change their own way of life, but also influence others for the better. You see, for example, that Gnaeus Cornelius, besides being a man of noble family, is well known in public life, and we ought surely to take human nature into account. The sword will not achieve all your purposes. It would be a great blessing if it served to make men see reason and to persuade or even compel them to love a ruler with genuine affection. But in practice, as it destroys the body of one man, so it will alienate the minds of the rest. The vengeance which people see carried out upon others does not bring them closer to anyone: instead it turns them into enemies because of their fears. That is

the effect produced by punishment. Those who receive forgiveness, on the other hand, not only repent – because they are ashamed to wrong their benefactors once again – but also repay them with many services, since they hope to receive still more kind treatment. For when a man has been rescued by one he has wronged, he believes that if he treats his saviour well, the latter's generosity will know no limit.

'Let yourself be convinced, then, dearest husband, and change your course. If you do, all your other actions which have made you unpopular will be believed to have been forced upon you, for it is in fact impossible for a man to guide a city as great as Rome from democracy to monarchy and accomplish such a change without bloodshed. But if you persist in the same course, you will be believed to have carried out these harsh measures deliberately.'

22.   Augustus took these words of Livia's to heart, and after giving the accused a warning, he released all of them, and even appointed Cornelius consul. Through these actions he succeeded so well in winning over this man and the others that none of them ever plotted against him later or was suspected of doing so. It was Livia herself who after having been instrumental in saving the life of Cornelius was subsequently to be accused of plotting the death of Augustus.

At this date when Gnaeus Cornelius and Valerius Messalla were consuls,[52] severe earthquakes took place, the waters of the Tiber rose and swept away the bridge, and the city became navigable for seven days. There was also a partial eclipse of the sun and the people suffered famine. In the same year Agrippa Postumus was enrolled among the youths of military age,[53] but was not granted any of the same privileges as his brothers. The senators watched the Circensian Games separately, and the knights were also separated from the rest of the populace, as is the custom at the present day.[54]

Since the most highly born families showed themselves reluctant to let their daughters enter the order of priestesses of Vesta, a law was passed allowing daughters of freedmen to become eligible. A large number presented themselves for this honour, and so lots were drawn in the Senate in the presence of the girls' fathers, if these were knights. But in the event no priestess was appointed from this class.

23.   The soldiers were greatly disappointed at the meagre sums which

were given them for their bounty for the wars which had been fought at that time, and none of them volunteered to bear arms for any period longer than the specified term of service. It was therefore decreed that 20,000 sesterces should be given to soldiers of the Praetorian Guard at the end of sixteen years' service, and 12,000 to the other soldiers when they had served for twenty. Twenty-three or, as others say, twenty-five legions recruited from the citizen body were then being maintained.[55] At present only nineteen remain, and these are as follows.

The Second, Augusta, with its winter quarters in Upper Britain; the three Thirds, the Gallica in Phoenicia, the Cyrenaica in Arabia, and the Augusta in Numidia; the Fourth, Scythica, in Syria; the Fifth, Macedonica, in Dacia; the two Sixths, one known as Victrix stationed in Lower Britain, the other, Ferrata, in Judaea; the Seventh, generally called Claudia, in Upper Moesia; the Eighth, Augusta, in Upper Germany; the two Tenths, one, Gemina, in upper Pannonia, and the other in Judaea; the Eleventh, Claudia, in Lower Moesia. I should explain that two legions were named after Claudius because they had not fought against the emperor in the rebellion led by Furius Camillus Scribonianus;[56] the Twelfth, Fulminata, in Cappadocia; the Thirteenth, Gemina, in Dacia; the Fourteenth, Gemina, in Upper Pannonia; the Fifteenth, in Cappadocia; the Twentieth, called both Valeria and Victrix, in Upper Britain. All these I believe, were the troops which Augustus took over and kept, together with the legion known as the Twenty-Second, which is quartered in Germany.[57] The legion I have entitled Valeria is not given this name by all, and in fact no longer uses that designation. At any rate these are the legions which are still in service today, out of those maintained by Augustus. Of the rest, some were disbanded altogether, others were amalgamated with other legions by Augustus himself and by later emperors, and this is how legions in that category have come to bear the name Gemina.

24. Now that I have once been led into providing an account of the legions, I shall also mention the others which exist today and describe how they were entitled by Augustus's successors. My object in doing this is that if anyone wishes to learn about them, he can easily find all the facts assembled in a single section of my book. Nero established the First legion, named Italica, which has its winter quarters in Lower Moesia; Galba the First, Adiutrix, with quarters in Lower Pannonia, and the Seventh, Gemina, in Spain; Vespasian the Second, Adiutrix, in Lower Pannonia,

the Fourth, Flavia, in Upper Moesia, and the Sixteenth, Flavia, in Syria; Domitian the First, Minervia, in Lower Germany; Trajan the Second, Aegyptia, and the Thirtieth, Germanica, both of which he named after himself;[58] Marcus Antoninus the Second, in Noricum, and the Third in Rhaetia, both of which are named Italica; and Severus the Parthicae, the First and Third, quartered in Mesopotamia, and the Second in Italy.

This is the total of the legions made up of regularly enrolled troops, and leaving out the city cohorts and the Praetorian Guard. At the time of Augustus's reign the legions I have mentioned constituted the standing army, whether their number was twenty-three or twenty-five. Besides these there were forces of infantry, cavalry and sailors drawn from the allies, whatever their numbers may have been, for I cannot give the exact figures. There were also the Praetorian Guards, ten thousand in number and organized in ten cohorts, and the city guards numbering six thousand and organized in four cohorts.[59] Finally there was a contingent of picked foreign horsemen, named Batavians after the island of Batavia in the Rhine, which produces excellent horsemen. I cannot give their exact strength, nor can I for the Evocati. Augustus was the first to employ this corps when he re-enlisted those troops who had served under Julius Caesar to fight against Antony, and he kept them in service afterwards. To this day they constitute a special corps and carry ceremonial rods as centurions do.

Augustus lacked the money to maintain all these troops, and he therefore laid before the Senate a proposal for a sufficient sum to be budgeted from year to year, so that there should be no shortage of funds to cover the soldiers' regular maintenance and periodic bonuses; this amount was to be provided from the taxes levied without requiring any further imposition on the public. Augustus then requested that the necessary allocation should be made. Meanwhile, when nobody declared himself willing to become a candidate for the office of aedile, some men who had previously served as quaestors and tribunes were compelled to hold the office by lot; this situation had often arisen in the past.

25. In the following year during the consulship of Aemilius Lepidus and Lucius Arruntius,[60] it became clear that no proposal for the funding of the military budget was going to please anybody; on the contrary, there was general resentment that such a measure was even being contemplated. Finally Augustus in his own name and in that of Tiberius made a sum of

money available to the treasury, and designated this fund the military treasury. He then directed that three of those who had served as praetors should be appointed by lot to administer the fund for three years; each would have two lictors on his staff and such further assistance as was appropriate.

The successive holders of this office were appointed in this way for many years, but today they are chosen by the emperor and are not attended by lictors. Augustus himself made a contribution to the fund and promised to renew this annually, and he also accepted voluntary contributions from kings and from certain communities. But he would take nothing from private citizens, even though large numbers of these offered money, at least, so they said. However, since even all these sources produced very little compared with the sums that were being spent and since some permanent provision was needed, he instructed the senators to search out sources of revenue, each acting independently of the others, to record these in memoranda and to give them to him to consider. This was not because he lacked ideas of his own, but rather because this was the most effective way of persuading them to choose the plan he had in mind. At any rate, when various men had put forward different schemes, he did not support any of these, but imposed a tax of five per cent on all inheritances and bequests left by people at their death, except those intended for the closest relations or for poor persons; he gave it out that he had found this tax set down among Julius Caesar's papers. It was, in fact, a measure which had been introduced once before, but had later been repealed and was now brought forward again. In this way, then, Augustus increased the public revenues. As for the expenditures, he appointed three former consuls chosen by lot to deal with them; with their help he reduced some items and abolished others.

26.   This matter of taxation was not the only cause of distress to the Romans, for there was also a severe famine. As a result of this the gladiators and the slaves to be put up for sale in the capital were removed to a distance of a hundred miles. Augustus and the other officials also dismissed the majority of their attendants, the courts were sent into recess, and senators were allowed to leave the city and go wherever they chose. In order not to impede the passing of decrees in their absence, it was ruled that all decisions reached by those senators who happened to be present at a meeting should be valid.[61] Besides this, former consuls were appointed

to supervise the distribution of bread and grain supplies so that only a specified quantity should be sold to each individual. Augustus, indeed, provided those who were already in receipt of doles of corn with as much again as their existing allowance. But when even that increase could not satisfy the general need, he forbade public banquets to be held on his birthday.

At this time many parts of the city were destroyed by fire. Augustus recruited a corps of freedmen consisting of seven divisions to bring help on such occasions, and appointed a knight to command them, expecting to disband them in a short time. But he did not do this, since he learned from experience that their assistance was most valuable and necessary, and so he kept them in service. These nightwatchmen exist to the present day as a special corps, in a sense: they are no longer recruited only from freedmen, but from the other classes as well. They have barracks in the city and are paid from the public treasury.

27. The mass of the people had suffered grievously from the famine, the taxes and the losses caused by the fires, and they now became restive. They not only openly discussed numerous plans for an uprising, but posted up at night even more numerous bulletins. It was said that these preparations were being managed by one Publius Rufus, but others also came under suspicion, for as Rufus could neither have planned any of these manifestations nor caused them to happen, it was believed that a revolution was being prepared by others using his name. Accordingly it was decreed that the matter should be investigated and rewards were posted for the giving of information. Reports began to come in, and on this account too the city was in a state of alarm. This atmosphere of crisis lasted until the shortage of grain was relieved, and gladiatorial games in honour of Drusus were presented by his sons, Germanicus Caesar and Tiberius Claudius Nero.

This commemoration of the memory of Drusus calmed the fears of the people, and so too did the dedication by Tiberius of the temple of Castor and Pollux.[62] On this building he inscribed not only his own name, calling himself Claudianus instead of Claudius because of his adoption into the family of Augustus, but also that of Drusus, his dead brother. Tiberius, I should mention, continued to carry out foreign campaigns, but also frequently visited the city whenever the occasion allowed. This was partly to attend to matters of public business, but chiefly because he feared that Augustus might, in consequence of his absence, show favour to somebody else.

These were the events which took place in the city in that year. In Achaea the governor of the province died in the middle of his term, and orders were sent to his quaestor and assessor, whom as I have explained we call legate, for the former to administer the territory as far as the isthmus of Corinth and the latter beyond it.[63] Herod of Palestine,[64] who was accused by his brothers of some misdemeanour or other, was exiled beyond the Alps, and his portion of the kingdom was annexed to the Roman state.

28.   During this period a number of wars also broke out. Pirates overran many regions, so that for some years Sardinia had no senator to govern the province; instead it was placed under military authority with knights in command. Not a few cities rose in rebellion, and in consequence in those provinces which were administered by the Roman people the same men held office for two years and were appointed by the emperor instead of being appointed by lot; those provinces which were controlled by Augustus were in any case allotted to the same officials for a longer period. However, I shall not describe all these matters minutely; many of the events which took place in individual regions are not worth mentioning, and no useful purpose would be served by recounting them in detail. I shall speak of those episodes which are memorable, but only in summary fashion, except for matters of the highest importance.

The Isaurians[65] began making marauding raids upon Roman territory, and they were drawn into the full rigour of war before being finally crushed. The Gaetulians were discontented with Juba, their ruler, and since they spurned the idea that they too should be governed by the Romans, they took up arms against him. They ravaged the neighbouring territory, killed many even of the Roman troops who were sent on an expedition against them, and built up so great a local ascendancy that Cornelius Cossus who overcame them received triumphal honours and an honorific title on this account.[66]

While these events were in train, campaigns were also being carried on against the Germans by various generals, and especially by Tiberius. He began by advancing to the river Visurgis and later as far as the Elbe, but these operations yielded no notable achievement. However, not only Augustus but also Tiberius was acclaimed as Imperator on account of this

campaign, and Gaius Sentius, the governor of Germany, was awarded
triumphal honours; this was because the Germans through their fear of
the Romans concluded not one truce but two. Peace was granted them a
second time in spite of their having broken the truce so quickly because
Dalmatia and Pannonia were by then in a state of violent upheaval,[67] and
the situation demanded an immediate response.

29.   The Dalmatians had for some time been restive because of the tribute
demanded from them, but had so far, however unwillingly, kept the
peace. But when Tiberius began his second campaign against the Germans,
Valerius Messallinus, the governor of Dalmatia, was sent out with him,
together with the majority of the Roman troops in the province, and the
Dalmatians were also ordered to send a contingent. When they mobilized
for this purpose and saw what a fine body of men of military age
they could muster, they waited no longer. A certain Bato, a native of
Desidiatia,[68] urged them to take up arms. At first a small number
responded and defeated the Romans who marched against them, and
following this success the rest of the people joined the rebellion. Next the
Breucians, a Pannonian tribe, chose another Bato as their commander and
attacked the town of Sirmium[69] and the Romans quartered there. They
did not capture it, however, for Caecina Severus, the governor of the
neighbouring province of Moesia, heard of the uprising, and making a
forced march engaged the enemy near the river Dravus[70] and defeated
them. However, the Dalmatians still cherished hopes that they could
resume the fighting in one way or another, especially as the Romans had
also suffered heavy losses, and so they applied themselves to summoning
their allies, and assembled as many as they could.

Meanwhile the Dalmatian leader, Bato, attacked Salonae,[71] where he
achieved nothing himself, since he was badly wounded by a stone missile,
but he sent out another raiding force which devastated the whole coast as
far as Apollonia. There, although he began by suffering a reverse, he in
turn overcame the Roman force which engaged his troops.

30.   When Tiberius heard of this defeat, he feared that the Dalmatians
might invade Italy, and accordingly he turned back from Germany, sent
Messallinus ahead and himself followed with the main body of his army.
However, Bato learned of his approach, and although not yet recovered
from his wound, marched out to face Messallinus. He gained the advantage

over him in open fighting, but was later defeated when the Romans set an ambush. After this he went to meet Bato the Breucian, formed an alliance with him to carry on the war, and occupied a mountain named Alma.[72] Here they were defeated in a short battle by Rhoemetalces the Thracian, who had been sent on by Severus as an advance force, but they fought strongly against Severus himself.

Later, when Severus returned to his province of Moesia because the Dacians and Sarmatians were ravaging it, and when Tiberius and Messallinus remained based upon Siscia,[73] the Dalmatians overran the territory of Rome's allies and induced many more to join the revolt. Although Tiberius brought his army close, the Dalmatians avoided a pitched battle and kept moving from place to place, devastating the country far and wide; they were thoroughly familiar with the region and lightly equipped, and so could easily move wherever they chose. When winter set in, they caused still greater havoc, for they even invaded Macedonia again. These Dalmatian forces were halted by Rhoemetalces and his brother Rhascyporis, who brought them to battle; as for the others, they did not rally to defend their territory when it was later devastated during the consulship of Caccilius Metellus and Licinius Silianus,[74] but took refuge in the mountain strongholds, and from there launched raiding expeditions whenever the opportunity arose.

31. When Augustus learned of these operations, he felt suspicious of Tiberius, who it seemed to him could easily have defeated the Dalmatians, but was deliberately marking time, using the war as an excuse to remain under arms for as long as possible.[75] He therefore sent out Germanicus, even though he was only a quaestor, and put him in command of an army recruited not only from free-born citizens but also from freedmen. The latter included former slaves, whom he had freed by taking them from their masters and mistresses according to the latter's census rating,[76] along with rations for six months. This was not the only step he took to meet the demands of the war. He also postponed the review of the knights, which was customarily held in the Forum, and besides this he made a vow in connection with the Megalensian Games, because some woman had incised various letters on her arm and given out some kind of divination. He had ascertained that this was not a case of divine possession, but that she had acted quite deliberately. However, since there was much unrest among the people both on account of the war and of the famine which

had once more overtaken them, he too made it appear that he believed the common report, and proceeded to take all the measures necessary to raise the spirits of the populace. To deal with the shortage of grain he appointed two former consuls as commissioners of the grain supply, and provided them with lictors. Then, as it was necessary to raise more money for the wars and to maintain the corps of nightwatchmen, he introduced a tax of two per cent on the sale of slaves. Besides this he directed that the money regularly allocated to the praetors for gladiatorial contests should no longer be spent for this purpose.

32.   The reason why he sent out Germanicus and not Agrippa Postumus for the campaign was that the latter possessed a disposition which was unfitted for command, and spent most of his time fishing, for which reason he dubbed himself Neptune. He was apt to give way to violent fits of anger, reviled Livia as a step-mother, and often blamed Augustus himself for having withheld from him the inheritance left by his father.[77] Since he could not be made to change his conduct for the better, he was disinherited and his property transferred to the military treasury. He himself was sent to Planasia, an island near Corsica.

These were the events which took place in Rome. After Germanicus had reached Pannonia, the various armies were converging upon each other from many sides.[78] The two Batos waited until Severus advanced from Moesia, and then launched a surprise attack while he was encamped near the Volcaean marshes.[79] Their onslaught dismayed the outposts stationed outside the entrenchments, and they drove these back inside, but when the troops in the camp stood firm, the attackers were defeated. After this the Romans divided their forces into flying columns, so as to overrun many parts of the country simultaneously. Most of these detachments achieved nothing worthy of note, at least at that time, but Germanicus defeated in battle and then harassed the Mazaei, a Dalmatian tribe.

33.   These were the military achievements of that year. During the consulship of Marcus Furius and Sextus Nonius[80] the Dalmations were anxious to make terms; this was because they had been stricken first by famine and then by the disease which followed it, since they were using for food roots and herbs that were unfamiliar. However, they did not approach the Romans, as they were hindered by those who had no hope

that their lives would be spared and held out in spite of their sufferings. There was one man named Scenobardus, who had given it out that he intended to change sides, and who had sent a message in this sense to Manius Ennius, the commander of the garrison in Siscia, as if he were ready to desert. Then he became frightened that he might be harmed before he could carry out his plan ...

[When at last the supply of food had improved in Italy, Augustus held games in the Circus in the name of Germanicus, who was the son of Drusus, and of his younger brother Claudius.[81] On this occasion an elephant overcame a rhinoceros, and a knight who had once been famous for his wealth fought in a single combat.

By this time Augustus was suffering from fatigue on account both of his age and of physical weakness, so that he was unable to deal with all individual cases or petitions which required his attention. He still continued with the help of his assistants to investigate judicial suits and to pass judgement, seated on the tribunal in the palace. However, he entrusted the reception of delegations sent to Rome by peoples and rulers to three former consuls; these men, sitting separately, gave audience to such embassies and replied to their petitions, except for matters concerning which the final decision had to be made by the Senate and the emperor.]

34. [At the meetings of the Senate] Augustus did not, however, deliver his opinion among the first, but among the last. His object was that all the senators should be enabled to arrive at their conclusions independently, and that nobody should depart from his own opinion as though he were under an obligation to agree with the emperor. He would often sit with the magistrates when they tried cases, and whenever those who were sitting in judgement with him found themselves divided in their opinions, the emperor's vote was given no more weight than that of any other judge. However, at the period which I am now describing, Augustus entrusted to the Senate the decision of most cases without his presence, and he ceased to attend the meetings of the popular assemblies. To replace this procedure he had in the previous year appointed all the officials who were to hold office, on account of the popular disturbances. In this year and in those following he merely posted a list recommending to the plebs and the people at large the candidates he supported. Nevertheless, in the direction of campaigns against enemies abroad, he travelled to Ariminum so as to be close at hand to give whatever advice was necessary against

both the Dalmatians and the Pannonians. When he left Rome prayers were offered up, and when he re-entered, the sacrifices customarily ordained on his return from enemy territory were carried out.

These were the events which took place in Rome. Meanwhile Bato, the Breucian leader who had betrayed Pinnes, and had been appointed to rule the Breucians as a reward, was captured by Bato the Dalmatian and put to death. The Breucian, it seems, had suspected the loyalty of his subject tribes, and had visited each of the garrisons to demand hostages. The Dalmatian Bato, having learned of his plan, laid an ambush for him, defeated him in battle and imprisoned him in a fortress. Later, when the Breucian was handed over by those inside the stronghold, Bato brought him before the army, and when he had been condemned, had him executed on the spot.[82] After this many of the Pannonians rose in revolt and Silvanus led an expedition against them, defeated the Breucians and won over some of the other rebellious tribes without fighting. When Bato learned this, he abandoned any hope of holding Pannonia, but occupied the passes leading to Dalmatia and devastated that country. After this the majority of the Pannonians came to terms with Rome, mainly because their country was being laid waste by Silvanus. However, a number of bands of outlaws continued to make marauding raids for a long while, as was normal after so widespread a revolt. This is indeed almost always the case not only among other peoples, but among these tribes in particular.

BOOK 56

The following is contained in the Fifty-Sixth Book of Dio's *Rome*:

1. While others put down these disorders, Tiberius returned to Rome after the winter in which Quintus Sulpicius and Gaius Sabinus took up office as consuls.[1] Even Augustus went out in person into the suburbs to meet him, accompanied him to the Saepta, and there greeted the people from a tribunal. After this he carried out all the other ceremonies which are appropriate to such occasions and arranged that the consuls should hold triumphal games. Then, since the knights in the course of the games had pressed him strongly to repeal the law concerning unmarried and childless individuals,[2] he assembled in one part of the Forum those of the equestrian order who were unmarried, and in another those who were married, including those who also had children. When he saw that the latter were far fewer in numbers than the former, he felt it keenly and spoke to them as follows:

2. 'Although there are few of you in all compared with the great mass of this city's population, and again far fewer than those who are unwilling to fulfil any of their duties, yet for this very reason I praise you all the more and feel deeply grateful because you have accepted your obligations and are helping to replenish your native land. For it is through men who live their lives in this way that the Romans of future years will become a

mighty people. At the beginning of our history we were no more than a small tribe, but when we engaged ourselves in marriage and begot children, we surpassed the rest of the world not only in the manly virtue of our citizens, but also in the size of our population. We should remember this and take consolation for what is mortal in our nature through a perpetual succession of generations, who will take up the torch like runners in a race. In this way we can with one another's help achieve immortality in that one respect in which we fall short of the blessed state of the gods.

'It was for this reason above all that the first and greatest god who shaped our being divided the mortal race into two, making one part male and the other female, and implanted in them love and the need for intercourse with one another. He made their association fruitful so that through the perpetual renewal of young life even the mortal nature of a man could, in a sense, be rendered eternal. In fact, even among the gods themselves, some are regarded as male and some female and, according to the legends handed down to us, some are thus the parents of others, and some the children. And so even among these beings, who have no need of such an arrangement, marriage and the procreation of children are reputed to be admired.

3.   'You have done well then, to follow the example of the gods and to emulate your fathers, so that just as they begot you, you may also give life to others; just as you regard them and name them as your ancestors, others may regard you and address you likewise. In this way the achievements which they valiantly wrought, made famous and handed down to you, you may likewise hand on to others; and the possessions which they acquired and left to you, you may also bequeath to your own descendants. Is there anything more admirable than a wife who is modest, who cares for her home, is equally versed in the management of her household and the upbringing of her children, can share with you the pleasures of health and tend you in sickness, be your partner in good fortune and comfort you in bad, moderate the madcap nature of youth and soften the crabbed severity of old age? Is it not a joy to acknowledge a child who possesses the qualities of both parents, to tend and educate a being who is both the physical and the spiritual image of yourself, so that, as it grows up, another self is created? Is it not blessed, on quitting this life, to leave behind as successor an heir both to your breed and your

property, one that is your own, born of your own essence, so that only the mortal element of you passes away, while you live on in the child who succeeds you? In this way, you do not fall a victim to the foreigner as in war, nor perish utterly as in a pestilence. Such private blessings are the reward of those who marry and beget children.

'But consider also the state, to which we owe many duties that may not come easily to us. How excellent, and how imperative it is, if cities and peoples are to exist, and if you are to rule others and the rest of the world is to obey you, that there should be a flourishing race of ours; such a race as will in time of peace till the soil, sail the seas, practise the arts and pursue handicrafts, and in time of war protect what we hold with an ardour which is all the greater because of the ties of blood, and which will bring forth others to take the places of those who fall.

'I address you as men – for it is only you of whom the word can rightly be used – and as fathers, for you are as worthy to hold the title as I myself. I love you and praise you for this, and I not only exalt you with the rewards I have already offered, but I shall honour you still further with other distinctions and offices. Thus you may not only enjoy great benefits yourselves, but hand them on undiminished to your children.

'Now I shall pass to the other group, whose actions in no way resemble yours, and who will be treated for that reason in exactly the opposite fashion. I do this so that you may understand, not only from my words but still more clearly from my actions, how far you excel them.'

4.   At the end of this speech he made gifts to some of his audience on the spot, and promised similar presentations to others. He then crossed to the second group, and spoke to them as follows:

'I have suffered a strange experience, and I do not know how to address you. As men? But you do not carry out any of the duties of men. As citizens? But so far as it depends on you, the city is wasting away. As Romans? But you are acting so as to obliterate our very name. Well, whatever you are, and by whatever name it pleases you to be called, I have, as I said, passed through a strange experience. The truth is that although I never cease my efforts to encourage you to increase our population, and am about to censure you, it distresses me to see that there are so many of you. I had far rather that the audience to which I have just spoken were as large as the one I now see before me, and that you either belonged with them, which would be best, or else did not exist at all. You have chosen to disregard both the providence of the gods and the devotion of your forefathers; your purpose is to extinguish our entire race and make it literally mortal, to put an end to the existence of the whole Roman nation. What human seed of any kind would be left, do you imagine, if all the world were to act as you do? For since you have become their rulers, you would rightly bear the responsibility for the universal collapse that would ensue. And if no others were to imitate you, would you not deserve to be hated for the very reason that you overlook what no one else would overlook, neglect what no one else would neglect, and introduce customs and practices which, if others were to follow, would lead to the extinction of all mankind, and if they were condemned, must result in your own punishment? We do not spare murderers because not all men commit murder, nor allow temple-robbers to go free because not all men rob temples. On the contrary, anyone who is found guilty of committing one of these forbidden acts is punished precisely on the ground that he alone, or together with a few others, does something which nobody else would do.

5.   'And yet if one were to spell out the greatest of crimes, the others are of no consequence compared with the action you are now taking, whether one examines them individually, or even sets all of them together against this one offence of yours. You are guilty of murder by not begetting in the first place those who should be your descendants; you are guilty of sacrilege by bringing to a close the names and distinctions of your ancestors; you are guilty in that you are causing your families, which were instituted by divine will, to disappear, and destroying the greatest of offerings to the gods – namely human life – and thus overthrowing their rites and their temples. Besides this, you are guilty of destroying the state by disobeying its laws, and of betraying your country by making her barren and childless – worse still you are obliterating her very existence by depriving her of those who would inhabit her in future. For a city is made up of human beings, not of houses or porticoes or market-places with no people in them.

   'Try to imagine, then, the anger which the great Romulus,[3] the founder of our race, would rightly feel, if he were to recall the circumstances in which he himself was born and could compare them with your situation, in which you refuse to beget children even in lawful wedlock. Would it not enrage the Romans who were his followers, if they knew that after

they had gone so far as to carry off foreign girls,[4] you by contrast have
no feeling even for those of your own race, and that after they had
engendered children even by the women of an enemy country, you refuse
to beget them even by women who are your fellow-citizens? What would
be the feelings of Curtius,[5] who consented to die to save married men
from being deprived of their wives? Or of Hersilia,[6] who waited upon
her daughter at the girl's wedding, and laid down for us all the rites of
marriage? Our fathers even went to war with the Sabines to win brides
for themselves, and came to terms with them when their wives and
children interceded with us. It was for this very purpose that they took
oaths and concluded various treaties, but you are casting away all their
efforts. And to what end? Is it your aim to dispense with the society of
women altogether, as the Vestal Virgins live without men? In that case,
you should be punished just as they are, if you offend in any way against
chastity.

6.   'I know that my words may sound harsh and bitter to you. But
consider first of all that physicians also treat many patients by means of
cautery and surgery when they cannot restore their health in any other
way; and secondly that I have no wish to speak in this fashion and take
no pleasure in doing so. Indeed, I must blame you for this reason too, that
you have provoked me into delivering a speech of this kind. So, if what
I have to say offends you, do not persist in conduct of this kind, which
must inevitably cause you to be despised. If my words wound some of
you, how much more do your actions wound not only me, but all the
rest of the Romans? And so, if you are truly aggrieved at what you have
heard, then change your way of life, so that I can praise and reward you.
Even you must be well aware that I am not hard by nature and that I have
carried out everything which it was proper for a good lawgiver to enact,
so far as was humanly possible.

'The truth is that even in times past no man was ever allowed to neglect
marriage and the procreation of children. From the earliest times, as soon
as government was first established, strict laws were laid down on these
matters, and afterwards many decrees were voted both by the Senate and
the people which there is no need for me to specify here. For my part, I
have increased the penalties for the disobedient, so that the fear of incurring
them may make you see reason: to the obedient I have offered more and
greater rewards than are given for any other meritorious act, in the hope

that for this reason if for no other you might be persuaded to marry and beget children.[7] In spite of this, you have made no effort to earn any of the rewards nor been deterred by any of the penalties; instead you have disdained all these measures and trodden them underfoot, as if you were not living in a community at all. You talk of this unconstrained and emancipated life you have chosen, without wives or children, but you are no different from outlaws or the most savage wild beasts.

7. 'Certainly it is not because you take pleasure in a solitary existence that you live without wives, for there is none among you who either eats or sleeps alone. What you want is complete liberty to lead an undisciplined and promiscuous life. And yet I even tolerated your wooing of girls who were still of tender years and not yet ready for marriage, so that by enjoying the name of fiancés you might live as family men should,[8] and I agreed that those who did not yet belong to the senatorial order could wed freedwomen. This enabled any man to marry within the law, whether for love or on account of any other attachment, if he so desired. And I did not restrict your freedom even to this extent, but first granted you three whole years and later two in which you could make your preparations. But even with all these concessions, neither by threats, nor exhortations, nor extensions of the time, nor entreaties could I achieve any result.

'You can see for yourselves how much more numerous you are than the married men, and yet you ought by this time to have provided us with as many descendants as you number yourselves, or rather with several times more. For how otherwise are families to continue? How can the state be preserved if we neither marry nor beget children? You surely do not expect men to spring up from the ground – as legend tells us – to inherit your goods and defend the common weal? And yet it is neither right nor honourable that our race should die out, the name of Romans disappear with us and the city be handed over to foreigners – to Greeks or even barbarians. Do we not free our slaves for this purpose above all, so as to create as many citizens as possible from their number? And do we not grant our allies a share in the government in order to increase the population? But you who are Romans from time immemorial and count the Marcii,[9] the Fabii, the Quintii, the Valerii and the Julii among your ancestors – do you really desire that your families and your names alike should perish with you?

8.   'For my part I feel ashamed that I have been obliged even to mention such a possibility. Rid yourselves of this obsession, then, and consider well that, with many people dying year by year through disease and in war, it is impossible for the city to maintain itself unless its population is replenished by a continual flow of new life.

'Let none of you suppose that I overlook the fact that marriage and the procreation of children have their vexatious and painful aspects. But remember this too, that we do not possess any other good which does not include some unpleasant element in its composition, and that even in our most abundant blessings are also implanted the most abundant and greatest evils. And so if you reject the latter, do not hunger after the former either, since virtually any achievement in which true excellence or pleasure resides demands that you exert yourself before, at the time of, and after its attainment. But there is no need to lengthen my speech by enumerating all these details. Even if there are various disagreeable elements which are inseparable from marriage and the procreation of children, reckon against these the corresponding advantages, and you will find that the latter are the more decisive and the more numerous. For besides all the other good things which naturally accompany this state of life, the rewards offered by the laws should persuade everyone to obey me; after all, many men are impelled even to suffer death for a mere fraction of these benefits. Is it not shameful then that those rewards which induce others to sacrifice their very lives should prove insufficient to persuade you to take wives and bring up children?

9.   'And so, my fellow-citizens – for I believe I may have persuaded you to stay in possession of your title as citizens and to take on that of men and fathers besides – I have censured you not for my own pleasure but from necessity, not as an enemy or as one who hates you, but rather out of love and the desire that there should be many more like you. My ideal is that we may have lawful homes to dwell in and houses full of descendants, that we may approach the gods together with our wives and children, that a man and his family should live together as partners who risk all their fortunes in equal measure, and likewise reap pleasure from the hopes they rest upon one another. How could I be a good ruler to you if I could bear to see your numbers growing ever smaller? How could I any longer properly be called father by you if you rear no children? And so, if you really feel affection for me, and above all if you have given me

this title not out of flattery but as an honour, make it your true desire to become both men and fathers. In this way you will not only share that title yourselves, but ensure that it is rightly applied to me.'

10. This was how he spoke to the two audiences of knights at the time. Later he increased the rewards given to those who had children, and for the rest he introduced a distinction between the married men and the unmarried by imposing different penalties on them. Besides this he allowed to those who were culpable in respect of being unmarried or childless a year's grace in which to obey him and avoid the penalties involved. The *Lex Voconia*[10] had laid it down that no woman could inherit property exceeding 100,000 sesterces in value, but Augustus allowed certain women to inherit larger sums, and he also granted the Vestal Virgins all the privileges which belonged to women who had borne children. As a result, the *Lex Papia Poppaea*[11] was drawn up by Marcus Papius Mutilus and Quintus Poppaeus Secundus, who held the consulship for a time during that year. It so happened that both these men were not only childless but not even married, and the necessity for the law became apparent from this situation. These were the events which took place in Rome.

11. In the meanwhile Germanicus captured the town of Splonum[12] among other places in Dalmatia, even though it was situated on ground that was well protected by nature, was strongly fortified by walls and contained a large garrison to defend it. Because of these factors he had been unable to achieve any success either with siege engines or by assaults, but he captured it as the result of the following episode. A German horseman named Pusio discharged a stone against the wall, and so shook the parapet that it at once collapsed and carried down with it a man who was leaning against it. At this the other defenders took fright, abandoned that section of the wall in panic and ran down to the citadel. Later they surrendered the citadel and themselves.

From there Germanicus's troops advanced to Raetinum, but on that occasion they came off less successfully. The enemy were overwhelmed by their numbers, and being unable to check their assault, set fire of their own accord both to the outer wall which encircled the town and to the adjoining houses. But they managed to control the flames so that they did not blaze up at once; thus for some while the fire continued unobserved, and having started it they withdrew to the citadel. The Romans, not knowing what had been done, charged into the city, expecting to sack the whole place without striking a blow. In this way they entered the area which was ringed with the flames, and since they had their attention fixed on the enemy, they saw nothing of the fire until they were encircled by it on all sides. Then they found themselves in mortal danger, being pelted with missiles by the enemy from above and injured by the flames around them. There was no safety if they remained where they stood, nor could they break out at any point without also risking harm. If they backed away out of range of the missiles they were burned by fire, or if they moved inwards from the flames they were struck down by the missiles; some, who were trapped in a confined space, even lost their lives from both causes at once, since they were wounded on one side and scorched on the other. The greater number of those who had rushed into the town perished in this way, but a few escaped by throwing dead bodies on to the flames and making a passage for themselves by using these as a causeway. The fire burned so fiercely that it was impossible even for those who had retreated into the citadel to stay there; instead they abandoned it in the night and hid themselves in caves under the rock. This was how the operations in that region progressed.

12.   The town of Seretium, which Tiberius had previously besieged but not captured, was now reduced, and thereafter a number of places were more easily secured. Yet in spite of these defeats the rest of the Dalmatians took up arms, the hostilities continued to drag on, and Italy was again stricken by famine, mainly on account of the war. Accordingly Augustus once more dispatched Tiberius to Dalmatia.[13] Tiberius recognized that the soldiers would not endure further delays and were eager to bring the campaign to an end in one way or another, even at some risk to themselves. He was afraid that if they all remained together they would mutiny. He therefore split his force into three corps. One of these he gave to Silvanus, another to Marcus Lepidus, while he himself assumed command of the third and marched against Bato, taking Germanicus with him.

The first two generals easily defeated their opponents in pitched battles, but Tiberius was obliged to traverse almost the whole country, as Bato decamped from place to place. Finally his adversary took refuge in Andetrium, a stronghold which had been built in the neighbourhood of Salonae itself, and there Tiberius encountered great difficulties when he settled down to a siege. The place had been built upon a rocky hill, which was strongly fortified, difficult to approach and encircled by deep ravines which were filled by rushing torrents. Besides this the enemy were stocked with all the supplies they needed; some of these they had already laid in, and more were still being conveyed to them from the mountains which were in their hands. Apart from these advantages they also harassed the Roman supply columns by means of ambushes. The consequence was that Tiberius, although supposedly besieging them, was himself beset with the problems of a beleaguered army.

13. He found himself unable to hit upon any plan of action and was baffled as to what to do next, for the siege was proving both futile and dangerous, while a retreat appeared disgraceful. This setback threw the soldiers into turmoil, and they raised an uproar so tremendous and so prolonged that the enemy, who were encamped at the foot of the fortress, lost their nerve and slipped away. Tiberius was at once angry and pleased. He called the soldiers together and delivered an address which was part praise and part reprimand. After this he took no reckless initiatives, but neither did he withdraw. He remained quietly where he was until Bato, having given up all hope of defeating him, sent a herald to ask for terms. He took this step because all but a few places he held had been captured, and because the force he commanded was weaker than the one he faced. However, he could not persuade the rest of the Dalmatians to ask for a truce, and so he left them and later refused to respond to other requests for help, although many were sent to him.

Tiberius now felt contemptuous of the force which still remained in the stronghold. He believed that he could overcome them without incurring many casualties, and disregarding the difficulties of the terrain, he made a frontal advance upon the fortress. Since there was no level ground ahead of him and the enemy would not come down to meet his troops, he seated himself on a platform in full view of both sides. He did this not only to watch the battle, since this would encourage his men to fight with more spirit, but also to be able to throw in support at the critical moment, if need arose. In fact, since he greatly outnumbered the enemy, he was holding a part of his force in reserve for this very purpose. The rest, who had formed up in a closely packed square, at first moved forward at a walk. But later their formation was broken up by the steep and uneven slope of the mountain, which contained many gullies and was also frequently split into ravines, so that some of the troops climbed more quickly and others moved more slowly.

14.   When the Dalmatians saw how the attack was developing, they took up position outside their wall at the top of the slope and hurled down volleys of stones upon the Romans. Some were discharged from slings and others rolled down. Besides these, loose wheels, whole waggons filled with rocks and circular chests fashioned to a design which is peculiar to that country and packed full of stones were all released down the hill. All these objects hurtling down simultaneously at great speed found their targets on a wide front with the impetus of a sling-shot; they reinforced the effect of the ground in separating the Romans from one another, and crushed their bodies. Others of the enemy were striking down many of their opponents with the spears and other missiles which they hurled at them.

Meanwhile fierce fighting was taking place as the one side strove to scale and capture the heights, and the other to repulse and hurl them back. At the same time those who were not taking part – both those who were watching the battle from the walls and those surrounding Tiberius – vied in supporting their comrades. Each side both individually and collectively urged on its men, trying to encourage those who fought bravely and reviling those who gave ground at any point. Those whose voices rose above the rest were at the same time calling upon the gods. Both were offering up prayers for the safety of the combatants at that moment and likewise both for the future, the one side begging for freedom and the other for peace.

The Romans would certainly have risked their lives in vain, since they were obliged to struggle against two factors at once – the difficult nature of the ground and the defensive formation of their opponents – if Tiberius had not prevented them from retreating by calling up frequent reinforcements; at the same time he managed to throw the enemy into confusion when he sent a detachment to a point where by making a wide detour the heights could be climbed. Through this manoeuvre the enemy were routed and could not even withdraw into the fortress; they had thrown off their armour so as to be unhampered by its weight and were scattered all over the mountain side. Their pursuers followed them everywhere, for they were determined to finish the war once and for all, and had no wish that their enemies should regroup and offer fresh resistance. They discovered most of them hiding in the woods and slaughtered them like wild beasts, after which they made prisoners of the men in the fortress who had surrendered.

15.   Tiberius was now engaged in dealing with those who had submitted and carrying out the terms of the capitulation, while Germanicus occupied himself with those who were still holding out, since they had many deserters in their ranks who would not allow them to make terms. He captured a place called Arduba, though he could not achieve this with his own force, in spite of the fact that he far outnumbered his opponents. The position had been strongly fortified, and at its base was almost entirely encircled, except for a short stretch, by a swiftly flowing river. However, the deserters quarrelled with the inhabitants, since the latter were anxious to make peace, and fighting broke out between them. The deserters were supported by the women in the stronghold, since these, contrary to the views of their menfolk, yearned for liberty and were willing to suffer any fate rather than slavery. A violent struggle followed, in which the deserters were overcome and surrendered, although some of them managed to escape. The women, on the other hand, snatched up their children and either threw themselves into the flames of the burning city, or leaped into the river below.

This was how that stronghold was captured, and afterwards the other places in the neighbourhood made terms with Germanicus of their own accord. After concluding these arrangements he rejoined Tiberius, while Postumius[14] completed the conquest of the rest of the region.

16.   In the meanwhile Bato sent his son Scevas to Tiberius with the offer that he would surrender himself and all his followers in return for a pardon.[15] After he had received a pledge, he entered the Roman camp by night, and on the following morning was brought before Tiberius, who was sitting on a tribunal. Bato asked nothing for himself, and even stretched out his neck as if he were awaiting the stroke of the sword, but he made a long speech in defence of his fellow-countrymen. Finally, when Tiberius asked him why his people had thought it right to rebel and to carry on the war against the Romans for so long, he replied, 'It is you Romans who are to blame for this. We are your flocks, yet you do not send dogs or shepherds to guard us, but wolves.'

In this way the war was brought to an end, but only after many lives had been lost and great expense incurred, for a very large number of legions were devoted to it and very little plunder was taken.

17.   On this occasion too it was Germanicus who made the announcement of the victory. Because of this success Augustus and Tiberius were authorized to add the title of Imperator to those they already held and to celebrate a triumph, and were awarded other honours besides, in particular two triumphal arches in Pannonia. These were the only distinctions out of the many voted to them that Augustus would accept. Germanicus received the triumphal decorations which were likewise conferred on the other commanders, and he was also given the rank of praetor and the privilege of casting his vote immediately after the former consuls and of holding the consulate at an earlier date than was customary. Tiberius's son Drusus, even though he had not served in the campaign, was granted the right to attend meetings of the Senate before becoming a senator, and to vote before the former praetors as soon as he should hold the office of quaestor.

18.   These decrees had scarcely been passed when the arrival of terrible news from the province of Germany prevented the festival from being held. What had been happening in Germany during this period was as follows. The Romans had a hold on parts of it, not whole regions, but merely those areas which happened to have been subdued, so that this fact has not received historical notice. Meanwhile bodies of troops were in the habit of wintering there, and cities were being founded; the barbarians were gradually re-shaping their habits in conformity with the Roman pattern, were becoming accustomed to hold markets and were meeting in peaceful assemblies. But they had not forgotten their ancestral customs, their native manners, their independent way of life, nor the power they had enjoyed through their strength in arms. So long as they were unlearning their customs little by little, by indirect means, so to speak, and were under careful surveillance, they did not object to the change in their manner of life, and were unconsciously altering their disposition.

But when Quintilius Varus became governor of the province of Germany,[16] and in the exercise of his powers also came to handle the affairs of these peoples, he tried both to hasten and to widen the process of change. He not only gave orders to the Germans as if they were actual slaves of the Romans, but also levied money from them as if they were subject nations. These were demands they would not tolerate. The leaders yearned for their former ascendancy, and the masses preferred their accustomed condition to foreign domination. They did not rise in open rebellion, because they saw that there were many Roman troops near the Rhine and many within their own territory. Instead, they received Varus, and by pretending that they would comply with all his orders, they lured him far away from the Rhine into the territory of the Cherusci and towards the river Visurgis.[17] There they behaved in a most peaceful and friendly manner, and made him feel confident that they could live in a state of subjection without the presence of soldiers.

19.   The result was that he did not keep his forces concentrated as was advisable in a hostile country, but dispersed many of his troops to those regions which lacked protection, supposedly to guard various vital positions, arrest outlaws or escort supply columns. Among those who were most deeply involved in the plot and took the lead in its planning and in the subsequent fighting were Arminius[18] and Segimerus; these men were constantly in Varus's company and often present in his mess. He thus became complacent to the point of rashness, and since he expected no harm, he not only disbelieved all those who suspected what was happening and urged him to be on his guard, but actually reproved them for being needlessly alarmed and for slandering his friends. Then an uprising broke out, the first to rebel being those peoples who lived at some distance from him. This had been deliberately contrived to entice Varus to march against them, so that he could the more easily be overwhelmed while he was crossing what he imagined to be friendly territory, instead of putting himself on his guard, as he would do in the event of the whole country taking up arms against him simultaneously.

And so the plan unfolded. The leaders escorted him as he set out, and then made their excuses for absenting themselves. This was to enable them, as they made out, to prepare their combined forces, after which they would quickly reassemble to support him. Then they took command of their troops which were already awaiting them in readiness somewhere. Next, after each community had slaughtered the detachments of Roman soldiers quartered with them, for which they had previously asked, they fell upon Varus in the midst of the forests, which at this point in his march were almost impenetrable. There, when they stood revealed as enemies instead of subjects, they dealt a succession of terrible blows to the Romans.

20.   The shape of the mountains in this region was irregular, their slopes
being deeply cleft by ravines, while the trees grew closely together to a
great height. In consequence the Romans, even before the enemy fell
upon them, were hard pressed by the necessity of felling trees, clearing
the tracks and bridging difficult stretches wherever necessary on their line
of march. They had with them many waggons and pack animals, as they
would for a journey in peace-time; they were even accompanied by
women and children and a large retinue of servants, all these being factors
which caused them to advance in scattered groups.

Meanwhile a violent downpour and storm developed, so that the
column was strung out even further; this also caused the ground around
the tree-roots and the felled trunks to become slippery, making movement
very dangerous, and the tops of the trees to break off and crash down
upon them creating great confusion. While the Romans were struggling
against the elements, the barbarians suddenly surrounded them on all sides
at once, stealing through the densest thickets, as they were familiar with
the paths. At first they hurled their spears from a distance, but as nobody
attacked them in return and many were wounded, the Germans closed in
to shorter range; for their part the Roman troops were not advancing in
any regular formation, but were interspersed at random with the waggons
and the non-combatants. This meant that they could not easily concentrate
their strength at any point, and since they were everywhere overwhelmed
by their opponents, they suffered many casualties and were quite unable
to counter-attack.

21.   Accordingly they pitched camp on the spot after taking possession of
a suitable place, so far as one could be found on wooded and mountainous
ground; afterwards they either burned or abandoned most of their
waggons and everything else that was not absolutely indispensable to
them. The next day they marched on in somewhat better order and even
broke out into open country, though they could not avoid suffering
casualties. Moving on from there they re-entered the woods, where they
fought back against their assailants, but suffered their heaviest losses in
this action. To enable the cavalry and infantry to make a combined charge
against the enemy they had to form up in a narrow space, and so frequently
collided with one another and with the trees. The fourth day saw them
still on the move, and again they experienced heavy rain and violent
winds, which prevented them from advancing or even finding a firm

foothold and made it impossible to wield their weapons. They could neither draw their bows nor hurl their javelins to any effect, nor even make use of their shields, which were completely sodden with rain. Their opponents, on the other hand, were for the most part lightly armed, and so could approach or retire without difficulty, and suffered far less from the weather.

Besides this the enemy's numbers had been greatly reinforced, since many of those who had at first hesitated now joined the battle in the hope of taking plunder. Their increased numbers made it easier to encircle and strike down the Romans, whose ranks by contrast had shrunk, since they had lost many men in the earlier fighting. And so Varus and all the senior officers, fearing that they would either be taken alive or slaughtered by their bitterest enemies – for they had already been wounded – nerved themselves for the dreaded but unavoidable act, and took their own lives.

22.   When this news spread to their men, none of the rest, even if strength remained, resisted any longer. Some followed the example of their general, others threw down their arms and allowed any who chose to slaughter them, since flight was out of the question, however much a man might desire it. So every soldier and every horse was cut down without resistance ...

[The barbarians seized all the Roman fortresses but one: it was because of the delay in this single instance that they neither crossed the Rhine nor invaded Gaul. They found themselves unable to capture this position because they did not understand the business of siege warfare, and also because the Romans employed a large number of archers, whose arrows repeatedly checked their attacks and caused them heavy losses ...

Later they learned that the Romans had stationed a garrison at the Rhine, and that Tiberius was approaching with a formidable army. At this most of the barbarians withdrew from the fort, and even the detachment which had been left there removed themselves to a safe distance, so that they should not suffer losses from sudden sorties on the part of the garrison. Then they closed the roads, hoping that they could overcome the defenders by cutting off their supplies. The Romans inside, so long as their food held out, remained on the spot and waited to be relieved. However, when no one arrived to rescue them and they began to suffer from hunger, they waited for a stormy night and made their escape. The troops of the garrison were only few in number and had

many non-combatants with them.] They managed to pass through the
enemy's first and second guard posts, but when they reached the third
their presence was discovered. This was because the women and children,
who were both frightened and exhausted, and troubled too by the darkness
and the cold, kept calling to the soldiers to come back. They would all
either have died or been captured if the barbarians had not given their
whole attention to seizing the plunder. This provided a chance for the
most vigorous to get some distance away, and when the buglers who
were with them blew the call to march in double time, this made the
enemy believe that a reinforcement had been sent by Asprenas. So the
barbarians abandoned their pursuit, and Asprenas, once he learned what
was happening, did in fact help them. Some of the prisoners were later
ransomed by their relatives and returned to Roman territory, a concession
which was granted provided that the men remained outside Italy.

23.   This arrangement took place later. At the time when Augustus
learned of the disaster which had befallen Varus, he rent his clothes,
according to some reports, and was overcome with grief. His feelings
were not only of sorrow for the soldiers who had perished, but of fear for
the provinces of Germany and of Gaul, above all because he expected that
the enemy would invade Italy and even attack Rome itself. There were
no able-bodied citizens of any fighting capacity left in reserve, and the
allied forces, such as were of any value, had suffered heavy losses.
However, he made such preparations as he could in the circumstances.
When no men of military age proved willing to be conscripted, he made
them draw lots. Through this arrangement, every fifth man of those
under thirty-five was deprived of his property and his civil rights, together
with every tenth man of those beyond that age. Finally, since even then
a great many men would not respond, he had a number put to death. He
then selected by lot as many as possible from those who had already
completed their military service and from the freedmen, and after enrolling them in the army, ordered them with all speed to the province of
Germany to join Tiberius. At this time there were many Gauls and
Germans actually living in Rome, some serving in the Praetorian Guard,
and others residing there for various reasons. Augustus feared that these
might start an uprising, and so despatched those who were serving in his
bodyguard to various islands, and ordered those who were unarmed to
leave the capital.

24.   These were the actions he took at that time, during which none of the usual observances were carried out, nor were the festivals celebrated. Later, when he received news that some of the soldiers had been saved, that the province of Germany was garrisoned and that the enemy had not ventured to advance even to the Rhine, his fears subsided and he paused to review the situation. It struck him that for such a great and overwhelming calamity to have taken place, the wrath of some divinity must have been incurred; besides, the portents which had been observed both before the defeat and afterwards made him inclined to suspect that some superhuman agency was at work. The temple of Mars in the field of that name had been struck by lightning; many locusts had flown into the very city and had been devoured by swallows; the peaks of the Alps had appeared to collapse upon one another and to send up three columns of fire; the sky was lit with flashes in many places and showers of comets appeared at one and the same time; spears seemed to fly through the air from the north and to fall in the direction of the Roman camps; bees formed their honeycombs about the altars in the camps; a statue of Victory which stood in the province of Germany facing the enemy's territory had been turned around so as to face Italy; finally there was an occasion when fighting broke out around the legionary standards in the Roman camps; the soldiers thought that the barbarians had attacked them, but this proved to be a false alarm . . .[19]

[Tiberius decided not to cross the Rhine, but stayed in his positions keeping watch to see that the barbarians did not cross either. For their part the enemy, knowing that he was there, did not venture to force a passage . . .

Meanwhile the popularity of Germanicus was increasing in Rome for a number of reasons, but in particular because he appeared in the courts on behalf of various people, and he did this as often before Augustus himself as before the other judges. In consequence, on one occasion when he was going to plead the case of a quaestor who had been charged with murder, the plaintiff became anxious that Germanicus's appearance would cause him to lose the suit if it came before the judges who normally heard such cases, and he wished to have it tried before Augustus. However his efforts were of no avail, for he did not succeed.]

25.   In the following year, besides the events already described, the temple of Concord[20] was dedicated by Tiberius and both his name and

that of his dead brother Drusus were inscribed on it. During the consulship of Marcus Aemilius and Statilius Taurus,[21] Tiberius and Germanicus (the latter holding proconsular rank) invaded Germany and overran parts of the territory. They did not win any pitched battles, however, since no German force engaged them, neither did they subdue any tribe. They feared that they might suffer another disaster, and so did not advance far beyond the Rhine. They remained in that region until late autumn and celebrated the birthday of Augustus, on which occasion they held a horse-race supervised by the centurions, and then returned.

In Rome, Drusus Caesar, Tiberius's son, became quaestor and sixteen praetors held office; this happened because that number of men had stood for the appointment and Augustus, amid the difficulties with which he was then faced, was reluctant to offend any of them. The same thing did not happen, however, in the years immediately following, but the number remained fixed at twelve for a long while.

Apart from these events which took place at that time, it was forbidden for the seers to prophesy to any single individual in private, or to prophesy concerning death, even if others were present. Now Augustus attached so little importance to such matters so far as concerned himself that he published in a declaration for all to read the aspect of the stars at the time of his own birth; however, he forbade the practice in general. He also made a proclamation to the subject nations, prohibiting them from conferring any honours upon an official appointed to govern them, either during his period of office or within sixty days of his departure. He did this because some governors by making preparations for testimonials and eulogies to be offered by their subjects were doing a great disservice.

The state's business with foreign delegations was handled as before by three senators,[22] and the knights were permitted to fight as gladiators, a concession which may surprise some people. It was made because some individuals were disregarding the penalty of disfranchisement which was normally imposed for this action. So permission was granted to take part in such contests, either because the prohibition seemed to have become ineffective and the offenders evidently needed a more severe deterrent, or else because it seemed possible that they might be persuaded to abandon the practice. The result was that they suffered death instead of disfranchisement, for they fought no less frequently than before, and the contests aroused great enthusiasm; even Augustus was in the habit of watching them with the praetors who supervised the combats.

26.   After this Germanicus received the office of consul,[23] even though he had never served as a praetor, and he held it throughout the year, not on account of his rank, but in the way that some other men at this time still officiated for the whole term. Germanicus achieved nothing of note, except that he remained active in the law-courts even during his term of office, since his colleague Gaius Capito was considered a nonentity.

Now Augustus, since he was growing old, wrote a letter in which he commended Germanicus to the Senate, and the Senate to Tiberius. He did not read it out himself, since he could not now make himself heard: it was read, as the custom had grown up, by Germanicus.[24] After this the emperor requested the senators, taking the war against the Germans as an excuse, not to pay their respects at his home, nor to feel offended if he ceased his practice of attending their public banquets. It had been their custom, especially whenever a session of the Senate was about to take place, to greet him not only in the Forum but sometimes also in the Senate-house itself, both when he entered it and again when he left the chamber. Indeed there were occasions when, as he was merely sitting or even lying down in the palace, not only the Senate but even the knights and many of the populace would come to salute him.

27.   Despite these disabilities, however, he fulfilled his duties no less meticulously than before. He allowed the knights to stand for the tribuneship.[25] And when he learned that a number of scurrilous pamphlets were being composed concerning certain people, he ordered them to be tracked down. Those that were found in the city he ordered to be burned by the aediles, those outside by the officials in each locality, and he punished some of the authors. Since there were many exiles who were either residing outside the areas to which they had been banished, or living in the prescribed places but in too luxurious a style, he directed that nobody who had been excluded from fire and water should live either upon the European mainland or on any island within fifty miles of it, except for Cos, Rhodes, Samos and Lesbos: I do not know why he made an exception in favour of these alone.[26] Besides this he issued an order to the exiles that they should not cross the sea to any other place, or possess more than one cargo vessel having a capacity of a thousand amphorae, or two craft propelled by oars; that they should not employ more than twenty slaves or freedmen and should not possess property worth more than 500,000 sesterces. Moreover he threatened to punish not only the

exiles themselves but all others who helped them in any way to break these ordinances.

These are the laws which he enacted and which I have described so far as is necessary for our history. At that time too a special festival was inaugurated by the actors and the breeders of race-horses. The games held in honour of Mars were conducted this time in the Forum of Augustus, because the Tiber had inundated the Circus, and were celebrated, after a fashion, by a horse-race and a public show at which wild beasts were killed. They were repeated, as custom required, and on this occasion Germanicus arranged for two hundred lions to be killed in the Circus. The basilica that is called Julia[27] was built in honour of Gaius and Lucius Caesar, and was dedicated in that year.

28. When Lucius Munatius and Gaius Silius had taken up office as consuls,[28] Augustus accepted a ten-year term as head of the state for the fifth time, though he was apparently reluctant to do so. He again conferred tribunician power upon Tiberius, and allowed Drusus, the former's son, to stand for the consulship two years later, even though he had never yet held the praetorship. Augustus also requested that twenty counsellors should be appointed annually, since by this time on account of his age he no longer visited the Senate-house except on rare occasions. Until then, it seems, fifteen such counsellors had assisted him for six months at a time.[29] It was further voted that all measures decided upon by Augustus in consultation with Tiberius and the above advisers, together with the serving consuls, the consuls designate, his adopted children and any other such persons as he might at any time call on for advice, should be treated as valid and as approved by the Senate as a whole. After he had gained through this decree the power which he had in effect possessed all along, he continued to transact the greater part of the business of state, even though he sometimes did so from a couch.

At this date the tax of five per cent[30] was almost universally felt to be an oppressive impost, and since it seemed likely that an uprising might take place, Augustus sent a message to the Senate ordering that body to find some alternative source of revenue. He did not act thus with any intention of abolishing the tax: his purpose was rather that when the senators had failed to discover any solution they considered preferable, they should ratify the original measure, however unwillingly, and that no blame should rebound upon him. He further forbade both Germanicus and Drusus to make any public reference to the subject; he was afraid that if they expressed an opinion it would be suspected that this was at his orders, and that the Senate would adopt that plan without exploring the problem any further. The matter was debated at length, and some proposals were put to Augustus in writing. When he discovered from these that the senators were willing to accept any form of tax rather than the existing one, he changed the incidence of the tax to a levy upon fields and houses. He then straightaway sent out officials all over the country to prepare schedules of the property both of individuals and of cities, but without disclosing a figure for the rate of tax, or how it would be imposed. [His aim was that the public, fearing that they were about to be taxed even more heavily, would choose the five per cent in preference, which was exactly what happened. This was how Augustus dealt with these problems.

29.   During a horse-race which took place at the festival of Augustalia, held in honour of Augustus's birthday, a madman seated himself in the chair dedicated to Julius Caesar, and taking his crown, put it on his own head.[31] This episode caused universal alarm, since it seemed to have some significance for the destiny of Augustus, as indeed proved to be the case. In the following year when Sextus Appuleius and Sextus Pompeius were consuls, Augustus set out for Campania, and having presided over the games at Neapolis, died soon afterwards at Nola.

Various omens which suggested this outcome for him had taken place; they were numerous and not difficult to interpret. For example there was a total eclipse of the sun and the greater part of the sky appeared to be on fire; glowing embers appeared to fall from it, and blood-red comets were seen. A meeting of the Senate had been summoned to offer up prayers on account of the emperor's illness;] the chamber was discovered to be closed, and an owl perched above it hooted. A thunderbolt struck Augustus's statue, which stood on the Capitol, and obliterated the first letter of the name Caesar. This caused the seers to prophesy that on the hundredth day after this event he would participate in a divine destiny. They drew this conclusion from the fact that the letter C stands for one hundred among the Latins, and that the rest of the word signifies 'god' among the Etruscans.

These portents appeared beforehand while Augustus was still alive; but in later times people noticed another significant coincidence which concerned the consuls for that year, and the later emperor, Servius Sulpicius Galba. The consuls who were then in office were in some way related to Augustus, and it was also on the first day of that year that Galba, who later became emperor, assumed the *toga virilis*.[32] Since he was the first Roman to occupy the imperial throne after the line of Augustus had died out, this caused some people to say that the synchronization of the date was no mere matter of chance, but that some divine purpose was at work.

30. So Augustus fell sick and died. Some suspicion attached itself to Livia concerning the cause of his death, because he had secretly sailed over to the island of Planasia to visit Agrippa Postumus, and it appeared that he was about to become completely reconciled with him.[33] Livia was afraid, some people allege, that Augustus might bring him back to make him emperor, and so she smeared with poison some figs which were still ripening on trees from which Augustus was in the habit of picking the fruit with his own hands. She then ate those which had not been smeared, and offered the poisoned fruit to him. At any rate, he fell sick from this or from some other cause. Then he sent for his associates, and told them of all that he wanted to be done. Finally he declared, 'I found Rome built of clay: I leave it to you in marble.' In this saying he was not referring literally to the state of the buildings, but rather to the strength of the empire. And when he asked them for some applause, as comic actors do at the end of a mime, he was in fact mocking very aptly the whole life of man.

So on the nineteenth day of August, the very day on which he had first become consul, Augustus passed away. He had lived for seventy-five years, ten months and twenty-six days – he had been born on the twenty-third of September – and had been sole ruler, reckoning from the time of his victory at Actium, for forty-four years, less thirteen days. His death, however, was not immediately made known. Tiberius was still in Dalmatia, and Livia concealed the news until he arrived back, since she feared that there might be some uprising. This, at any rate, is the account given by most writers, including the most trustworthy ones. However, there are some who maintain that Tiberius was present during the emperor's illness and received various instructions from him.

The body of Augustus was conveyed from Nola by the most prominent men of each city in succession. When it reached the neighbourhood of Rome, the knights received it into their charge and carried it by night into the city. On the next day the Senate held a meeting, to which most of its members came wearing the dress which belongs to the knights, while the magistrates wore the senatorial habit, except for the toga which carried a purple border. Tiberius and his son Drusus wore grey garments. They too offered up incense, but did not employ a flute-player. Most of the senators sat in their accustomed places, while the consuls sat below, one on the bench occupied by the praetors, the other on that of the tribunes. After this Tiberius was formally absolved for having touched the body, an action which is not permitted, and for having escorted it.

32.   ... [Drusus took Augustus's will from the Vestal Virgins, with whom it had been deposited, and brought it into the Senate. Those who had witnessed it examined the seals, and then it was read out for the Senate to hear.

... It was Polybius, a freedman created by the emperor, who read the will, since it was not considered fitting for a senator to deliver any announcement of this kind. The document revealed that Augustus had left two-thirds of his estate to Tiberius and the rest to Livia, according to one report. In order that she should benefit to some extent from his estate, Augustus had sought permission from the Senate to bequeath to her this proportion since it was more than the amount allowed by law.[34] These two, then, were named as his heirs. Augustus also specified that many articles and sums of money should be given to many different people, both relatives and others who were unconnected by blood, including not only senators and knights but also foreign rulers. He left 40,000,000 sesterces to the Roman people, and in the case of the army 1,000 sesterces to each member of the Praetorian Guard, half that amount to the urban cohorts, and to the rest of the citizens enrolled in the legions 300 sesterces each. There were also children whose fathers had made Augustus their heir while the children were still young, and for these he directed that the whole amount together with interest should be repaid, when they reached manhood. He had practised this principle even in his lifetime: whenever he inherited the estate of anyone who had descendants, he invariably restored it in full to the man's offspring, immediately if they were already grown up, and otherwise later. However, although he treated the children of others in this way, he did not bring back his daughter from exile – although he did consider her worthy to receive gifts; he also gave orders that she should not be buried in his tomb. These were the provisions revealed in his will.

33.   Four documents were then brought in, and Drusus read out these. The first specified the arrangements for his funeral. The second recorded all the acts which he had carried out, and he directed that these should be inscribed on bronze columns, which were to be set up in front of his mausoleum.[35] The third was devoted to an account of military matters, of the revenues and the public expenditure, the amount of money in the treasuries, and all the other details of this kind which concerned the administration of the empire. The fourth contained instructions and commands for Tiberius and for the public at large. One of these enjoined them not to grant liberty to many slaves, so as to avoid filling the city with a nondescript rabble, and another to limit the numbers admitted to citizenship, so as to preserve a significant distinction between Roman citizens and the peoples of the subject nations. He urged them to entrust the conduct of the affairs of state to all who possessed the capacity to grasp the issues at stake and to act, and never to allow this executive power all to depend upon one person. If this principle were adopted, no one would aspire to set up a tyranny, nor on the other hand would the state founder if one man were removed. He gave it as his view that they should be satisfied with the possessions they now held, and should in no way seek to enlarge the empire beyond its present limits. It would become difficult to defend, he told them, and for this reason they would risk losing what was already theirs. This was the principle which he had in fact always observed himself, not only in word but in deed; at least, it had been open to him to annex many territories from the barbarian world, but he had not wished to do so. These, then, were his injunctions.

34.   After this his funeral took place. A couch was made of ivory and gold and spread with a pall of purple and gold. Beneath the covering his body was hidden in a coffin; above it a wax effigy, clad in triumphal dress, was displayed. This image was carried from the palace by the officials who had been appointed for the following year;] another one of gold was borne from the Senate-house, and yet a third was placed on a triumphal chariot. Behind these were conveyed the images of Augustus's ancestors, of his deceased relatives, except for that of Julius Caesar, because he had been ranked among the demi-gods, and finally those of the other Romans of the past who had distinguished themselves in some way, beginning with Romulus himself. An image of Pompey was also displayed, and all the nations which he had added to the empire were included

in the procession, each represented by an image which possessed some indigenous characteristics. After these followed all the other items in the pageant mentioned above. When the couch had been placed in full view on the Rostra of the orators,[36] Drusus read a pronouncement from there, and from the other Rostra, the Julian, Tiberius delivered the following address, in accordance with a decree:

35.   'Drusus has spoken to you of those matters concerning the divine Augustus which it is fitting for relatives to touch upon in their private capacity. But the Senate has rightly judged that his death deserves some form of public eulogy as well. I recognize that it was appropriate for this speech to be entrusted to me – for who other than his son and successor would it be more proper to invite to praise him? Still, I feel no confidence that my capacity to deal with the subject matches either your desires or his merits. Indeed, if I were about to speak in the presence of strangers, I should have deep misgivings that, when they heard my speech, they might judge that his deeds were no more remarkable than my account of them. But as it is, I am heartened by the fact that my words will be addressed to you, who are thoroughly familiar with all his achievements, who have witnessed them at first hand, and who for that reason have found him worthy of the praises I shall utter. And you will judge his excellence not merely from what I say, but from what you yourselves know, and you will reinforce my discourse by whatever it may lack from your memory of events. So, in this sense too, the eulogy will be a public one: I shall, like the leader of a chorus, give out the principal theme, and you will join in and chant the rest of the refrain. On this score, at least, I have no fears, either that you will consider it a weakness on my part that I cannot completely satisfy your desires, or that you yourselves will feel any jealousy towards one whose excellence so far surpassed your own. We all understand that even if all mankind were gathered together, they could not pronounce a tribute worthy of him; for your part you will gladly yield to him his triumphs, and so far from feeling envious that not one of you could equal him, will rather rejoice in the fact of his surpassing greatness. Indeed, the greater he appears when you compare him to yourselves, the greater will seem the benefits which he conferred, so that there will be no rancour in your hearts through any sense of feeling diminished by comparison with him, but rather pride on account of the good things you have received at his hands.

36. 'I shall begin at the point where he began to take part in public life, that is from the first years of his manhood. For this is one of Augustus's greatest achievements, namely that at the moment when he had only just left boyhood behind him and had scarcely arrived at man's estate, he devoted himself to his education for as long as public affairs were well directed by that demi-god, Julius Caesar. But when, after the conspiracy against Caesar, the whole commonwealth was thrown into turmoil, he not only amply avenged his father's death, but also gave you help at a time of dire need. In doing this he showed no fear of the number of his enemies, nor shrank from the magnitude of the problems which faced him, nor hesitated on account of his own immaturity.

'And yet what exploit of comparable greatness was achieved by Alexander of Macedon or by Romulus, who have the reputation beyond all others of having performed some outstanding deed of prowess in their youth? I shall pass over these, in case, by merely making the comparison and citing them as examples, I might be regarded – especially by you who know the facts as well as I do – as diminishing the virtues of Augustus. It is only if I were to match him with Hercules and his labours that I might be considered to be making a just comparison. But even then I should not fulfil my purpose, since Hercules during his childhood only fought with serpents, and in his manhood with a stag or two, and a boar, which he killed, and of course a lion, but this he did unwillingly, and under orders. Augustus, on the other hand, was dealing not with beasts but with men, and acting of his own free will, and by waging war and devising laws he did nothing less than save the commonwealth, and thereby gained great renown for himself. So it was on account of these services that you chose him as praetor and appointed him consul, at an age when some men are unwilling to serve even as private soldiers.

37. 'This, then, was how Augustus's political life began, and it is also the beginning of my account of him. Soon after, he perceived that the largest and most influential part of the people and of the Senate was on his side, but that Lepidus and Antony, Sextus Pompeius, Brutus and Cassius were creating factions in order to attain power. He feared that Rome might become embroiled in many wars simultaneously, and civil wars at that, and would thus become deeply divided and exhausted beyond all prospect of recovery, and he handled these men with consummate judgement, and in the manner which most benefited the state. He first

drew to his side those powerful figures who were endangering the state's very existence, and with their help conquered the others in war; then, having eliminated one group, he freed us in turn from the other men of power. He decided, although against his will, to sacrifice a few men to the vengeful desires of his colleagues[37] in order to save the people as a whole, and he showed an accommodating attitude to each of them in turn so as not to have to oppose all at once. He did not profit personally from these arrangements, but the outcome was of great benefit to us all.

'And yet I need not enlarge upon his successes in war, either in civil conflict or in fighting foreign enemies: the former should never have occurred in the first place, and as for the latter, the benefits which Roman arms have won for our people speak more eloquently than words. Now such successes depended to a great extent upon chance, and since they were won with the help of many Roman citizens and allies, Augustus must share the credit with all of these; and hence there are various other men with whose exploits his might be compared. I shall not dwell upon these achievements, then, for they have been described in many books and in works of art, and you can both read of them and see them represented.

'It is rather those deeds which are peculiar to Augustus – in other words those never performed by any other man – which have not only enabled our city to survive after experiencing many dangers of every kind, but have even made it stronger and more prosperous, and it is these alone I shall mention. To recount them will not only create for him a renown which is unsurpassed: it will give to the older men among you an unreserved pleasure and to the younger a positive lesson in the character and the composition of our government.

38.   'Consider, then, this Augustus, whom you judged to be worthy of his title for the reasons I have just described. As soon as he had put an end to the civil wars, in which his actions and experiences were not those which he himself desired but which the gods imposed upon him, he first of all spared the lives of most of his adversaries who had survived the various battles; in this respect he took the opposite course to that of Sulla, who was known as the Fortunate. I need not enumerate each example of his clemency – for everyone knows of the case of Sosius, of Scaurus, the brother of Sextus Pompeius, and above all of Lepidus, who lived on for

so many years after his defeat and continued to be high priest for the whole of his life.

'Again, although Augustus honoured his comrades in arms with many generous rewards, he never allowed them to indulge in any insolent behaviour. You are very well acquainted with the men in this category, especially Maecenas and Agrippa, so that here too I need not mention their names. Moreover Augustus possessed these two qualities which were never before united in any one man. I know there have been victors who spared their enemies, and others who did not allow their comrades to abuse their advantage, but these combined virtues have never been consistently and uniformly practised by one and the same man. For example, Sulla and Marius nursed a hatred against even the sons of those who had fought them, and I need not mention the instances of other and lesser men. Pompey and Caesar did not, generally speaking, give way to hatred in this fashion, but they allowed their friends on not a few occasions to do things which did not accord with their own principles. But this man so combined and mingled these two qualities that he enabled his opponents to feel they had been victorious rather than defeated, and proved to his comrades in arms that virtue is truly rewarded by Fortune.

39. 'After he had wrought all these achievements, calmed by acts of humanity all the discord which was the legacy of civil strife, and pacified his victorious troops by means of a generous settlement, he could by virtue of his efforts and of the armed strength and the money at his command have proclaimed himself the supreme and sole ruler, which indeed the course of events had made him. Yet he refused, and like a good physician who takes in hand a body wasted by sickness and cures it, he first brought back to health and then returned to your keeping the whole system of government. The importance of this action you can understand best if you recall that our ancestors praised Pompey, and also the Metellus[38] who rose to power at that time, because they demobilized of their own free will the armies with which they had fought the war. Now if these men who commanded only a small force recruited specifically for that campaign, and who were faced by rivals who would not let them do otherwise, acted thus and were praised for that reason, how can we do justice to the magnanimity shown by Augustus? He commanded your entire army, whose strength you know; all the financial resources of Rome, an immense sum, were under his control; he had no need to fear

or suspect any man; he might have ruled alone, and everyone would have approved; yet he decided not to do this, and instead laid down the arms, the money and the provinces before you.

'For your part, you made a wise and far-sighted decision when you declined this proposal and would not let him withdraw into private life: you knew very well that a democracy would never be able to reconcile such an immense variety of interests, but that they were most likely to be safeguarded by the leadership of one man. Accordingly you refused to go back to a state of affairs which appeared to promise independence, but in reality offered only perpetual strife between factions. When you chose Augustus, whose powers had been tested by the success of his own actions, you obliged him for a time at least to rule over you. Then when you discovered that he governed even better than before, you called upon him for a second, third, fourth and fifth time to continue in charge of affairs.

'And this was only reasonable, for who would not choose to be granted safety without effort, prosperity without danger, and to enjoy the abundant blessings which flow from settled government, without being a prey to the unceasing anxieties which it brings? Who succeeded better than Augustus in ruling over his own household, not to mention an empire of so many other beings? He took it upon himself to defend and uphold the safety of those provinces which were rebellious and at war, and gave back to you those which were peaceable and created no danger. And although he maintained such a great number of soldiers as a standing army to fight on your behalf, he never allowed them to cause harm to any Roman citizen; he trained them to be the most redoubtable protectors against alien races, while to their fellow-citizens at home they were unarmed and unwarlike.

'As for the senators, he did not deprive them of the right to cast lots for the governorships of the provinces, but offered them additional rewards in recognition of excellence; and when the Senate's decrees needed to be passed, he did not abolish their right to vote, but even added safeguards to protect their freedom of speech. He took those questions which were difficult to decide out of the hands of the people, and transferred them to the clearly defined jurisdiction of the courts, but he preserved for the people the prestigious dignity of holding elections for the offices of state. On these occasions he strove to instil into the citizens the love of honour rather than of party strife, and in the case of the candidates to replace the element of greed in their contests for office with a regard for their good name.

'He increased his own wealth by dint of sober living, but spent it freely for the public need, and while he handled the public funds as carefully as if they were his own, he refused to make use of them, on the grounds that they belonged to others. He repaired all the public works which had suffered damage, but deprived none of the original builders of the glory of having founded them. He also erected many new buildings, some in his own name and some in that of others, or else allowed those others to build them; in this he was constantly mindful of the public good, but grudged no one the fame which resulted from these public benefactions.

'He pursued any lapses from the moral code on the part of his own family with great severity, but he treated the offences of others with charity. Those who showed qualities of excellence he acknowledged without hesitation as possessing standards which equalled his own, but he did not find fault with those who followed a different mode of life. Even among the men who conspired against him, he punished only those whose lives would have been of no benefit, even to themselves, and his treatment of the rest was such that for many years afterwards they could find no grounds, either true or false, for attacking him. It is not surprising that plots should have been formed against him at times, for not even the gods can please all alike. The excellence of good rulers, however, shows itself in their own virtuous actions, not in the misdeeds committed by others.

41. 'I have spoken, Quirites, only of Augustus's greatest and most outstanding qualities, and this too only in summary fashion, for the task of chronicling all his qualities minutely, one by one, would require many days. What is more, I know well that although I have touched only upon these few subjects, yet these will spur you to recall all the rest in your own minds, and thus you may feel that I have in a sense spoken of all the others as well. Neither I as the speaker nor you as my audience have been stirred by any spirit of boasting; my purpose has rather been that his many noble achievements should receive the tribute of everlasting glory in your hearts.

'But how can I refrain from mentioning his senators as well? Without doing harm to any man, he purified the Senate of the scum which had risen to the surface as a result of the various party factions, and by this action regenerated the character of the remainder, raised its quality by increasing the property qualification and enriched it by grants of money. He cast his vote on an equal footing with his colleagues, and took part with them in divisions of the house. He always communicated to them all the greatest and most important issues, either in the Senate-chamber or else at his house, where he received different members at different times on account of his age and physical weakness.

'And how can I refrain from mentioning the rest of the Roman people? He provided for them public works, distributions of money, games, festivals, amnesties, an abundance of the necessities of life, and security, not only from wrongdoers and foreign enemies, but even from the acts of the gods, as they occur by day and night. And I must not leave out the allies: he enabled them to live in freedom without incurring dangers and in alliance with Rome without cost to themselves. Likewise the subject nations: none of them were ever treated with arrogance or suffered abuse at his hands.

'How too could I forget to mention a man who lived his private life in poverty and used his wealth only for public service; who treated himself with austerity but others with lavish generosity; who took upon his own shoulders every hardship and danger for your sake, but would not burden you with the labour of accompanying him when he left the city or meeting him when he returned; who on holidays received even the masses into his own house, but on other dates greeted the Senate only in its own chamber?

'How could I pass over the multitude of laws which he enacted, and the exactitude of their provision? They offered to those who had suffered wrong compensations that were sufficient, and for the wrongdoers penalties that were not inhuman. Should I not mention too the rewards he offered to those who married and had children? Or the prizes given to the soldiers without causing deprivation to anyone else? Or the fact that he remained content with those possessions which Rome had acquired once and for all by force of necessity, but declined to conquer additional territory, which once annexed might appear to have enlarged our empire, but might have caused us to lose what we already held? Or how he always shared the joys and the sorrows, the jests and the serious counsels of his closest friends and, in a word, allowed all those who could offer any useful suggestion to utter their thoughts freely? Or how he praised those who spoke the truth, but detested flatterers? Or how he gave away to many people large sums of money from his own means, and how whenever he received a bequest from men who had children, he restored it all to the children? No speaker could be so forgetful as to leave such actions unmentioned.

'This, then, was why you had good reason to make him your leader and the father of the people, why you honoured him with so many distinctions and such a number of consulships, and why you finally made him a demi-god and declared him to be immortal. And so it is right that we should not mourn for him, but that while we now return his body to nature, we should glorify his spirit for all time as that of a divine being.'

42.   This was the speech which Tiberius read. Afterwards the same bearers as before took up the couch and carried it through the Porta Triumphalis,³⁹ as had been directed by a decree of the Senate. The whole Senate was present and walked in the funeral procession. So too did the equestrian order, their wives, the Praetorian Guard and indeed virtually all who were in Rome at the time. When the bier had been placed on the pyre in the Campus Martius, all the priests marched around it first, then came the knights, not only those who were to be senators but the others as well, and then the infantry of the Praetorian Guard circled it at a run and threw on to it all the triumphal decorations which any of them had ever received from the emperor for an act of valour. After this the centurions took torches, again in accordance with a senatorial decree, and set fire to the pyre from below. So it was consumed, and an eagle released from it flew aloft to bear the emperor's spirit to heaven. When these ceremonies had been completed, all the others departed, but Livia remained on the spot for five days, attended by the most distinguished of the knights; then she had his bones gathered up and placed in his tomb.

43.   The mourning prescribed by the law was carried on only for a few days by men, but the women continued it for a whole year, in accordance with a decree. At the time there were not many who mourned the dead man with genuine emotion, but later all came to do so. Augustus had been easily approachable by all alike, and he had made a practice of aiding many people with sums of money. He bestowed signal honours upon his friends, and he felt real pleasure when they shared their opinions openly with him. Besides the examples I have already related, there was one which concerned Athenodorus. This man was once carried into Augustus's

room in a covered litter, as if he were a woman. He suddenly leaped out of it with a drawn sword and cried out, 'Are you not afraid that someone might come in like this and kill you?' Augustus was not in the least angry, but even thanked him for the warning. These qualities of his were remembered, and also the fact that he never gave way to uncontrolled rage against those who had done him any wrong, and kept faith even with those who did not deserve it. There was, for example, a robber named Corocotta, who flourished in Spain, and who had made Augustus so angry at first that he had offered a reward of 1,000,000 sesterces for his capture alive. But later when the robber came to him of his own accord, Augustus not only did him no harm, but actually enriched him by the sum offered as a reward.

The Romans felt his death as a great loss, both for these reasons and for others besides. By dint of combining monarchy with democracy, he saved their freedom for them and at the same time established order and security, so that they were delivered alike from the lack of authority which prevails in a democracy and from the excess of it in a tyranny, and could live in a state of freedom enjoyed with moderation and under a monarchy which held no terrors for them; they were subjects of royalty without being slaves, and citizens of a democracy without suffering discord.

44.   If any of them remembered Augustus's deeds during the civil wars, they attributed them to the pressure of circumstances. They judged it right to base their view of his disposition on what he did after he had come into the undisputed possession of supreme power, for here in truth there was an immense contrast. Anyone who examines his actions in detail can confirm this. But to sum them up briefly, I may say that he resolved the strife between the rival factions, remodelled the system of government in such a way as to equip it with the maximum of power and greatly strengthened it. For this reason, even if an occasional deed of violence did occur, such as is apt to happen in exceptional situations, it would be fairer to lay the blame on the circumstances rather than on him.

One of the factors that contributed to his glory, and by no means the least, was the length of his reign. The great majority of those who had lived under the republic were now dead, and the most influential of them too. The later generation knew nothing of that form of government: they had been brought up entirely or very largely under the conditions which prevailed during the principate, and so not only did they find no objection to them since they were now familiar, but even rejoiced in them, since they saw that their present situation was preferable and more free from fear than those times of which they knew from hearsay.

45.   Although the people recognized these things during Augustus's lifetime, they understood them more completely after his death, for human nature is so constituted that it is not so keenly aware of its good fortune in times of prosperity as it is of what it has lost when misfortune strikes. This is what happened at that time in the case of Augustus. When they learned by experience that his successor Tiberius was a very different kind of ruler, they longed for the man who was gone. Indeed it was immediately possible for people of intelligence to judge the change in the situation. For example, when the consul Pompeius set out to meet the men who were carrying Augustus's body, he received a blow on the leg and had to be carried back in a litter with the bier. And at the very first meeting of the Senate after the emperor's death, an owl sat on the roof of the Senate-house and uttered many ill-omened cries. At any rate the characters of the two men were so completely different that the suspicion was current that Augustus knew Tiberius's nature very well, and had deliberately made him his successor to exalt his own reputation.

46.   It was only at a later date that these rumours began to circulate. At the time the Senate declared Augustus to be immortal, assigned to him sacred rites and priests to perform them, and appointed Livia, who had already been named Julia and Augusta, to be his priestess. They also authorized her to be attended by a lictor whenever she exercised her sacred office. For her part she presented a certain Numerius Atticus, a senator and former praetor, with 1,000,000 sesterces, because he testified on oath that he had seen Augustus ascending to heaven in the same way, as tradition has it, as occurred in the case of Proculus[40] and Romulus.[41] A shrine voted by the Senate and built by Livia and Tiberius was erected to his memory in Rome, and others in many different places; some of the communities built these of their own accord, others only under orders. Besides this, the house at Nola in which Augustus had died was dedicated to him as a precinct. While the shrine was being constructed for him in Rome, the Senate placed a golden image of him lying on a couch in the temple of Mars, and to this they decreed all the honours which were later to be conferred upon his statue.

Other decrees concerning Augustus directed that his image was not to be borne in the procession at any man's funeral, that the consuls should celebrate his birthday with games such as the Ludi Martiales, and that the tribunes, because of their sacrosanctity, should have charge of the Augustalia. These officials carried out all the ceremonies in the customary manner, including even the wearing of triumphal robes at the horse-race, except that they did not ride in the chariot.[42] Besides these arrangements Livia held a private festival in his honour at the palace which lasted for three days, and this ceremony is still carried out by the reigning emperor down to the present day.

47.   These were the decrees which were passed in memory of Augustus, nominally by the Senate, but in fact by Tiberius and Livia. This was because some men made one suggestion and some another, and finally the Senate decreed that Tiberius should be sent proposals in writing from the senators, and then select whichever he preferred. I have also mentioned Livia's name, because she took a share in the proceedings, as if she possessed full powers.

Meanwhile the populace raised a riot because at the celebration of the Augustalia one of the actors refused to enter the theatre for the fee which he had been offered. The disturbance did not cease until the tribunes summoned a meeting of the Senate on the same day, and appealed to it to allow them to spend more than the sum authorized by law. Here ends my account of Augustus.

NOTES

BOOK 50

1. The last two chapters of Book 49 and the first of Book 50 deal with events taking place in 33 B.C. But in the opening sentences of ch. 1 Dio looks back to an earlier phase of the civil wars, broadly speaking the situation which followed the elimination of Lepidus from the Triumvirate in 36 B.C. Sextus Pompeius was executed in 35 B.C. and the king of Armenia captured in 34. In the second paragraph of ch. 1 the narrative returns to 33 B.C., with its analysis of the breakdown of the relationship between Antony and Octavian.

2. After his defeat by Agrippa in the naval battle of Naulochus (36 B.C.) Sextus fled from Sicily to Asia Minor. There he intrigued against Antony and offered his services to the king of Parthia to repel Antony's expedition. He was finally captured by Antony's subordinate, Titius, and executed at Miletus (35 B.C.).

3. Artavasdes I, king of Armenia, had in 36 B.C. offered his support to Antony, which encouraged the latter to embark on the invasion of Parthia. During the campaign Artavasdes defected from his alliance. A force of Armenian cavalry had been assigned to protect Antony's siege-train; when the escort was withdrawn, the siege-train was attacked and Antony's whole expedition endangered. In 34 B.C., supported by the king of Media Atropatene, Antony returned to Armenia. Artavasdes was persuaded to come to a conference at which he was arrested. He was later brought to Alexandria to be led in Antony's triumph, and was finally executed after the battle of Actium on Cleopatra's orders.

4. In the Sicilian campaign of 36 B.C. Lepidus was nominally supporting Octavian against Sextus Pompeius. When Pompeius was defeated, Lepidus was tempted to challenge Octavian in an effort to restore his declining power in the Triumvirate. But his soldiers went over to Octavian. Lepidus's life was spared, but he was dismissed from the Triumvirate, and although he could scarcely be stripped of the office of Pontifex Maximus, was forced to spend the rest of his life in Circeii, a seaside town south of Rome; he died in 12 B.C.

5. It is worth noting that, in spite of the Donations of Alexandria (see following note), Octavian's overt propaganda campaign against Antony had in 33 B.C. scarcely begun. The crucial moment arrived at the beginning of the consulship of Sosius and Ahenobarbus in 32.

6. In the winter of 34 B.C. Antony held a ceremony, later known as the Donations of Alexandria. At this he declared that Cleopatra had been Julius Caesar's wife by a Macedonian marriage – she was of royal Macedonian descent – and that her son Ptolemy Caesar (Caesarion) was Julius Caesar's legitimate son. Cleopatra was pronounced Queen of Kings and Ptolemy Caesar King of Kings: they were to be joint rulers of Egypt and Cyprus. Antony's eldest son by Cleopatra, Alexander the Sun (aged six), was given the kingdom of Armenia, the overlordship of Media and Parthia and an Armenian bodyguard. Their second son, Ptolemy Philadelphus (aged two), was given the Egyptian possessions in Syria and Cilicia, and the overlordship of all other rulers in Asia Minor from the Euphrates westward to the Hellespont. Their daughter, Cleopatra the Moon, Alexander's twin, was given the territories of Cyrenaica and Libya.

In Roman law, Antony's legitimate children were those born to his Roman wives, namely Fulvia and Octavia. In later history the emperors Caligula, Claudius and Nero were directly descended from Antony and Octavia.

In Cleopatra's case, at the time of Julius Caesar's death his legal wife was Calpurnia, and Cleopatra's legal husband was her consort, Ptolemy XIII. Besides exalting Cleopatra's position, Antony's purpose, according to Dio's comment, was to disparage Octavian as an adopted, not a real son of Julius Caesar. However, in Caesar's will Octavian was named as his principal heir, and there was no mention of Cleopatra.

7. Gnaeus Domitius Ahenobarbus was the Enobarbus whom Shakespeare portrays as Antony's devoted supporter. He was a successful commander, especially at sea, who had first taken the side of Brutus and Cassius and had charge of their fleet. Even after their defeat at Philippi he continued to harass Octavian's forces in the Adriatic. In 40 B.C. he joined Antony, was included in an amnesty for former republicans and was appointed governor of Bithynia.

8. Gaius Sosius was one of Antony's ablest subordinates. In 38 B.C. Antony had appointed him governor of Syria and Cilicia. There he led a campaign against Antigonus, whom the Parthians had installed, with the support of the Jews, as king of Judaea. His operations were aided by Herod the Great, who had become one of Antony's firmest adherents. Sosius captured Jerusalem in 37. Antony had entrusted to Sosius and Ahenobarbus an account of his Eastern settlement for this to be ratified by the Senate. As a result of Octavian's management of the second session of the Senate, and the subsequent flight of Antony's supporters, these proposals for the East were never presented. By the time of the third session, the

opportune arrival of Titius and Plancus had placed vital information in Octavian's hands (see following notes).

9. The consuls presided in alternate months: Ahenobarbus, the senior, had taken January.

10. Marcus Titius had served as quaestor in Antony's Parthian campaign in 37–36 B.C. In the following year he had Sextus Pompeius executed in Miletus. After Actium, Octavian appointed him governor of Syria.

11. Lucius Munatius Plancus, Titius's uncle, was one of the most adroit 'fence-sitters' and trimmers of the period of the civil wars; his defection to Octavian must have been noted by many as an ominous sign for Antony's prospects. He had first joined Antony in 43 B.C. and was consul in 42 with Lepidus. He commanded several legions in Italy and was associated with Antony's brother Lucius and Antony's wife Fulvia in the fighting against Octavian in 41. Later he governed Asia, and then Syria, in Antony's interest. In 32 Antony sent Octavia formal letters of divorce, and this may have prompted Titius's and Plancus's decision, since it showed that Antony was irrevocably committed to Cleopatra. In 27 Plancus proposed that the title Augustus should be conferred upon Octavian. In 22 he was appointed censor.

12. These actions may be seen as part of a campaign of psychological warfare on Octavian's part. Antony still had the consuls and many senators on his side. For the clash to be represented as a just war, Antony must be shown as a degenerate Roman, seeking to subvert the supremacy and the liberty of his compatriots, and to transfer world power from the Tiber to the Nile. He must be depicted as morally in the wrong and morally the aggressor. Although a properly witnessed will existed, we do not know that Octavian's spoken version was an accurate one.

13. Under the agreements reached between Antony, Octavian and Sextus Pompeius in 39 B.C. consuls had been designated for each of the years 38–31 B.C. (See Dio, Book 48, ch. 35; Appian, *Civil Wars*, Book 5, ch. 73.) Antony's coinage shows that he regarded himself as still holding the consulship (for the third time) in 31 B.C.

14. The Roman goddess of war, regarded sometimes as the wife, sometimes as the sister, of Mars.

15. A member of the college of priests who represented the Roman people in their dealings with other nations, for instance in the formal declaration of war and peace, or the conclusion of treaties.

16. The gymnasiarch was the president of the Gymnasium, which was a kind of cross between Sandhurst and a sixth-form college and was attended by the young men of Greek origin and citizen status (that is, the Alexandrian elite). Its social importance was high and the post of gymnasiarch correspondingly prestigious.

17. What was especially repugnant was the word's association with the institution of kingship, which the Romans held in perpetual abhorrence.

18. In the Graeco-Egyptian culture of Egypt, Osiris and Dionysus were often identified with one another as deities, and also associated with the cult of ruler-worship. The rulers of the Hellenistic kingdoms ever since the time of Alexander the Great had come to be regarded as gods on earth, gods made manifest in living beings. Antony had been received as the New Dionysus at Ephesus in 41 B.C. Cleopatra's father, Ptolemy Auletes, was referred to as the New Dionysus. The word Osiris signifies the Occupier of the Throne. On the same principle the god's partner, Isis, was often identified with the queen, whether consort or regnant, and Cleopatra followed this practice.

19. The Romans used this phrase as a term of abuse. Cleopatra was, in fact, of Macedonian descent, and had no Egyptian blood at all.

20. The modern Bologna. This region contained a large number of Antony's 'clients', that is, long-standing adherents of his ancestors and himself. Suetonius, however, states (*Divus Augustus* 17) that Octavian's generosity to the Bononians consisted in excusing them from swearing the oath of allegiance he imposed on Italy and the western provinces.

21. The two areas of Africa directly administered by Rome were the provinces of Cyrenaica and 'Africa', that is to say the coastal strip which corresponds roughly to the modern Tunisia.

22. Originally the ruler of Mauretania, who had fought on Julius Caesar's side at the battle of Munda (45 B.C.), where Caesar defeated the republican forces under Gnaeus and Sextus Pompeius, the sons of Pompey the Great. He was later driven from Mauretania by his brother Bocchus, who supported Octavian. Bogud joined Antony and commanded the naval station at Methone, an important staging post on Antony's supply route from Egypt. (See ch. 11.)

23. Antony's financial resources were always stronger than Octavian's, thanks to the immense wealth of the Egyptian throne.

24. The great race-track which occupied the hollow between the Palatine and Aventine hills. The length of the arena was over 700 metres and it is estimated to have held some 200–250,000 spectators. It was used for chariot-racing, and is not to be confused with the Colosseum, built A.D. 72–80, which was especially used for gladiatorial contests.

25. The Albanian coast north of Corcyra (Corfu). It is most improbable that Antony considered an invasion of Italy in the autumn of 32. His fleet, if it was doing more than reconnoitring, may have been seeking to establish control of the eastern coast of the Adriatic as far north as possible, in order to deny Octavian

the chance of an easy crossing the next spring from Brundisium to Apollonia. (See also note 32 below.)

26. During the winter of 41–40 B.C. Antony's brother Lucius had been besieged by Octavian in Perusia and surrendered in 40.

27. See note 13 above.

28. In 45 the Senate had voted that a gilded throne and crown should be set for Caesar at all public games and theatrical performances. It is possible that after his death and subsequent deification a crowned image of him was substituted. (Appian, *Civil Wars*, Book II, ch. 106.3.28.)

29. The goddess Hope had several temples in Rome.

30. Normally Roman citizens living in Italy were exempt from direct taxation, but the Triumvirate of Antony, Octavian and Lepidus had been obliged to resort to various special levies to pay for the civil wars. Thus in 43 all property-owners with an estate of over 400,000 sesterces were required to pay a year's income. The proscriptions of 42 were likewise intended to raise funds.

31. 31 B.C.

32. Both Antony and Octavian had embarked on a strategic gamble. Antony, by setting up his bases in southern Greece and abandoning the Adriatic and the Via Egnatia, which commanded the approaches to Macedonia and Thrace, was banking on lengthening Octavian's sea communications: the risks involved in long voyages were great. Octavian was aiming at an early finish to the campaign, and in this context it could be argued that the factors of time and money were on Antony's side. The line of supply for his army was guarded by a chain of naval stations, of which Methone was one of the southernmost on the route taken by the corn ships from Egypt. The loss of this base was thus a very serious reverse. Antony's strategy was logical, but was upset by Agrippa's brilliant seamanship.

33. Octavian by no means used his whole military resources. His army has been estimated at 80,000 infantry and 12,000 cavalry, and his fleet at 400 ships. Antony had mustered 100,000 infantry, of whom perhaps three-quarters were legionaries, 12,000 cavalry and a fleet of 500 vessels.

34. Octavian regarded Apollo as a deity especially protective towards himself and his family. He had already vowed a temple to him on the Palatine hill in 36 B.C., which was eventually dedicated in 28.

35. Malaria is likely, with much stagnant water present; also dysentery.

36. Quintus Dellius had been employed by Antony on various special missions. He had escorted Cleopatra to Tarsus in 41 B.C. for the celebrated encounter with Antony in her barge on the river Cydnus. He had been sent to Artavasdes I to bring him to the conference in Media, at which the king was arrested in 34. Both Dellius and Amyntas went over to Octavian.

37. A striking inconsistency in the narrative. In Book 51, ch. 2, Dio reports that Octavian spared Sosius's life after Actium; this is confirmed by other contemporary sources.

38. Antony reduced his fleet to some 230 vessels to oppose Octavian's 400. He embarked some 20,000 soldiers, including 2,000 archers and slingers. Octavian had about 37,000 troops on his ships.

39. Here Antony was certainly on stronger ground. Octavian lacked the money rather than the manpower to sustain a long campaign.

40. Antony was now fifty-two, Octavian thirty-one.

41. The battle was fought in October 42. It was largely due to Antony's generalship that the republican forces of Brutus and Cassius were defeated.

42. In August 36 Sextus Pompeius defeated Octavian off the eastern coast of Sicily. But in September Agrippa won the decisive naval battle of the campaign at Naulochus, a little further north.

43. It is very unlikely that any ancient ship had more than three banks of oars, and absolutely certain that the higher figures – 'forty' is cited in the Ptolemaic navy – cannot have referred to the number of banks. The most likely explanation of the numeral is that ships were classified according to the numbers of rowers on each *vertical set* of oars. A trireme did indeed have three banks of oars, but only one man per oar. A 'four' (quadrireme) had two banks of oars with two men per oar, a 'six' either three banks with two men per oar or more probably two banks with three men per oar, and so on. Three-banked ships needed extremely well-trained crews, as the heyday of trireme warfare in the fifth century B.C. made clear. It is therefore unlikely that the large ships of the first century B.C., often manned by pressed men and freed slaves, were more than double-banked. Antony's flagship, a 'ten', will then have had two banks of oars with five men to an oar.

44. Pyrrhus (319–272), king of Epirus, was one of the most brilliant Greek generals of the generation which succeeded that of Alexander the Great. In 281 he invaded Italy at the invitation of the Tarentines to help them against the Romans. His use of the phalanx and of elephants at first disconcerted the Romans, and he defeated them at Heracleia in 280. But both there and in later battles his losses were very heavy. Finally the Romans defeated him at Beneventum in 275, and he returned to Epirus in 274 with barely a third of his original army.

45. Philip V of Macedon (230–179 B.C.) engaged in the first and second Macedonian wars with Rome (214–205 and 200–197 B.C.), and was decisively defeated by T. Quinctius Flamininus at the battle of Cynoscephalae (197 B.C.).

46. Perseus, the son of Philip V and last king of Macedon, was defeated by Aemilius Paullus at the battle of Pydna (168 B.C.), and was deposed.

47. Antiochus III, king of Syria, who reigned 223–187 B.C., had allied himself with Philip V to partition the possessions of the Ptolemies. After the second Punic war he gave refuge to the exiled Hannibal, and was at war with Rome from 192–189 B.C., when he was defeated by Lucius Scipio at the battle of Magnesia.

48. The war against Numantia in north-eastern Spain was brought to a successful conclusion in 133 B.C. by Scipio Aemilianus (185–129 B.C.), one of the sons of Aemilius Paullus. He besieged the city, starved it into submission, and finally destroyed it.

49. The Romans fought three wars against Carthage – 265–241 B.C., 218–202 B.C. and 149–146 B.C.; at the end of the third war Carthage was razed to the ground.

50. A tribe from northern Germany. Together with the Teutones, the Cimbri invaded Gaul in 109 B.C., where they defeated several Roman armies. They and the Ambrones were repulsed by Marius at Aquae Sextiae, the modern Aix, in 102, and still more decisively beaten at Vercellae in the Po valley in 101.

51. The references to the Gauls, the Britons and the Rhine relate to Julius Caesar's campaigns.

52. Octavian himself fought the Pannonians, a tribe inhabiting north-western Jugoslavia, in 35 B.C. (See Book 49, ch. 36.)

53. 'Imperator' was a title of honour conferred by acclamation on their general by the troops after a decisive victory. The prolonged commands of the last years of the republic made it possible for a man to win more than one such acclamation. By the time of Actium Octavian had won five, Antony four. Octavian had also, in the early thirties, converted the word into a permanent attribute of his own, a talisman of victory, by adopting it as a sort of first name and becoming known as Imperator Caesar.

54. The names given to Alexander and Cleopatra, Antony's twin children by Cleopatra.

55. A reference to the Donations of Alexandria (see note 6 above).

56. Antony married Octavia in 39 B.C.

57. The elder Antonia was born in 39, the younger in 36.

58. A port at the east of the Nile delta. Like Corinth, it was well known for its large cosmopolitan sea-faring population and its riotous night-life.

59. The modern Modena. During the civil wars Antony was defeated there by Octavian's troops in April 43, but in fact the veterans of Mutina had been discharged by Octavian after his defeat of Sextus Pompeius in 36.

60. In the summer of 36 B.C. Antony led an expedition to invade Parthia. In

August he attempted to besiege the palace at Phraaspa, but without success; he was obliged to retreat in winter, and his army suffered heavy losses.

61. These charges were a routine part of Roman political abuse and should not be taken seriously.

62. In the autumn of 44 B.C. Antony left Rome to collect four legions from Brundisium and lead them to his province of Cisalpine Gaul, but two of them deserted to Octavian *en route*.

63. Lucius Scipio – brother of the great Publius Scipio (Africanus), the conqueror of Hannibal – was consul in 190 B.C., and was appointed to lead an expedition with Publius against Antiochus III. Sulla (138–78), Lucullus (110–56) and Pompey the Great (106–48) all conducted successful campaigns in Asia. The argument is that the province of Asia produces immense wealth, but its inhabitants are of little military value as allies.

64. Inhabitants of a region in north-western Jugoslavia, corresponding roughly to the modern Slovenia.

65. A tribe inhabiting the modern Croatia. Dalmatia preserves its name to this day. Octavian campaigned against all these tribes and the Pannonians in 35–33 B.C.

66. Dio's narrative of the battle is muddled, and in parts fanciful. With the help of Plutarch's *Life of Antony* (ch. 65ff.), sense can be made of it. Octavian's aim was to draw Antony out into open water and use his numerical superiority to outflank him. Antony wished to stay inshore, with his wings protected by land on either side of the narrows, and use the advantage of his heavier ships. Eventually, since it was he who wanted the battle, he had to advance. By edging north and west with his right wing, he opened a gap in the middle of the line through which Cleopatra's ships, lying in rear, could suddenly sail when the moment was ripe; and at the same time he also gained distance to windward, so that it was easier for the queen's ships, and for any others which could disengage and follow them, to round under sail the great mass of Leucas to southward. This plan worked fairly well. Cleopatra's squadron, with the pay chest on board, got away and Antony managed to extricate himself and several of the other ships. Of the rest, some were sunk and the remainder eventually surrendered. Antony and Cleopatra thus escaped with about a third of the 230 ships that had rowed out of the Gulf that morning. Dio has composed a set-piece on the battle in the manner of Thucydides, but this was not a naval engagement on the grand scale, rather a blockade-breaking attempt. As such, it was fairly successful, considering the hopelessness of Antony's position, embayed on a lee shore and facing superior forces. Cleopatra's 'treachery' in fleeing is of course a misrepresentation by the victors, while Dio's embellishment of the end of the battle with the horrors of fire receives no

confirmation from any other source and probably arises from a wish to make such an important battle suitably memorable.

BOOK 51

1. See Book 50, note 43.

2. Perhaps some 130 out of Antony's 230 which took part in the battle surrendered. Most of these were burned, as Octavian had no use for them.

3. In 29 B.C.

4. See Book 50, ch. 13. Amyntas deserted to Octavian with Dellius.

5. Archelaus, king of Cappadocia.

6. The king of Cilicia, who had been killed in the sea battle with Agrippa just before Actium.

7. Iamblichus was the ruler of Emesa in Syria, executed by Antony shortly before Actium for suspected treachery. Antony had been incited to do this by Alexander.

8. Towns in Crete which had declared for Octavian before Actium.

9. See Book 50, note 37.

10. The third wife of Pompey the Great. He divorced her for her liaison with Julius Caesar, but later, for political reasons, married Caesar's daughter, Julia.

11. Gaius Scribonius Curio had been elected tribune in 51 B.C. He used his tribunician powers to veto the motion that Caesar must return home from his province of Gaul. His action enabled Caesar to remain on the spot in command of the legions stationed there. He later took part in the civil wars on Caesar's side, but was killed by Pompey's supporters at the battle of Utica in Africa (49 B.C.).

12. January, 30 B.C.

13. Marcus Licinius Crassus had joined Antony after the defeat of Sextus Pompeius in 36 B.C., but went over to Octavian before Actium. He was the grandson of the Crassus who was defeated and killed by the Parthians at Carrhae (53 B.C.) and who had been the associate of Pompey and Julius Caesar in the so-called 'First Triumvirate'.

14. The loyalty of the legions, and hence Octavian's prospects, depended to a great extent at this time on whether he could secure the treasure of the Ptolemies.

15. To avoid the stormy passage round the southern extremity of the Peloponnese.

16. See Book 50, note 3. Artavasdes had been detained in Alexandria ever since Antony had brought him there in 34 B.C.

17. The inhabitants of Nabataea, a territory which extended from southern Jordan to the head of the Gulf of Eilat. Its ruler, Malchus, had long been an enemy of

Cleopatra. He had withheld from her the revenues due from the bituminous deposits in his territory, for which he had been punished by Herod.

18. What Dio refers to as the Red Sea is now known as the Persian Gulf: what we call the Red Sea he calls the Arabian Gulf.

19. A city in Mysia on the south coast of the Sea of Marmara.

20. Other sources give his first name as Decimus. He was the last of Caesar's murderers to survive.

21. Asclepius, the Greek god of healing, son of Apollo and Coronis, was worshipped throughout the Greek world and after the fourth century B.C. at Rome under the name of Aesculapius. There was a famous sanctuary of his at Cos; the island also contained the medical school established by Hippocrates (c. 460–377 B.C.).

22. Gaius Cornelius Gallus (69–c. 26 B.C.) was a noted poet and friend of Virgil. We know nothing of his military and administrative career before this, but to command an army, as a mere knight, was an extraordinary achievement.

23. The modern Sollum, near the western frontier of Egypt.

24. The port at the most easterly mouth of the Nile. Modern historians question whether Cleopatra surrendered it: Octavian may well have had to take it by storm. These chapters contain many items which could be Octavian's propaganda.

25. The brother-in-law of Maecenas. According to Plutarch, *Antony* (ch. 79), the interview was begun by Proculeius. He then handed over to Gallus, the general who had defeated Antony at Paraetonium, so that he himself could gain surreptitious entry by ladder while Cleopatra was distracted.

26. This refers to the power which she had exercised over Julius Caesar: it was now Octavian who had power over her.

27. According to Egyptian religious tradition the asp was the divine minister of the Sun-god, and its effigy encircled the royal diadem of Egypt to protect its wearer. The symbolic significance of its bite in this context was that the Sun-god had rescued his daughter from humiliation and taken her to himself.

28. This seems unlikely. Octavian may well have reflected that to lead Cleopatra in his triumph might cause a revulsion of feeling in her favour; this had happened in the case of Arsinoe, Cleopatra's half-sister, when she had been paraded in Caesar's triumph in 47 B.C. There was also the question of how to treat Cleopatra in future, Octavian's most pressing need was to capture the treasure of the Ptolemies intact; this achieved, Cleopatra's suicide solved many problems. Dolabella's visit, described in Plutarch, *Antony* (ch. 84), may well have been arranged to warn her that she would shortly be taken to Rome; then she was left free to contrive how to end her life.

29. Shakespeare, relying upon Plutarch, says that Cleopatra's Roman lovers had been Julius Caesar, Gnaeus Pompey and Mark Antony. In the lines

> ... great Pompey
> Would stand and make his eyes grow in my brow;
> There would he anchor his aspect ...
>
> (I.v.31–3)

Shakespeare has misidentified Pompey the Great with his elder son, Gnaeus, who took command of the Alexandrian fleet in 49–48 B.C. and was killed at Munda in 45 B.C. This tradition is nowhere mentioned by Dio: in this context he is alluding to Julius Caesar, Mark Antony and Octavian.

30. Antyllus was Antony's eldest son by his first wife, Fulvia, and his legitimate heir, and, since he was a Roman citizen, Octavian may have regarded him as even more dangerous than Caesarion. The betrothal had been a political arrangement, made in 37, to seal the compact of Tarentum.

31. Caesarion had been acknowledged by Antony as Julius Caesar's son, and in this sense he was a rival to Octavian, Caesar's adopted son. Both Caesarion and Antyllus paid the penalty for being adult sons of their fathers.

32. Juba was a Numidian prince. The kingdom of Mauretania had been seized by Bocchus, an adherent of Octavian's, from his brother Bogud, who supported Antony. On Bocchus's death in 25 B.C., Octavian bestowed the kingdom upon this Juba (Juba II), in compensation for the confiscation by Rome of his paternal realm in 41.

33. Iullus Antonius, born in 42 B.C., escaped the fate of his brother Antyllus because he had been brought up in Italy by his step-mother Octavia. Under Roman law a freedman was bound to leave half his property to his patron, until Octavian altered the rules.

34. Artavasdes, king of Media Atropatene, must be distinguished from the king of Armenia of the same name, who was executed by Cleopatra in 31. The Median had been expelled by the Parthians in 31.

35. The god Apis was incarnate as a live bull.

36. Julius Caesar, when he had left a garrison in Egypt in 47 B.C., had decided that he could not entrust the governorship of the province (because of its immense resources, especially in grain) to any senator, and Octavian took the same view. Cornelius Gallus, his first appointment, was a knight. The governor was styled prefect, which marked the personal nature of his appointment by, and responsibility to, the emperor, and the post always remained non-senatorial.

37. Dio is here anachronistic. The idea of an Egyptian senator would have been unthinkable to the Romans of Augustus's day. The first man from the Greek East

to enter the Senate was a Phrygian, L. Servenius Cornutus, during the reign of Nero (Syme, *Tacitus*, 509, n. 4).

38. And hence without the local autonomy commonly enjoyed by cities under Roman rule.

39. A thousand sesterces was just over a year's regular pay for a legionary.

40. Nicopolis: see ch. 1 above.

41. To improve the irrigation and hence the agriculture of the province.

42. See Introduction (p. 13). Dio is wrong to say that the other tribunes did not possess authority up to a mile beyond the city limits.

43. The 'vote of Athena' may be taken as a casting vote or as an overruling (cassatory) vote. Both interpretations are difficult, the former because such a vote could very seldom be used, the latter because it would give immense powers and undermine the importance of the courts.

44. The closing of the temple of Janus celebrated, above all, the end of the civil wars. It did not signify, of course, that all fighting was to cease: military commands on the frontiers remained active. The purpose of the taking of the augury, which could be performed only in times of peace, was to ask what prayers could be offered for the safety of the state. It had last been taken in 63 B.C.

45. A Celtic tribe, inhabiting lands in eastern Gaul, west of the Rhine, which contain the modern city of Trier.

46. This tribe inhabited a coastal strip in north-west Spain, facing the Bay of Biscay.

47. Their lands lay immediately south of the territory of the Cantabri, and east of that of the Astures.

48. Inhabitants of the modern province of Asturias in north-west Spain, west of the territory of the Cantabri.

49. 30–29 B.C.

50. Octavia's son by her first marriage, born in 42 B.C.

51. Pannonia was a territory in the north-west of modern Jugoslavia, bounded on the north and east by the Danube, and on the south by the Sava. Octavian campaigned there in 35, but the region was only pacified some thirty years later by Tiberius. Dalmatia corresponds roughly to its modern boundaries. Octavian campaigned there in 34 B.C.

52. A small tribe living immediately south of the Pannonians. Octavian led a hard-fought campaign there in 35 B.C.

53. A small tribe whose territory lay on the coast of the modern Belgium.

54. A powerful group of Germanic tribes inhabiting a region between the Rhine and the Elbe.

55. Dio is in error here. Carrinas celebrated his triumph nearly a year later, on 14 July 28 B.C., and there is no evidence to suggest that Octavian attempted to appropriate the credit.

56. Octavian, by placing the magistrates behind him in the ceremonial order, demonstrated his position as head of state, and destroyed the fiction that they had come out of the city to greet him and lead him in.

57. The interest of the Suebian and Dacian prisoners is that they were newly sent back by Carrinas (see ch. 21) and Crassus (see ch. 23ff.) respectively, and emphasized that Roman armies had reverted to their traditional role of defeating foreigners and extending the bounds of empire.

58. Consul in 37 and 30 B.C. and one of Octavian's ablest generals and administrators. He commanded a force in Illyricum in 34 B.C., and distinguished himself in the Actium campaign (see Book 50, ch. 13) and in operations in Spain in 29 B.C.

59. The spoils traditionally awarded to the commander-in-chief of a Roman army who kills in single combat the ruler of a people at war with Rome. The feat had been achieved only three times in the history of Rome: by Romulus, by Cornelius Cossus in the fifth century and by M. Claudius Marcellus in 222 B.C. Octavian's claim that Crassus could not qualify for this honour, because he was not fighting under his own auspices, was of doubtful validity (see Livy, Book IV, chs. 20 and 32), but he could not allow himself to be outshone at the very moment of his triple triumph.

60. Crassus indubitably *won* a salutation as 'Imperator' from his troops, and indubitably triumphed. Since the latter was the greater honour, to strip him of the lesser was senseless. Dio probably means, if he is not in error, that only Octavian used 'Imperator' as a title preceding his name (see Book 50, note 53).

61. In 43 B.C. Gaius Antonius, Mark Antony's brother, was defeated in Macedonia.

BOOK 52

1. Dio is surveying the whole period from the traditional date of the foundation of Rome (753 B.C.) to 28 B.C. The period referred to as the rule of the war-lords dates approximately from the end of the seventies B.C. and thereafter, when the ascendancy of the Senate, which Sulla had strengthened, came to be threatened by political leaders such as Pompey, Crassus and Caesar, who exercised major military commands.

2. Dio's conclusion refers to the achievements of the Greek city states. He omits

to mention their failure to combine to defend their interests, or the achievements of the Macedonian monarchy, which conquered them in the fourth century B.C.

3. The patron–client relationship (*clientela*) was a cornerstone of Roman social and political life. To confer favours (*beneficia*) was to place others under the obligation of repaying them, and enhanced the status and power of the patron. The Roman plebs became collectively the clients of the emperor: he gave them bread and circuses, they gave him their support.

4. Gaius Marius (156–86 B.C.) was elected, against all recent precedent, to a run of consulships to save Italy from invasion by nomadic northern tribes. He finally defeated them in his fifth consulship, and when elected to a sixth in 100 B.C., virtually *honoris causa*, was in a position to dominate the state by reason of his alliance with the democratic leaders, Saturninus and Glaucia. Unable to stomach their unconstitutional and violent behaviour, he suppressed them forcibly with the backing of the majority of the Senate. He then retired peacefully from the scene, as a consul should, at the end of the year. Dio chooses to ignore the events which led to the civil war of 88–82 and Marius's seventh consulship in 86.

5. Lucius Cornelius Sulla (138–78 B.C.), after defeating the younger Marius in 82 B.C., emerged as the victor of the civil wars of that period. He was created dictator, but after imposing laws which ensured the control of affairs by the Senate, he laid down his office in 80 B.C.

6. Metellus Pius, who fought on Sulla's side against Marius and in the Social War was consul in 80 B.C. He died (peacefully) *c.* 64 B.C.

7. Pompey the Great (106–48 B.C.) was elected consul with Crassus in 70 B.C. and overthrew the regime established by Sulla. But neither then nor in 60 B.C., when he formed the First Triumvirate with Crassus and Julius Caesar, did he claim the political power which his spectacular military successes in Spain and Asia might have put within his grasp. In 52 he was elected sole consul, and thereafter manoeuvred by his senatorial supporters into challenging Caesar for supremacy, a decision which led to his downfall.

8. Lucius Cornelius Cinna (*c.* 130–84 B.C.) supported Marius and the democratic faction. He was elected consul in 87; his colleague Octavius represented the aristocratic party. Expelled from Rome by his fellow-consul, he collected an army, was joined by the elder Marius, defeated Octavius and established a reign of terror in Rome. He was re-elected consul in 86 together with the elder Marius, who died soon after. He continued to hold power until 84, when he was murdered by his troops.

9. The younger Marius returned with his father to Rome in 87 from Africa, where they had taken refuge from Sulla. He was elected consul for 82, but was defeated and killed by Sulla in that year.

10. Gnaeus Pompeius Strabo (*c.* 135–87 B.C.) was the father of Pompey the Gr[...]
Consul in 89 and commander of an army operating against the Italian insurgen[...]
(see note 17 below), he engineered the murder by his troops of Q. Pompeius
Rufus, consul in 88, when the latter came to take over command from him. He
then played an ambiguous part when the Marians attacked Rome in 87 (see note
8 above), and is suspected of trying to create a powerful position for himself, but
he died before Rome fell. (Another possible Strabo is C. Julius Caesar Strabo
Vopiscus, who helped precipitate the civil strife of 88 by standing for the
consulship before he was legally qualified to do so.)

11. Quintus Sertorius (125–72 B.C.) was a brilliant soldier with a special aptitude
for guerrilla warfare, and for training foreign troops, notably the Spaniards. He
belonged to the party of Marius, and when Italy had been lost he campaigned
successfully in Spain against the senatorial generals, Metellus and Pompey. He
was assassinated by some of his own Roman officers.

12. Marcus Furius Camillus commanded the Roman army which took Veii in
396 B.C. By using white horses at his triumph he was felt to have trespassed upon
the privileges of the gods. This was not, however, the reason for his exile, which
arose from a prosecution concerned with misappropriation of booty.

13. Dio seems to be making an inaccurate reference to events which followed the
defeat of king Antiochus III by Lucius and Publius Scipio (Africanus) in 190 B.C.
In 187 Lucius was saved only by a tribune's veto from an enormous fine for
misappropriation of money, and in 184 Publius was charged with corrupt dealings
with the king. He took his stand on his past services to Rome, refused to answer
the charge before the people, and withdrew to his estate at Liternum in Campania,
where he died in the following year. Neither Lucius nor Publius was 'deposed
from power' except in an informal sense.

14. In ch. 13 above, Agrippa cites the careers of Marius and Sulla to arrive at a
conclusion precisely the opposite of Maecenas's. No other authority cites this
tradition of Sulla's suicide.

15. M. Aemilius Lepidus, consul in 78, agitated for the repeal of some of Sulla's
laws even before Sulla died early in that year.

16. See note 11, ch. 13 above.

17. This allusion harks back to one of the most crucial struggles for political rights
ever fought in Roman history. This was the Social War (90–80 B.C.), in which
the Italian communities fought for Roman citizenship and for voting rights in
the popular assemblies. These rights were eventually conceded at the time, but
full assimilation took two generations.

18. In the early republic the city prefect represented the consuls when both were
absent from Rome. The post became superfluous when another regular annual

perium, the praetorship, was intended in 366 B.C. Augustus, ... ve felt the need for some kind of official representative when ... Rome for long periods. He appointed Messalla Corvinus in ... after a few days, apparently uncertain of his authority), and ... Taurus in 16–13 B.C. But he was *not* absent when L. Calpurnius Piso was made prefect in A.D. 12, and this marks the conversion of the post into a permanent long-term judicial and administrative appointment of a nature quite foreign to the republican constitution. Piso continued to be prefect until his death in A.D. 32.

19. Dio here reveals the age to which he himself belonged, when knights had come to hold some of the most powerful offices of state. In 28 B.C. it would have been inconceivable for any non-senator, indeed anyone who had not been consul, to have occupied a post of the nature here described.

20. No such post as this is known in the Augustan constitution, though its duties were embraced by the traditional censorship. Augustus was keen enough to carry out the enumerative role of the censor, because it was creditable to count more citizens than ever before and thus show the state to be stronger than ever before; but he was embarrassed by having to pass ethical judgements on the fitness of other members of the Roman upper class to be senators or knights, and tried various expedients to avoid acting the judge. The censorship was the most prestigious of all the regular republican magistracies, partly because of the high standards of behaviour and morality its holders were expected to enforce, and therefore themselves possess, and partly because a pair of censors were elected only once in every five years.

21. The Praetorian Guard consisted at this time of nine cohorts, each 1,000 strong. Never more than three of these cohorts were stationed in Rome, the others in various Italian towns.

22. The night watch (*Vigiles*) was not instituted until A.D. 6. It then consisted of seven cohorts each of 1,000 freedmen, commanded by a prefect of equestrian rank.

23. Such cases are attested by inscriptions of Augustan date.

24. Augustus was at all times sternly opposed to indolence and effeminacy in any form. See his speech, Book 56, chs. 1–10.

25. When a standing army was recognized towards the middle of Augustus's reign, it had a strength of twenty-eight legions, half of which were stationed in the provinces of the northern frontiers from Gaul to Macedonia.

26. The Roman people in fact ceased to act as a judicial assembly *c.* 100 B.C. and as an electoral body in A.D. 14. The last known law passed by the people is of A.D. 98, but the assembly met on occasion until the third century.

27. See Book 44, chs. 2–5. However, other evidence seems to show that it was Octavian who converted 'Imperator' into a permanent title in the early thirties B.C. (cf. Book 50, note 53).

28. By the *Lex Saenia* of 29 B.C. Certain religious offices could be held only by patricians.

29. Julius Caesar had founded a colony of veterans at Carthage in 44 B.C., calling it Concordia Julia.

30. The island of Ischia.

BOOK 53

1. 29 B.C.

2. Bundles of rods bound around an axe, which signified the ultimate powers of the magistrates – the rods for scourging before an execution, the axe for beheading. In earliest republican times the consuls had exercised power in alternate months: the ruling consul was escorted by twelve lictors carrying the fasces, the other only by an attendant. Later both were attended by lictors, who preceded the ruling and followed the non-ruling consul, but the monthly alternation of precedence persisted (see Book 50, ch. 2). Octavian used twenty-four lictors up to 29 B.C., twelve thereafter.

3. Taken by the consul at the end of his term, testifying before the gods that he had done nothing contrary to the laws or to the well-being of the republic.

4. Treated any other colleague with such deference.

5. The elder Marcella. Agrippa was previously married to Caecilia Attica, daughter of Cicero's friend, Atticus.

6. This had last been carried out in 69 B.C. Augustus took a census twice subsequently, in 8 B.C. and A.D. 14.

7. The temple had been vowed to Apollo in 36 B.C., after the site had been struck by lightning, but inevitably acquired the function of a thank-offering for Apollo's favour in granting Octavian victory at Actium, a place sacred to the god.

8. The manuscripts read 'during Augustus's life-time'.

9. Under the republic a senator had to possess the equestrian property qualification of 400,000 sesterces. In practice more was needed, and Augustus later created a senatorial qualification of 1,000,000 sesterces. Grants such as the ones here mentioned recognized that impoverishment in a period of civil war was a matter of bad luck, and that senators did not deserve to lose their status on that account.

10. In the late republic the aedileship had come to be regarded as an opportunity to buy votes for the praetorship, principally by lavish spending on the public

games for which the aediles were responsible. Julius Caesar exploited the aedileship in this way.

11. This probably means that Augustus designated which of the already elected praetors was to be *praetor urbanus*. This was the senior praetorship and in the republic had been held by the man who headed the poll.

12. In Sulla's time a college of priests of Isis had been founded in Rome and by 48 B.C. a shrine existed. This did not mean that the cult received the approval of the state. Octavian regarded the worship of Isis and other Oriental cults as a threat to his aim of restoring the ancient Roman traditions and moral values. His programme of repairing the temples was another facet of the same policy.

13. *Destiny* is contrasted with *fortune* (later in the same paragraph): the former suggests the immovable nature of fate, the latter its unpredictable aspect.

14. Octavian was only eighteen when he came forward as Julius Caesar's heir.

15. '*freedom . . . the republic . . .*' Octavian is alluding here to the end of the rule of the Triumvirs, which represented provisional and arbitrary government, and his own *de facto* continuation of it. He was claiming to be restoring constitutional government. He had started the process with the acts described in chs. 1–2.

16. Julius Caesar considerably increased the size and reduced the powers of the Senate; he also showed notable clemency towards his senatorial opponents. Octavian strengthened its prestige by purging unworthy members, increasing the number of patricians (see Book 52, ch. 42) and helping its members financially. But Octavian is also referring to benefits such as peace, which affected all alike.

17. An anachronism: the territory was not finally subdued until Tiberius's campaigns of 7–9 B.C., although Octavian had campaigned in the area in 35–33 B.C.

18. Conquered by Marcus Licinius Crassus, 29–28 B.C. (see Book 51, chs. 23–27).

19. Pharnaces II, king of Pontus, was defeated by Julius Caesar in 47 B.C., the occasion of the latter's *Veni, Vidi, Vici* dispatch.

20. King of Numidia, defeated by Julius Caesar at Thapsus, 46 B.C.

21. Possibly another anachronism. The negotiations with Phraates, king of Parthia, for the return of the standards and prisoners captured from Antony and earlier from Crassus, were not concluded until 20 B.C. However, Augustus had made an arrangement in 30 B.C. whereby he kept one of Phraates's sons as a hostage (see Book 51, ch. 18).

22. References to Julius Caesar's campaigns in Britain and Germany. In the latter Caesar constructed a bridge over the Rhine in ten days.

23. The legendary defender of the Sublician bridge over the Tiber against the Etruscan army. See Livy, Book II, ch. 10, and Macaulay's *Lays of Ancient Rome*.

24. Mucius Scaevola, captured by the Etruscans, demonstrated that they had no hope of making him talk, by holding his hand in the fire. Porsenna, much impressed, set him free.

25. Another legendary hero. When a chasm opened in the Forum, the seers declared that this could not be closed unless Rome's most precious possession were thrown in. Marcus Curtius rode into the abyss, whereupon the earth closed over him.

26. A Roman general in the first Punic war. Legend relates that after being captured and released on parole, he returned to Carthage to face torture and death rather than urge unfavourable terms on his compatriots.

27. Publius Decius Mus, consul in 295, his father, consul in 340, and his son of the same name, consul in 279, are respectively credited with having brought about the defeat of the Gauls, the Latins and Pyrrhus.

28. Julius Caesar accepted divine honours in his lifetime (see Suetonius, *Julius Caesar*, ch. 76).

29. 'Weaker' and 'stronger' in this passage mean provinces containing weaker or stronger military forces.

30. These regions, which had become provinces in 66 and 74 respectively, formed a single province from Augustus's time.

31. These kingdoms had been organized as a province by Pompey in 62 B.C.

32. In 36 B.C. Agrippa had invited the Ubii, allies of Rome since 52, to cross the Rhine and settle on the western bank. The Ubii, to whom the Sugambri and other tribes east of the Rhine were hostile, gladly accepted the offer.

33. The valley between the Lebanon and Anti-Lebanon mountains.

34. Inhabited by warlike tribes. They suffered a preliminary subjugation in 35–33 B.C. but rebelled in 14 and 12 B.C. and in A.D. 6.

35. See ch. 26 and Book 54, ch. 9, for examples.

36. That is both the 'weaker' and the 'stronger', or 'senatorial' and 'imperial', to adopt the terminology of later historians.

37. Gnaeus Cornelius Gallus (see Book 51, ch. 17).

38. See Book 54, ch. 16, and Book 56, chs. 1–10, for Augustus's views concerning marriage and children. Dio here anticipates details of the fully developed imperial administrative system, which were not in existence in 27 B.C.

39. Twelve.

40. The Latin title is *legati propraetore*.

41. Dio is mistaken in his explanation. It is true that in the very early republic

praetor, not *consul*, was the title of the supreme magistrate and commander of the citizen army, but after 366 B.C. the title *praetor* was used to designate a new magistracy junior to the consuls. The reason that Augustus's *legati* were *propraetore* was that since he himself was consul or proconsul, his subordinates had to be of lower rank. The Greek term for *praetor* is *strategus* (= general), which adds conviction to Dio's explanation.

42. Authority to condemn to death and execute – the *ius gladii* – held good in the provinces over Romans only on military service. Thus Pilate as procurator of Judaea had *ius gladii* over Jesus Christ as a Jew, but his successor, Festus, was obliged to allow Paul as a Roman citizen to appeal to Caesar.

43. Dio means the adjective *quinque fascalis* found on some inscriptions. It was not an official title.

44. In 27 B.C. there were ten senatorial provinces. Besides the two consuls, eight praetors were appointed yearly, ten from 23 B.C. and twelve by at least A.D. 11.

45. That is provided the latter were not Roman citizens who had appealed to the emperor.

46. *Legati* of the governor: they assisted him with judicial business.

47. See Book 52, chs. 19–20, 25.

48. In 18 B.C.

49. The imperial *decennalia* were not a regular celebration until the time of Antoninus Pius.

50. This is Dio's description, phrased two centuries later. Octavian would not, of course, have used these words. The laurel symbolized victory, while the crown of oak leaves (*corona civica*) was given to a soldier who saved a fellow-citizen's life.

51. The title was objectionable because of the despotic rule practised by the Etruscan kings.

52. The term is used advisedly to denote the authority temporarily granted to an elected official, as distinct from *dominatio*, which was what the emperors possessed.

53. See ch. 18. Augustus himself conducted a census three times, in 28 B.C., 8 B.C., and A.D. 14. He probably took a specific grant of censorial power in 28 B.C., but he informs us in the *Res Gestae*, ch. 8 that he acted by consular authority in 8 B.C. and A.D. 14.

54. Until and including the reign of Nero, the emperors as descendants of the Julio-Claudian line were unquestionably patricians. Thereafter it could be assumed that, as the emperor had the power to make patricians, he was one himself.

55. The phrase in Latin is *Princeps legibus solutus est*, Ulpian, *Digest*, 1.3.31 (*c*. A.D. 220).

56. The title *Pater Patriae*, Father of his Country, was formally conferred upon Augustus in 2 B.C.

57. The publication *Acta Senatus* (Proceedings of the Senate) first published by Julius Caesar, had been discontinued by Octavian. But the *Acta* could be consulted with the permission of the city prefect, and Dio would have had access. It was, of course, an official publication, and hence liable to be edited.

58. For example, Sejanus, who attained great power under Tiberius, or the influential freedmen employed by Claudius.

59. According to Valerius Maximus, II, 6.11, the Celtiberian tribe thought it dishonourable to survive a battle, if the leader, whose life they had vowed to preserve, was killed.

60. Under the republic the Senate had acted as a court of arbitration between municipalities in Italy. Under the empire its judicial functions grew, and it became the court in which persons accused of treason were tried and sentenced, as in the case of Gallus, and later Sejanus.

61. In the matter of elections to the magistracies, Augustus followed the precedent set by Julius Caesar; see Suetonius, *Julius Caesar*, ch. 41.

62. 27 B.C.

63. The Mulvian Bridge.

64. The modern Rimini, situated at the end of the Via Flaminia.

65. Britain at this time harboured rebellious Gauls. One of the reasons for Claudius's invasion of Britain in A.D. 43 was the refusal of the Britons to surrender fugitives from Roman authority. The Britons were also technically in default of tribute imposed by Julius Caesar in 54 B.C.

66. 26 B.C.

67. Statilius Taurus had been consul in 37 B.C., had played an important part in the campaign against Sextus Pompeius in 36, and commanded part of the land forces at Actium. In 29 he had conducted a successful campaign in Spain.

68. The buildings known as the Saepta Julia, erected on the Campus Martius and used as polling enclosures by the popular assemblies for the elections to the offices of state. In 54 B.C. Julius Caesar had begun to rebuild the original wooden structure in stone and marble. The work was continued by Lepidus in 36 and completed by Agrippa.

69. Gnaeus Cornelius Gallus was one of the most brilliant and versatile figures of his time. For his activities in Egypt, see Book 51, chs. 9 and 17. He was also a

distinguished elegiac post. Virgil dedicated his Tenth Eclogue to him and Ovid praised him highly. He committed suicide in 27 B.C.

70. Aedile in 20 B.C. Fire-fighting had hitherto been the business of the *Tresviri Nocturni*. After entrusting this responsibility to the aediles (see also Book 54, ch. 2), Augustus later transferred it to the night watch, a corps founded in A.D. 6 (see Book 55, ch. 26). Rufus became praetor in 19 B.C. and tried to stand for the consulship in the following year. This was contrary to the law, because there was supposed to be a two-year interval between offices, and the officiating consul forbade his candidature. Rufus then formed a conspiracy against Augustus: it was detected and the plotters executed.

71. He had been one of Antony's supporters, and had also served him as envoy to Media in 35 B.C. He was not punished by Octavian after Actium, and ruled for many years as an ally of the Romans.

72. A primitive tribe of mountaineers who inhabited the valleys on the Italian side of the Great St Bernard Pass and frequently raided the inhabitants of the foothills of the Pennine Alps and the neighbouring lowlands.

73. In 25 B.C.

74. The modern Aosta.

75. Tiberius was serving for the first time as a military tribune. The aedileships here referred to of Tiberius and Marcellus were probably those of Augusta Emerita in its foundation year.

76. Juba's father had supported Pompey against Julius Caesar and committed suicide after the defeat of the Pompeians at Thapsus (46 B.C.). In consequence much of Juba's territory in Numidia had been incorporated into the Roman province of Africa. The son was compensated with territory in Gaetulia (southern Algeria) and in Mauretania (northern Algeria and Morocco).

77. Bocchus had reigned over eastern Mauretania; Bogud, Antony's ally killed at Methone in 31 B.C., over western Mauretania.

78. Another former ally of Antony, who had ruled Galatia, Lycaonia, Pamphylia and Pisidia since 36 B.C. After Actium, Octavian allowed him to keep his territories. He was killed in a local campaign in 26 B.C.

79. Dio refers to tribes whom we speak of as Germans as Celts. The reference to the Alps and the fact that Vinicius is elsewhere said to have held his command in Gaul suggests that these tribesmen inhabited a mountain region on the north-western slopes of the Alps.

80. As commander-in-chief. See Book 50, note 53.

81. The temple had been closed in 29 B.C. to signal the end of the civil wars (see Book 51, ch. 20). Before Augustus's lifetime it had been closed only twice, in the reign of king Numa and at the end of the first Punic war.

82. The bathers were subjected to hot air and sweated profusely, as in the modern sauna.

83. Mars was the father of Romulus, and the Romans were often referred to as the children of Mars. Venus was the mother of Aeneas, and thus divine ancestress of the Julian family.

84. The Pantheon which exists today was built by Hadrian on the site of Agrippa's.

85. Julius Caesar had received divine honours in his lifetime, and so qualified for admission to the Pantheon. Augustus and Agrippa were seen as door-keepers to the temple.

86. Messalla had fought on Brutus's side at Philippi, where he had captured Octavian's camp. In 36 B.C. he attached himself to Octavian, and held the consulship in 31 B.C.

87. This became a regular practice in Augustus's lifetime, but Tiberius did not adopt it, arguing that it was wrong to commit the Senate to all his decisions.

88. The minimum age prescribed for holding magistracies in the republic had been reduced by five years by Augustus, so that the normal ages were now 25 for the quaestorship and 37 for the consulship. Both Marcellus and Tiberius were born in 42 B.C., the latter on 16 November. Tiberius, holding the quaestorship in 23, did not in fact attain his twentieth year (that is reach his nineteenth birthday) until just before his year of office expired. It is just possible that Tiberius held his quaestorship in 22, though it is beyond doubt that Marcellus's aedileship was in 23.

89. This man is otherwise unknown. Perhaps a mistake for L. Aelius (Lamia) or Quintus Aemilius (Lepidus), consul in 21 B.C.

90. The south-western part of the Arabian peninsula. Aelius Gallus had succeeded Cornelius Gallus as Prefect of Egypt in 26 B.C. The expedition seems to have been inspired by a speculative quest for fabled wealth, not unlike that of Raleigh's for El Dorado. According to Strabo, XVI, ch. 4, the expedition's difficulties were caused by the treachery of the Nabataean Syllaeus, upon whom Gallus was relying to guide the march.

91. A coastal town on the African shore of the Red Sea. Gallus may have advanced as far as Aden. Augustus himself says his forces advanced as far as Mariba (*Res Gestae*, 26. 5).

92. In 23 B.C.

93. An anachronistic phrase in 23 B.C. See Introduction pp. 12–13.

94. The so-called *breviarium imperii*, which recorded the military and financial resources of the empire (see Suetonius, *Augustus*, ch. 101).

95. The *ius annuli aurei*, the privilege of senators, magistrates and knights. The

right of the ring raised Musa from the status of *libertinus* (freedman) to *ingenuus* (a man born of free parents).

96. In the autumn of 23 B.C.

97. Marcellus was curule aedile at the time of his death, and was due to superintend the games. The carrying in of these emblems was intended to indicate that he was present in spirit.

98. The offices Augustus held could not be bequeathed.

99. It would have been regarded as ill-omened.

100. There is evidence that Agrippa's real mission at this time was to negotiate with the king of Parthia for the return of the Roman standards captured from Crassus in 53 B.C., from Decidius Saxa in 40 and from Antony in 35. He appears to have held a general power of command (*imperium*) over all the Eastern provinces.

101. According to Velleius (II. 89. 4), Augustus added two praetors to the republican eight. It seems likely that there were eight from 27 to 23 B.C., and that two were added for the purpose stated by Dio (*praetores aerarii*). Later in the reign the number crept up to twelve, and once to sixteen (Book 56, ch. 25). Augustus's improvement of the administration of the state created a large number of posts of praetorian rank, and the praetorship became the 'career grade' for a senator.

102. Augustus had chosen 1 July for the Feriae Latinae, which took place on the Alban Mount, south of Rome. This public holiday was a movable festival, and he had probably fixed the date so as to make his abdication from power effective for the second half of the year.

103. Although the powers of the consuls were much reduced, the prestige of the office was still great.

104. Dio's words are 'be a tribune', although he states below (and in ch. 17 above) that the emperors never took the office, although they exercised the power.

105. Known as the *ius relationis*. The introduction of measures was the function of the presiding magistrates, the consuls. If Augustus were no longer to be consul, he needed some degree of control over the proceedings of the Senate. In 19 B.C. he was granted consular power for life.

106. Proconsular *imperium* could be held only outside the official boundary (*pomoerium*) of the city of Rome. An ordinary proconsul would assume it on leaving for his province and lay it down on returning, before he came into the city. In the case of Augustus, it would be very inconvenient for him to have to lay it down and reassume it every time he went in or out of Rome. He had hitherto, as consul, not had this problem, since consular *imperium* was valid both within and without the city.

107. *imperium maius.*

108. This was especially true of his dealings with the Senate. Julius Caesar had treated the Senate with much less consideration.

109. In 30 B.C. Tiridates had rebelled against Phraates, the king of Parthia, had been defeated and had taken refuge in Syria. Augustus had allowed him to stay, but had given him no support. Meanwhile Phraates's son had since 30 B.C. been detained in Rome as a hostage.

110. See Book 54, ch. 8, and note 100 above.

111. The office of curule aedile was more prestigious in terms of insignia and privileges than that of plebeian aedile. The former had originally been open only to patricians, but was later extended to include plebeian candidates.

112. During the absence of the consuls at the Alban Mount (see note 102 above) they were represented in Rome by a prefect of the city. This had become a purely honorific appointment and was regularly held by a young noble.

113. The Pons Sublicius.

BOOK 54

1. 22 B.C.

2. Julius Caesar had only recently accepted the dictatorship for life when he was murdered, and the feeling of the senatorial class against the potential of the office was so great that Antony abolished it by law in 44 B.C. Thus not only was it politically dangerous for Augustus to become dictator, it was technically unconstitutional without a new law. Dio's argument that it was unnecessary is quite correct, but this was not the most important consideration.

3. Paullus Aemilius Lepidus (consul in 34 B.C.) was the son of L. Aemilius Paullus (consul in 50 B.C.), a man notorious for having been proscribed by his brother, the Triumvir. If the son *was* proscribed, as Dio asserts, he must have been soon pardoned. The proscribed brother of the other consul was Lucius Plautius Plancus. For Lucius Munatius Plancus, see Book 50, note 11.

4. Augustus's denial ensured Primus's condemnation, since Primus had broken the law which forbade a governor to make war outside his province without express authorization. Augustus was in a difficult position, because he had no constitutional authority in Macedonia, which was a senatorial province. So if he had, without reference to the Senate, given Primus the permission necessary, he had blatantly overstepped the limits of his powers. Many modern historians date the trial to 23, since by 22 Augustus had in fact acquired the right to give such orders to governors of senatorial provinces. However, it is only necessary for the date of Primus's offence to lie before mid-23, and there would be nothing unusual

in a governor who laid down office say in the spring of 23 not being brought to trial until a year or so later.

5. Both in Dio and in other authorities there is some confusion concerning Murena's name. The most likely hypothesis is that his full name was L. Terentius Varro Licinius Murena and that he was the brother of A. Terentius Varro Murena, who fought a campaign against the Salassi in 25 B.C., and though elected to the consulship for 23 B.C., never in fact took up office.

6. For Terentia, Maecenas's wife and Murena's sister, see also Book 54, ch. 19, and for Proculeius Book 51, ch. 11. The latter must have been Murena's half-brother.

7. See Book 53, ch. 25, for Augustus's earlier campaigns against these tribes.

8. On the Upper Nile below the First Cataract, and a little north of Philae. Modern research places the Ethiopian invasion in 25 B.C. The Ethiopians were tempted to invade because Aelius Gallus's expedition to Arabia had weakened the Roman forces garrisoning Egypt. The Ethiopian attack mentioned in the last sentence of ch. 5 was a second invasion in 22 B.C.

9. The capital of northern Ethiopia.

10. 21 B.C.

11. At this time Augustus was especially concerned to reach a settlement for the eastern frontier, that is Armenia and Parthia. See ch. 8.

12. The object was to strengthen the imperial succession. Julia bore Agrippa three sons, Gaius (20 B.C.–A.D. 4), Lucius (17 B.C.–A.D. 2) and Agrippa Postumus (12 B.C.–A.D. 14). Agrippa's divorced wife was the elder Marcella, who was subsequently married to her step-brother, Iullus Antonius.

13. See Book 53, note 12.

14. The prefect had the responsibility of assuming charge of the city while the consuls were absent at the celebrations of the Latin Festival on the Alban Mount. The office was by this time purely honorific.

15. In 40 B.C., when Perusia was captured by Octavian's troops, Livia had fled with her first husband, Tiberius Claudius Nero, and her two-year-old son, Tiberius, later the emperor, to take refuge in Greece.

16. In 20 B.C.

17. The legionary standards and the prisoners taken by the Parthians after the defeats of Crassus at Carrhae (53 B.C.), Decidius Saxa in Syria (40 B.C.) and Antony in Armenia and Media (36 B.C.). See Books 51, ch. 18; 53, ch. 33.

18. This temple of Mars Ultor is depicted on coins which were issued to commemorate the recovery of the standards. It was a small round shrine, which

lost its *raison d'être* when the large temple of Mars Ultor, vowed by Augustus on the field of Philippi in 42 B.C., was eventually completed and dedicated in 2 B.C., along with the new Forum in which it stood. For Jupiter Feretrius, see Book 51, ch. 24.

19. The minor form of triumph known as an *ovatio*.

20. The so-called *milliarium aureum* stood at the north end of the Forum near the temple of Saturn, at the point where all the great roads met. It was a column covered with gilt bronze, and engraved with the names of the principal cities of the empire with their distances from Rome, these being measured from the city gates.

21. His father of the same name, the ruler of Emesa, had been executed by Antony for treachery in 31 B.C. before Actium (see Book 50, ch. 13).

22. The son of the Tarcondimotus, who was killed fighting for Antony in the naval battle against Agrippa in 31 B.C. (see Book 50, ch. 14).

23. Herod the Great (73–4 B.C.), at this time the king of Judaea. The territory of Ituraea, ruled by Zenodorus, stretched from the Lebanon/Anti-Lebanon valley down to Jordan.

24. Tiberius had brought a force from Macedonia to use against Parthia, if necessary.

25. The Greek goddesses Demeter and Persephone, whose mysteries were celebrated at Eleusis.

26. 19 B.C.

27. The younger brother of Tiberius and father of the future emperor Claudius.

28. This marked an important stage in the re-shaping of Augustus's powers, which had been in progress since 23, the critical year of Caepio's conspiracy and Augustus's nearly fatal illness. After his recovery, he had resigned the consulship and been granted tribunician and proconsular powers for life (see Book 53, ch. 32, but also Book 54, ch. 12). However, within the capital the consuls were the chief magistrates, and in particular enjoyed precedence in bringing business before the Senate. In 23 he had been granted the right to bring forward one item of business at each session, and in 22 the right to convene the Senate whenever he chose (see Book 54, ch. 3). Now he was given the right to sit between the two consuls of the year, and to be attended by lictors. However, Dio seems to be wrong about the censorship and curatorship of morals, which Augustus denies having accepted (*Res Gestae* 6).

29. Book 54, ch. 6.

30. 18 B.C.

31. In 29 B.C. (see Book 52, ch. 42). Augustus had then managed to reduce the Senate to about 800 members. Between 80 and 49 B.C. its size had been about 600.

32. The former Triumvir.

33. The conspiracy had been detected and suppressed by Maecenas in 31.

34. At Circeii, between Naples and Rome.

35. A distinguished jurist, whose father, a staunch republican, had committed suicide after Philippi.

36. Because of the oath which the first thirty had taken to select the best men.

37. A reference to the important *Lex Julia de maritandis ordinibus*. This was later amended by the *Lex Papia Poppaea* of A.D. 9 (see Book 56, ch. 10), and it is difficult to distinguish the exact provisions of the *Lex Julia*. By it unmarried men and women were debarred from certain categories of inheritance and from full participation in civic life (see below, ch. 30, end). On the positive side it removed certain restrictions on marriage, modified the laws of inheritance so as to favour parenthood, and offered both men in public life, and freedmen, privileges of different kinds, if they became fathers.

38. The point of this story is that Augustus had behaved in exactly this way when he married Livia early in 38 B.C.

39. That is, each man served for three months. Dio's Greek almost certainly means that to be eligible for the post a man must have been praetor three years or more previously. In terms of age, the post was thus of the same seniority as the consulship.

40. See ch. 6 above, note 14. Because the Feriae lasted more than one day, and the prefecture was honorific, it was possible to appoint a different prefect for each day and effectively destroy the fiction that this was a serious office.

41. The Sibyl of Cumae was a famous oracular prophetess, reputedly of immense age. One of the Sibyls had come to Tarquin II, then the Etruscan king of Rome, and offered nine volumes of prophecies at a high price. When he declined, she burned three books, and offered the remaining six at the same price. Tarquin finally bought the last three before they were burned. The books were kept in the temple of Jupiter Capitolinus, until Augustus moved them to his Palatine temple of Apollo, and were consulted at times of national crisis.

42. In 17 B.C.

43. Roman boys assumed the *toga virilis* at the age of fifteen.

44. The Secular Games, a festival lasting for three days, but only held at very long intervals: the two preceding observances had been in 249 and 146 B.C. They were to mark the beginning of a new *saeculum*, that is a new century or new age.

45. Lucius Domitius Ahenobarbus, consul in 16 B.C. He was the son of Antony's

renegade general, and the husband of Antony's daughter by Octavia, Antonia the elder.

46. In his *Life of Solon* Plutarch records (ch. 25) that after passing his great legislative programme, Solon took leave of absence of the Athenians for ten years. In that time he calculated that they would have become accustomed to his laws.

47. The name Quirinus was given to Romulus after his deification.

48. One of Augustus's ablest generals and administrators. For his achievements see Book 53, note 67.

49. See Book 51, ch. 1.

50. The year 17–16 B.C.

51. 'Gaius' is wrong, but the name it conceals is unidentifiable.

52. 'Germany' includes territory to the west of the Rhine.

53. Not securely identifiable. Perhaps Lake Garda, possibly Lake Geneva.

54. The modern Posilippo.

55. In 7 B.C. See Book 55, ch. 8.

56. See Book 54, ch. 7.

57. 14 B.C.

58. The Cimmerian Bosporus is the modern Strait of Kerch, which connects the Sea of Azov, known to the ancients as the Maeotic Lake, with the Black Sea. The tribes mentioned here inhabited part of the Crimean peninsula and the coastal region east of the Strait. Asander had ruled the kingdom since 44 B.C. and had been recognized by Antony. Although Augustus sanctioned the union of Polemon and Dynamis, the couple separated after a year and resumed war. In 8 B.C. Polemon was captured and killed by the Bosporans. Finally Dynamis obtained the throne as a vassal of Rome, and ruled until her death in A.D. 8.

59. 13 B.C. Varus later served as legate in Syria at the time of the birth of Christ, and finally in Germany, where he committed suicide after his defeat by Arminius in A.D. 9. See Book 56, chs. 18–21.

60. Lucius Cornelius Balbus, the nephew of Julius Caesar's famous engineer, came from an eminent and wealthy Spanish family of Gades (Cadiz). He had celebrated a triumph in 19 B.C. for his victory over the Garamantes, a tribe inhabiting the southern Libyan desert; in that year he had built the theatre here referred to, which was dedicated in 13 B.C.

61. It was the custom for boys of distinguished birth, even before assuming the *toga virilis* at fifteen, to join societies which gave training in horsemanship and physical fitness. They displayed their prowess in the 'Troy Game', which might be compared to a modern military tournament or tattoo. At seventeen they passed

into the *collegia iuvenum*, an ancient organization, which was extended throughout
Italy and encouraged martial prowess. Augustus gave it his active patronage and
chose the title of *princeps iuventutis* as an honour for Gaius and Lucius.

62. 13 B.C.

63. A high priest who was concerned with conducting sacrifices.

64. His Pannonian campaign began in January, 12 B.C.

65. The Quinquatrus (19–23 March) was a festival held in honour of Minerva,
equated by the Romans with Athena. Ovid confirms that in Augustan times
gladiatorial combats were held at the Quinquatras (*Fasti*, III, 811–14).

66. To pay for the maintenance of the baths.

67. Known as Agrippa Postumus. For his later career see Books 55, ch. 32, and
56, ch. 30.

68. The festivals were important: the Megalenses (4–10 April), the Cereales (12–
19 April) and the Florales (28 April–3 May). Augustus did not want ostentatious
mourning by the leading men. Funeral games for Agrippa were not held until 7
B.C. (see Book 55, ch. 8).

69. The word is derived from the Greek adjective *kometes*, meaning long-haired,
and referring to the fiery track left by the star in the sky.

70. See above, ch. 10, note 28.

71. The transmitted text of Dio says the opposite, 'chosen by lot and not
appointed', but since this was the normal procedure for the province of Asia, we
may infer that the Greek is corrupt. Other instances are known in the Augustan
period of governors being appointed instead of being selected by lot when there
was some emergency.

72. Vipsania was Agrippa's daughter by his first marriage to Caecilia Attica,
daughter of Cicero's great friend and correspondent, T. Pomponius Atticus.
Agrippa's second marriage was to Augustus's niece, the elder Marcella (see ch. 6,
note 12 above), and his third to Julia. Tiberius's young son was Drusus: the as yet
unborn child is not heard of again, and presumably died young.

73. The 'lake' has been variously interpreted as meaning either the Zuyder Zee,
or the bay at the mouth of the river Ems.

74. In 11 B.C.

75. The Lippe.

76. The Weser.

77. The Alme.

78. Dio places this uprising in 11 B.C., but the war is known to have lasted for
three years, and 11 may have been the last.

79. Iullus Antonius and (probably) M. Valerius Messalla Barbatus, both ex-consuls.

80. L. Cornelius Merula, suffect consul in 87 B.C., who abdicated his office and committed suicide in the same year. This priest (*flamen Dialis*) was not allowed to ride a horse, look upon a dead body, or spend more than three consecutive nights out of his own bed. These restrictions were not attractive to ambitious members of an imperialistic and warlike aristocracy.

81. Drusus's campaigns may be summarized as follows. The expedition of 12 B.C., described in ch. 32, was mainly a reconnaissance: it took him as far as the North Sea. In 11 B.C. he bridged the Lippe and advanced as far east as the Weser, but had to fight his way back, and was nearly trapped at Arbalo. In 10 B.C., starting from Moguntiacum (Mainz), he subdued the Chatti, before returning to Rome to become consul. His last and most ambitious campaign of 9 B.C. is described in Book 55, ch. 1.

BOOK 55

1. 10 B.C.

2. Mark Antony's son by Fulvia. He lost his life in 2 B.C. in the scandal concerning Julia's lovers.

3. The temple was triple: the side chambers belonged to Juno and Minerva.

4. The Elbe.

5. The Riesengebirge.

6. Dio means that Augustus could not perform the customary ceremonies, presumably because he was in mourning, and therefore had to remain outside the *pomoerium*, the sacred boundary of the city (see ch. 5 below).

7. The *ovatio*.

8. Book 54, note 37 mentions the privileges granted to fathers of large families by the *Lex Papia Poppaea* (see also Book 56, ch. 10) of A.D. 9. Evidently something similar had been included in the *Lex Julia* of 18 B.C., although there is no other evidence for it, and Dio may have made a mistake over the date at which Livia received this honour.

9. A tablet covered with gypsum, used as a public notice board.

10. It would no longer merely carry *senatus auctoritas*, but become a *senatus consultum*.

11. In the absence of both consuls, a praetor could preside over and bring proposals before the Senate. Such a situation was extremely unlikely to arise under the

Augustan regime. Hence the special (and inappropriate) privilege granted, of bringing in business when, presumably, not presiding.

12. 9 B.C.

13. Instead of into the temple of Jupiter Capitolinus.

14. The text of the decree is quoted by Macrobius (*Saturnalia* 1.12.35). It gives various reasons for the change of name (including Augustus's first consulship), but the only battle mentioned is the capture of Alexandria in 30 B.C.

15. 8 B.C.

16. 7 B.C.

17. A hall within the complex of buildings associated with the Porticus Octaviae in the southern Campus Martius.

18. This is the portico built on the site of Vedius Pollio's mansion (see Book 54, ch. 23).

19. The name is derived from *diribere* – to sort. The building was used for the sorting of the voters' ballots. The roof was destroyed by fire in A.D. 80.

20. See Book 53, ch. 23, note 68.

21. These were called *regiones*, which were further subdivided into 265 *vici*. Each *vicus* was supervised by four *magistri*, chosen each year by the local inhabitants.

22. 6 B.C.

23. Octavian, born on 23 September 63 B.C., had become consul in 43 B.C., aged nineteen.

24. Tigranes II, the younger son of Mark Antony's enemy, Artavasdes, had been placed on the Armenian throne in 20 B.C., supported by Tiberius's expeditionary force (see Book 54, ch. 9). See also note 36 below.

25. Dio here uses the terminology of his own age, by which 'Caesar' meant 'emperor-designate', and had become a simple title.

26. Roman boys assumed the *toga virilis* after completing their fifteenth year, the age which Gaius had then reached.

27. An honorary title created by Augustus (see Book 54, note 61). The troop of cavalry referred to is a division of the annual parade of the equestrian order (*transvectio equitum*). One could compare Gaius's command to that of a squadron of the Household Cavalry at the Trooping of the Colour.

28. 2 B.C. There is a large gap in the text at this point.

29. Augustus himself says so (*Res Gestae* 15. 4).

30. In early times a nail was driven each year into the side of the shrine of Jupiter Capitolinus, to keep an official count of the years. After lapsing for a time, the

practice was revived on the occasion of great disasters or dangers, as a propitiatory rite. It was an Augustan innovation to transfer it to mark the close of a *lustrum*, and to give the duty of driving in the nail to the censors.

31. Senators were barred from tendering for public contracts, since they were (collectively) responsible for the oversight of these.

32. Then ten years old.

33. An artificial lake was excavated beside the Tiber for this spectacle, and afterwards converted into a memorial garden for Gaius and Lucius.

34. The platforms from which orators spoke in the Forum. They were so called because they had originally been adorned with the beaks of warships captured from the people of Antium in 336 B.C.

35. 1 B.C. This is where the first of several manuscript leaves is lost.

36. After the death of Tigranes II in 6 B.C., the anti-Roman faction had gained the upper hand and placed on the throne his son, Tigranes III, whose consort was his daughter Erato. Augustus had replaced him with his Romanized uncle, Artavasdes, who was in turn unseated by this Parthian invasion, after which Tigranes III appears to have been briefly reinstated, before meeting his end (see ch. 10A below).

37. Livia Julia, sister to Germanicus and Claudius. She was no more than thirteen at this time. Later she became the wife of Tiberius's son Drusus, her first cousin.

38. In 2 B.C. there had been a revolution in Parthia. The old king, Phraates IV, had been murdered, and had been succeeded by his illegitimate son, Phrataces, who because of his lowly birth did not enjoy the support of the Parthian nobility. About 10 B.C. Phraates had sent his four legitimate sons out of the country and placed them under Roman protection, precisely in order to discourage the hopes of potential usurpers. It was because Phrataces regarded the residence of his half-brothers in Rome as a threat to his own security that he pressed for their return.

39. Other sources suggest that this refers to Artavasdes, the Roman-backed candidate for the Armenian throne, mentioned in note 36.

40. The trouble-makers referred to in this incomplete paragraph are presumably either the Marmaridae or some other native tribe of the interior of Africa, or a group of brigands or other fugitives from the law. In the context the cities mentioned must be those of Cyrene, since only Cyrene and modern Tunisia (termed 'Africa' by the Romans) were normally governed by senators, and 'Africa', being an armed province, had no need of help from Egypt, whereas Cyrene had no regular garrison.

41. Lucius Domitius Ahenobarbus was the son of Antony's renegade general (see Book 50, note 7). He was married to Augustus's niece Antonia (who was also

Antony's daughter), and had been consul in 16 B.C. This expedition belongs to the decade between 7 B.C. and A.D. 2, during which Dio's record of affairs in Germany is meagre. It has been conjectured that one purpose of this campaign was to reconnoitre a route for an advance from the Danube valley to the middle reaches of the Elbe.

42. Tigranes III.

43. A rival claimant to Phraates IV for the Parthian throne. Augustus had granted him refuge in Syria in 30 B.C. (see Book 51, ch. 18).

44. A.D. 2.

45. A Mede, to be distinguished from the Armenian of the same name, mentioned in ch. 10, note 39.

46. Gaius died in A.D. 4, Lucius in A.D. 2.

47. A.D. 4. This was Tiberius's first return to the field since his voluntary exile in Rhodes. In this campaign he advanced as far as the Weser. In A.D. 5 he defeated the Langobardi and reached the Elbe. In A.D. 6 he began a combined advance with Gaius Sentius Saturninus against the territory of Maroboduus (Bohemia), but was obliged to halt and turn south because of the outbreak of rebellion in Dalmatia (ch. 29).

48. See Book 52, ch. 42.

49. See Book 54, chs. 1–2.

50. The law referred to by Dio is the *Lex Aelia Sentia*.

51. His full name was Gnaeus Cornelius Cinna Magnus.

52. A.D. 5.

53. Agrippa Postumus was then seventeen.

54. Senators and knights had sat in reserved front seats at theatrical performances since 67 B.C., but the same privilege at the Circus was only now extended to them.

55. Twenty-five is correct for the number of legions left after Varus lost XVII, XVIII and XIX in Germany in A.D. 9. See Book 56, ch. 18ff.

56. Furius Camillus Scribonianus, another descendant of Pompey, had, when governor of Dalmatia, taken part with Annius Vinicianus in a conspiracy against the emperor Claudius. The emperor rewarded the two legions which had rejected Camillus's appeal to mutiny.

57. Dio is wrong. The Twenty-Second legion (Primigeneia) was raised by Claudius. The Augustan Twenty-Second was called Deiotariana.

58. Traiana and Ulpia respectively.

59. Under Augustus there were nine praetorian cohorts and three urban cohorts,

which were numbered consecutively I–XII. There was a fourth urban cohort at Lyon numbered XIII, to ensure the security of the mint. The praetorians were the emperor's guards and went with him on campaign; the urban cohorts were to keep the city safe and orderly, and always stayed in or just outside Rome.

60. A.D. 6.

61. A quorum had been imposed in 11 B.C. (see Book 54, ch. 35).

62. On 27 January (*Fasti Praenestini*).

63. Dio mentions this because the normal practice would have been for the quaestor to take over the whole province.

64. The reference is to Archelaus, a son of Herod the Great, who used the name of Herod on his coinage.

65. An especially turbulent group of tribes, much addicted to brigandage, who inhabited a mountainous region on the borders of Lycaonia, Pamphylia, Pisidia and Cilicia in southern Asia Minor.

66. Gaetulicus.

67. As noted in ch. 13, note 47, it was the outbreak of this revolt which forced Tiberius to break off his campaign in Bohemia.

68. The revolt of the Dalmatian Bato began in the south, but the Romans regarded the Pannonians in the north of the country as the greater threat.

69. Near the modern Belgrade.

70. The Drava.

71. The modern Split.

72. A little north of Belgrade.

73. The modern Sisak near Zagreb. Tiberius and Messallinus had succeeded in joining forces there.

74. A.D. 7. The manuscripts give Licinius's cognomen wrongly as Silanus.

75. Tiberius's strategy was to bar the route to Italy and reduce the rebels by hunger, rather than risk pitched battles and substantial losses. Augustus's correspondence with him, quoted in Suetonius, *Tiberius*, ch. 21, does not suggest that there was a crisis of confidence between the two. But public feeling in Rome, exacerbated by food shortages, plague and taxation, and accustomed to rapid successes in Germany, may have become restive. Suetonius describes this rebellion as the most bitterly fought of all the foreign wars since Rome had defeated Carthage.

76. This was in effect a compulsory levy of the slaves and their maintenance upon the wealthier Romans.

77. Augustus had adopted Tiberius and Agrippa Postumus as his sons in A.D. 4. One effect of this was that property owned by the adoptees (and it was very considerable) passed back into the control of their new 'father'.

78. Germanicus's hastily assembled force had joined Tiberius in the north-west at Siscia.

79. Meanwhile Severus, the governor of Moesia, had been reinforced by the arrival of Plautius Silvanus from Asia, and could now muster five legions. The combined forces of the two Batos barred their passage west of Sirmium: the Volcaean marches are situated in this area in the valley of the Sava. The Roman victory enabled Tiberius and Severus to join forces at Siscia, raise their strength to ten legions and regain the initiative against the rebels.

80. A.D. 8.

81. The future emperor Claudius. This paragraph (from Xiphilinus) may belong to A.D. 6 (see ch. 27 above).

BOOK 56

1. A.D. 9.

2. Probably the *Lex Julia de maritandis ordinibus* (see Book 54, note 37).

3. Romulus's birth is the subject of various conflicting myths. The one which, according to Plutarch, received the widest credence relates that the descendants of Aeneas, the brothers Amulius and Numitor, contended for the ancestral kingdom of Alba. Amulius won, and in order to pre-empt the succession, made Numitor's daughter, Silvia, a priestess of Vesta. When she was found to be pregnant, she claimed that the father was Mars. According to some accounts, she had been raped by Amulius. Her twin sons, Romulus and Remus, were exposed, but were rescued by Faustulus, a swineherd in Amulius's employment. (Plutarch, *Life of Romulus*, chs. 2–4).

4. Augustus is referring to the rape of the Sabine women, to provide womenfolk for the newly founded Rome.

5. See Book 53, note 25.

6. One version of the story of Hersilia, a Sabine woman, is that she became Romulus's wife. She had a daughter named Prima, who can, in the legend, plausibly figure as the first girl born to the new community to be married. So whatever Hersilia did on this occasion would set a precedent. (See Plutarch, *Life of Romulus*, ch. 14.)

7. See Book 54, ch. 16.

8. The *Lex Julia* laid it down that betrothal to a girl not yet of marriageable age (that is, under 12) counted as marriage for the purposes of the law.

9. With the exception of the Julii these are all families prominent in the history of the epic days of the early republic.

10. A law passed in 169 B.C. which had strictly limited the extent to which women could benefit from wills. It appears from Cicero (*De Republica*, III. 17) that Dio has mistaken the 100,000 asses census qualification of the highest property class for a figure in sesterces governing how much a woman could inherit. The *Lex Voconia* forbade a woman to be instituted heir, or to receive a legacy of more than the sum left to the heir. It was an attempt by the Roman upper class to prevent their women from acquiring economic power.

11. This law, passed in A.D. 9, substantially modified the *Lex Julia*. Concessions were made to bachelors and spinsters concerning their rights of inheritance, and also to the partners of childless marriages. The period after which women, following divorce or widowhood, were expected to find a new husband was extended, and further inducements to marriage were offered to spinsters. Women, both born free and freed, were offered further concessions if they increased their families.

12. Dio devotes much space to Germanicus's part in this campaign, but in fact he arrived only during the final stages of the rebellion, and was mainly concerned with 'mopping-up' operations.

13. Tiberius had returned to Rome in the winter of A.D. 8–9 (see ch. 1) leaving Aemilius Lepidus in command of his headquarters at Siscia. In this final three-pronged offensive, Lepidus advanced from the north-west, Silvanus from the north-east, Tiberius with Germanicus from the south.

14. Gaius Vibius Postumus appears to be meant. He had held a consulship in A.D. 5.

15. After the campaign Tiberius treated Bato generously and gave him a house in Ravenna.

16. See Book 54, note 59. He was married to Augustus's grand-niece. Although certainly culpable in the handling of his forces, he seems in his performance as a governor to have been made a scapegoat for the errors of Roman policy. Other sources suggest that he did not administer or tax his province oppressively: the catastrophe originated rather from the mistaken view that Germany could be assimilated into the Roman imperial system as quickly as Gaul had been.

17. The Weser.

18. Arminius, whom Velleius calls 'son of Segimerus', was the chief of the Cherusci. He had actually received Roman citizenship and ranked as a knight. In A.D. 14 after Augustus's death Germanicus led a fresh expedition into German

territory, and later built a mound over the unburied bones of Varus's troops. But in A.D. 15 Arminius held him to an indecisive battle at Idistaviso, near Minden. Arminius was killed by his own kinsmen in A.D. 19.

19. There is a gap in the manuscript at this point. The following two paragraphs are inserted from summaries preserved in other sources, and the continuous narrative resumes at ch. 25 with the opening of the year A.D. 11.

20. The temple of Concord had been erected by L. Opimius, consul in 121 B.C., at the head of the republican Forum. This refurbishment was elaborate and the surviving architectural fragments are of high quality.

21. A.D. 11.

22. See Book 55, ch. 33 (A.D. 8).

23. A.D. 12.

24. This could mean one of two things: either that Germanicus, as consul, read Augustus's letter just as he would have read any other communication from a magistrate to the Senate; or else that ever since his quaestorship in A.D. 7 Germanicus had read Augustus's missives to the Senate. Against the latter is the fact that Germanicus had been campaigning in Germany in A.D. 9 and 11.

25. See also Book 54, ch. 30.

26. 'Exclusion from fire and water' (*ignis et aquae interdictio*) was the ancient technical term for banishment. Augustus had also introduced a milder penalty, relegation to a specified spot (generally an island) which did not involve loss of all citizen rights. It is likely that Dio is confusing regulations made for the two different categories.

27. The Basilica Julia in the republican Forum was rebuilt by Augustus in honour of Gaius and Lucius after a fire. There was also a portico or loggia in the Forum, which unlike the Basilica was always known by their names, that is, *Porticus Gai et Luci*.

28. A.D. 13.

29. See Book 53, ch. 21.

30. Augustus had introduced this tax in A.D. 6 to finance the defence budget. See Book 55, ch. 25.

31. See Book 50, ch. 10, note 28.

32. See Book 55, ch. 9, note 26.

33. See Book 55, ch. 32.

34. See ch. 10 above, note 10.

35. The text of this document has survived. It is known as the *Res Gestae*, or

Monumentum Ancyranum, from the place of discovery of the most important copy, and was set up not only as Augustus had directed, but also in various cities of the empire, probably in precincts dedicated to the worship of Roma and Augustus, as at Ancyra (Ankara).

36. See Book 55, note 34.

37. A euphemistic allusion to the proscriptions carried on under the Triumvirate, in which Augustus had certainly taken his share.

38. Quintus Caecilius Metellus, known as Creticus, for his conquest of the island in 67 B.C.

39. The gate in the old city wall through which triumphal processions always passed.

40. A Roman senator, to whom Romulus is said to have declared his desire to be worshipped as Quirinus.

41. When Romulus died, he disappeared suddenly and completely. Plutarch discusses the alternative possibilities concerning his end – that he was murdered by senators, or carried up to heaven (*Life of Romulus*, chs. 27–28).

42. At the opening procession of the games, the presiding magistrate rode in a triumphal chariot, wearing triumphal garb. Cf. Juvenal, *Satires* X, 36–40.

CHRONOLOGICAL TABLE

B.C.	ROME	B.C.	THE WEST	B.C.	THE EAST
63	23 September. C, Octavius ('Octavian') born.				
49	Civil war between Julius Caesar and Pompey begins.			48	Caesar defeats Pompey at Pharsalus. Pompey is murdered in Egypt.
		45	Caesar defeats Pompey's sons at Munda.		
44	15 March. Caesar murdered in Rome. Octavian returns and adopts the name of Caesar. Antony given a five-year command of Cisalpine and Transalpine Gaul. Octavian opposes Antony, raises an army and allies himself with the senatorial group led by Cicero.			44–43	Brutus and Cassius gather troops.
43	JANUARY: Octavian granted *imperium* by the Senate. APRIL: Siege and battle of Mutina. The consuls Hirtius and Pansa killed. AUGUST: Octavian takes his first consulship. NOVEMBER: The				

B.C.	ROME	B.C.	THE WEST	B.C.	THE EAST
	Triumvirate of Antony, Octavian and Lepidus formed. The proscriptions begin.				
42	Julius Caesar deified. Tiberius born.	42	Sextus Pompeius in control of Sicily	42	OCTOBER: Battle of Philippi. Brutus and Cassius commit suicide.
41	Civil war between Octavian and Lucius Antonius, who is besieged in Perusia.			41	Antony in Asia Minor, meets Cleopatra at Tarsus and visits Alexandria.
				41–40	The Parthians invade Asia Minor.
40	Perusia captured. Octavian marries Scribonia. Antony returns to Italy from Alexandria. Treaty of Brundisium between Antony and Octavian. Antony marries Octavia.			40	Herod named King of Judaea by the Romans.
39	Pact of Misenum between Octavian, Antony and Sextus Pompeius. Birth of Julia.			39	Antony's general Ventidius defeats the Parthians in the Taurus mountains
				39–38	Antony's generals drive the Parthians out of Syria. Pacorus, king of Parthia, killed.
38	Octavian marries Livia. Civil war between Octavian and Sextus Pompeius.				
37	The Triumvirate renewed at the Treaty of Tarentum.	37	Octavian defeated by Sextus Pompeius off Messina.	37	Antony leaves Octavia and joins Cleopatra.
		36	Agrippa defeats Sextus Pompeius off	36	Antony invades Parthia, fails to

B.C. ROME	B.C. THE WEST	B.C. THE EAST
		capture Phraaspa and is forced to retreat through Armenia.
	Naulochus (Sicily). Lepidus deposed from the Triumvirate.	
	35–34 Octavian campaigns successfully in Illyria and Dalmatia.	35 Sextus Pompeius captured and executed in Asia Minor.
		34 Antony occupies Armenia and captures King Artavasdes. The Donations of Alexandria.
33 Octavian consul for the second time. Aedileship of Agrippa. Relations between Octavian and Antony deteriorate rapidly.		33 Antony campaigns in Armenia.
32 Both consuls and more than a third of the Senate join Antony. Both sides prepare for war.		32 Antony divorces Octavia. Antony and Cleopatra winter in Greece.
31 Octavian consul for the third time, followed by successive consulships until 23 B.C. Maecenas in charge of Rome during Octavian's absence.		31 APRIL: Octavian crosses the Adriatic to Epirus. Agrippa captures Antony's naval station at Methone. SEPTEMBER: Battle of Actium. Antony's troops in Greece and Cyrenaica go over to Octavian. Antony and Cleopatra flee to Egypt.
		31–30 The Parthians overrun Armenia.
30 Tribunician power	30–29 Crassus's campaigns	30 Cleopatra plans but

B.C. ROME	B.C. THE WEST	B.C. THE EAST
conferred on Octavian for life.	or 29–28 in the Balkans against the Bastarnae, Getae and other tribes.	has to abandon escape to the East. SUMMER: Octavian invades Egypt. AUGUST: Suicide of Antony and Cleopatra. Octavian takes possession of the treasure of the Ptolemies.
29 Octavian returns and celebrates his triumph. Temples of Divus Julius and Minerva dedicated. Dio's imaginary debate between Agrippa and Maecenas.		29 Octavian in Syria and Asia.
28 Temple of Apollo dedicated. Celebrations in commemoration of Actium. Census and review of the Senate.		28 or 27 Recall of Cornelius Gallus from Egypt.
27 Allotment of the imperial and senatorial provinces: the 'first settlement'. Octavian granted *imperium* for ten years and the name Augustus; he leaves for Gaul and Spain. Crassus's triumph celebrated. Probably, suicide of Gallus.	27 Augustus holds a census in Gaul.	
26 The Saepta dedicated.	26–25 Augustus campaigns in Spain against the Cantabri and Astures.	26 Polemon, king of Pontus, enrolled as an ally of Rome.

B.C. ROME	B.C. THE WEST	B.C. THE EAST
	Terentius Varro subdues the Salassi.	
		26–25 Aelius Gallus's expedition against Arabia Felix.
25 Augustus's daughter Julia marries Marcellus. The Basilica of Neptune, Baths of Agrippa and the Pantheon dedicated.		25 Death of Amyntas of Galatia. The territory comes under Roman rule.
24 Augustus returns from Spain.	24 Revolt of Astures and Cantabri suppressed.	
23 Augustus seriously ill. Conspiracy of Caepio and Murena. Second constitutional settlement: Augustus resigns the consulship, is granted *imperium maius* everywhere outside Rome. His years of tribunician power reckoned from this year. Death of Marcellus.		23–22 Agrippa receives enhanced *imperium* and administers the East from Lesbos.
22 Augustus refuses the dictatorship and perpetual consulship. Paullus Aemilius Lepidus and Lucius Munatius Plancus appointed censors. Temple of Jupiter Tonans dedicated. Civil disturbances in Rome.	22 AUTUMN: Augustus visits Sicily.	
21 Agrippa recalled to take charge of affairs.		21 Augustus winters in Greece.

B.C.	ROME	B.C.	THE WEST	B.C.	THE EAST
	He marries Julia.				
20	Praetorship of Egnatius Rufus. Birth of Gaius to Julia.			20	Augustus in Asia Minor. The Parthians return Roman prisoners of war and captured standards. Augustus's eastern settlement establishes Tarcondimotus as ruler of Cilicia, Iamblichus of Emesa, Archelaus of Lesser Armenia, Mithridates of Commagene. Tiberius invades Armenia and reinstates Tigranes as king.
19	Attempt of Egnatius to become consul. Augustus returns to Rome and receives consular powers.	19	Agrippa pacifies Gaul and subdues the Cantabri in Spain. Balbus's expedition against the Garamantes.		
18	Augustus's *imperium maius* renewed for ten years. Agrippa granted tribunician power for five years. Reviews of the Senate.				
18–17	Augustus's social and moral reforms (*Leges Juliae*) passed.				
17	The Ludi Saeculares held. Augustus adopts his grandsons Gaius and Lucius.				
		16	Augustus visits Gaul and supervises	16	Agrippa in the East.

B.C.	ROME	B.C.	THE WEST	B.C.	THE EAST
			campaigns. Publius Silius subdues revolts by Alpine tribes of the Camunni and Vennii, and brings the Norici under Roman rule. Uprisings quelled in Spain, Dalmatia, Macedonia and Thrace.		
		15	Tiberius and Drusus campaign in Alpine territories in preparation for invasion of Germany.	15	Agrippa visits Jerusalem.
14	Basilica of Aemilius Paullus burned down and rebuilt.			14	Agrippa assigns the Bosporan kingdom to Polemon, king of Pontus.
13	Tiberius appointed consul. Theatre of Marcellus dedicated. Review of the Senate. Agrippa granted *imperium maius* and his tribunician power renewed.	13–12	WINTER: Agrippa sent to Pannonia to quell threatened rebellion.		
12	Temple of Vesta dedicated. Death of Agrippa. Augustus succeeds Lepidus as Pontifex Maximus.	12–9	Campaigns of Tiberius in Pannonia, and Drusus in Germany.		
11	Augustus carries out census of property. Tiberius marries Julia.				
		9–8	Tiberius campaigns in Germany against		

B.C. ROME	B.C. THE WEST	B.C. THE EAST
	the Sugambri	
8 Augustus's *imperium maius* renewed. Death of Maecenas.	8–7 Tiberius campaigns on the Rhine.	8 King Polemon of Pontus captured and put to death by Dynamis in the Cimmerian Bosporus.
7 Tiberius consul for the second time and celebrates triumph. The Campus of Agrippa and the Diribitorium dedicated. Widespread fires in Rome.		
6 Tiberius granted tribunician power. He retires to Rhodes.		6 Death of Tigranes, king of Armenia. The Armenian revolt.
5 Gaius enrolled among youths of military age, declared *princeps iuventutis* and designated consul for A.D. 1.		4 Death of Herod the Great.
2 Lucius introduced to public life and designated consul for A.D. 4. Temple of Mars Ultor and Forum of Augustus dedicated. Augustus named *Pater Patriae*. Julia banished to Pandateria.		2 King Phraates of Parthia murdered; succeeded by Phrataces
		1 Revolts in Parthia and Armenia.
A.D.	**A.D.**	**A.D.**
		1 Augustus and Roman troops driven out of Armenia.

A.D.	ROME	A.D.	THE WEST	A.D.	THE EAST
					Gaius sent to Syria.
2	Tiberius returns to Rome.	2	Death of Lucius at Massilia.	2–3	Gaius's campaigns in Parthia. He is wounded.
3	Augustus's *imperium maius* renewed.				
4	Augustus adopts Tiberius, who is required to adopt Germanicus. Conspiracy of Gnaeus Cornelius. *Lex Aelia Sentia.*	4	Tiberius dispatched to take command in Germany; advances to the Weser.	4	Gaius dies at Limyra.
	Augustus holds a census of property.	5	Tiberius reaches the Elbe.		
6	The *aerarium militare* (soldiers' pension fund) created. Widespread fires and famine. The post of Prefect of the Night Watch established.	6	Revolts in Pannonia and Dalmatia. Tiberius moves from Germany against them. Revolt of the Gaetulians against Juba subdued.	6	Judaea becomes a Roman province.
7–8	Banishment of Agrippa Postumus, the younger Julia and Ovid.	7	Germanicus sent to Dalmatia with troops hurriedly raised in Rome. Dalmatians and Pannonians defeated at the Volcaean marshes.		
		8	The Pannonians surrender.		
9	The *Lex Papia Poppaea* passed.	9	Revolt in Dalmatia subdued. Varus defeated in Germany and commits suicide: three legions lost.		
10	Temple of Concord dedicated to the Concordia Augusta.	10–11	Tiberius and Germanicus hold the Rhine frontier and make a limited counter-attack.	10–11	Aspurgus wins control of the Bosporan kingdom.

A.D. ROME	A.D. THE WEST	A.D. THE EAST
12 Germanicus consul for the first time. Tiberius's second triumph.		
13 Augustus's *imperium maius* and Tiberius's tribunician power renewed. An equal *imperium maius* conferred on Tiberius.	13 Germanicus assumes command on the Rhine.	
14 Death of Augustus.		

LIST OF CONSULS

B.C

28 imp. Caesar (vɪ); M. Agrippa (ɪɪ)
27 imp. Caesar (vɪɪ); M. Agrippa (ɪɪɪ)
26 imp. Caesar Augustus (vɪɪɪ); T. Statilius Taurus
25 imp. Caesar Augustus (ɪx); M. Junius Silanus
24 imp. Caesar Augustus (x); C. Norbanus Flaccus
23 imp. Caesar Augustus (xɪ); A. Terentius Varro Murena
   suffecti: Cn. Calpurnius Piso; L. Sestius Quirinus
22 M. Claudius Marcellus; L. Arruntius
21 Q. Aemilius Lepidus; M. Lollius
20 M. Appuleius; P. Silius Nerva
19 C. Sentius Saturninus; Q. Lucretius Vespillo
18 P. Cornelius Lentulus Marcellinus; Cn. Cornelius Lentulus
17 C. Furnius; C. Junius Silanus
16 L. Domitius Ahenobarbus; P. Cornelius Scipio
   suffectus: L. Tarius Rufus
15 M. Livius Drusus Libo; L. Calpurnius Piso Frugi
14 M. Licinius Crassus Frugi; Cn. Cornelius Lentulus Augur
13 Ti. Claudius Nero; P. Quinctilius Varus
12 M. Valerius Messalla Barbatus; P. Sulpicius Quirinius
   suffecti: C. Valgius Rufus; C. Caninius Rebilus; L. Volusius Saturninus
11 Paullus Fabius Maximus; Q. Aelius Tubero
10 Iullus Antonius; Africanus Fabius Maximus
9 Nero Claudius Drusus; T. Quinctius Crispinus
8 C. Marcius Censorinus; C. Asinius Gallus
7 Ti. Claudius Nero (ɪɪ); Cn. Calpurnius Piso
6 C. Antistius Vetus; D. Laelius Balbus
5 imp. Caesar Augustus (xɪɪ); L. Cornelius Sulla
   suffecti: L. Vinicius; Q. Haterius; C. Sulpicius Galba
4 C. Calvisius Sabinus; L. Passienus Rufus
   suffecti: C. Caelius; Gaius Sulpicius
3 L. Cornelius Lentulus; M. Valerius Messalla Messallinus
2 imp. Caesar Augustus (xɪɪɪ); M. Plautius Silvanus
   suffecti: L. Caninius Gallus; C. Fufius Geminus; Q. Fabricius
1 Cossus Cornelius Lentulus; L. Calpurnius Piso
   suffecti: A. Plautius; A. Caecina Severus

A.D.

1 C. Caesar; L. Aemilius Paullus
   suffectus: M. Herennius Picens

A.D.

2   P. Vinicius; P. Alfenus Varus
     suffecti: P. Cornelius Lentulus Scipio; T. Quinctius Crispinus
3   L. Aelius Lamia; M. Servilius
     suffecti: P. Silius; L. Volusius Saturninus
4   Sext. Aelius Catus; C. Sentius Saturninus
     suffecti: Cn. Sentius Saturninus; C. Clodius Licinus
5   L. Valerius Messalla Volesus; Cn. Cornelius Cinna Magnus
     suffecti: C. Vibius Postumus; C. Ateius Capito
6   M. Aemilius Lepidus; L. Arruntius
     suffectus: L. Nonius Asprenas
7   Q. Caecilius Metellus Creticus Silanus; A. Licinius
       Nerva Silianus
8   M. Furius Camillus; Sext. Nonius Quinctilianus
     suffecti: L. Apronius; A. Vibius Habitus
9   C. Poppaeus Sabinus; Q. Sulpicius Camerinus
     suffecti: M. Papius Mutilus; Q. Poppaeus Secundus
10   P. Cornelius Dolabella; C. Junius Silanus
     suffecti: Ser. Cornelius Lentulus Maluginensis; Q. Junius Blaesus
11   M. Aemilius Lepidus; T. Statilius Taurus
     suffectus: L. Cassius Longinus
12   Germanicus Caesar; C. Fonteius Capito
     suffectus: C. Visellius Varro
13   C. Silius; L. Munatius Plancus
     suffectus: A. Caecina Largus
14   Sext. Pompeius; Sext. Appuleius
15   Drusus Caesar; C. Norbanus Flaccus
     suffectus: M. Junius Silanus

NOTE: If a consulship became vacant during the year through the death or
resignation of the holder, the man elected to fill the vacancy was termed *suffectus*
(substitute).

KEY TO PLACE NAMES

	MODERN NAME OR REGION	MAP
Athlula	Town in Arabia	—
Augusta Emerita	Merida	10
Augusta Praetoria	Aosta	1
Aventine Hill	Rome	11
Baetica	Seville/Cordoba	10
Basilica of Neptune	Rome	11
Basilica of Paullus	Rome	11
Bastarnae	W. Ukraine	9
Batavia	S. Netherlands, Maas/Waal region	2
Baths of Agrippa	Rome	11
Belgica	Belgium	2
Bessi	W. Thrace	8
Bithynia	N.W. Anatolia	4
Bononia	Bologna	1
Bosphorus, Cimmerian	Kerch Straits	9
Bosphorus, Thracian	Bosphorus	4
Breuci(ans)	Central Dalmatia	—
Britain	Britain	2
British Ocean	North Sea	2
Brundusium	Brindisi	1
Campania	Campania	1
Campus Martius	Rome	11
Camunni	Swiss Alps	—
Canopus	Aboukir	7
Cantabri	Oviedo/Santander	10
Capitol	Rome	11
Capitoline Hill	Rome	11
Cappadocia	E. Anatolia	5
Capreae	Capri	1
Carthage	Ras Kartadjina	6
Ceraunian Mts	N.W. Greece	8
Chatti	Upper Weser	3
Chauci	Lower Weser/Elbe	3
Chersonesus	Dardanelles, N. shore	4
Cherusci	Middle Weser	3

	MODERN NAME OR REGION	MAP
Chios	Chios	4
Cilicia	S. Anatolia	5
Cimbri	a wandering tribe probably originating from the region of Jutland	—
Circus Flaminius	Rome	11
Circus Maximus	Rome	11
Coele Syria	Syria/Lebanon	5
Commagene	E. Anatolia	5
Concordia, Temple of	Rome	11
Corinth	Corinth	8
Corsica	Corsica	1
Cos	Cos	4
Crete	Crete	8
Cydonia	Town in Crete	8
Cyprus	Cyprus	5
Cyrenaica	Cyrenaica	—
Cythera	Cythera	8
Cyzicus	Bal Kiz (near Bandirma)	4
Dacia	Central Rumania	—
Dalmatia	Dalmatia	1
Daphne	Town near Antioch	5
Dardani	E. Yugoslavia	—
Dentheleti	S.W. Bulgaria	—
Diribitorium	Rome	11
Dravus, R.	Drava R., Slovenia	—
Dyrrachium	Durazzo (Albania)	—
Egypt	Egypt	7
Elephantine	Town on the Nile S. of Assuan	7
Ephesus	Ephesus	4
Epirus	Epirus	8
Eretria	Town on island of Euboea	8
Eridanus R.	Po R.	1
Ethiopia	Ethiopia	7
Etruria	Tuscany/Lazio	1
Euphrates R.	Euphrates R.	5

	MODERN NAME OR REGION	MAP
Lycia	S. Anatolia	4
Macedonia	Macedonia	8
Maedi	S. Bulgaria	—
Marcomanni	Czechoslovakia	3
Mars Ultor, Temple of	Rome	11
Mauretania	Morocco	6
Mausoleum of Augustus	Rome	11
Mazaei	Bosnia, nr Banjaluka	1
Mediolanum	Milan	1
Mesopotamia	Mesopotamia	5
Methone	Modon, S. Peloponnese	8
Moesia	N. Bulgaria/E. Yugoslavia	—
Mutina	Modena	1
Mysians	W. Anatolia	—
Napata	Town in Ethiopia	—
Neapolis	Naples	1
Nicaea	Town in N. Anatolia	4
Nicomedia	W. Anatolia, near Izmir	4
Noricum	E. Austria/Slovenia	3
Numidia	N. Algeria	6
Palatine Hill	Rome	11
Palatium	Rome	11
Palestine	Israel	5
Pamphylia	W. Anatolia	4
Pandateria	Pantelleria, island W. of Ischia	—
Pannonia	N. Yugoslavia/W. Hungary	1
Pantheon	Rome	11
Paphlagonia	N. Anatolia/Black Sea	—
Paphos	Town in W. Cyprus	—
Paraetonium	Sollum, Egypt	—
Paros	Paros	8
Parthia	Iraq/Iran	5
Patrae	Patras	8
Pausilypon	Posilipo	1b

	MODERN NAME OR REGION	MAP
Sinope	Sinob	5
Sirmium	Mitrovica, N. Serbia	1
Siscia	Siszeg, Serbia	1
Spain	Spain	10
Splonum	Dalmatia	—
Sugambri	Sieg-Lahr region, E. of Bonn	3
Surrentum	Sorrento	1b
Syracuse	Syracuse	1
Syria	Syria	5
Tarentum	Taranto	1
Tarraco	Tarragona	10
Tauromenium	Taormina	1
Tencteri	Sieg-Lahr region, E. of Bonn	3
Theatre of Marcellus	Rome	11
Theatre of Pompey	Rome	11
Thrace	Thrace	4,8
Tiber	Tiber	1,11
Tyre	Tyre	5
Vaccaei	Zamora/León region	10
Vandalic Mts	Riesengebirge, Germany	3
Venus, Temple of	Rome	11
Vesta, Temple of	Rome	11
Via Flaminia	Rome	11
Visurgis R.	Weser	—
Volcaean Marshes	Lower Sava R., nr Cibalae (Vincovci)	—

PANNONIA

R. Drava

•Siscia

R. Sava

Sirmium

R. Danube

•Mazaei

ILLYRICUM

N

D A L M A T I A

•Salonae

Trimerus

APULIA

MNIUM

Dyrrachium

ua •Beneventum

MPANIA

polis

Barium

Apollonia

Brundisium

CALABRIA

Tarentum

LUCANIA

Thurii

Rhegium

t Aetna △

Tauromenium

Y

Syracuse•

ITALY

0   100   200 km

0   50   100 miles

North-Western Europe

Mona

BRIGANTES

R. Trent

DECANGI
ORDOVICES

FRISII

L. Flevo

R. Severn

ICENI

SILURES

BRITAIN

Verulamium

TRINOVANTES

Camulodunum

BATAVI

Londinium

British

Ocean

LOWER AND UPPER GERMANY

Arduenna
Forest

TREVERI

British

BELGICA

LUGDUNENSIS

Alesia

ANDECAVI
R. Loire

TURONES

SENONES

SEQUANI

Augustodunum

AEDUI

R. Saône

N

SANTONES

Lugdunum

Vienna

AQUITANIA

R. Rhône

NARBONENSIS

Massilia

Pyrenees

NEARER

Numantia

SPAIN

Termes

Tarraco

0   100   200   300 km

0   100   200 miles

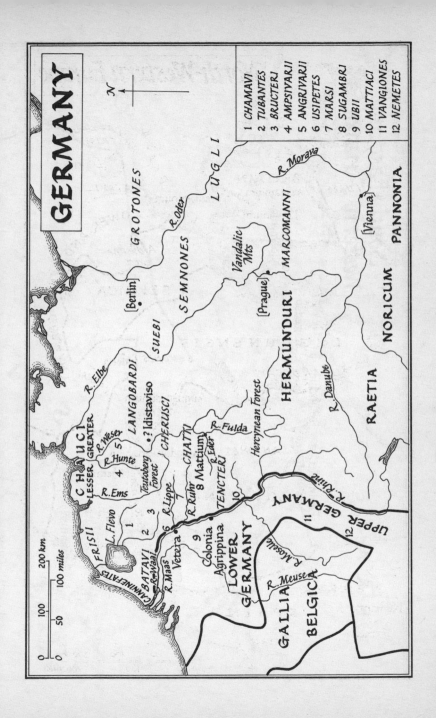

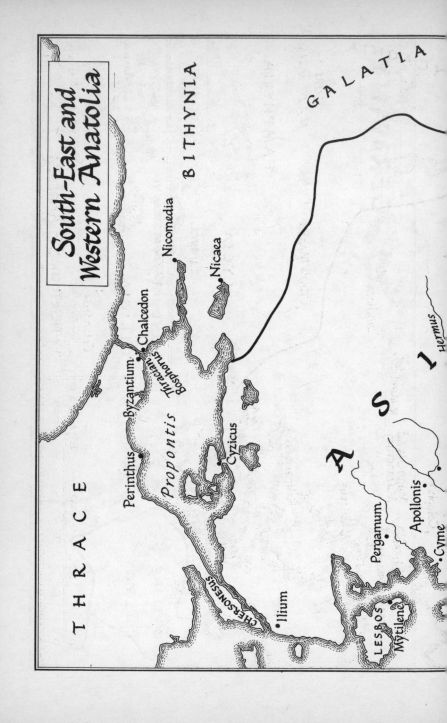

South-East and
Western Anatolia

THRACE

GALATIA

BITHYNIA

Nicomedia

Nicaea

Chalcedon

Byzantium

Perinthus

Thracian
Bosporus

Propontis

Cyzicus

CHERSONESUS

Ilium

ASIA

Hermus

Pergamum

Apollonis

Cyme

LESBOS

Mytilene

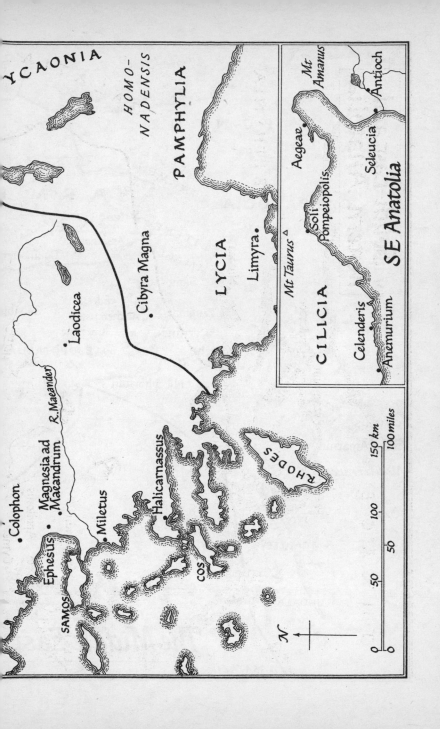

LYCAONIA

HOMO-
NADENSIS

PAMPHYLIA

Mt
Amanus

Antioch

Aegeae

Seleucia

SE Anatolia

Soli
Pompeiopolis.

LYCIA

Mt Taurus △

Limyra.

CILICIA

Cibyra Magna

Celenderis

Anemurium.

Laodicea

R. Maeander

Colophon

Magnesia ad
Maeandrum

Ephesus

Miletus

Halicarnassus

SAMOS

RHODES

COS

N

150 km

100 miles

50   100   150

0   50   100

The Middle East

Caucasus Mountains
Pass
IBERIA
R. Kura

Gorneae?
Artaxata
olandum?
Mt Ararat
IA
R. Aras

ALBANIA

Caspian

Sea

MEDIA

ATROPATENE

MARDI

Gaugamela
IABENE
Gt Zab
nus

MEDIA

Ecbatana

LAN EMPIRE

Halus?
Artemita
△Sunbula Mt

Ctesiphon
eleucia ad Tigrim

R. Tigris

N

ELYMAEI

Persian Gulf

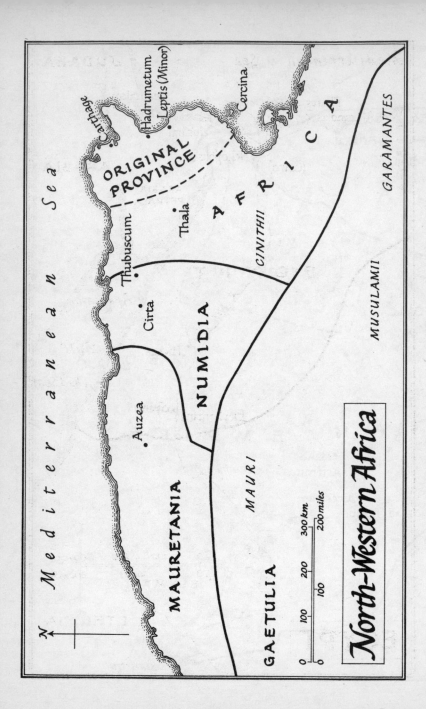

North-Western Africa

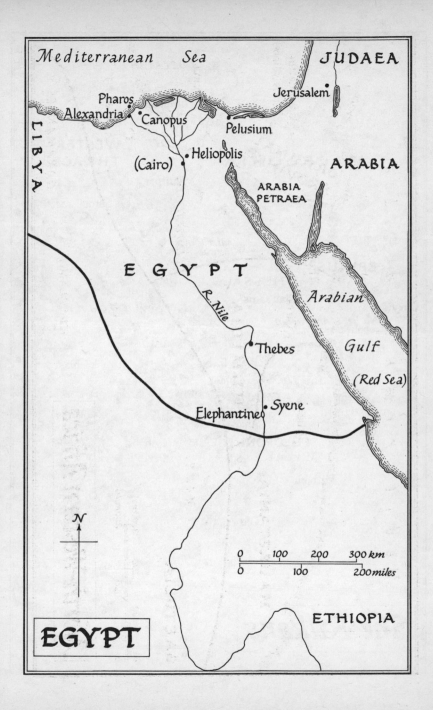

COELALETE

Philippopolis
BESSI   ODRYSIANS
DII   WESTERN
THRACE

MACEDONIA

Philippi

Samothrace

Ceraunian
Mts
EPIRUS   THESSALY
Gulf of
Thermae
Gulf of
Torone

Pharsalus   *Aegean*

Corcyra
Paxos
Nicopolis   Ambracian
Gulf
Actium

Lesbos

Delphi   Thebes
Eretria

Chios

EUBOEA

ATTICA
Patrae   Aegium
Athens   Sea
ACHAIA   Piraeus
Corinth   Aegina   Tenos
Argos   Delos
PELOPONNESE   Cythnos   Paros
Messene   Seriphos   Amorgos
Sparta

Ionian Sea

Methone

N

Cythera

Cydonia
CRETE

The Balkans

0   100   200 km
0   50   100 miles

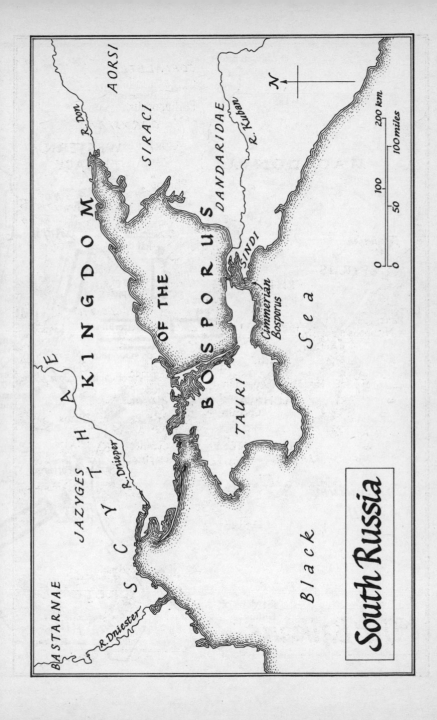

South Russia

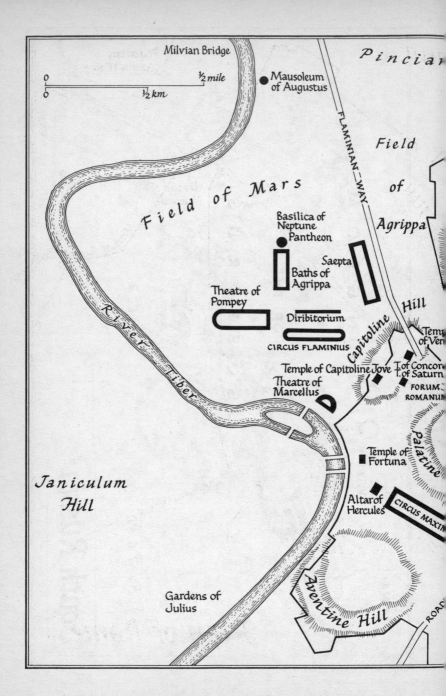

Hill

Praetorian
(Guards) Camp

Gardens of
Maecenas

Marcian Aqueduct

Viminal Hill

Viminal Hill

Esquiline Hill

Temple of Mars Ultor

Fora (squares) of
Julius and Augustus

Basilica of Paullus

Temple of Janus

ED WAY

ple of
esta

tium

Amphitheatre

N

ASINARIAN WAY

Caelian Hill

APPIAN WAY

Plan of Rome

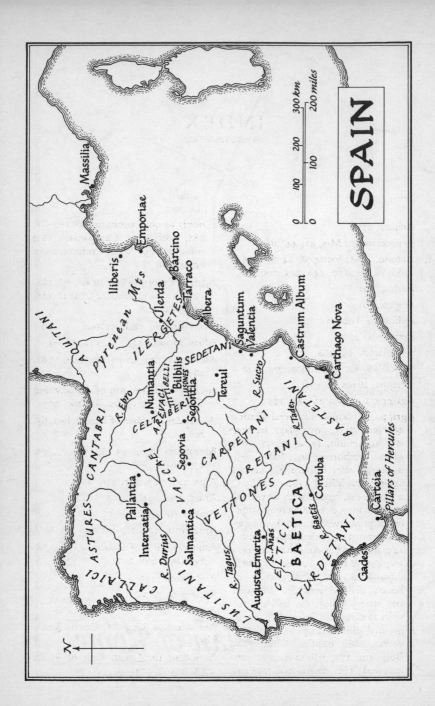

SPAIN

300 km
200 miles

200

100

100

0

Massilia

Iliberis

Emporiae

Pyrenean Mts

Barcino

Ilerda

Tarraco

ILERGETES

Ibera

R. Ebro

Saguntum

Valencia

AQUITANI

Numantia

CELTIBERI

AREVACI

Bilbilis

SEDETANI

Castrum Album

Carthago Nova

TITTI

Tereul

R. Sucro

BELLI

LUSONES

Segontia

CANTABRI

VACCAEI

Segovia

CARPETANI

R. Jader

ORETANI

BASTETANI

Pallantia

VETTONES

Intercatia

ASTURES

R. Durius

Salmantica

CELTICI

Corduba

R. Tagus

Augusta Emerita

R. Anas

BAETICA

R. Baetis

TURDETANI

CALLAICI

LUSITANI

Gades

Cartcia

Pillars of Hercules

N

INDEX

FOR THE BEST IN PAPERBACKS, LOOK FOR THE 🐧

In every corner of the world, on every subject under the sun, Penguin represents quality and variety – the very best in publishing today.

For complete information about books available from Penguin – including Puffins, Penguin Classics and Arkana – and how to order them, write to us at the appropriate address below. Please note that for copyright reasons the selection of books varies from country to country.

In the United Kingdom: Please write to *Dept E.P., Penguin Books Ltd, Harmondsworth, Middlesex, UB7 0DA*.

If you have any difficulty in obtaining a title, please send your order with the correct money, plus ten per cent for postage and packaging, to *PO Box No 11, West Drayton, Middlesex*

In the United States: Please write to *Dept BA, Penguin, 299 Murray Hill Parkway, East Rutherford, New Jersey 07073*

In Canada: Please write to *Penguin Books Canada Ltd, 2801 John Street, Markham, Ontario L3R 1B4*

In Australia: Please write to the *Marketing Department, Penguin Books Australia Ltd, P.O. Box 257, Ringwood, Victoria 3134*

In New Zealand: Please write to the *Marketing Department, Penguin Books (NZ) Ltd, Private Bag, Takapuna, Auckland 9*

In India: Please write to *Penguin Overseas Ltd, 706 Eros Apartments, 56 Nehru Place, New Delhi, 110019*

In the Netherlands: Please write to *Penguin Books Netherlands B.V., Postbus 195, NL–1380AD Weesp*

In West Germany: Please write to *Penguin Books Ltd, Friedrichstrasse 10–12, D–6000 Frankfurt/Main 1*

In Spain: Please write to *Longman Penguin España, Calle San Nicolas 15, E–28013 Madrid*

In Italy: Please write to *Penguin Italia s.r.l., Via Como 4, I-20096 Pioltello (Milano)*

In France: Please write to *Penguin Books Ltd, 39 Rue de Montmorency, F-75003 Paris*

In Japan: Please write to *Longman Penguin Japan Co Ltd, Yamaguchi Building, 2–12–9 Kanda Jimbocho, Chiyoda-Ku, Tokyo 101*

PENGUIN ARCHAEOLOGY

The Dead Sea Scrolls in English G. Vermes

This established and authoritative English translation of the non-biblical Qumran scrolls – offering a revolutionary insight into Palestinian Jewish life and ideology at a crucial period in the development of Jewish and Christian religious thought – now includes the Temple Scroll, the most voluminous scroll of them all.

Hadrian's Wall David J. Breeze and Brian Dobson

A penetrating history of the best-known, best-preserved and most spectacular monument to the Roman Empire in Britain. 'A masterpiece of the controlled use of archaeological and epigraphical evidence in a fluent narrative that will satisfy any level of interest' – *The Times Educational Supplement*

Before Civilization The Radiocarbon Revolution and Prehistoric Europe
Colin Renfrew

'I have little doubt that this is one of the most important archaeological books for a very long time' – Barry Cunliffe in the *New Scientist*. 'Pure stimulation from beginning to end ... a book which provokes thought, aids understanding, and above all is immensely enjoyable' – *Scotsman*

The Ancient Civilizations of Peru J. Alden Mason

The archaeological, historical, artistic, geographical and ethnographical discoveries that have resurrected the rich variety of Inca and pre-Inca culture and civilization – wiped out by the Spanish Conquest – are surveyed in this now classic work.

PENGUIN HISTORY

The Germans Gordon A. Craig

An intimate study of a complex and fascinating nation by 'one of the ablest and most distinguished American historians of modern Germany' – Hugh Trevor-Roper

Imperial Spain 1469–1716 J. H. Elliot

A brilliant modern study of the sudden rise of a barren and isolated country to the greatest power on earth, and of its equally sudden decline. 'Outstandingly good' – *Daily Telegraph*

British Society 1914–1945 John Stevenson

A major contribution to the *Penguin Social History of Britain*, which 'will undoubtedly be the standard work for students of modern Britain for many years to come' – *The Times Educational Supplement*

A History of Christianity Paul Johnson

'Masterly ... It is a huge and crowded canvas – a tremendous theme running through twenty centuries of history – a cosmic soap opera involving kings and beggars, philosophers and crackpots, scholars and illiterate *exaltés*, popes and pilgrims and wild anchorites in the wilderness' – Malcolm Muggeridge

The Penguin History of Greece A. R. Burn

Readable, erudite, enthusiastic and balanced, this one-volume history of Hellas sweeps the reader along from the days of Mycenae and the splendours of Athens to the conquests of Alexander and the final dark decades.

A History of Latin America George Pendle

'Ought to be compulsory reading in every sixth form ... this book is right on target' – *Sunday Times*. 'A beginner's guide to the continent ... lively, and full of anecdote' – *Financial Times*

FOR THE BEST IN PAPERBACKS, LOOK FOR THE 🐧

PENGUIN HISTORY

The Penguin History of the United States   Hugh Brogan

'An extraordinarily engaging book' – *The Times Literary Supplement*. 'Compelling reading ... Hugh Brogan's book will delight the general reader as much as the student' – *The Times Educational Supplement*. 'He will be welcomed by American readers no less than those in his own country' – J. K. Galbraith

The Making of the English Working Class   E. P. Thompson

Probably the most imaginative – and the most famous – post-war work of English social history.

The Waning of the Middle Ages   Johan Huizinga

A magnificent study of life, thought and art in 14th- and 15th-century France and the Netherlands, long established as a classic.

The City in History   Lewis Mumford

Often prophetic in tone and containing a wealth of photographs, *The City in History* is among the most deeply learned and warmly human studies of man as a social creature.

The Habsburg Monarchy 1809–1918   A. J. P. Taylor

Dissolved in 1918, the Habsburg Empire 'had a unique character, out of time and out of place'. Scholarly and vividly accessible, this 'very good book indeed' (*Spectator*) elucidates the problems always inherent in the attempt to give peace, stability and a common loyalty to a heterogeneous population.

Inside Nazi Germany   Conformity, Opposition and Racism in Everyday Life
Detlev J. K. Peukert

An authoritative study – and a challenging and original analysis – of the realities of daily existence under the Third Reich. 'A fascinating study ... captures the whole range of popular attitudes and the complexity of their relationship with the Nazi state' – Richard Geary

Aeschylus	**The Oresteia** **(Agamemnon/Choephori/Eumenides)** **Prometheus Bound/The Suppliants/Seven** **Against Thebes/The Persians**
Aesop	**Fables**
Apollonius of Rhodes	**The Voyage of Argo**
Apuleius	**The Golden Ass**
Aristophanes	**The Knights/Peace/The Birds/The Assembly** **Women/Wealth** **Lysistrata/The Acharnians/The Clouds/** **The Wasps/The Poet and the Women/The Frogs**
Aristotle	**The Athenian Constitution** **The Ethics** **The Politics**
Aristotle/Horace/ Longinus	**Classical Literary Criticism**
Arrian	**The Campaigns of Alexander**
Saint Augustine	**City of God** **Confessions**
Boethius	**The Consolation of Philosophy**
Caesar	**The Civil War** **The Conquest of Gaul**
Catullus	**Poems**
Cicero	**The Murder Trials** **The Nature of the Gods** **On the Good Life** **Selected Letters** **Selected Political Speeches** **Selected Works**
Euripides	**Alcestis/Iphigenia in Tauris/Hippolytus/The** **Bacchae/Ion/The Women of Troy/Helen** **Medea/Hecabe/Electra/Heracles** **Orestes/The Children of Heracles/** **Andromache/The Suppliant Woman/** **The Phoenician Women/Iphigenia in Aulis**

PENGUIN CLASSICS

Hesiod/Theognis	**Theogony and Works and Days/Elegies**
'Hippocrates'	**Hippocratic Writings**
Homer	**The Iliad**
	The Odyssey
Horace	**Complete Odes and Epodes**
Horace/Persius	**Satires and Epistles**
Juvenal	**Sixteen Satires**
Livy	**The Early History of Rome**
	Rome and Italy
	Rome and the Mediterranean
	The War with Hannibal
Lucretius	**On the Nature of the Universe**
Marcus Aurelius	**Meditations**
Martial	**Epigrams**
Ovid	**The Erotic Poems**
	The Metamorphoses
Pausanias	**Guide to Greece** (in two volumes)
Petronius/Seneca	**The Satyricon/The Apocolocyntosis**
Pindar	**The Odes**
Plato	**Georgias**
	The Last Days of Socrates (Euthyphro/The Apology/Crito/Phaedo)
	The Laws
	Phaedrus and Letters VII and VIII
	Philebus
	Protagoras and Meno
	The Republic
	The Symposium
	Timaeus and Critias
Plautus	**The Pot of Gold/The Prisoners/The Brothers Menaechmus/The Swaggering Soldier/Pseudolus**
	The Rope/Amphitryo/The Ghost/A Three-Dollar Day

FOR THE BEST IN PAPERBACKS, LOOK FOR THE 🐧

PENGUIN CLASSICS

Saint Anselm	**The Prayers and Meditations**
Saint Augustine	**The Confessions**
Bede	**A History of the English Church and People**
Chaucer	**The Canterbury Tales**
	Love Visions
	Troilus and Criseyde
Froissart	**The Chronicles**
Geoffrey of Monmouth	**The History of the Kings of Britain**
Gerald of Wales	**History and Topography of Ireland**
	The Journey through Wales and
	The Description of Wales
Gregory of Tours	**The History of the Franks**
Henryson	**The Testament of Cresseid and Other Poems**
Walter Hilton	**The Ladder of Perfection**
Julian of Norwich	**Revelations of Divine Love**
Thomas à Kempis	**The Imitation of Christ**
William Langland	**Piers the Ploughman**
Sir John Mandeville	**The Travels of Sir John Mandeville**
Marguerite de Navarre	**The Heptameron**
Christine de Pisan	**The Treasure of the City of Ladies**
Marco Polo	**The Travels**
Richard Rolle	**The Fire of Love**
François Villon	**Selected Poems**

FOR THE BEST IN PAPERBACKS, LOOK FOR THE 🐧

PENGUIN CLASSICS

ANTHOLOGIES AND ANONYMOUS WORKS

The Age of Bede
Alfred the Great
Beowulf
A Celtic Miscellany
The Cloud of Unknowing and Other Works
The Death of King Arthur
The Earliest English Poems
Early Christian Writings
Early Irish Myths and Sagas
Egil's Saga
King Arthur's Death
The Letters of Abelard and Heloise
Medieval English Verse
Njal's Saga
Seven Viking Romances
Sir Gawain and the Green Knight
The Song of Roland

FOR THE BEST IN PAPERBACKS, LOOK FOR THE 🐧

PENGUIN CLASSICS

Pliny	**The Letters of the Younger Pliny**
Plutarch	**The Age of Alexander** (Nine Greek Lives)
	The Fall of the Roman Republic (Six Lives)
	The Makers of Rome (Nine Lives)
	The Rise and Fall of Athens (Nine Greek Lives)
	On Sparta
Polybius	**The Rise of the Roman Empire**
Procopius	**The Secret History**
Propertius	**The Poems**
Quintus Curtius Rufus	**The History of Alexander**
Sallust	**The Jugurthine War** and **The Conspiracy of Cataline**
Seneca	**Four Tragedies** and **Octavia**
	Letters from a Stoic
Sophocles	**Electra/Women of Trachis/Philoctetes/Ajax**
	The Theban Plays (King Oedipus/Oedipus at Colonus/Antigone)
Suetonius	**The Twelve Caesars**
Tacitus	**The Agricola** and **The Germania**
	The Annals of Imperial Rome
	The Histories
Terence	**The Comedies** (The Girl from Andros/The Self-Tormentor/The Eunuch/Phormio/The Mother-in-Law/The Brothers)
Thucydides	**The History of the Peloponnesian War**
Tibullus	**The Poems** and **The Tibullan Collection**
Virgil	**The Aeneid**
	The Eclogues
	The Georgics
Xenophon	**A History of My Times**
	The Persian Expedition

Molière	**The Misanthrope/The Sicilian/Tartuffe/A Doctor in Spite of Himself/The Imaginary Invalid**
	The Miser/The Would-be Gentleman/That Scoundrel Scapin/Love's the Best Doctor/Don Juan
Michel de Montaigne	**Essays**
Marguerite de Navarre	**The Heptameron**
Blaise Pascal	**Pensées**
Marcel Proust	**Against Saint-Beuve**
Rabelais	**The Histories of Gargantua and Pantagruel**
Racine	**Andromache/Britannicus/Berenice**
	Iphigenia/Phaedra/Athaliah
Arthur Rimbaud	**Collected Poems**
Jean-Jacques Rousseau	**The Confessions**
	A Discourse on Equality
	The Social Contract
Jacques Saint-Pierre	**Paul and Virginia**
Madame de Sevigné	**Selected Letters**
Voltaire	**Candide**
	Philosophical Dictionary
Émile Zola	**La Bête Humaine**
	Germinal
	Nana
	Thérèse Raquin